ALSO AVAILABLE FROM TOKYOPOP®

MANGA

.HACK//LEGEND OF THE TWILIGHT BRACELET (September 2003)
@LARGE (COMING SOON)
ANGELIC LAYER*
BABY BIRTH* (September 2003)
BATTLE ROYALE*
BRAIN POWERED*
BRIGADOON* (August 2003)
CARDCAPTOR SAKURA
CARDCAPTOR SAKURA: MASTER OF THE CLOW*
CHOBITS*
CHRONICLES OF THE CURSED SWORD
CLAMP SCHOOL DETECTIVES*
CLOVER
CONFIDENTIAL CONFESSIONS*
CORRECTOR YUI
COWBOY BEBOP*
COWBOY BEBOP: SHOOTING STAR*
DEMON DIARY
DIGIMON*
DRAGON HUNTER
DRAGON KNIGHTS*
DUKLYON: CLAMP SCHOOL DEFENDERS*
ERICA SAKURAZAWA*
FAKE*
FLCL* (September 2003)
FORBIDDEN DANCE* (August 2003)
GATE KEEPERS*
G GUNDAM*
GRAVITATION*
GTO*
GUNDAM WING
GUNDAM WING: BATTLEFIELD OF PACIFISTS
GUNDAM WING: ENDLESS WALTZ*
GUNDAM WING: THE LAST OUTPOST*
HAPPY MANIA*
HARLEM BEAT
I.N.V.U.
INITIAL D*
ISLAND
JING: KING OF BANDITS*
JULINE
KARE KANO*
KINDAICHI CASE FILES, THE*
KING OF HELL
KODOCHA: SANA'S STAGE*
LOVE HINA*
LUPIN III*
MAGIC KNIGHT RAYEARTH* (August 2003)
MAGIC KNIGHT RAYEARTH II* (COMING SOON)
MAN OF MANY FACES*
MARMALADE BOY*
MARS*
MIRACLE GIRLS
MIYUKI-CHAN IN WONDERLAND* (October 2003)
MONSTERS, INC.
PARADISE KISS*
PARASYTE
PEACH GIRL
PEACH GIRL: CHANGE OF HEART*
PET SHOP OF HORRORS*
PLANET LADDER*
PLANETES* (October 2003)
PRIEST
RAGNAROK
RAVE MASTER*
REALITY CHECK
REBIRTH
REBOUND*
RISING STARS OF MANGA
SABER MARIONETTE J*
SAILOR MOON
SAINT TAIL
SAMURAI DEEPER KYO*
SAMURAI GIRL: REAL BOUT HIGH SCHOOL*
SCRYED*
SHAOLIN SISTERS*
SHIRAHIME-SYO: SNOW GODDESS TALES* (Dec. 2003)
SHUTTERBOX (November 2003)
SORCERER HUNTERS
THE SKULL MAN*
THE VISION OF ESCAFLOWNE
TOKYO MEW MEW*
UNDER THE GLASS MOON
VAMPIRE GAME*
WILD ACT*
WISH*
WORLD OF HARTZ (COMING SOON)
X-DAY* (August 2003)
ZODIAC P.I. *

For more information visit www.TOKYOPOP.com

*INDICATES 100% AUTHENTIC MANGA (RIGHT-TO-LEFT FORMAT)

CINE-MANGA™

CARDCAPTORS
JACKIE CHAN ADVENTURES (COMING SOON)
JIMMY NEUTRON (September 2003)
KIM POSSIBLE
LIZZIE MCGUIRE
POWER RANGERS: NINJA STORM (August 2003)
SPONGEBOB SQUAREPANTS (September 2003)
SPY KIDS 2

NOVELS

KARMA CLUB (COMING SOON)
SAILOR MOON

TOKYOPOP KIDS

STRAY SHEEP (September 2003)

ART BOOKS

CARDCAPTOR SAKURA*
MAGIC KNIGHT RAYEARTH*

ANIME GUIDES

COWBOY BEBOP ANIME GUIDES
GUNDAM TECHNICAL MANUALS
SAILOR MOON SCOUT GUIDES

5-12-03

KING OF HELL

VOLUME 2

BY
RA IN-SOO

&
KIM JAE-HWAN

LOS ANGELES • TOKYO • LONDON

Translator - Lauren Na
English Adaptation - R.A. Jones
Associate Editors - Paul Morrissey & Tim Beedle
Retouch and Lettering - Tom Misuraca
Cover Layout - Patrick Hook
Graphic Designer - Mark Paniccia

Editor - Mark Paniccia
Managing Editor - Jill Freshney
Production Coordinator - Antonio DePietro
Production Manager - Jennifer Miller
Art Director - Matthew Alford
Editorial Director - Jeremy Ross
VP of Production - Ron Klamert
President & C.O.O. - John Parker
Publisher & C.E.O. - Stuart Levy

Email: editor@TOKYOPOP.com
Come visit us online at www.TOKYOPOP.com

A ⊙ **TOKYOPOP**® Manga
TOKYOPOP® is an imprint of Mixx Entertainment, Inc.
5900 Wilshire Blvd. Suite 2000, Los Angeles, CA 90036

ISBN: 1-59182-188-6

First TOKYOPOP® printing: August 2003

10 9 8 7 6

Printed in the USA

Story Thus Far

In life, Majeh was a gifted swordsman. In death, he acts as a whimsical reaper for the King of Hell, collecting the souls of the dead to bring them to the netherworld.

All this changes when a mysterious rift opens up between Hell and Earth and evil spirits begin escaping into the mortal realm. Commanded by the King of Hell to destroy these demons and seal the rift, Majeh runs into a young scam artist and helps to change her life. He also discovers that the King has sent a spy named Samhuk to make sure he's not screwing off. Once caught, Samhuk is made into a reluctant assistant by Majeh. This prompts Samhuk to unsuccessfully request a transfer of duty.

While tailing an evil spirit, Majeh and Samhuk run across a 300-year-old man who is ready to be taken to the next world. But when the old man tires of Majeh's antics, he commands a mysterious warrior to take on the unpredictable and capricious swordsman from beyond.

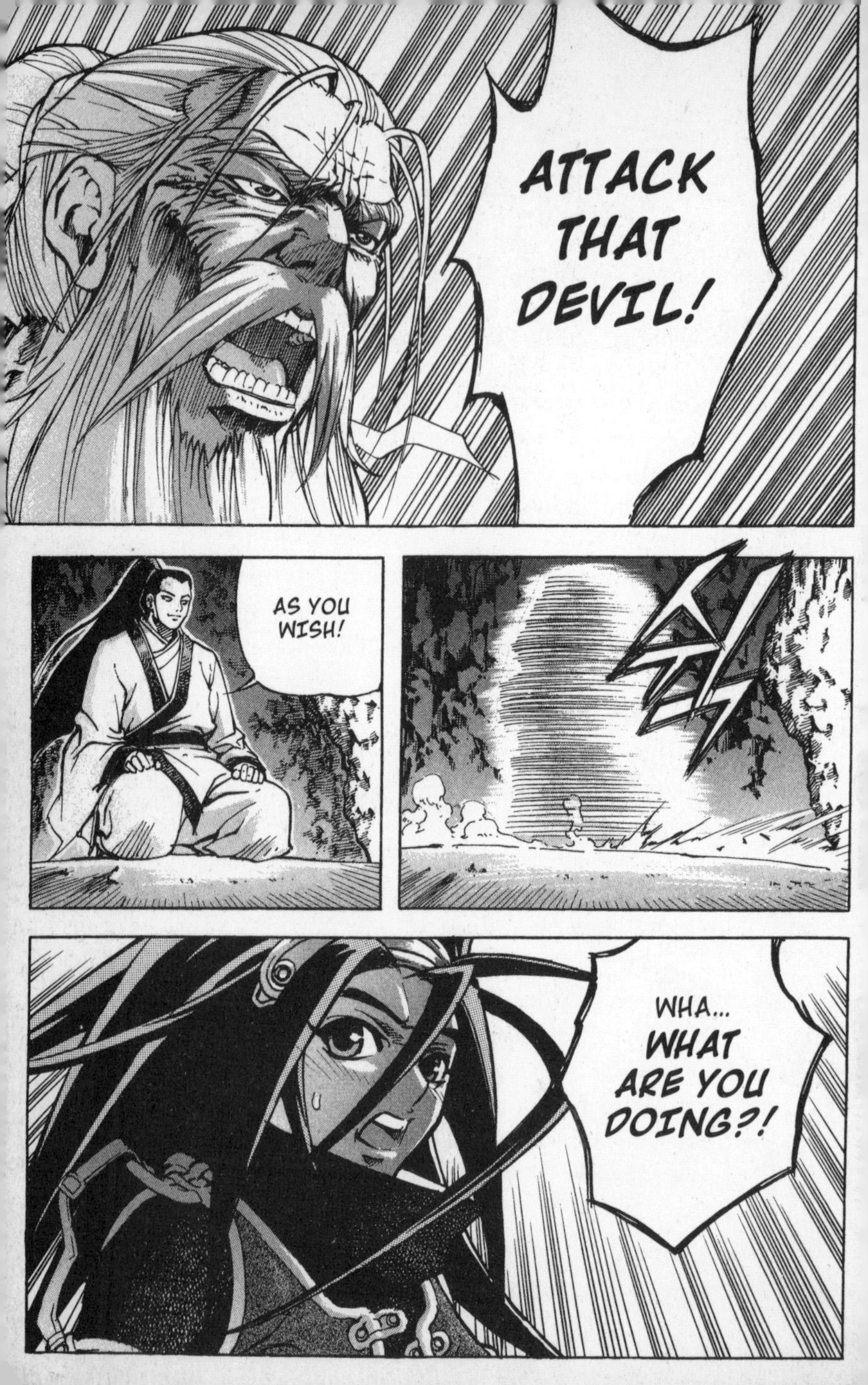
ATTACK THAT DEVIL!
AS YOU WISH!
WHA... WHAT ARE YOU DOING?!

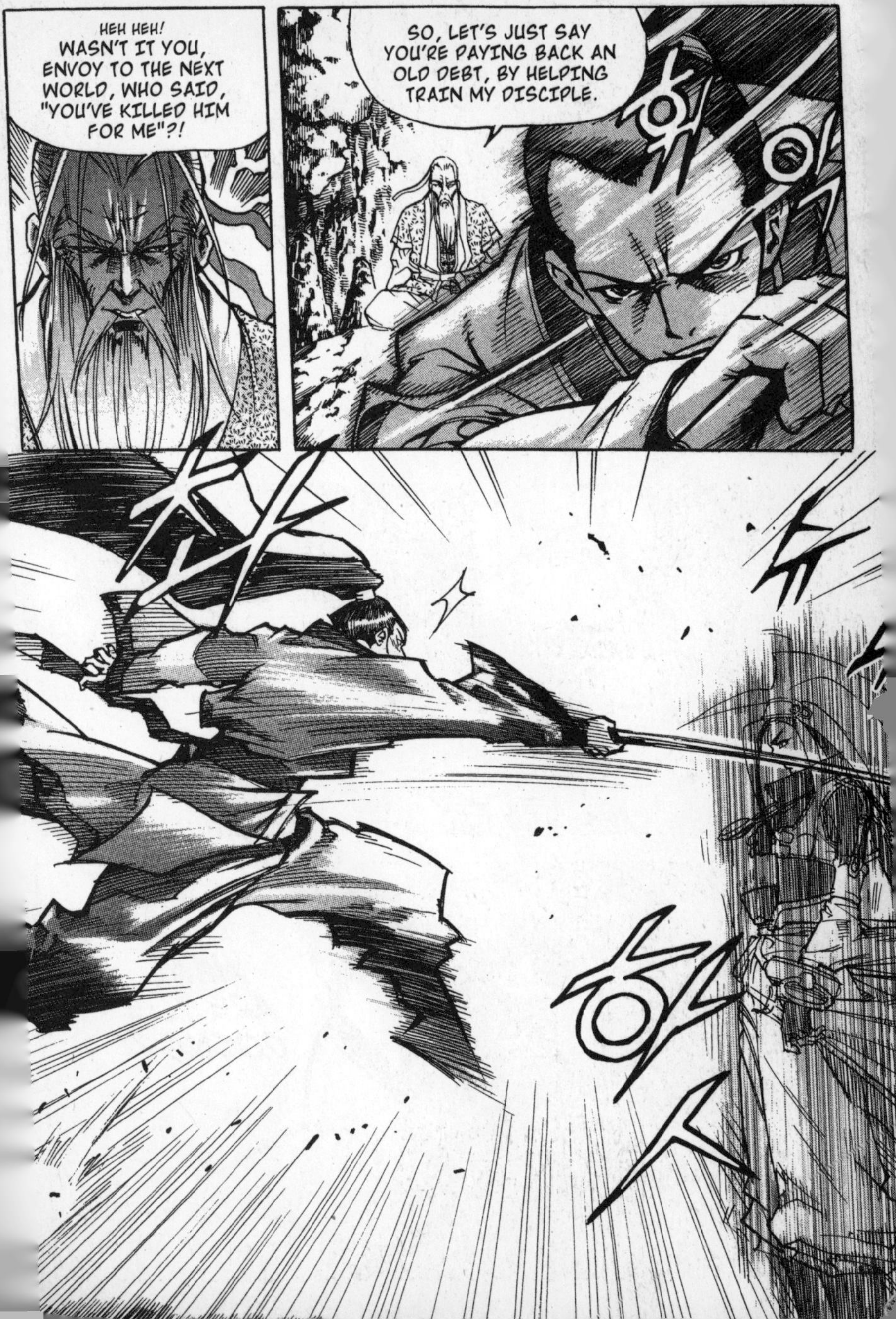
HEH HEH! WASN'T IT YOU, ENVOY TO THE NEXT WORLD, WHO SAID, "YOU'VE KILLED HIM FOR ME"?!
SO, LET'S JUST SAY YOU'RE PAYING BACK AN OLD DEBT, BY HELPING TRAIN MY DISCIPLE.

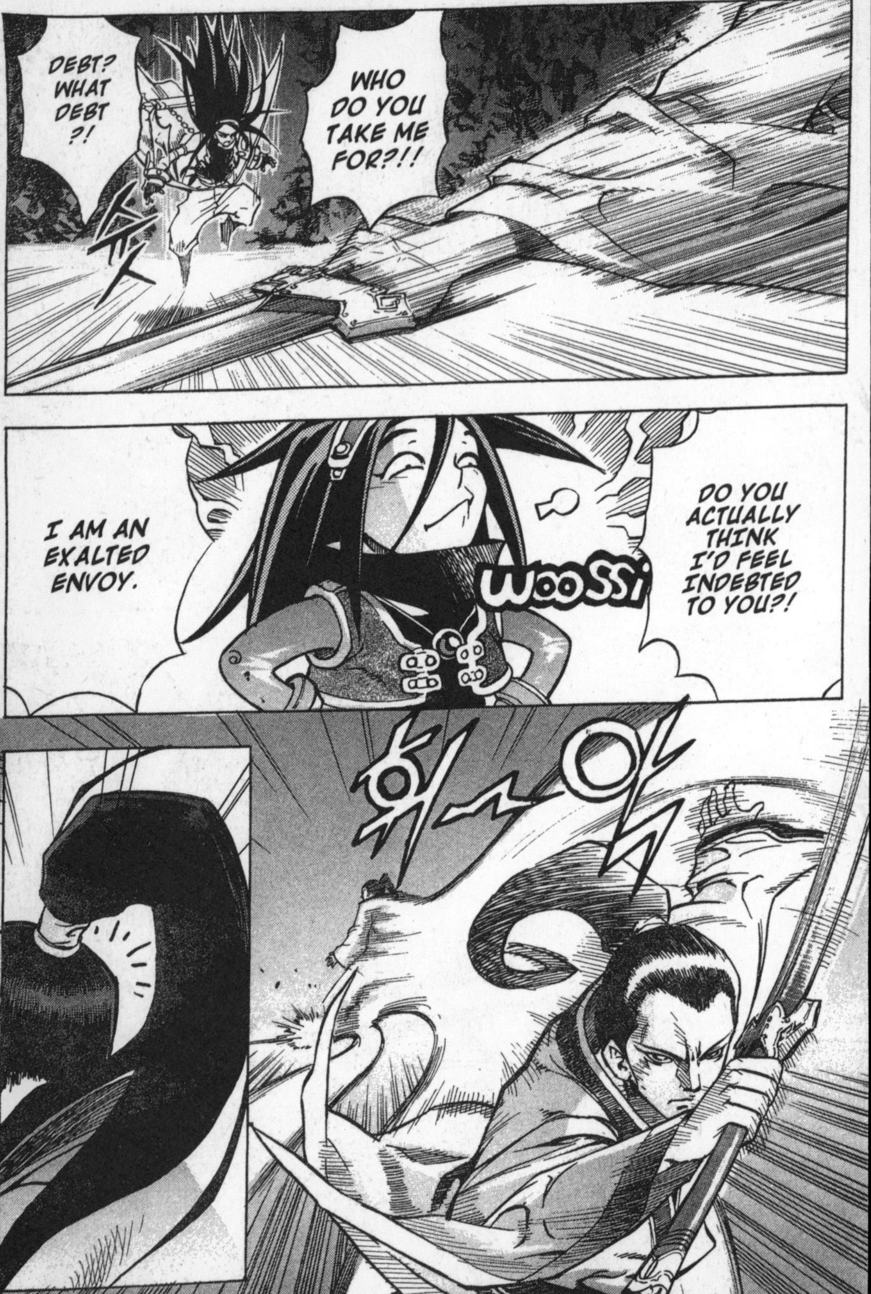
DEBT? WHAT DEBT?!
WHO DO YOU TAKE ME FOR?!!
I AM AN EXALTED ENVOY.
WOOSSi
DO YOU ACTUALLY THINK I'D FEEL INDEBTED TO YOU?!

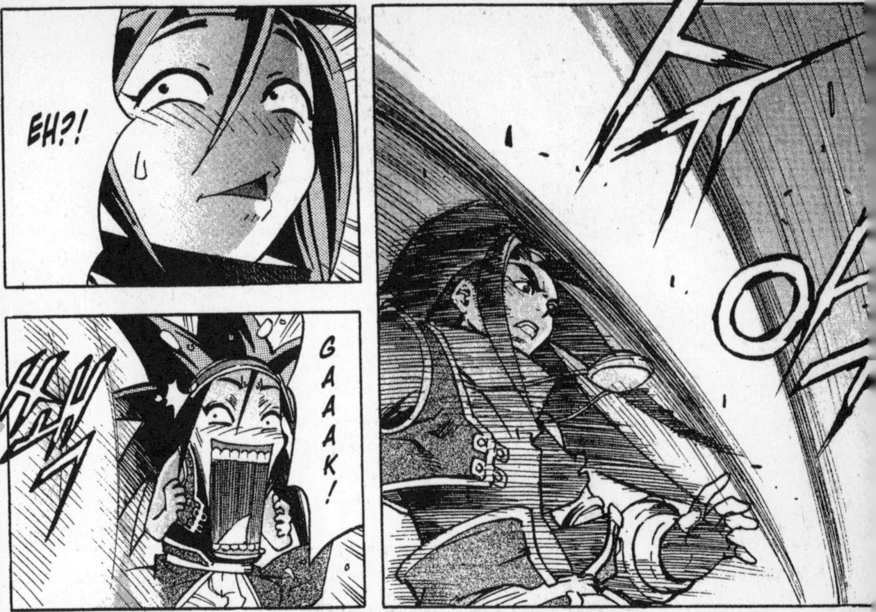
EH?!
GAAAK!

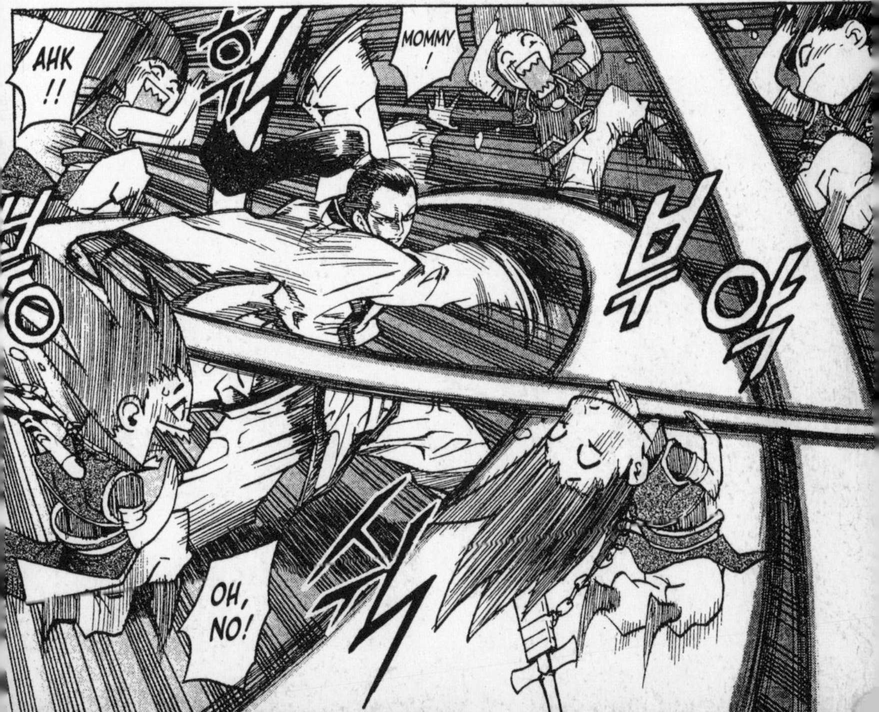
AHK !!
MOMMY !
OH, NO!

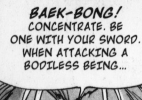

BAEK-BONG! CONCENTRATE. BE ONE WITH YOUR SWORD. WHEN ATTACKING A BODILESS BEING...

...YOU MUST GATHER ALL YOUR ENERGY AT THE TIP OF YOUR SWORD AND YOUR HEART MUST FOCUS ON YOUR MIND...!

DAMMIT! WHAT ARE YOU DOING?! ARE YOU TELLING HIM HOW TO KILL ME?!

HAR HAR! WHY ALL THE FUSS? YOU SEEM TO BE ELUDING HIS SWORD ADMIRABLY.

TELL HIM TO STOP!!

AAAK!

SERVES YOU RIGHT, HEH-HEH!

LOOK HERE!

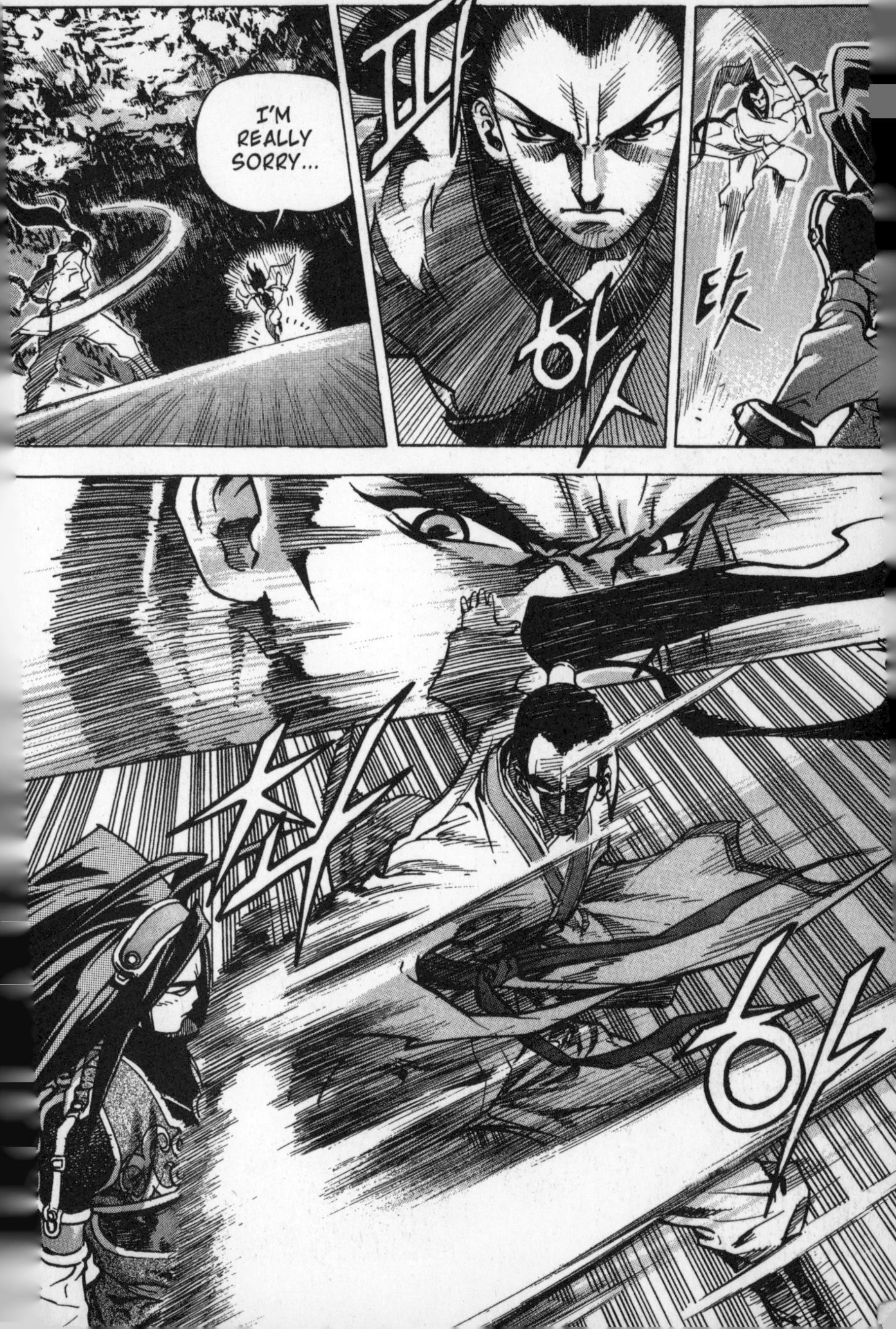
I'M REALLY SORRY...

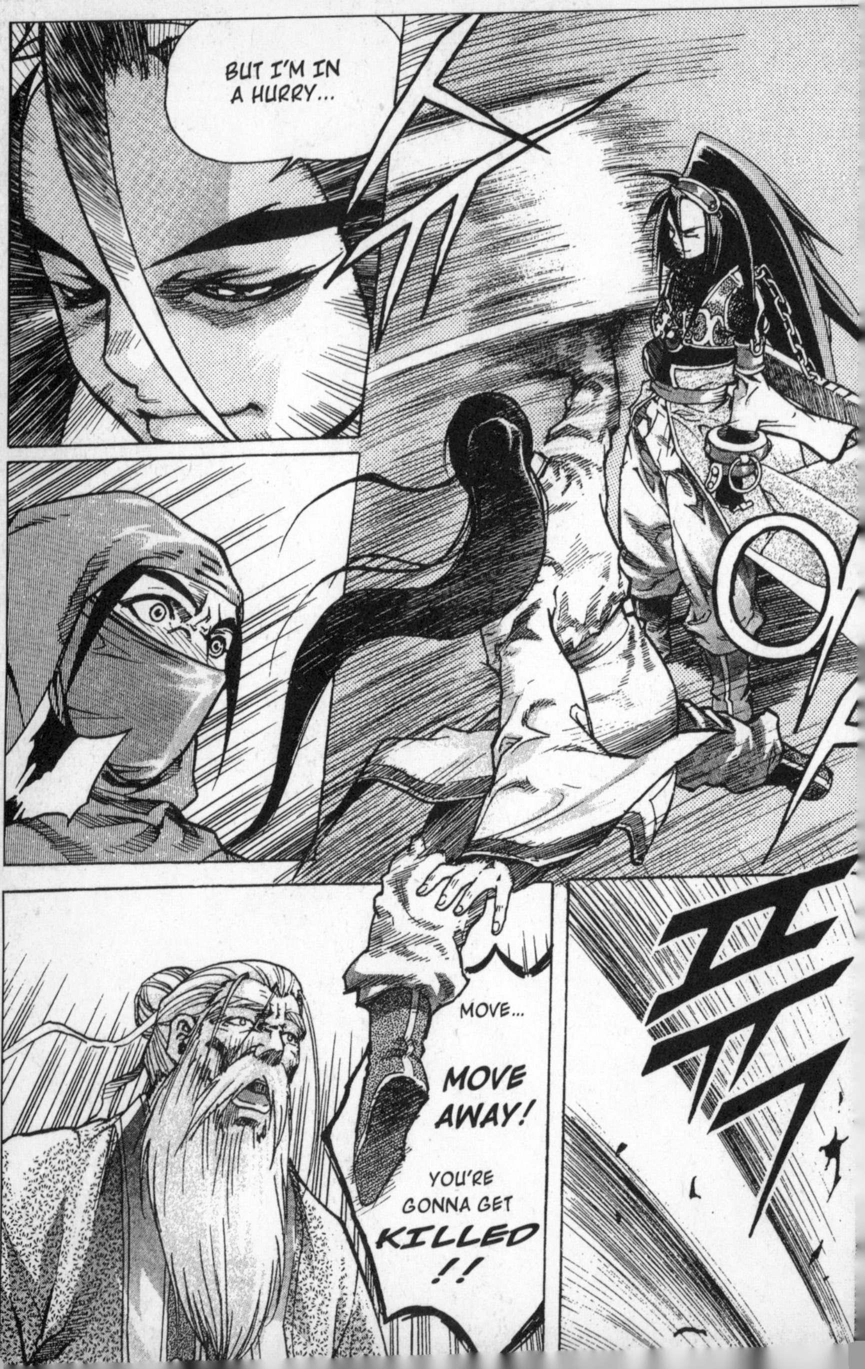
BUT I'M IN A HURRY...
MOVE...
MOVE AWAY!
YOU'RE GONNA GET KILLED!!

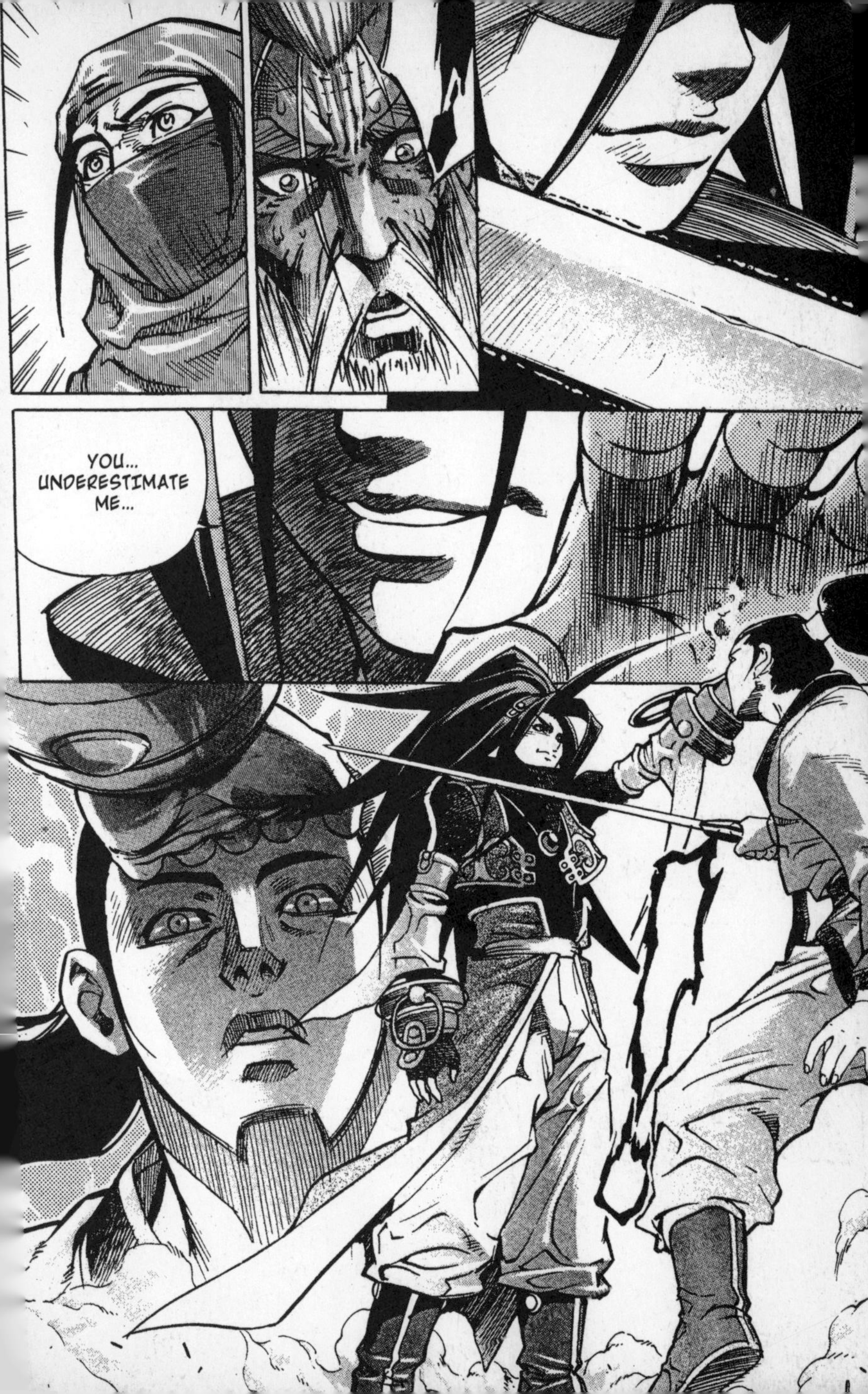
YOU... UNDERESTIMATE ME...

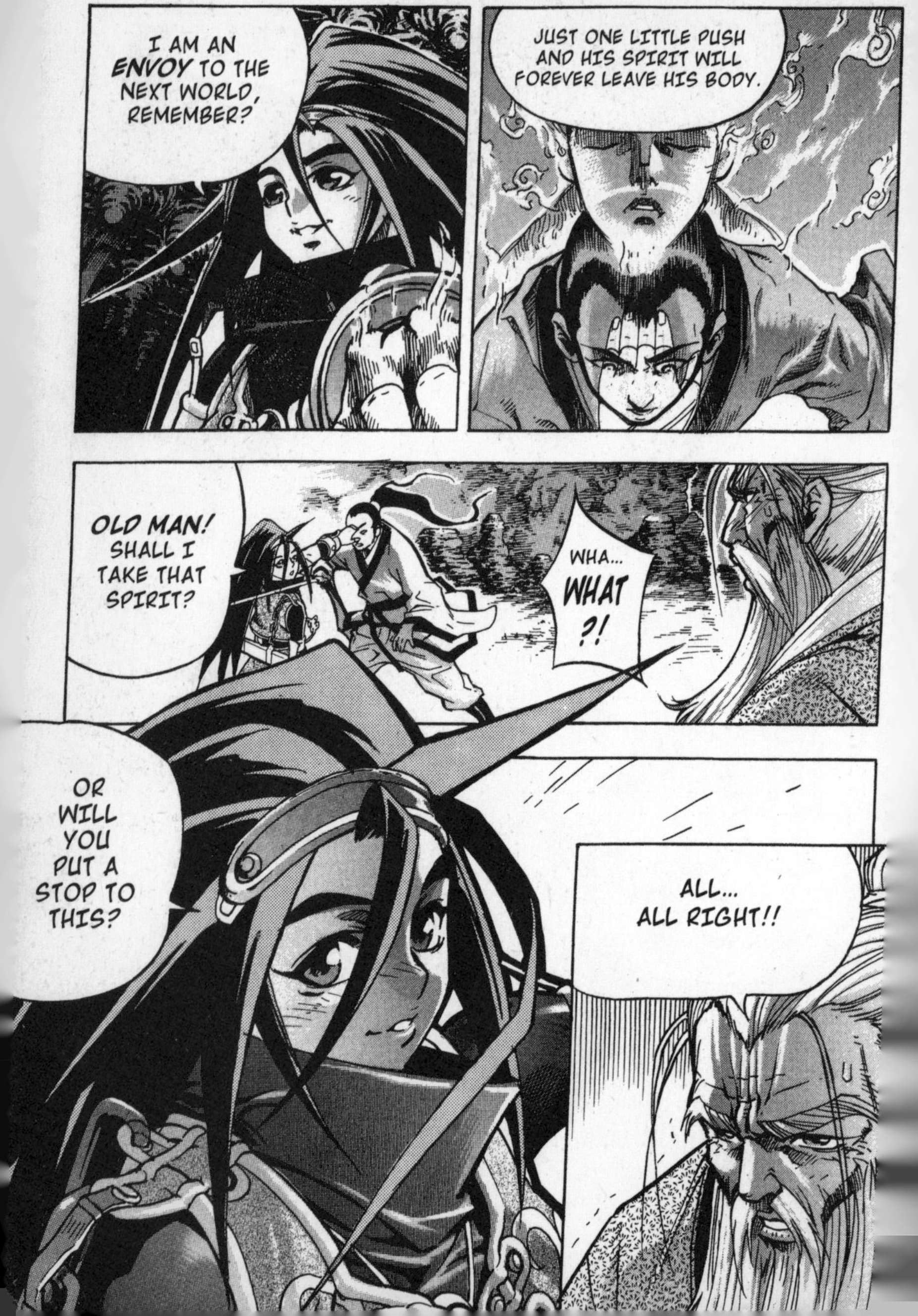
I AM AN ENVOY TO THE NEXT WORLD, REMEMBER?
JUST ONE LITTLE PUSH AND HIS SPIRIT WILL FOREVER LEAVE HIS BODY.
OLD MAN! SHALL I TAKE THAT SPIRIT?
WHA... WHAT ?!
OR WILL YOU PUT A STOP TO THIS?
ALL... ALL RIGHT!!

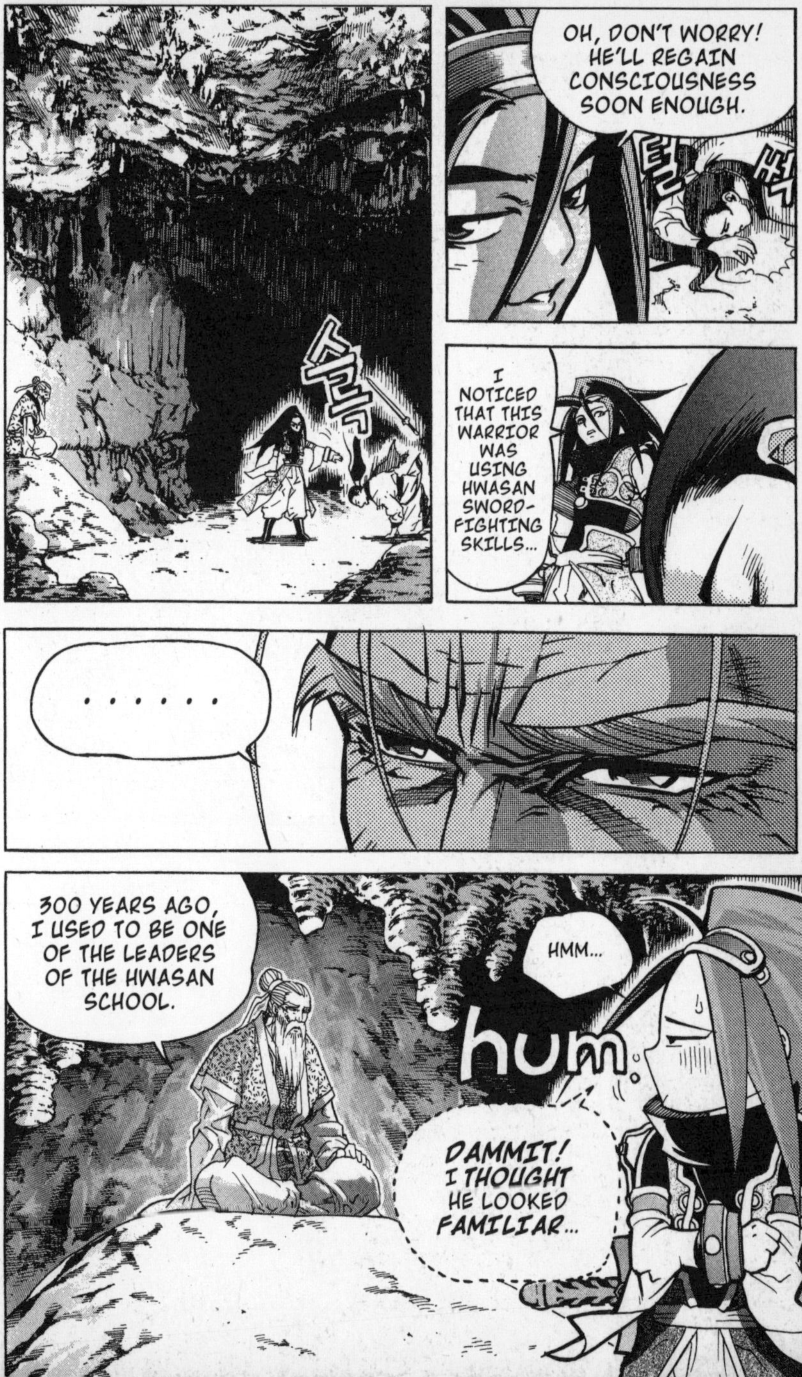
OH, DON'T WORRY! HE'LL REGAIN CONSCIOUSNESS SOON ENOUGH.
I NOTICED THAT THIS WARRIOR WAS USING HWASAN SWORD-FIGHTING SKILLS...
......
300 YEARS AGO, I USED TO BE ONE OF THE LEADERS OF THE HWASAN SCHOOL.
HMM...
hum.
DAMMIT! I THOUGHT HE LOOKED FAMILIAR...

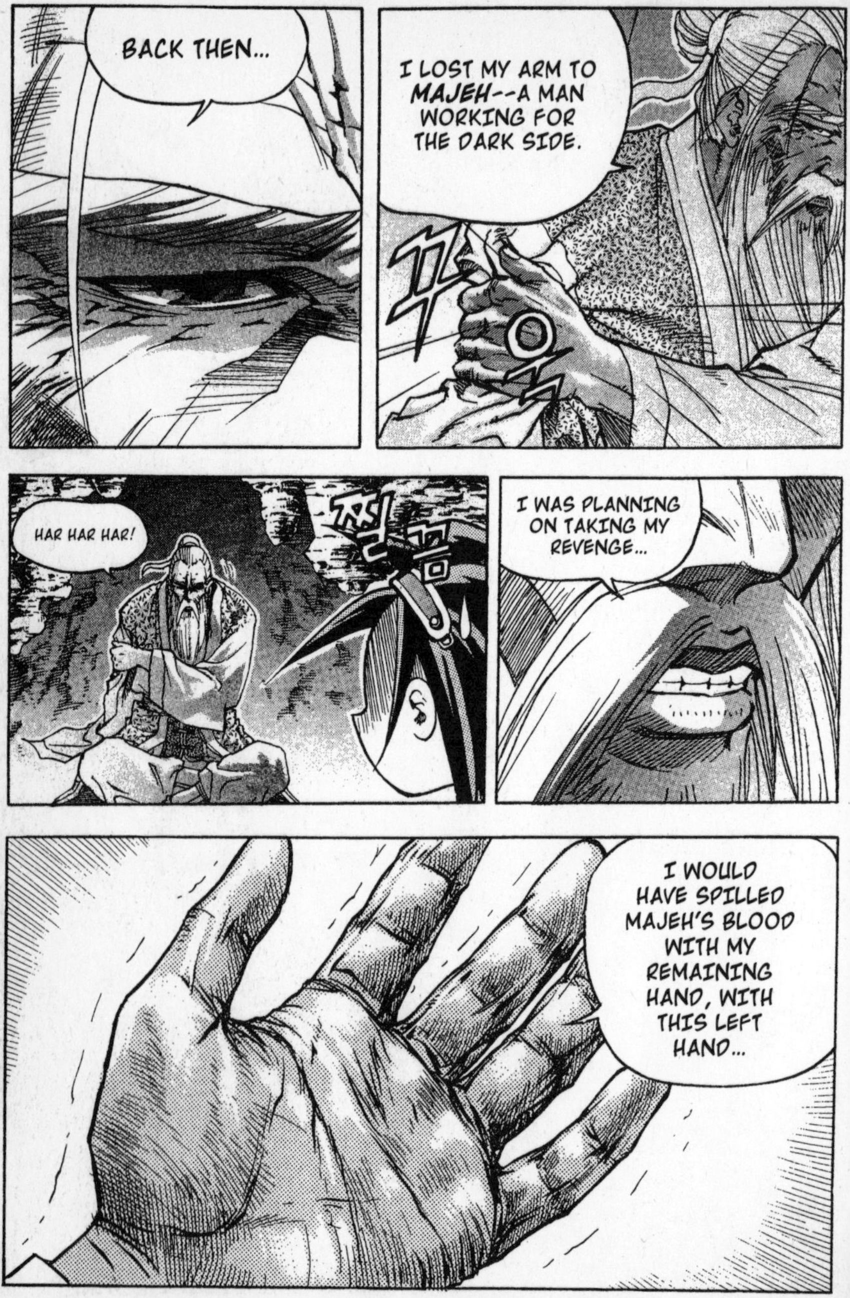
BACK THEN...
I LOST MY ARM TO MAJEH--A MAN WORKING FOR THE DARK SIDE.
HAR HAR HAR!
I WAS PLANNING ON TAKING MY REVENGE...
I WOULD HAVE SPILLED MAJEH'S BLOOD WITH MY REMAINING HAND, WITH THIS LEFT HAND...

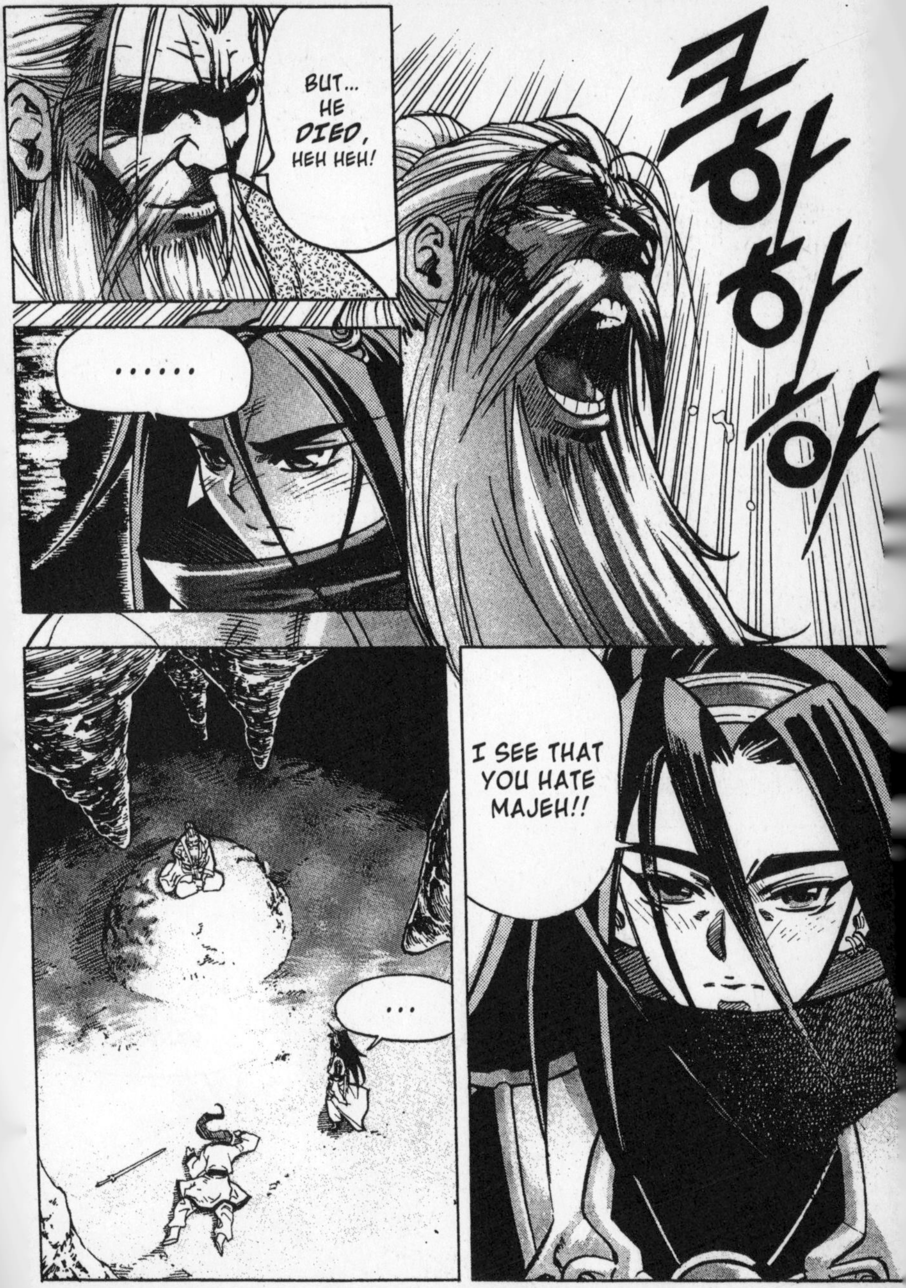
BUT... HE DIED, HEH HEH!
......
크하하하
...
I SEE THAT YOU HATE MAJEH!!

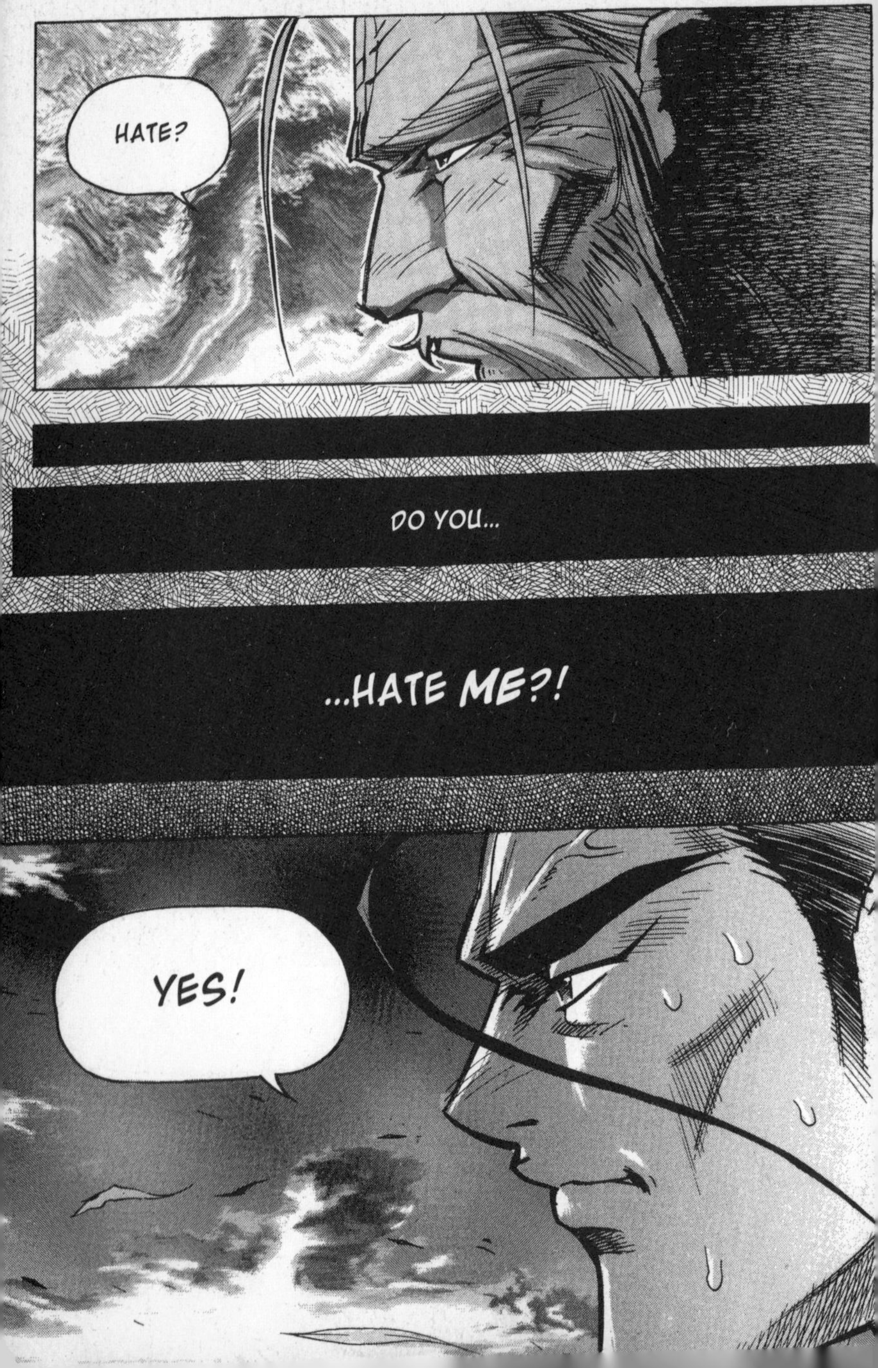
HATE?
DO YOU...
...HATE ME?!
YES!

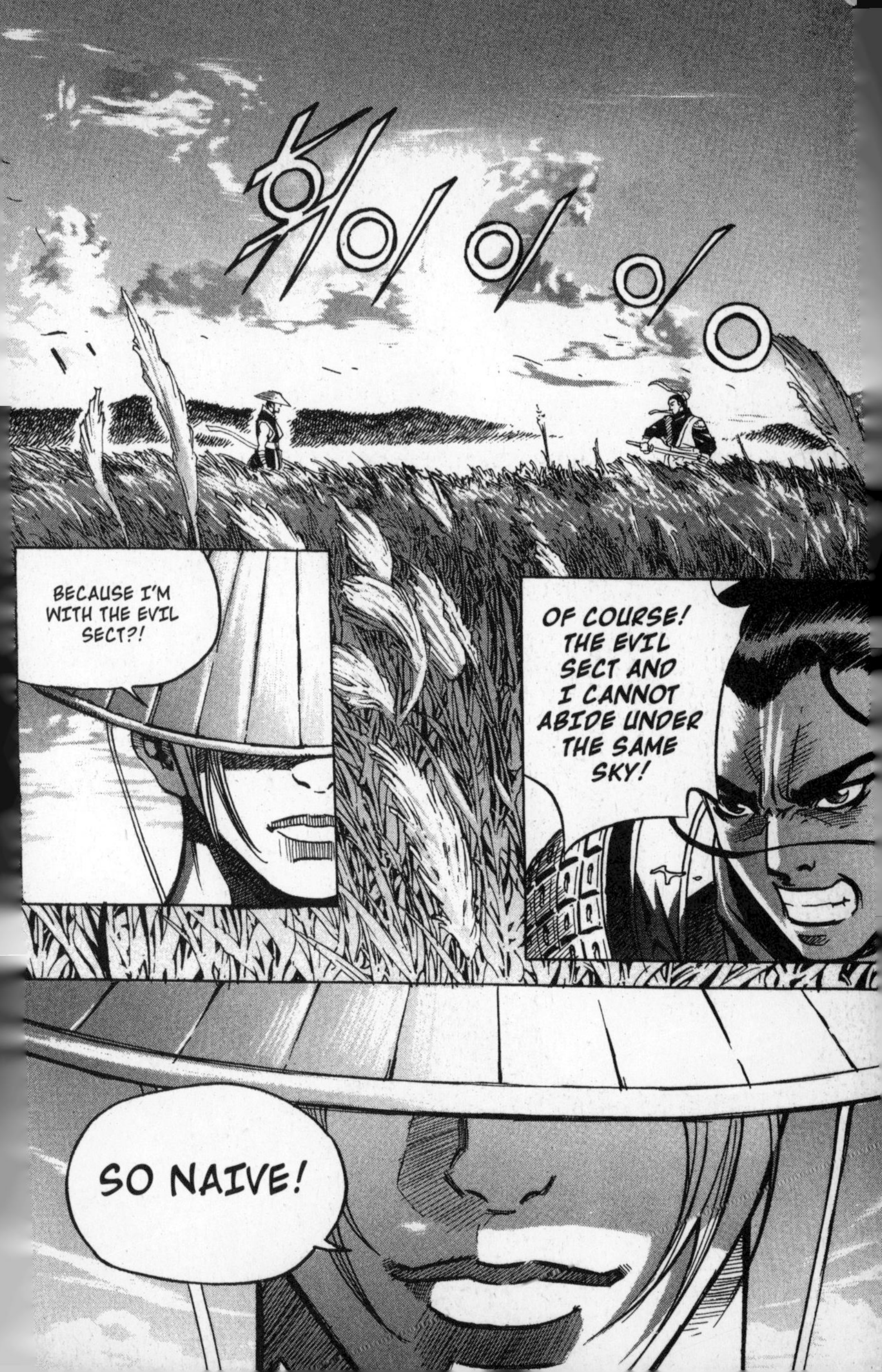
BECAUSE I'M WITH THE EVIL SECT?!
OF COURSE! THE EVIL SECT AND I CANNOT ABIDE UNDER THE SAME SKY!
SO NAIVE!

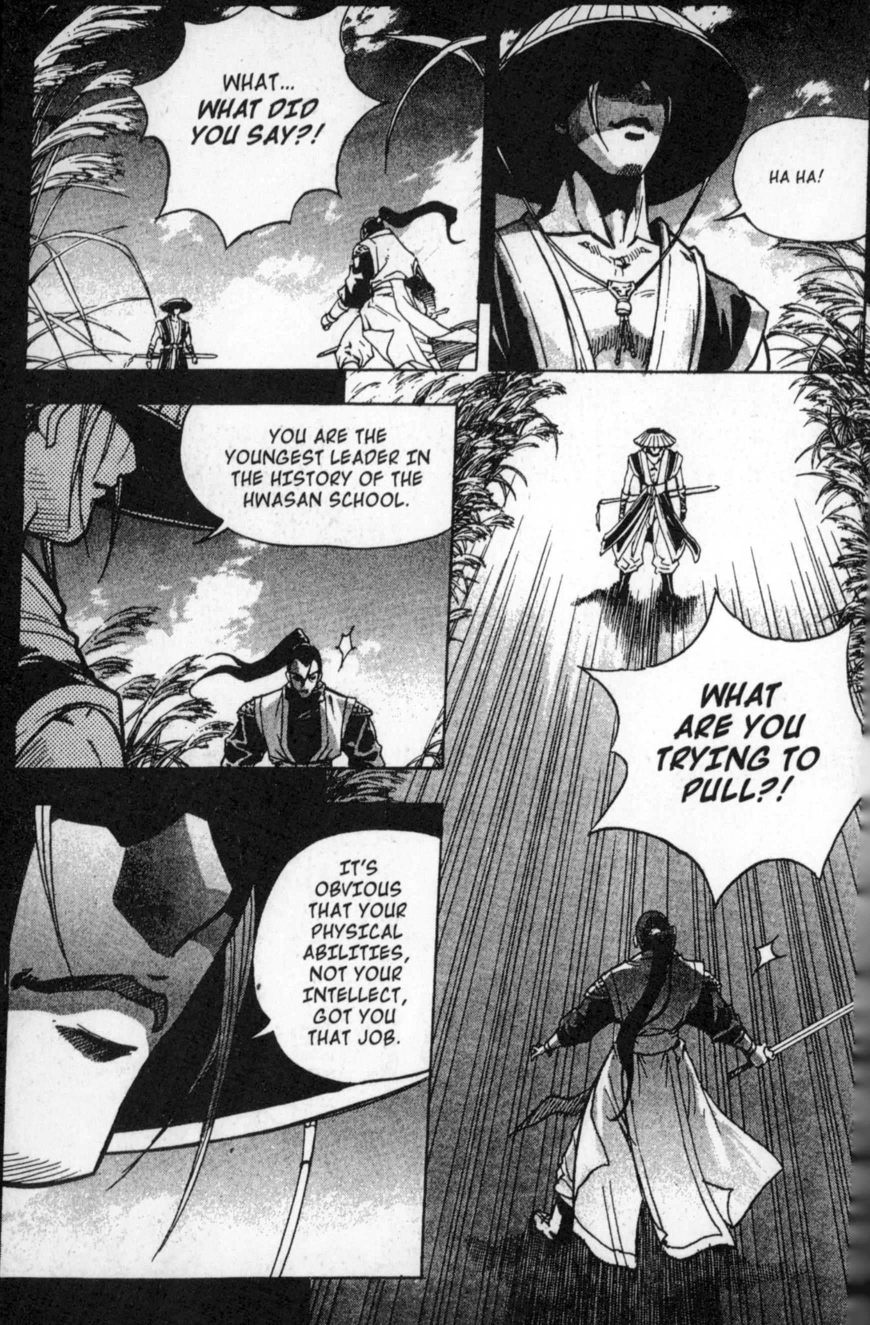
WHAT... WHAT DID YOU SAY?!
HA HA!
YOU ARE THE YOUNGEST LEADER IN THE HISTORY OF THE HWASAN SCHOOL.
IT'S OBVIOUS THAT YOUR PHYSICAL ABILITIES, NOT YOUR INTELLECT, GOT YOU THAT JOB.
WHAT ARE YOU TRYING TO PULL?!

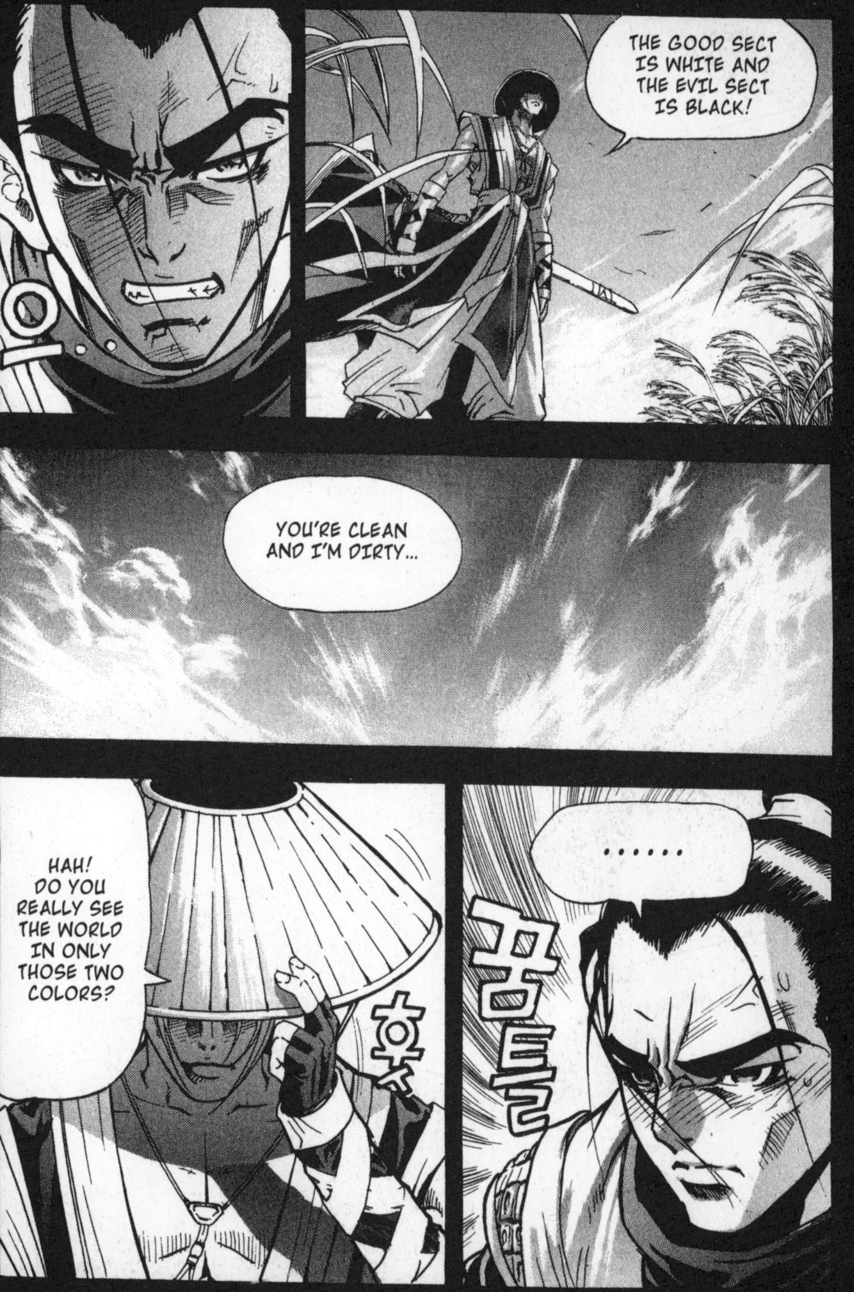
THE GOOD SECT IS WHITE AND THE EVIL SECT IS BLACK!
YOU'RE CLEAN AND I'M DIRTY...
HAH! DO YOU REALLY SEE THE WORLD IN ONLY THOSE TWO COLORS?
......

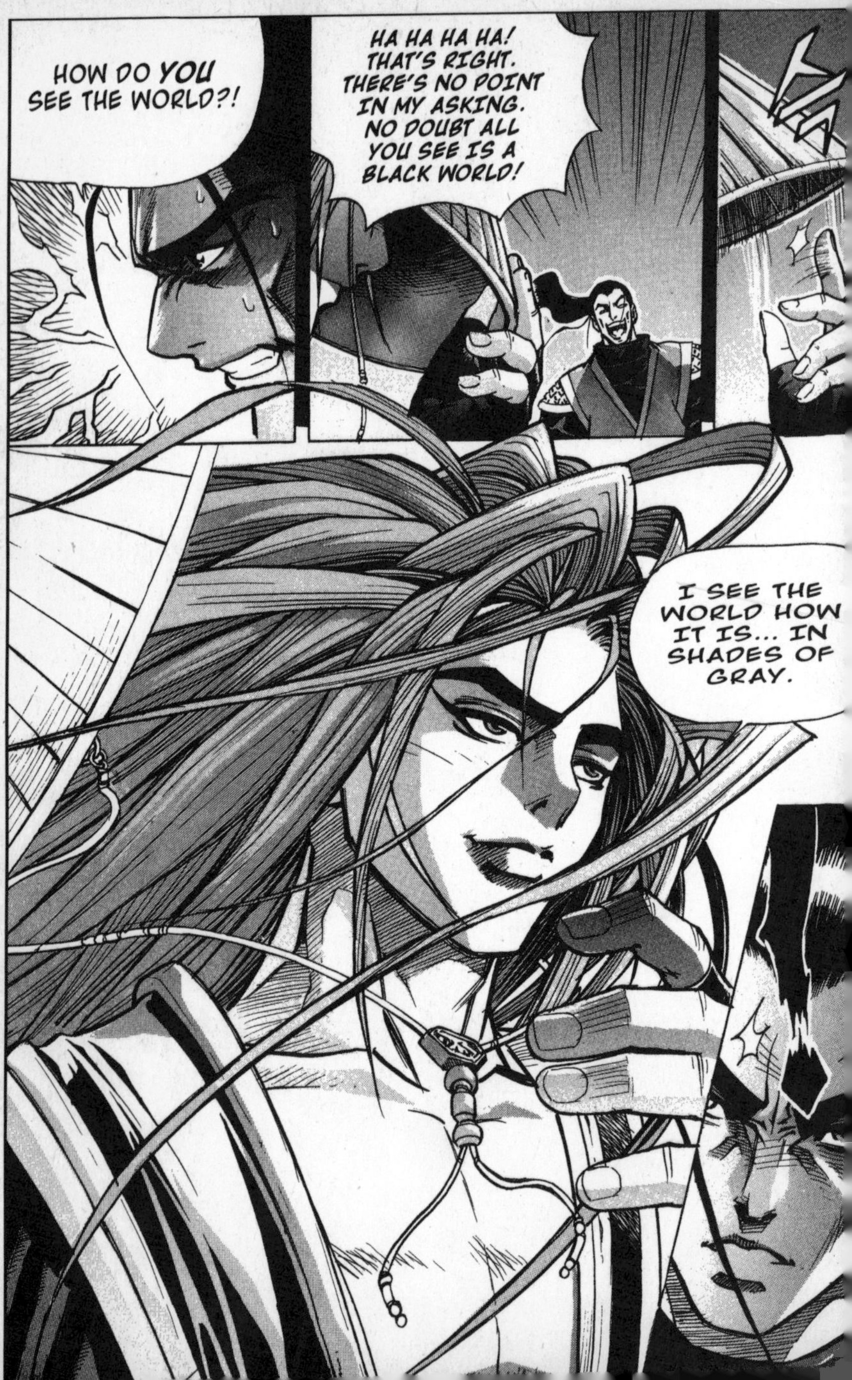
HOW DO YOU SEE THE WORLD?!
HA HA HA HA! THAT'S RIGHT. THERE'S NO POINT IN MY ASKING. NO DOUBT ALL YOU SEE IS A BLACK WORLD!
I SEE THE WORLD HOW IT IS... IN SHADES OF GRAY.

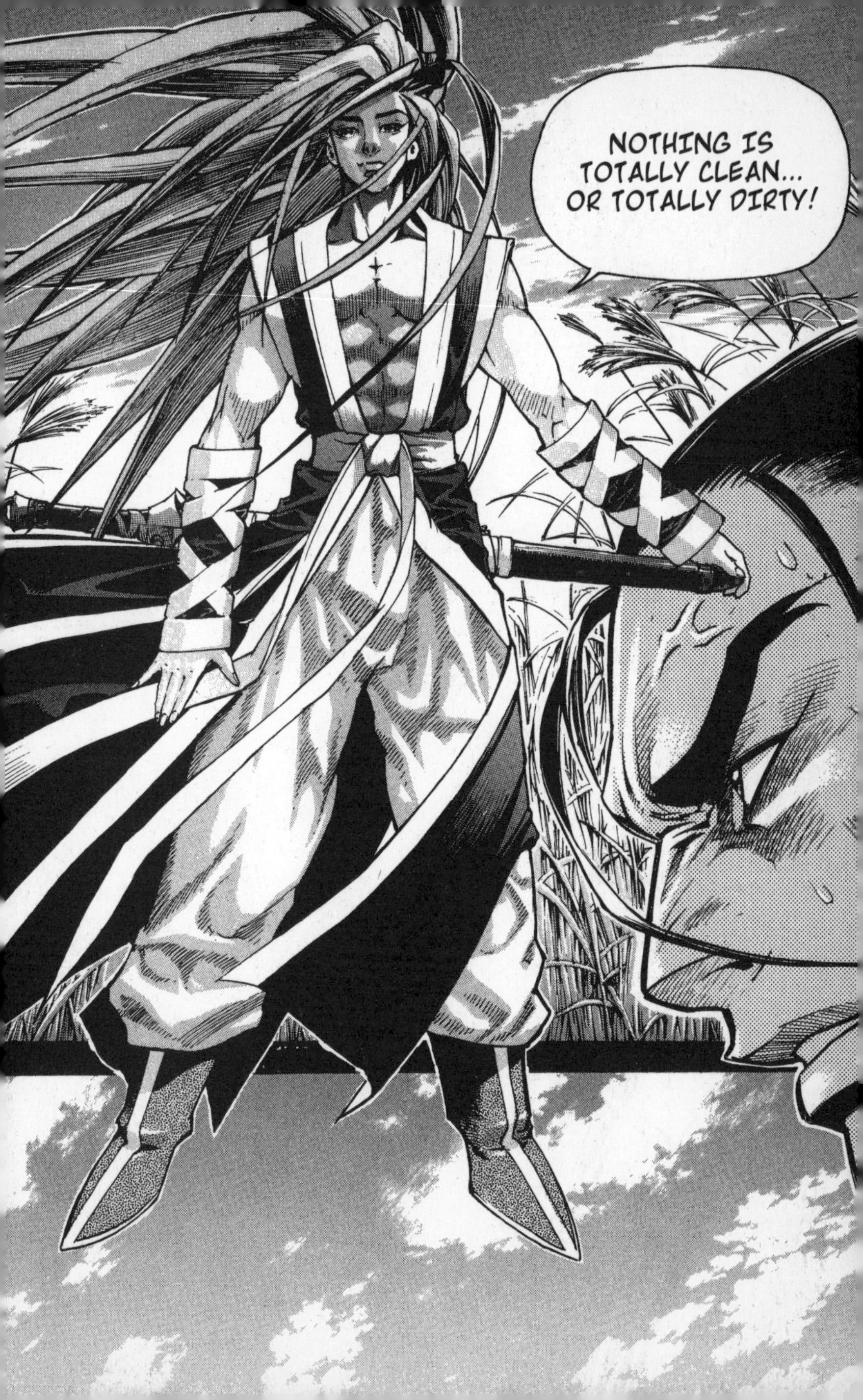
NOTHING IS TOTALLY CLEAN... OR TOTALLY DIRTY!

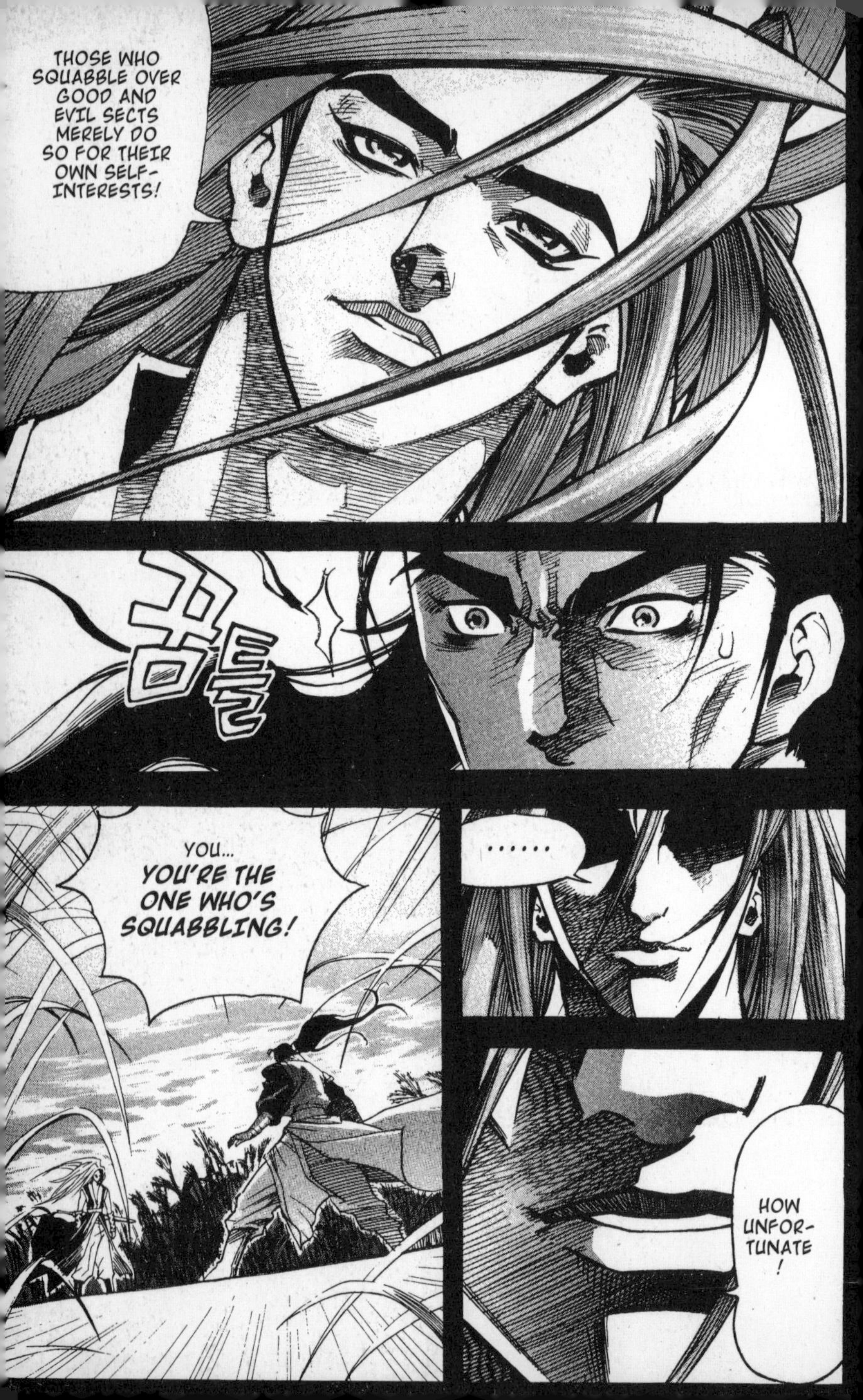
THOSE WHO SQUABBLE OVER GOOD AND EVIL SECTS MERELY DO SO FOR THEIR OWN SELF-INTERESTS!
YOU... *YOU'RE THE ONE WHO'S SQUABBLING!*
......
HOW UNFOR-TUNATE!

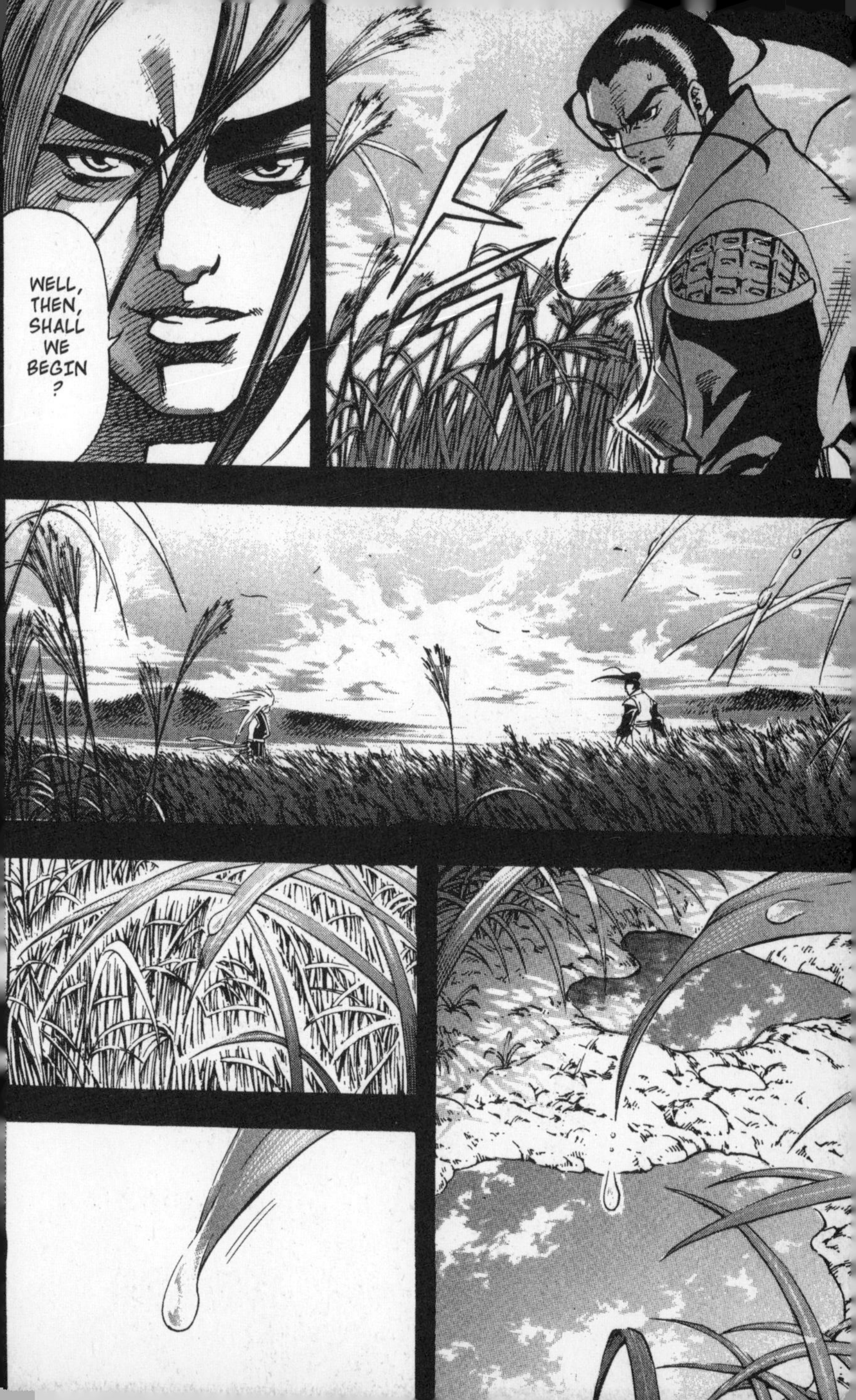
WELL, THEN, SHALL WE BEGIN?

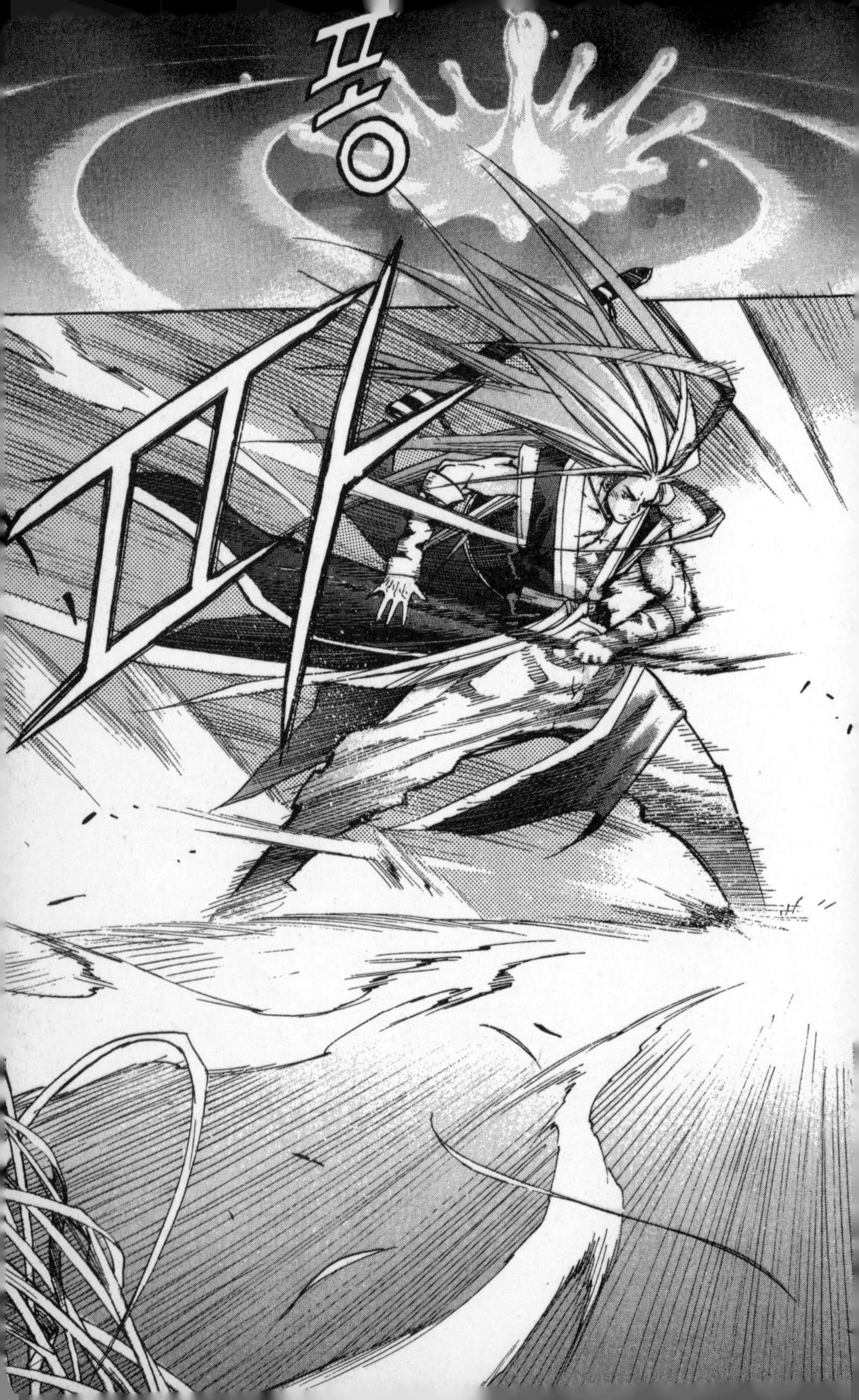
퐁
파

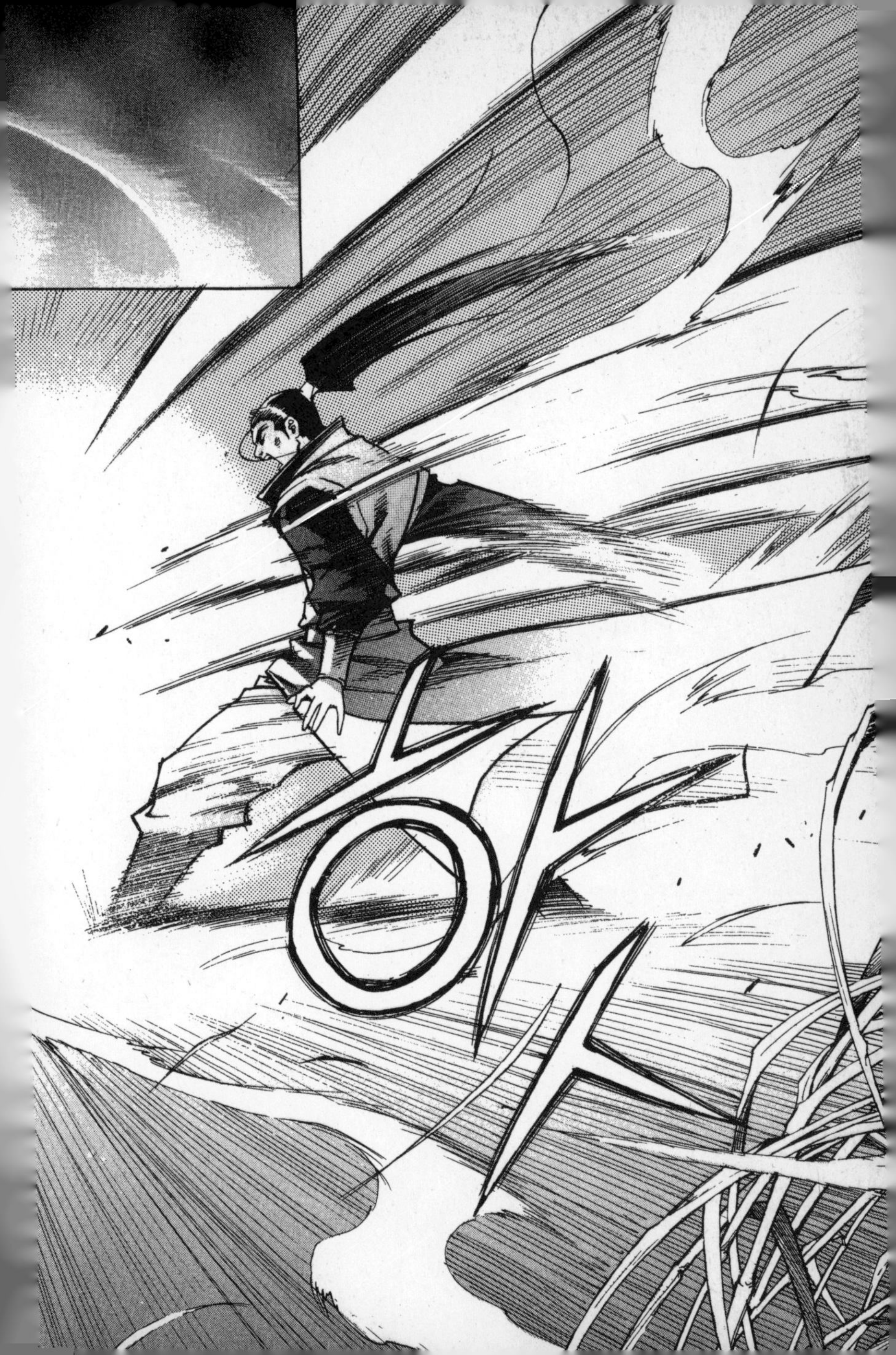

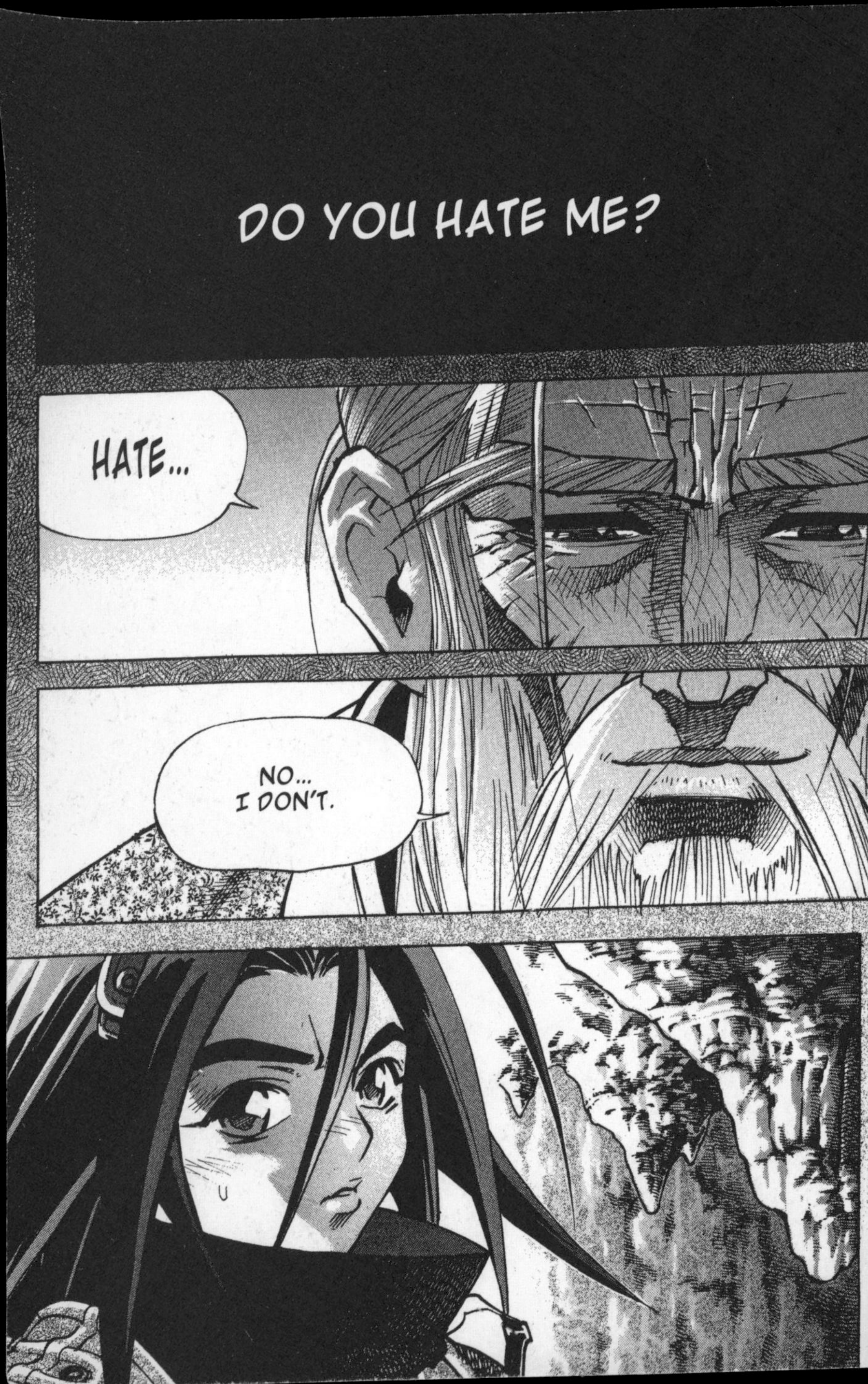
DO YOU HATE ME?
HATE...
NO... I DON'T.

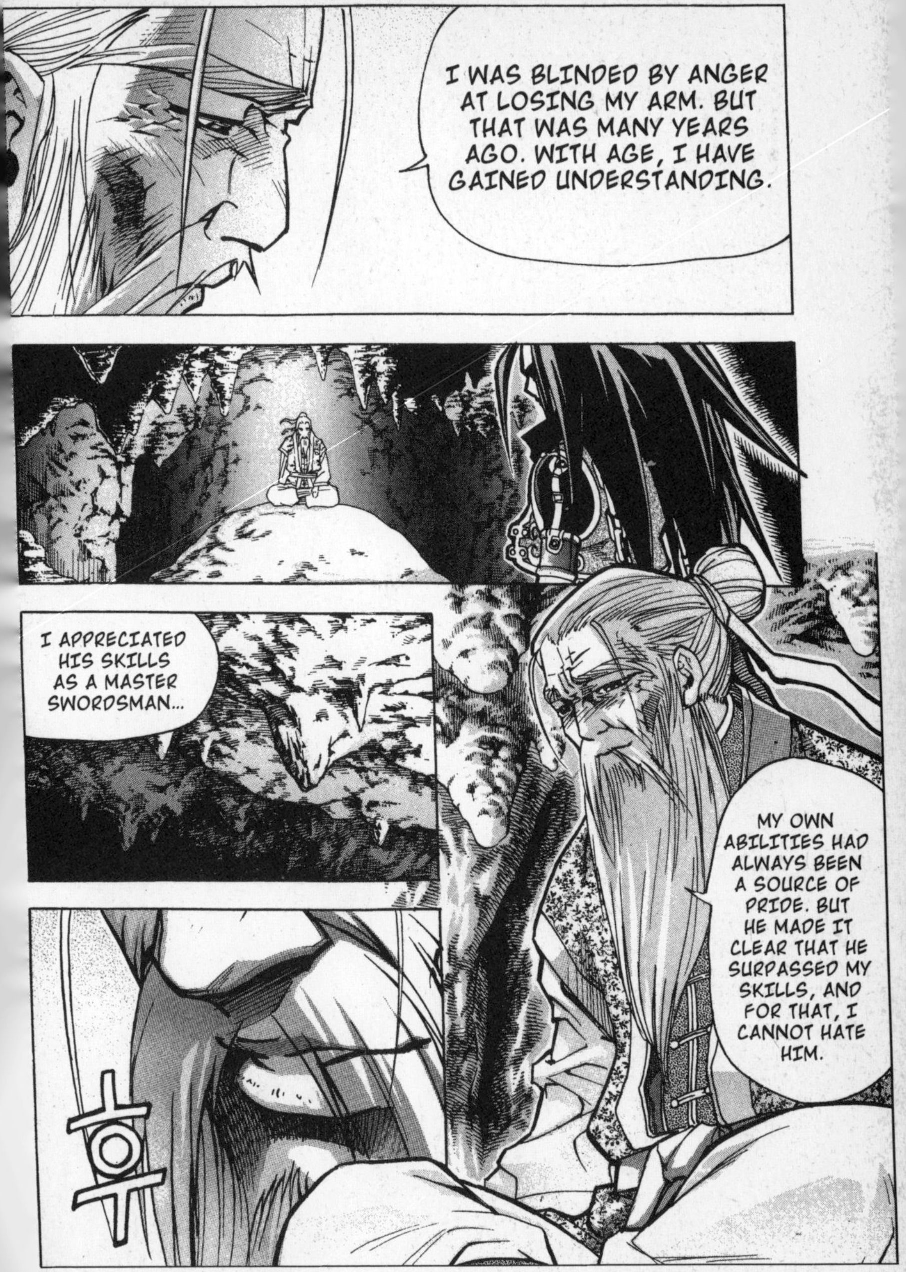

I WAS BLINDED BY ANGER AT LOSING MY ARM. BUT THAT WAS MANY YEARS AGO. WITH AGE, I HAVE GAINED UNDERSTANDING.
I APPRECIATED HIS SKILLS AS A MASTER SWORDSMAN...
MY OWN ABILITIES HAD ALWAYS BEEN A SOURCE OF PRIDE. BUT HE MADE IT CLEAR THAT HE SURPASSED MY SKILLS, AND FOR THAT, I CANNOT HATE HIM.

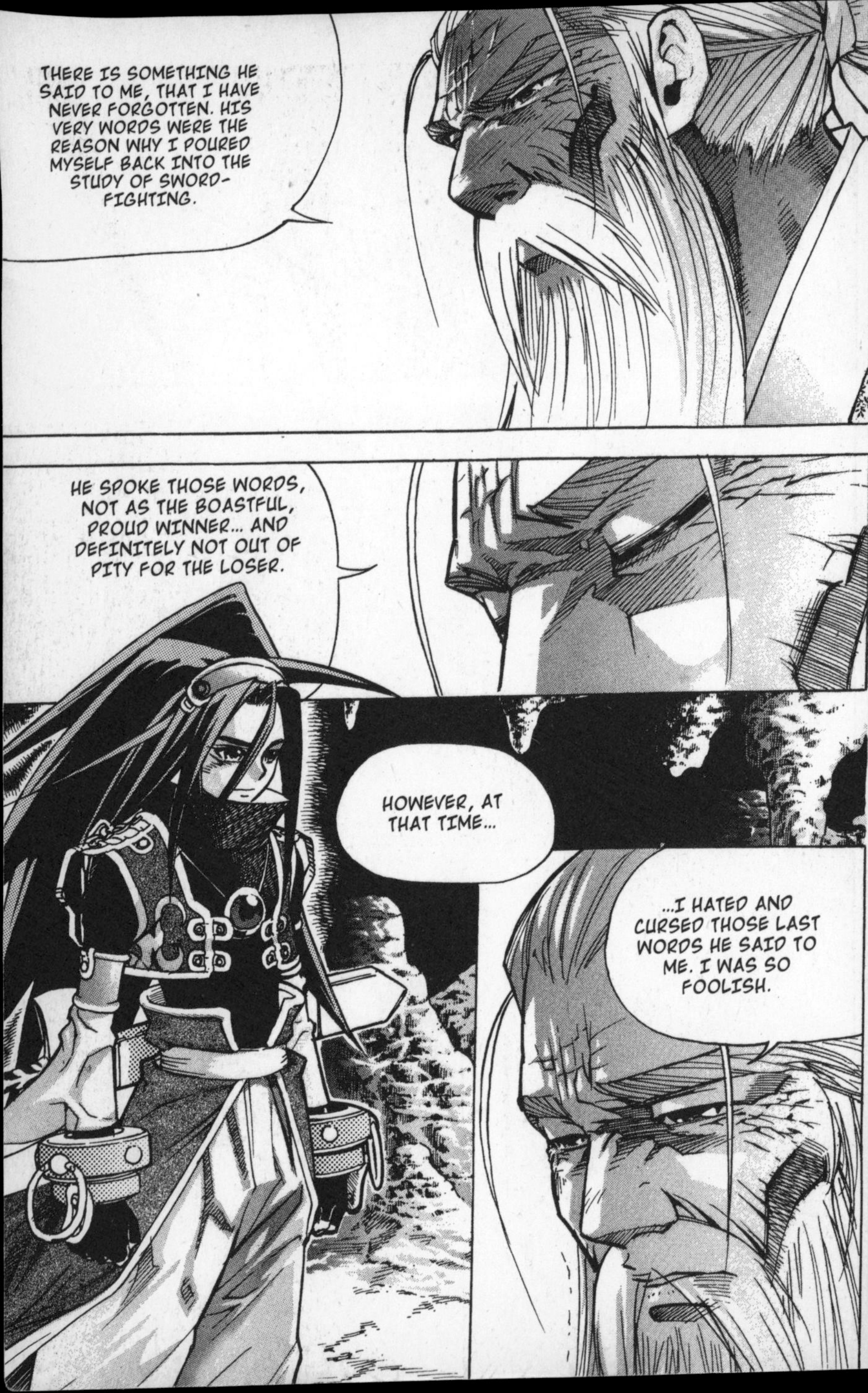
THERE IS SOMETHING HE SAID TO ME, THAT I HAVE NEVER FORGOTTEN. HIS VERY WORDS WERE THE REASON WHY I POURED MYSELF BACK INTO THE STUDY OF SWORD-FIGHTING.
HE SPOKE THOSE WORDS, NOT AS THE BOASTFUL, PROUD WINNER... AND DEFINITELY NOT OUT OF PITY FOR THE LOSER.
HOWEVER, AT THAT TIME...
...I HATED AND CURSED THOSE LAST WORDS HE SAID TO ME. I WAS SO FOOLISH.

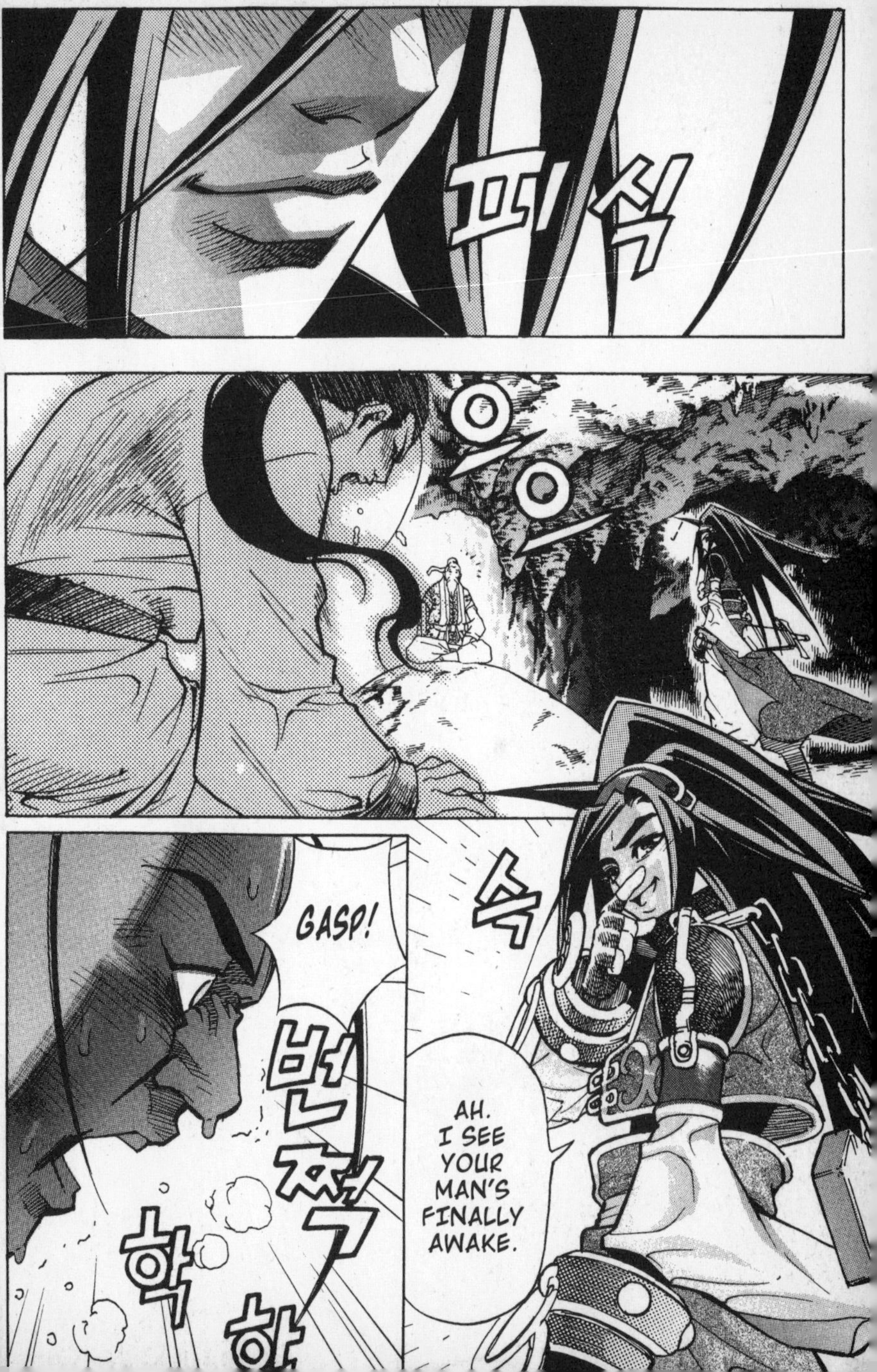
피식
응응
GASP!
번쩍
헉 헉
슥
AH. I SEE YOUR MAN'S FINALLY AWAKE.

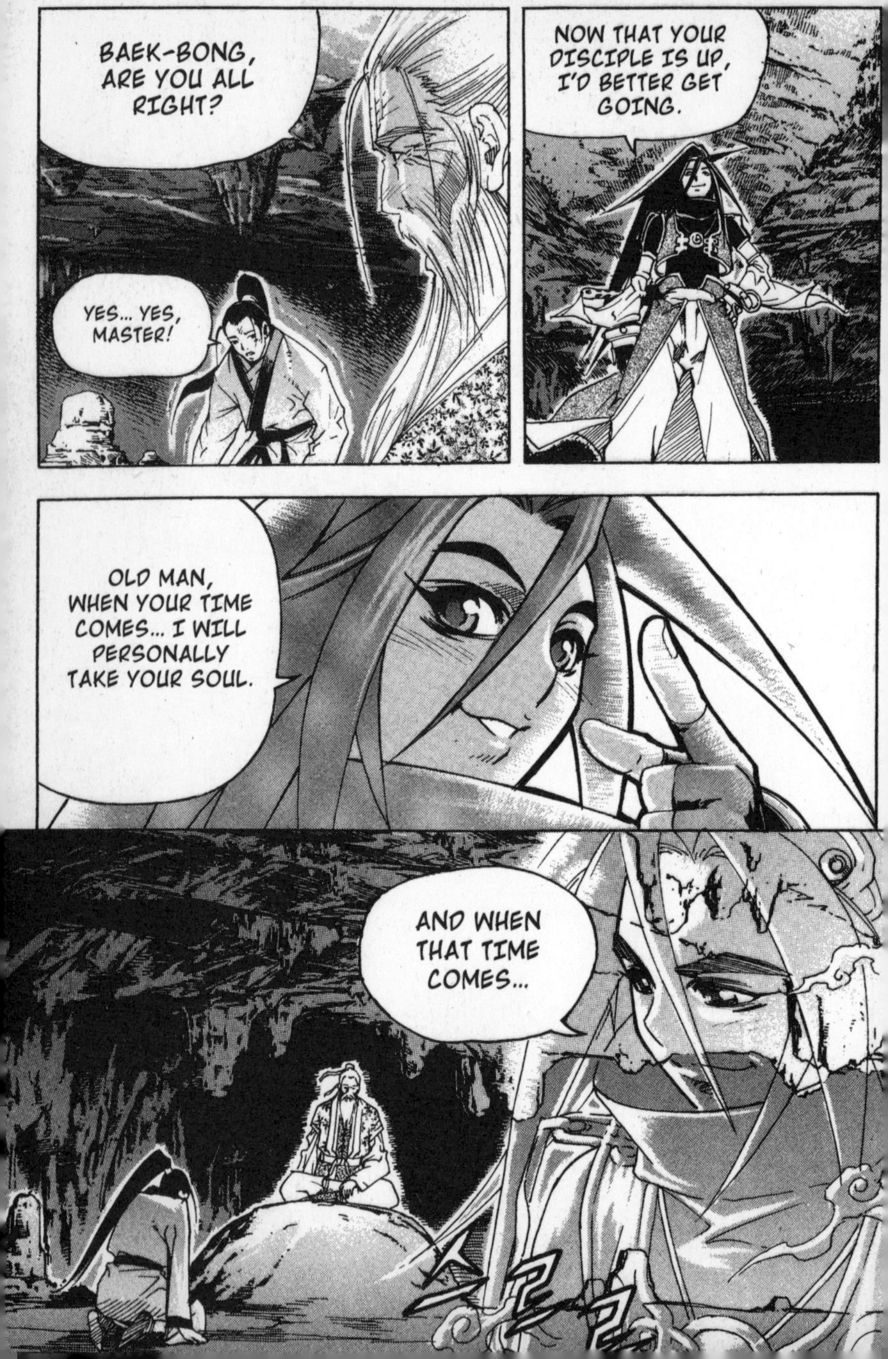
BAEK-BONG, ARE YOU ALL RIGHT?
YES... YES, MASTER!
NOW THAT YOUR DISCIPLE IS UP, I'D BETTER GET GOING.
OLD MAN, WHEN YOUR TIME COMES... I WILL PERSONALLY TAKE YOUR SOUL.
AND WHEN THAT TIME COMES...

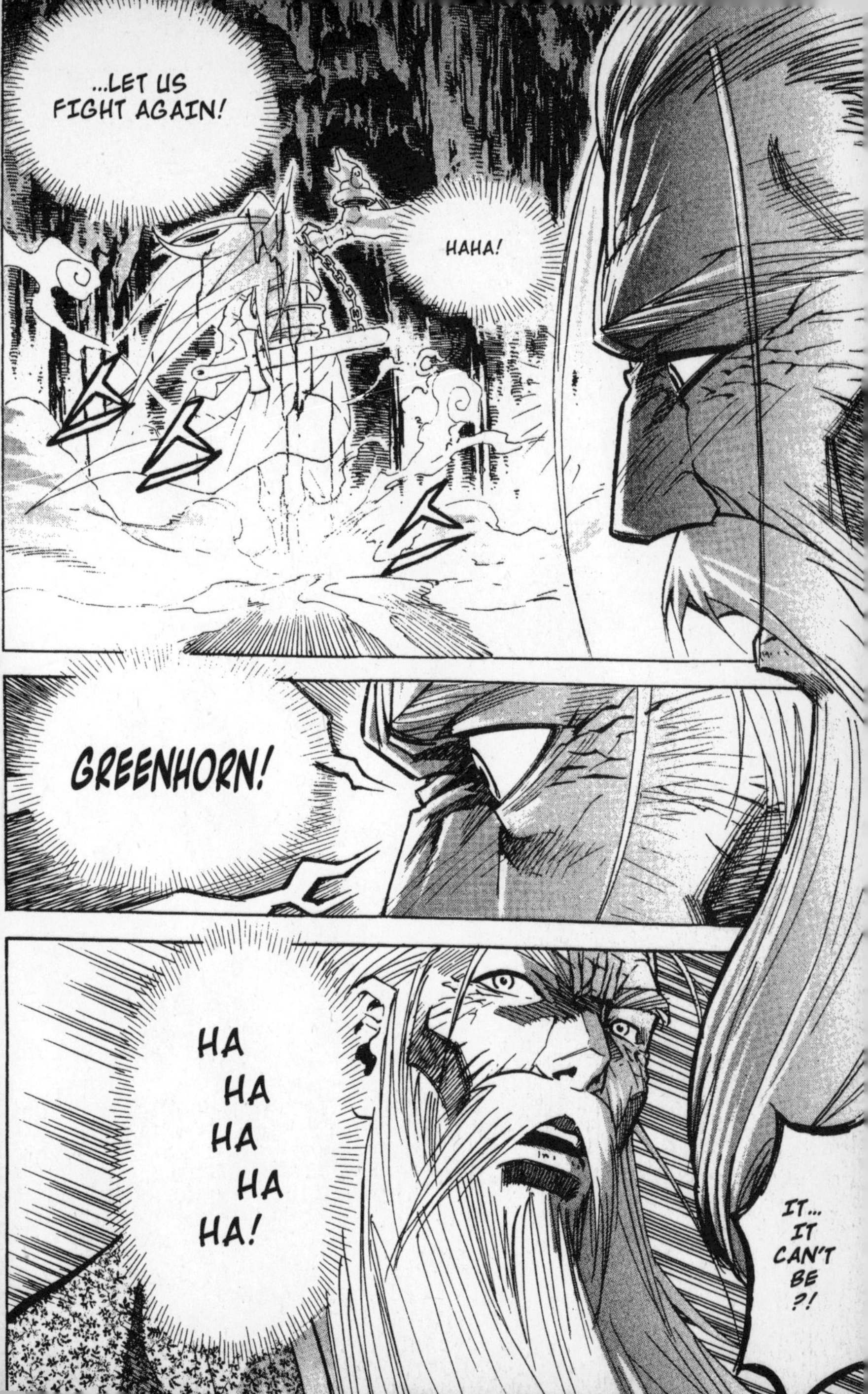
...LET US FIGHT AGAIN!
HAHA!
GREENHORN!
HA HA HA HA HA!
IT... IT CAN'T BE ?!

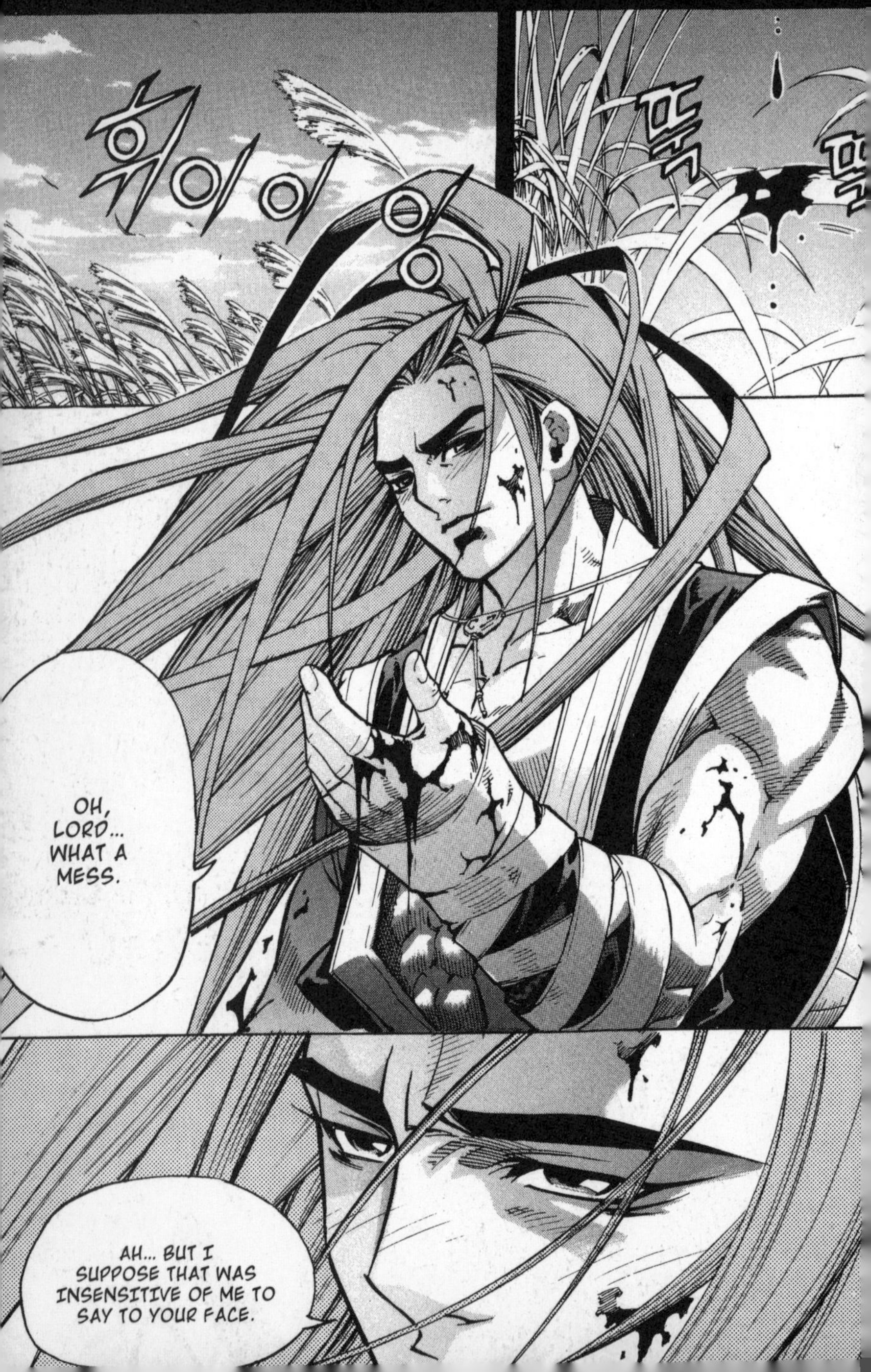
휘이이잉
뚝
뚝
OH, LORD... WHAT A MESS.
AH... BUT I SUPPOSE THAT WAS INSENSITIVE OF ME TO SAY TO YOUR FACE.

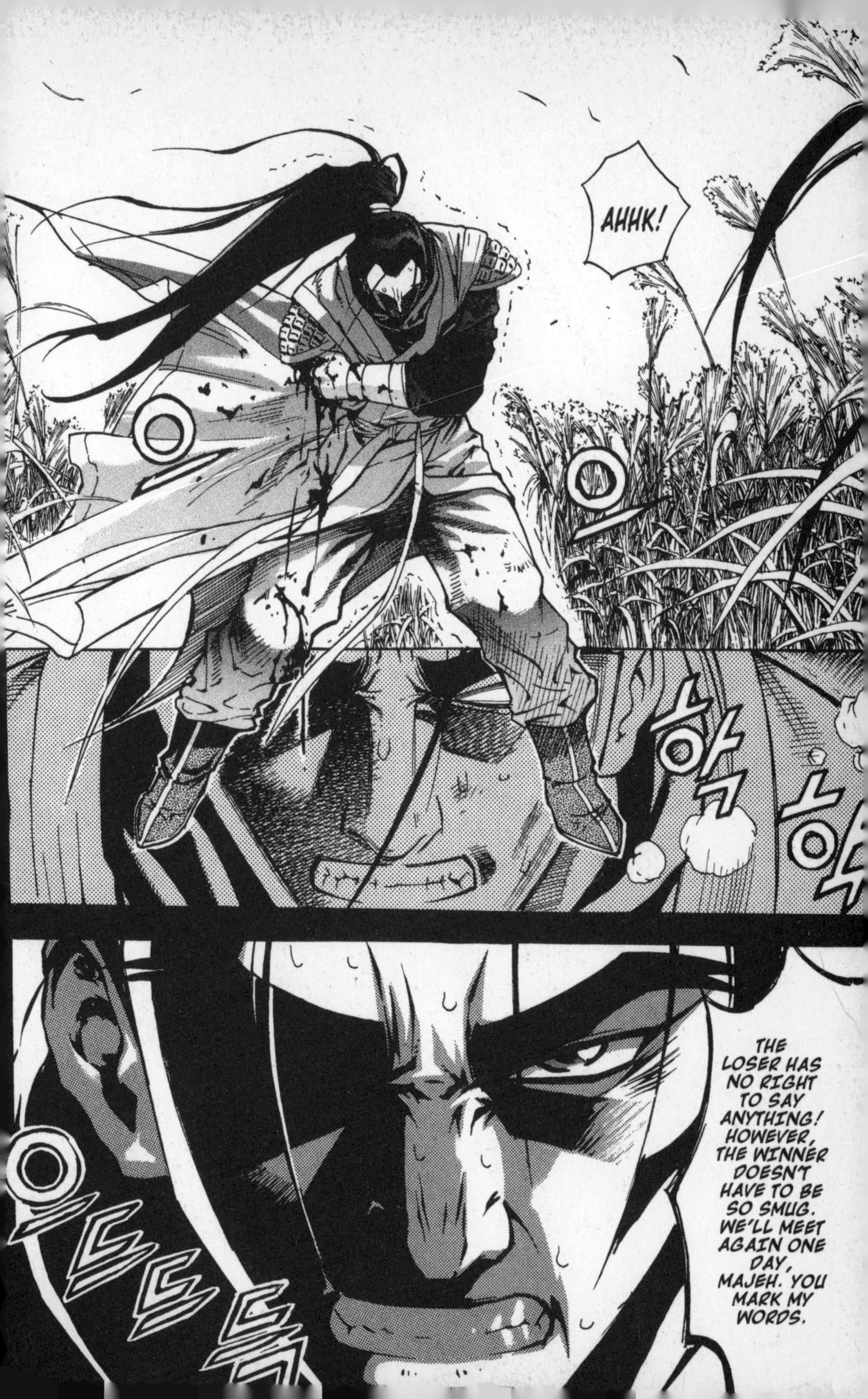
AHHK!
THE LOSER HAS NO RIGHT TO SAY ANYTHING! HOWEVER, THE WINNER DOESN'T HAVE TO BE SO SMUG. WE'LL MEET AGAIN ONE DAY, MAJEH. YOU MARK MY WORDS.

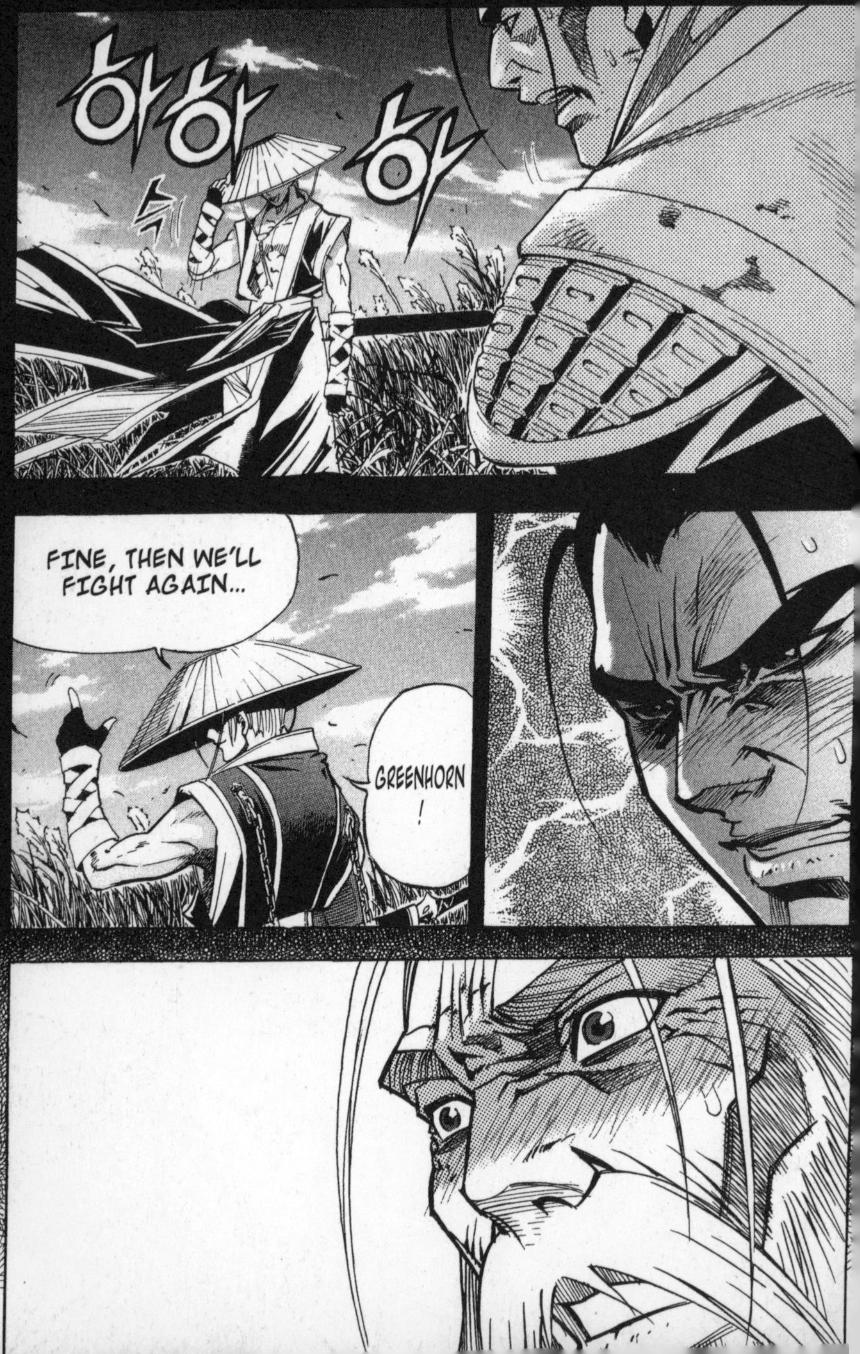
하하하
흐
FINE, THEN WE'LL FIGHT AGAIN...
GREENHORN!

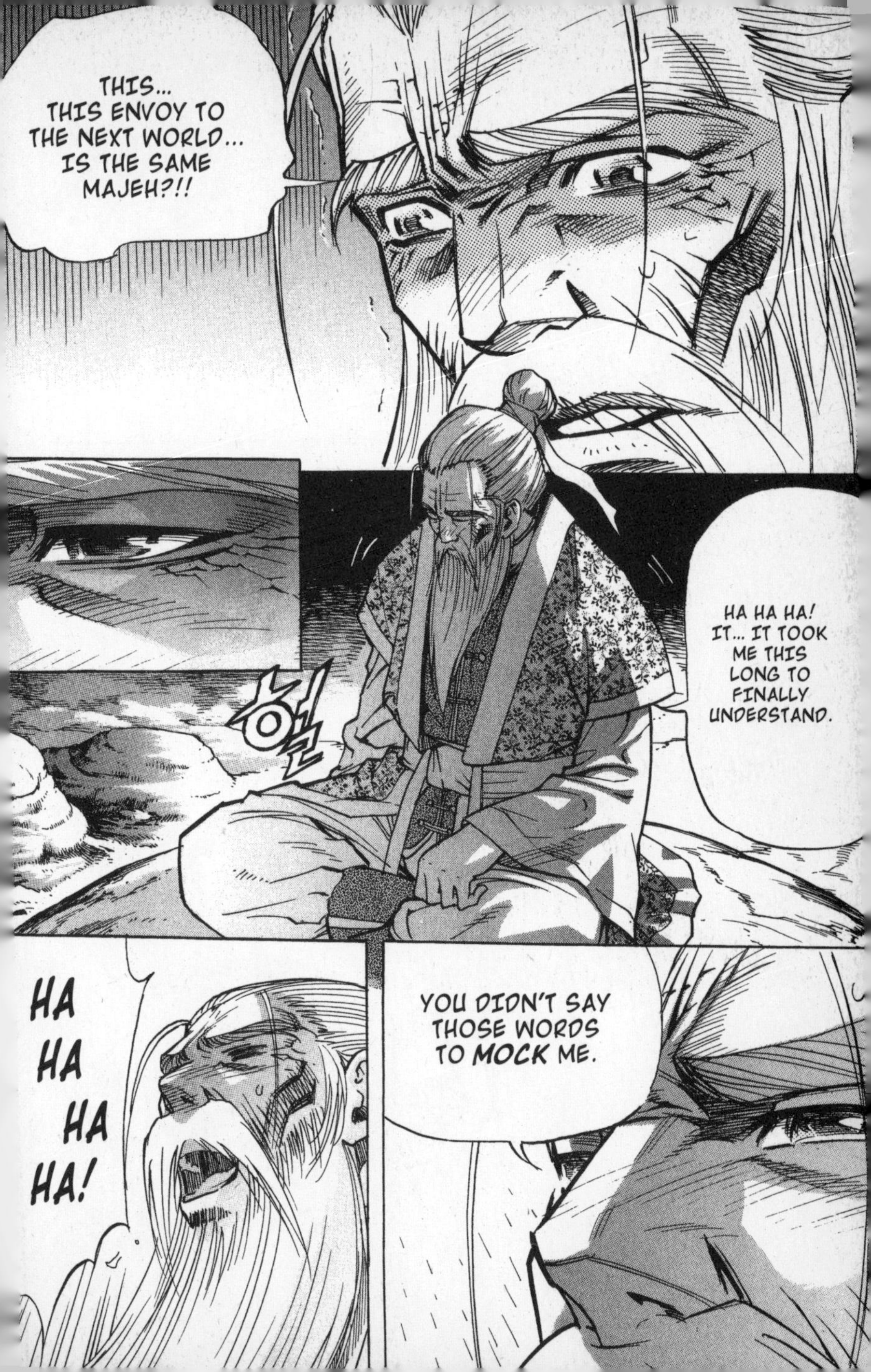
THIS... THIS ENVOY TO THE NEXT WORLD... IS THE SAME MAJEH?!!
HA HA HA! IT... IT TOOK ME THIS LONG TO FINALLY UNDERSTAND.
HA HA HA HA!
YOU DIDN'T SAY THOSE WORDS TO MOCK ME.

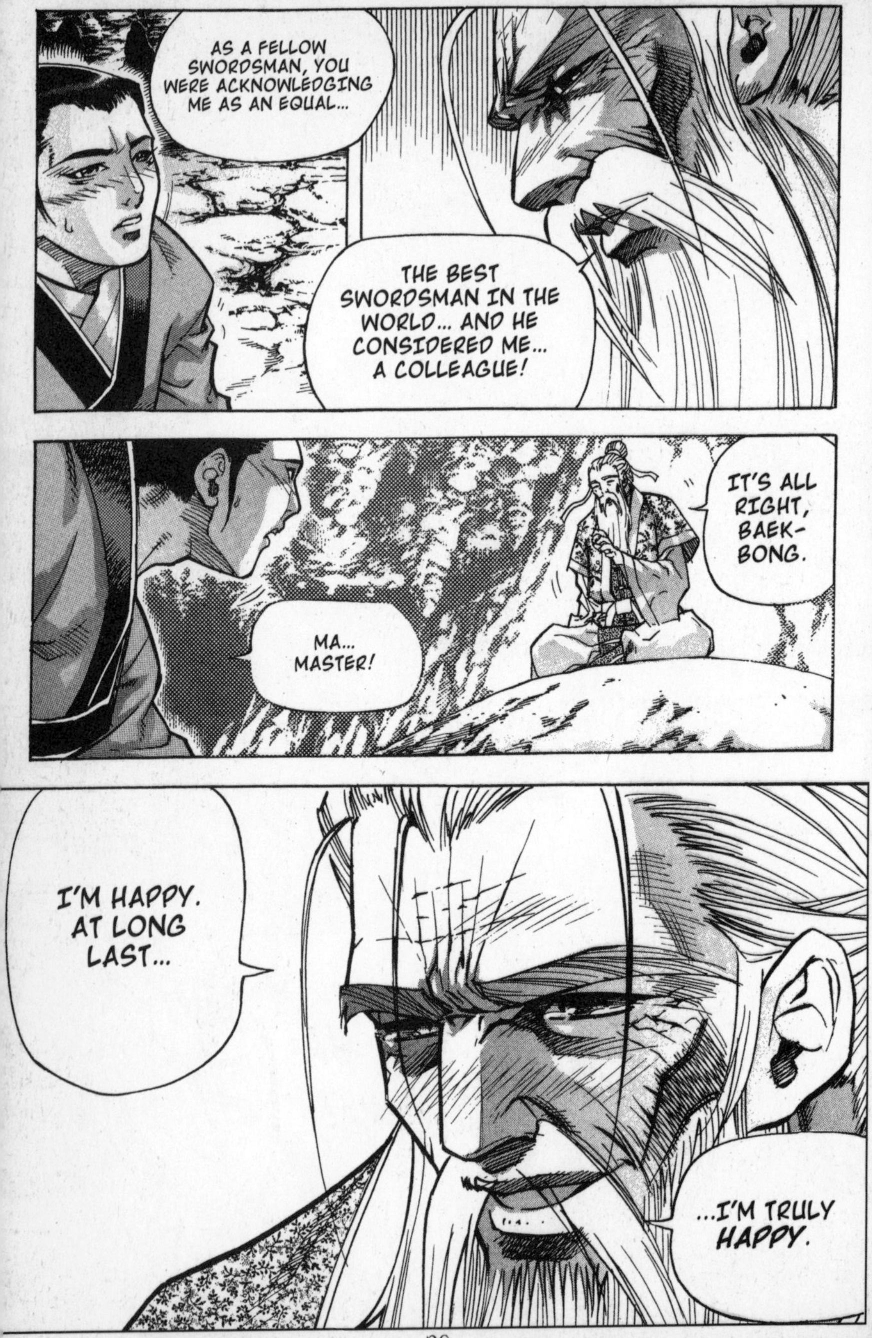
AS A FELLOW SWORDSMAN, YOU WERE ACKNOWLEDGING ME AS AN EQUAL...
THE BEST SWORDSMAN IN THE WORLD... AND HE CONSIDERED ME... A COLLEAGUE!
MA... MASTER!
IT'S ALL RIGHT, BAEK-BONG.
I'M HAPPY. AT LONG LAST...
...I'M TRULY HAPPY.

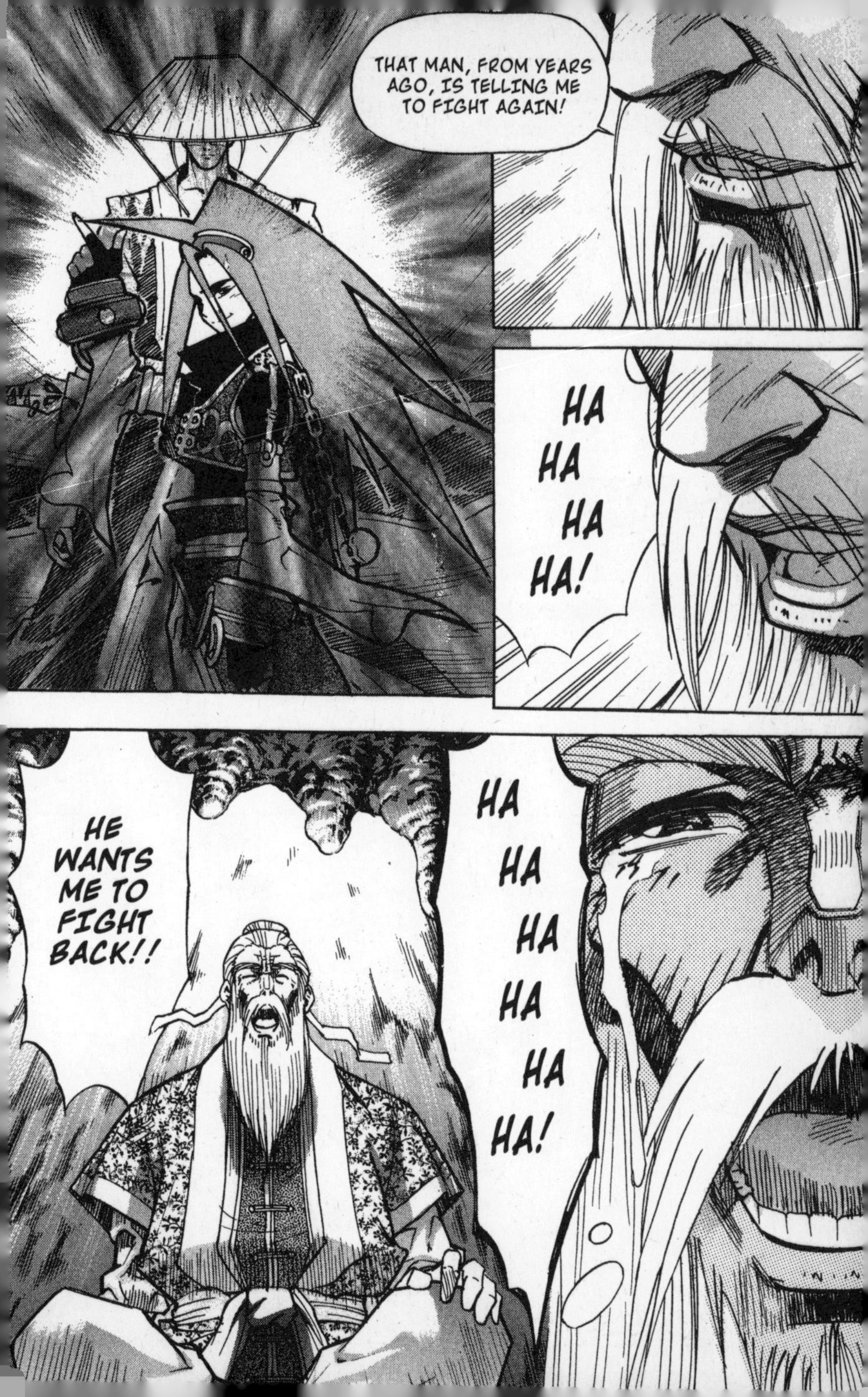
THAT MAN, FROM YEARS AGO, IS TELLING ME TO FIGHT AGAIN!
HA HA HA HA!
HE WANTS ME TO FIGHT BACK!!
HA HA HA HA HA HA!

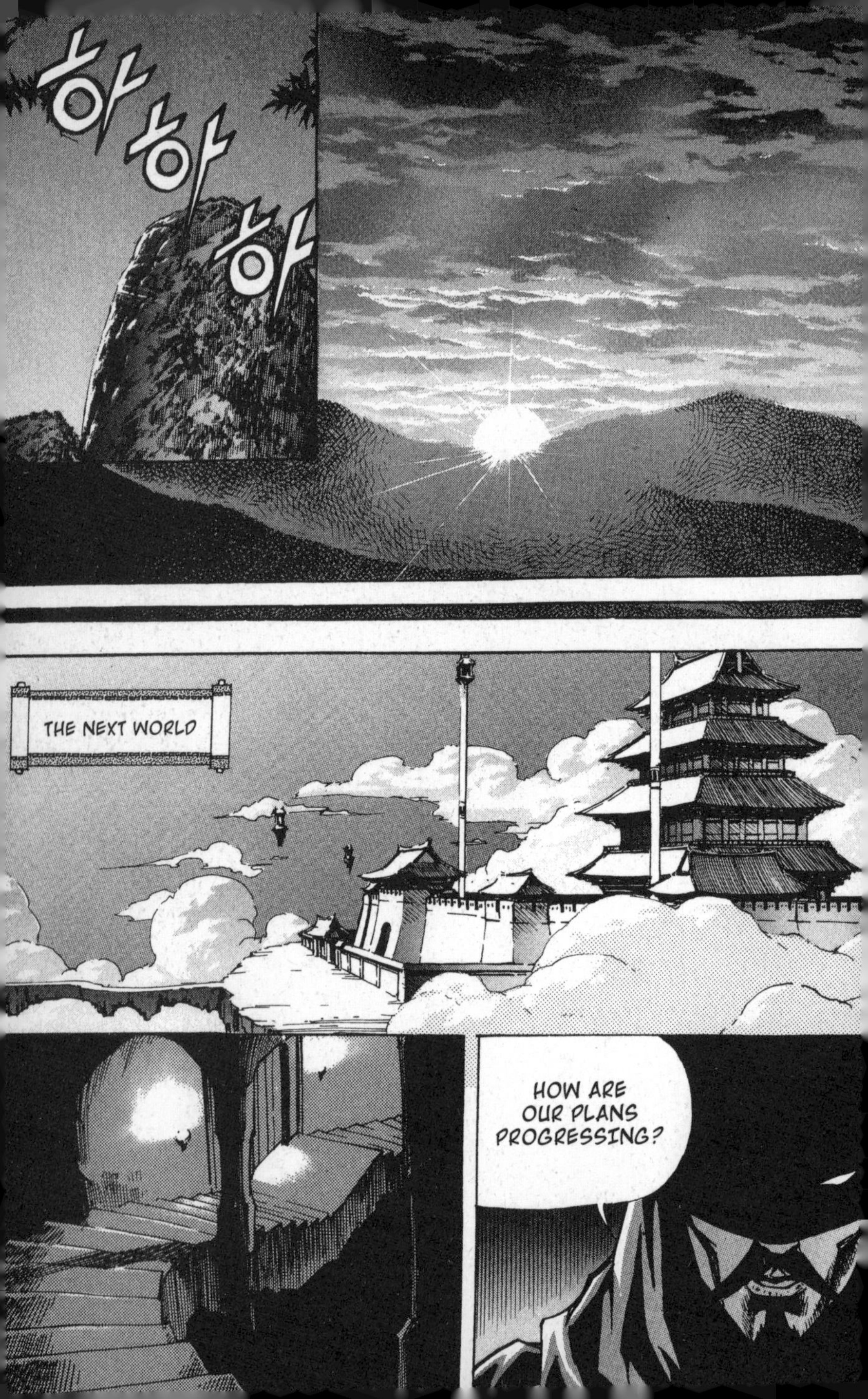

하하하
THE NEXT WORLD
HOW ARE OUR PLANS PROGRESSING?

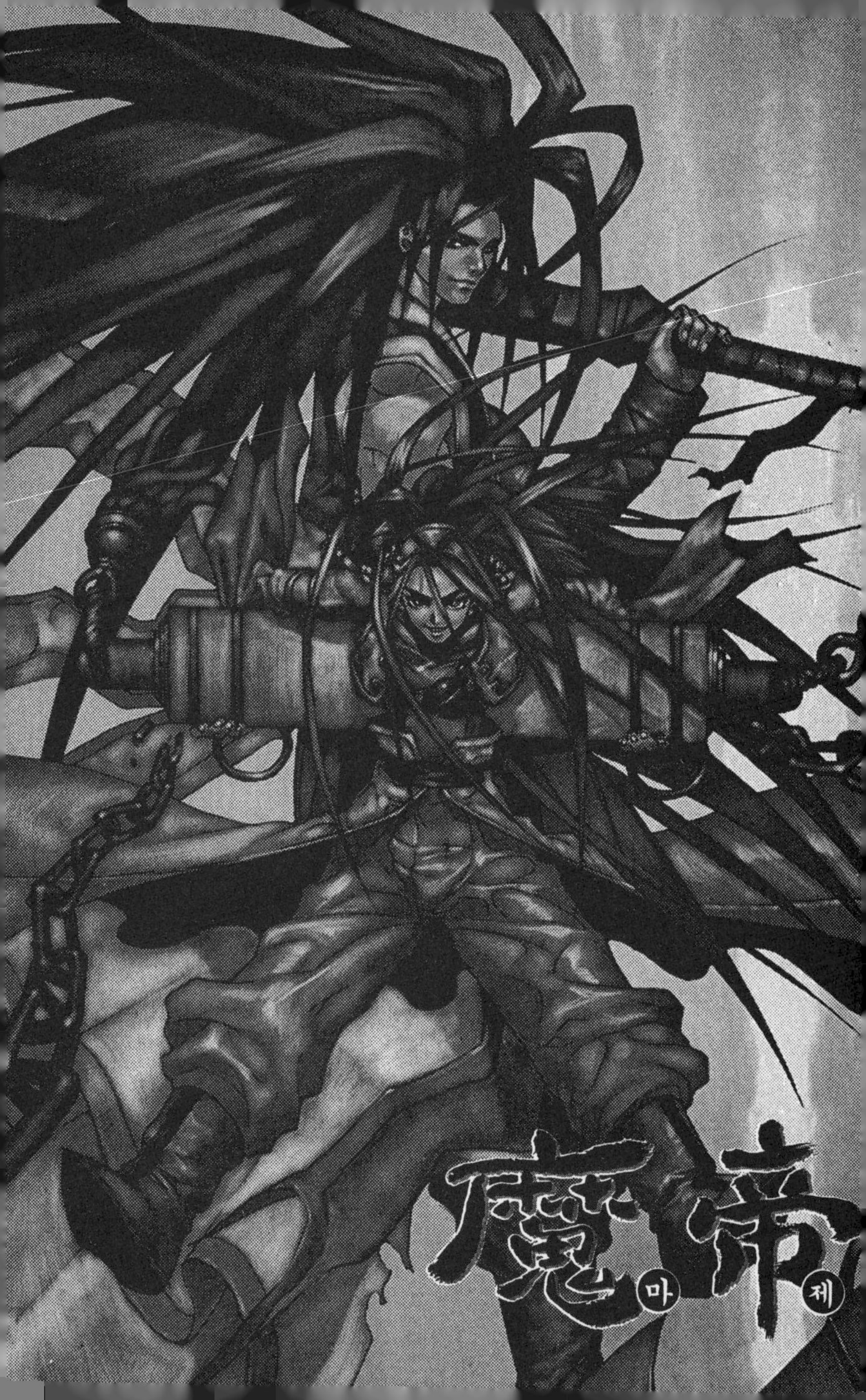

魔帝
마 제

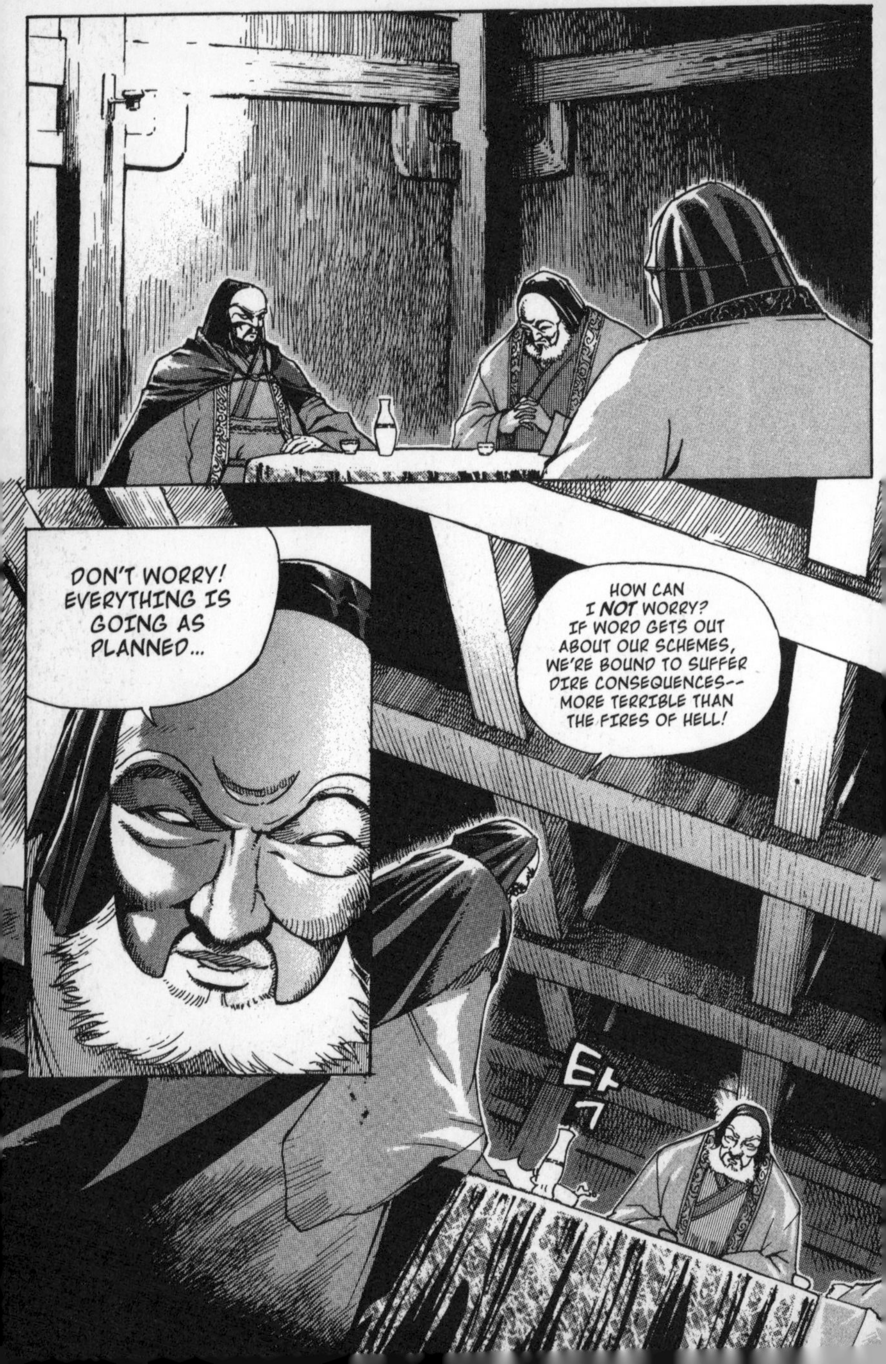
DON'T WORRY! EVERYTHING IS GOING AS PLANNED...
HOW CAN I **NOT** WORRY? IF WORD GETS OUT ABOUT OUR SCHEMES, WE'RE BOUND TO SUFFER DIRE CONSEQUENCES-- MORE TERRIBLE THAN THE FIRES OF HELL!
탁

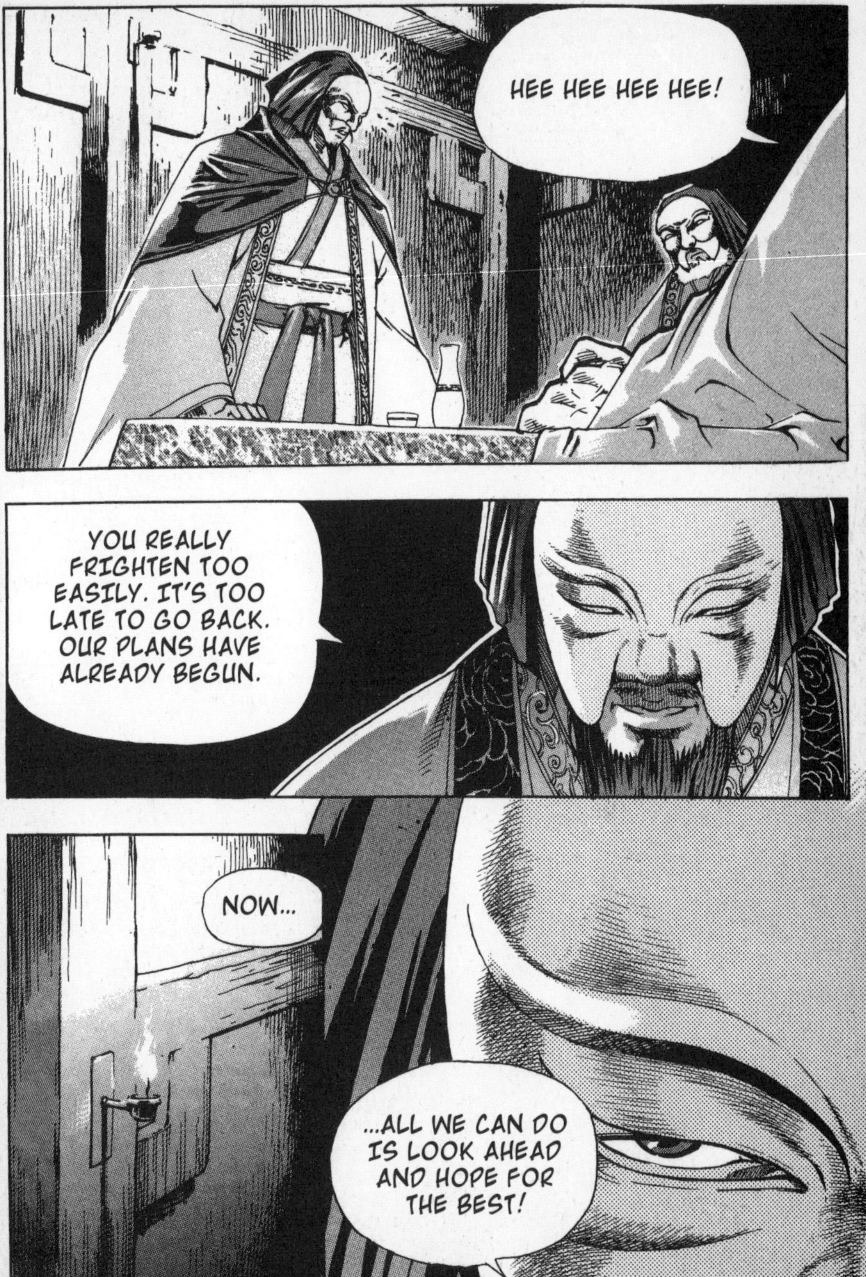
HEE HEE HEE HEE!
YOU REALLY FRIGHTEN TOO EASILY. IT'S TOO LATE TO GO BACK. OUR PLANS HAVE ALREADY BEGUN.
NOW...
...ALL WE CAN DO IS LOOK AHEAD AND HOPE FOR THE BEST!

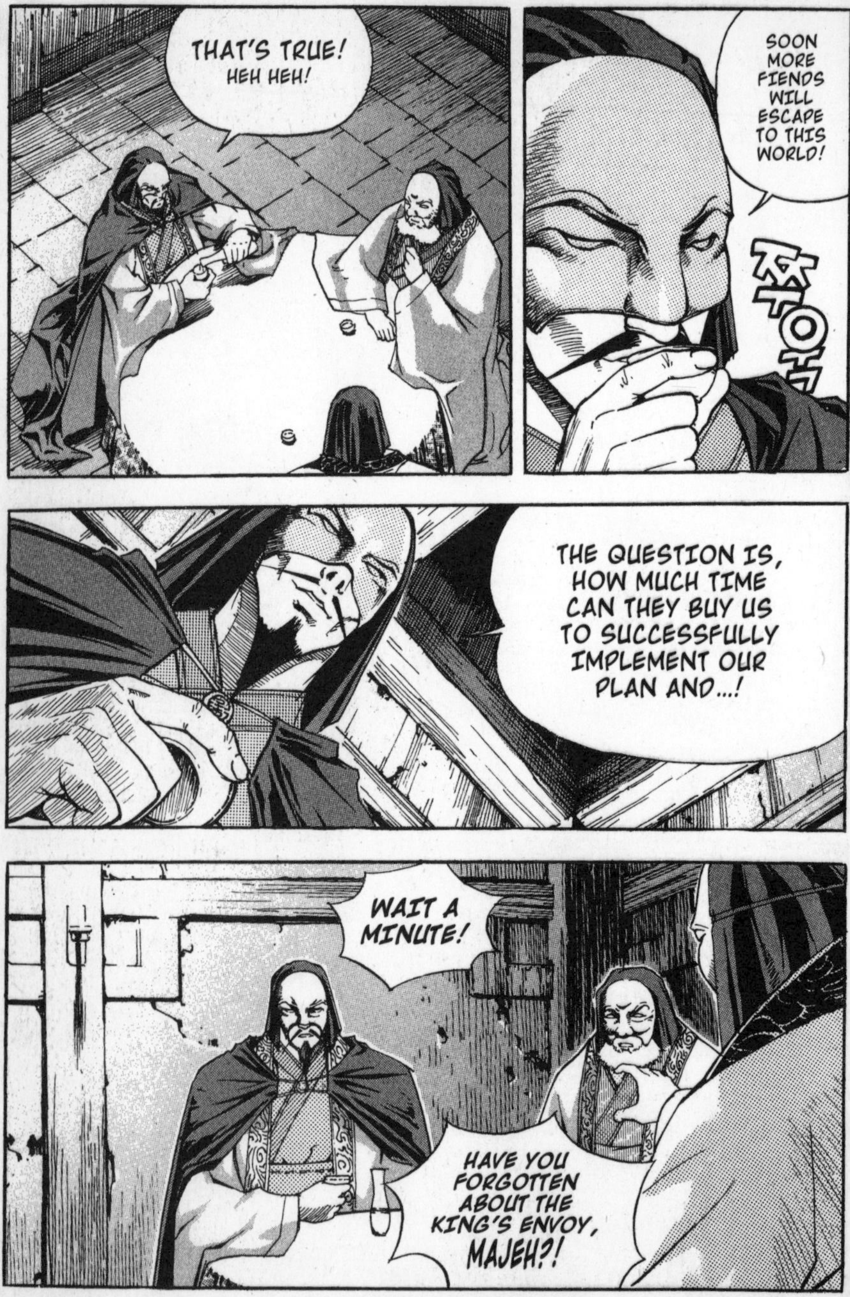
THAT'S TRUE! HEH HEH!
SOON MORE FIENDS WILL ESCAPE TO THIS WORLD!
THE QUESTION IS, HOW MUCH TIME CAN THEY BUY US TO SUCCESSFULLY IMPLEMENT OUR PLAN AND...!
WAIT A MINUTE!
HAVE YOU FORGOTTEN ABOUT THE KING'S ENVOY, MAJEH?!

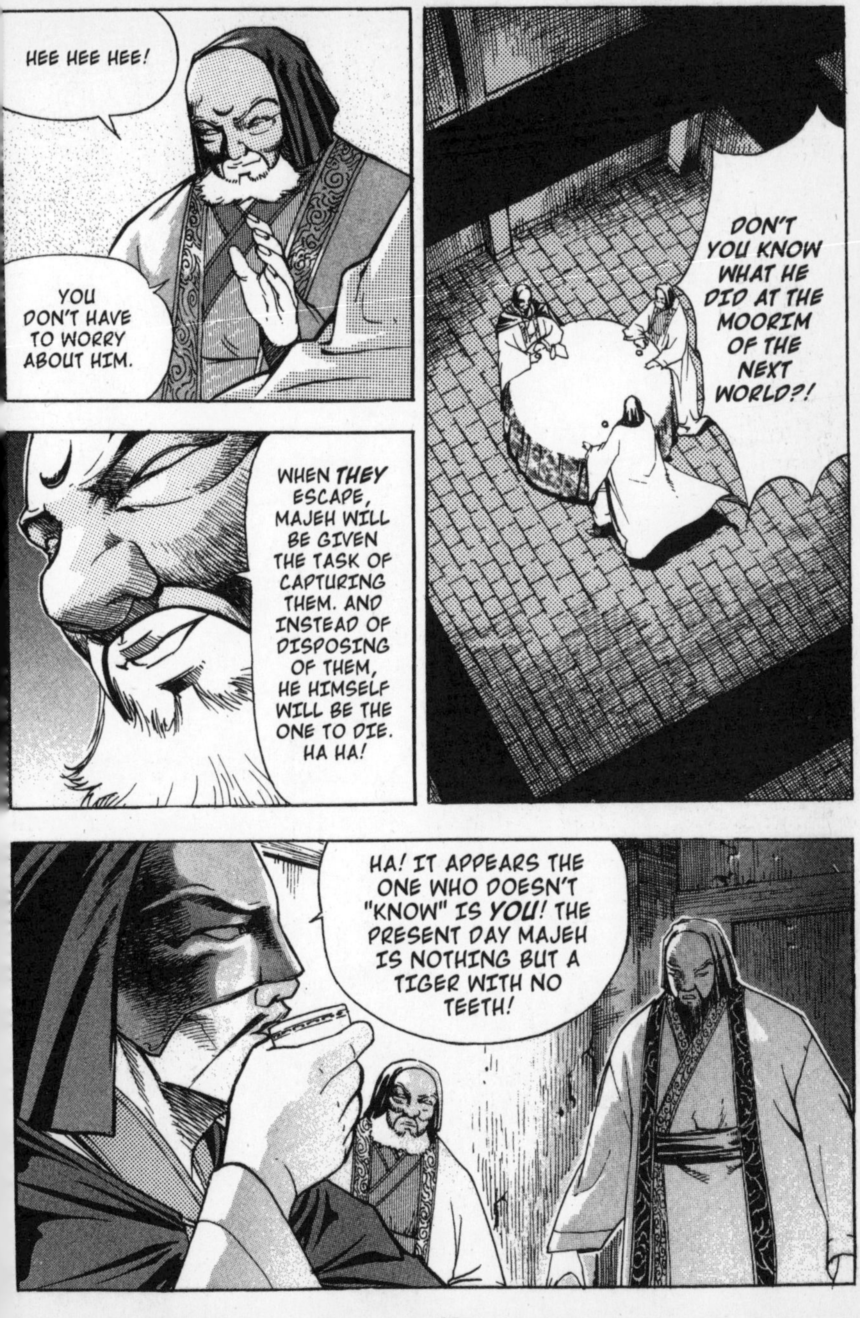
HEE HEE HEE!
YOU DON'T HAVE TO WORRY ABOUT HIM.
WHEN *THEY* ESCAPE, MAJEH WILL BE GIVEN THE TASK OF CAPTURING THEM. AND INSTEAD OF DISPOSING OF THEM, HE HIMSELF WILL BE THE ONE TO DIE. HA HA!
DON'T YOU KNOW WHAT HE DID AT THE MOORIM OF THE NEXT WORLD?!
HA! IT APPEARS THE ONE WHO DOESN'T "KNOW" IS *YOU*! THE PRESENT DAY MAJEH IS NOTHING BUT A TIGER WITH NO TEETH!

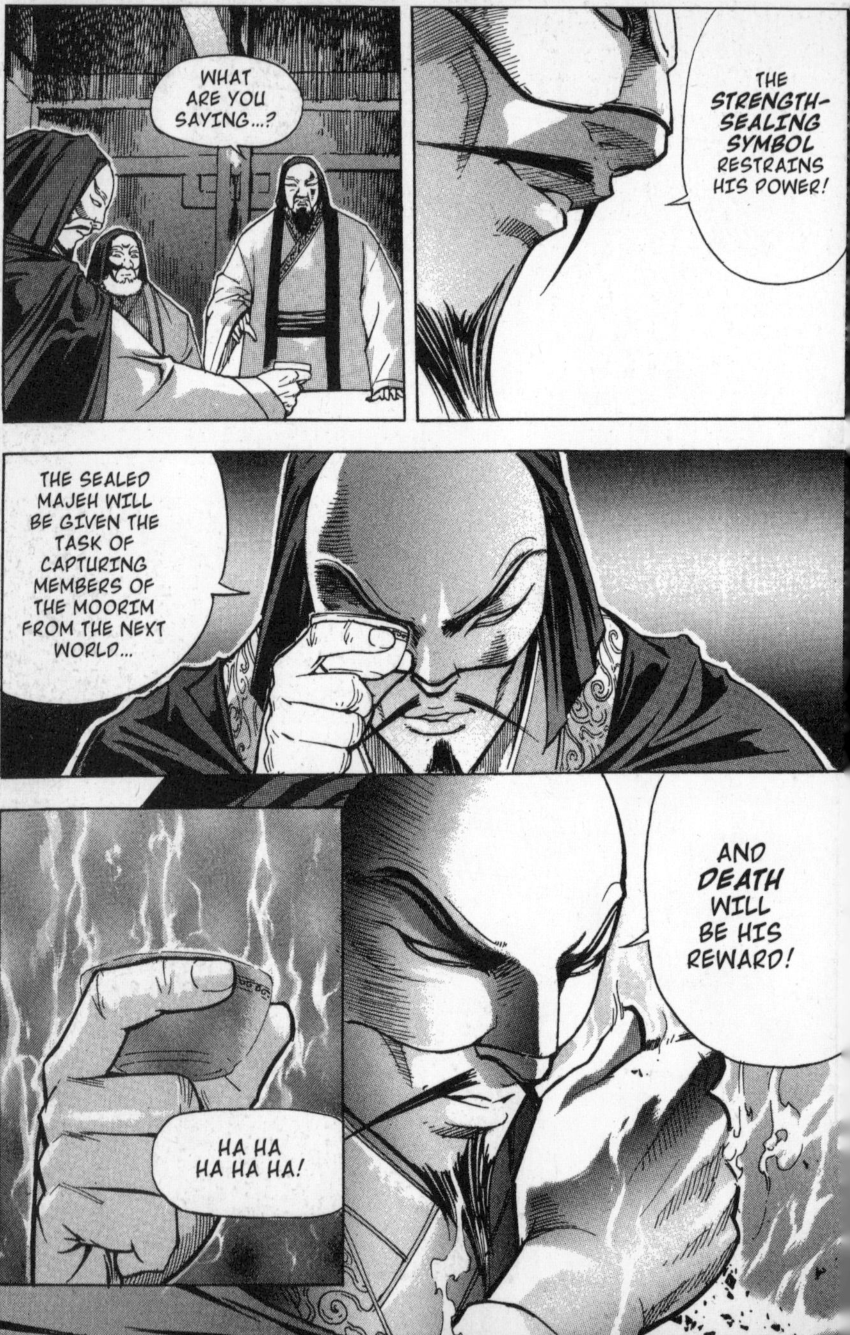
WHAT ARE YOU SAYING...?
THE STRENGTH-SEALING SYMBOL RESTRAINS HIS POWER!
THE SEALED MAJEH WILL BE GIVEN THE TASK OF CAPTURING MEMBERS OF THE MOORIM FROM THE NEXT WORLD...
AND DEATH WILL BE HIS REWARD!
HA HA HA HA HA!

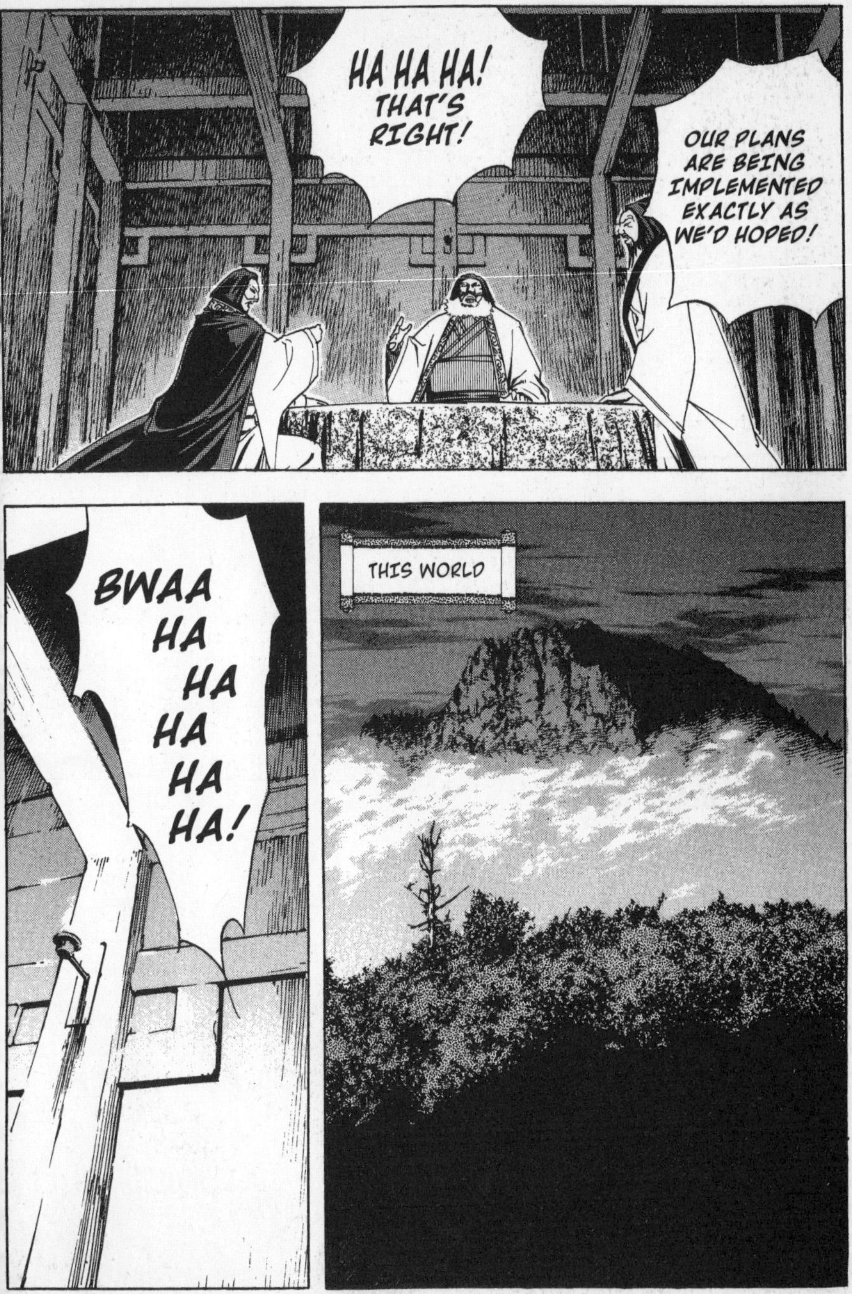
HA HA HA! THAT'S RIGHT!
OUR PLANS ARE BEING IMPLEMENTED EXACTLY AS WE'D HOPED!
BWAA HA HA HA HA HA!
THIS WORLD

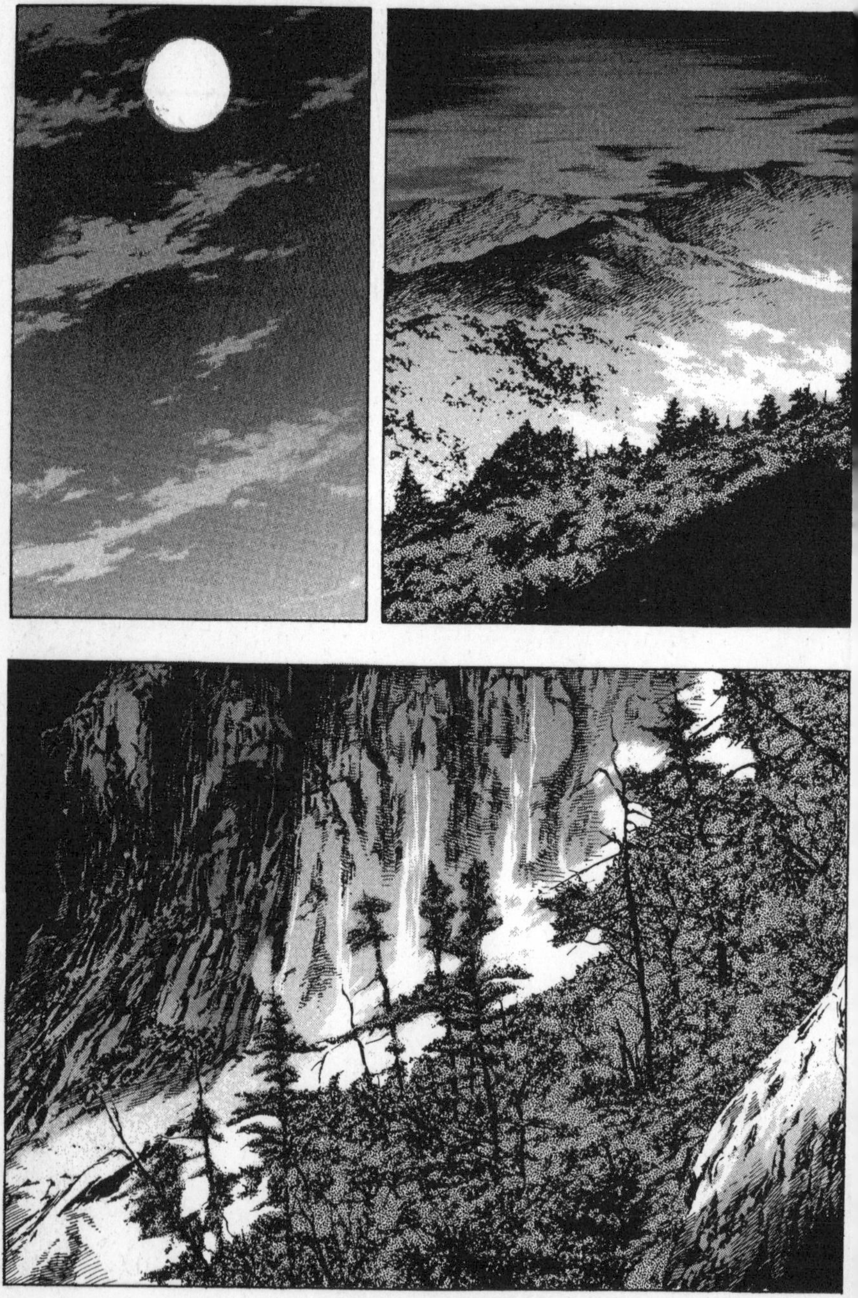

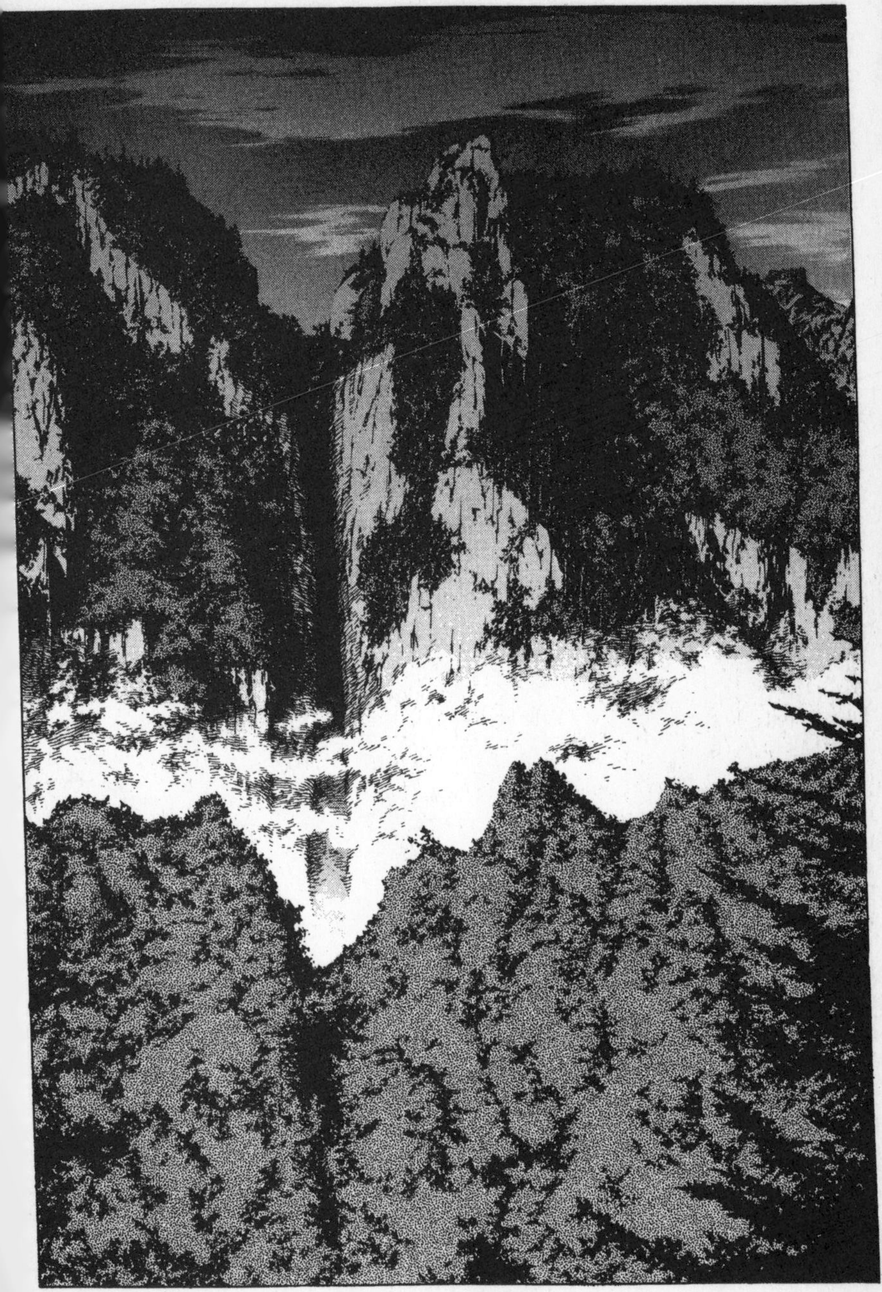

BEWARMOOYIBGOK:
"UNLESS YOU ARE A MOON, YOU CAN NOT ENTER"

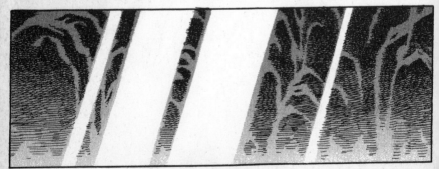

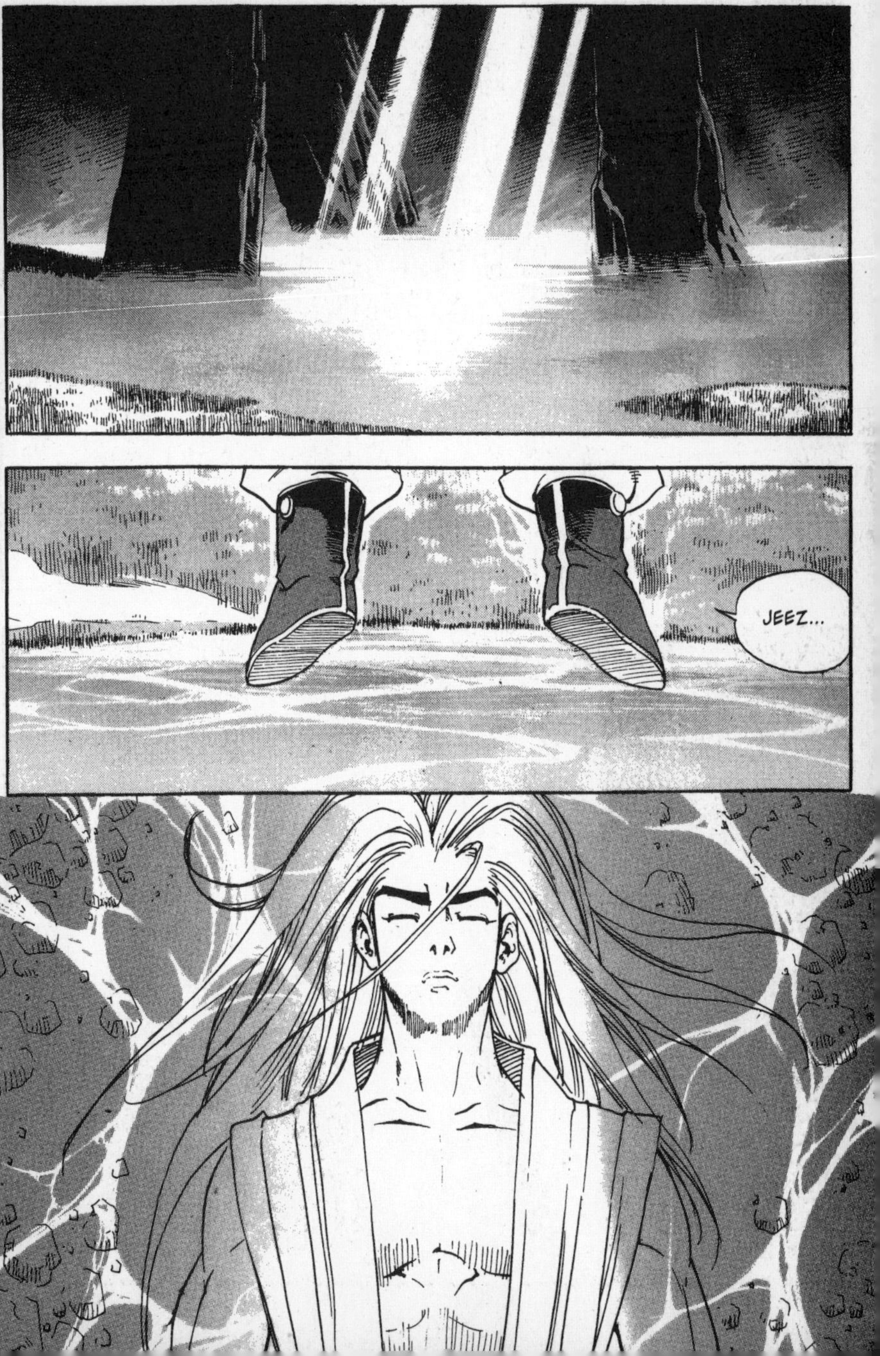
JEEZ...

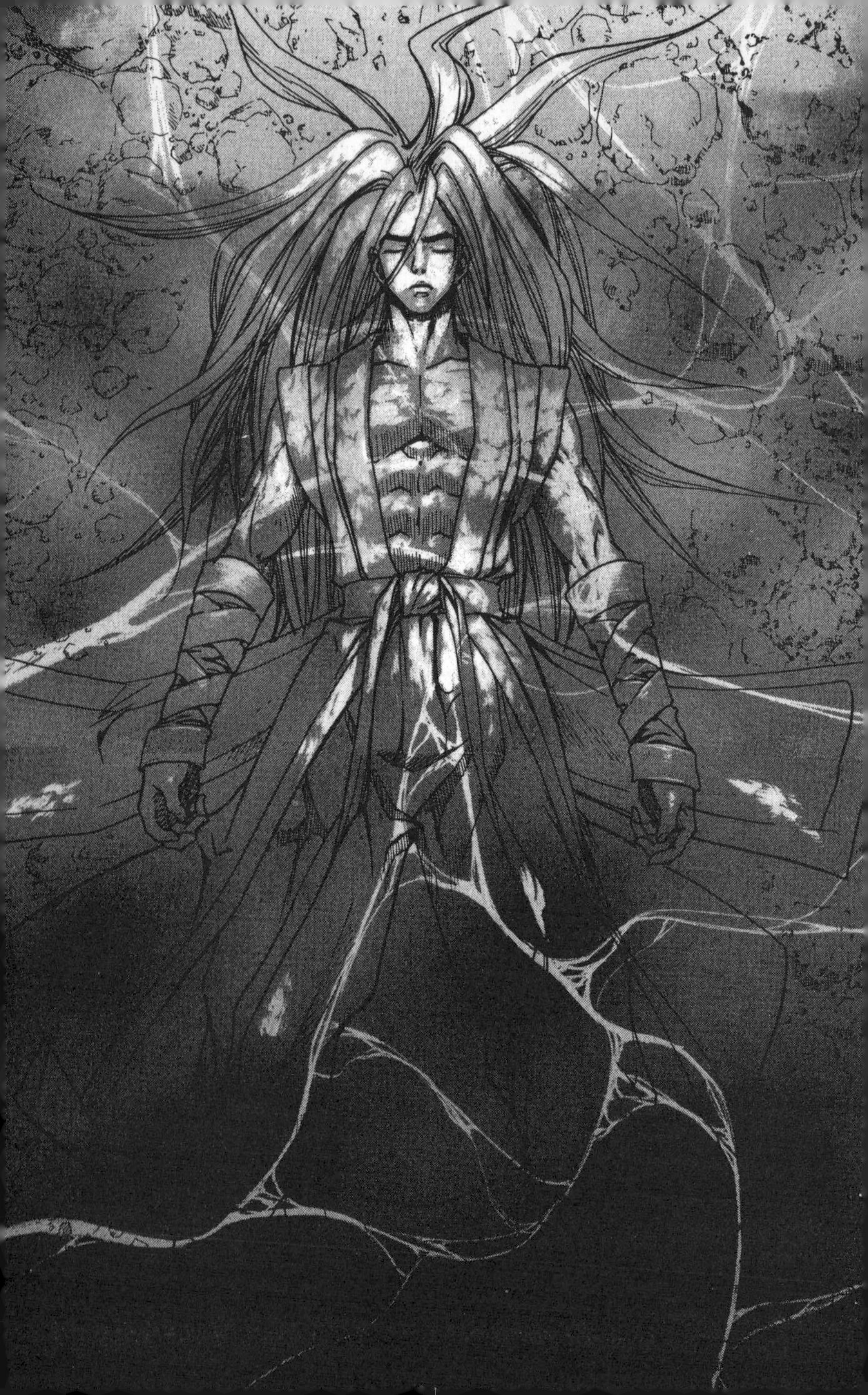

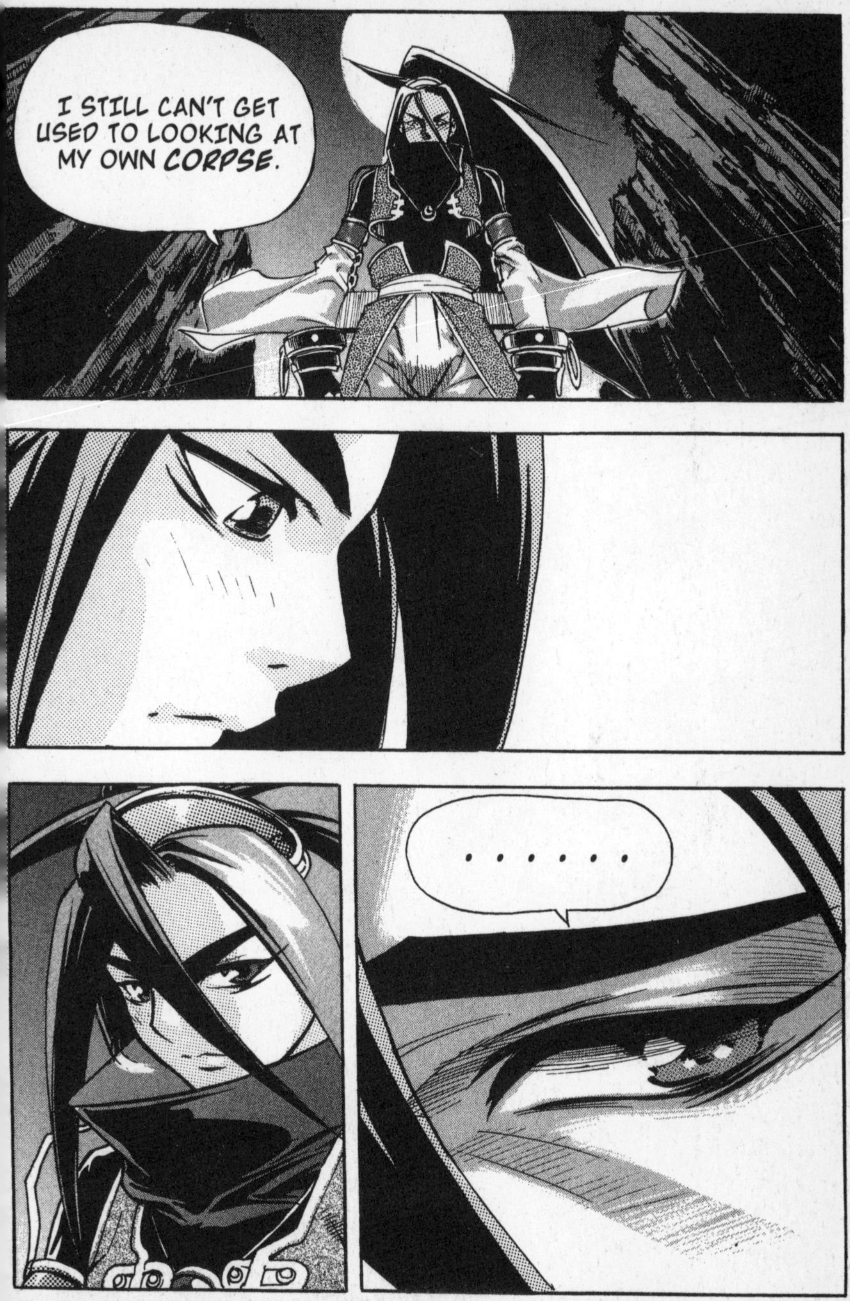
I STILL CAN'T GET USED TO LOOKING AT MY OWN CORPSE.
......

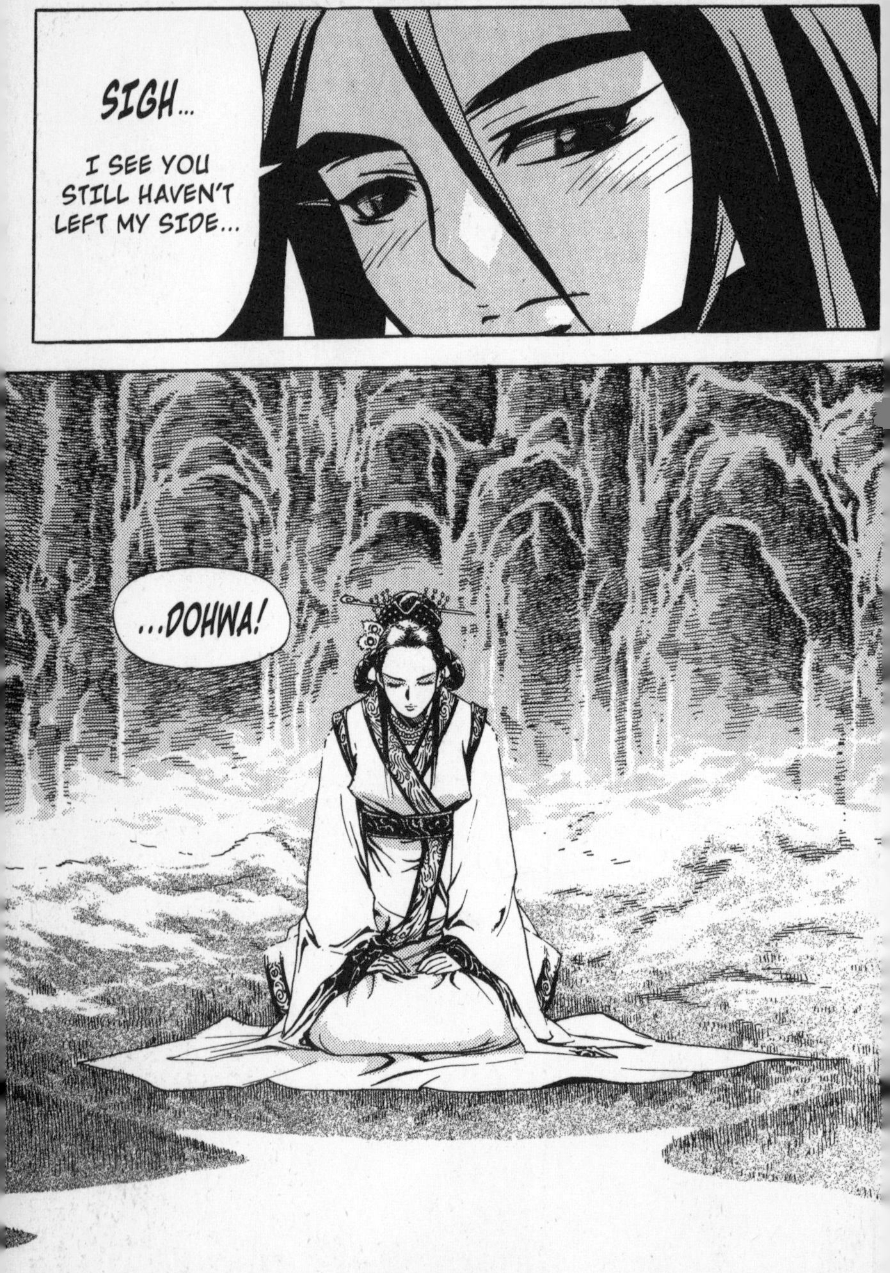
SIGH...
I SEE YOU STILL HAVEN'T LEFT MY SIDE...
...DOHWA!

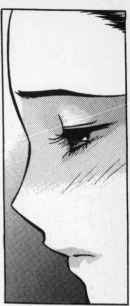

IT WOULD HAVE BEEN BETTER IF YOU *HAD* LEFT, CENTURIES AGO. NOW, IF YOU EVER DO ATTEMPT TO LEAVE...YOU'LL *DIE*.

AND IT'S ALL MY FAULT...

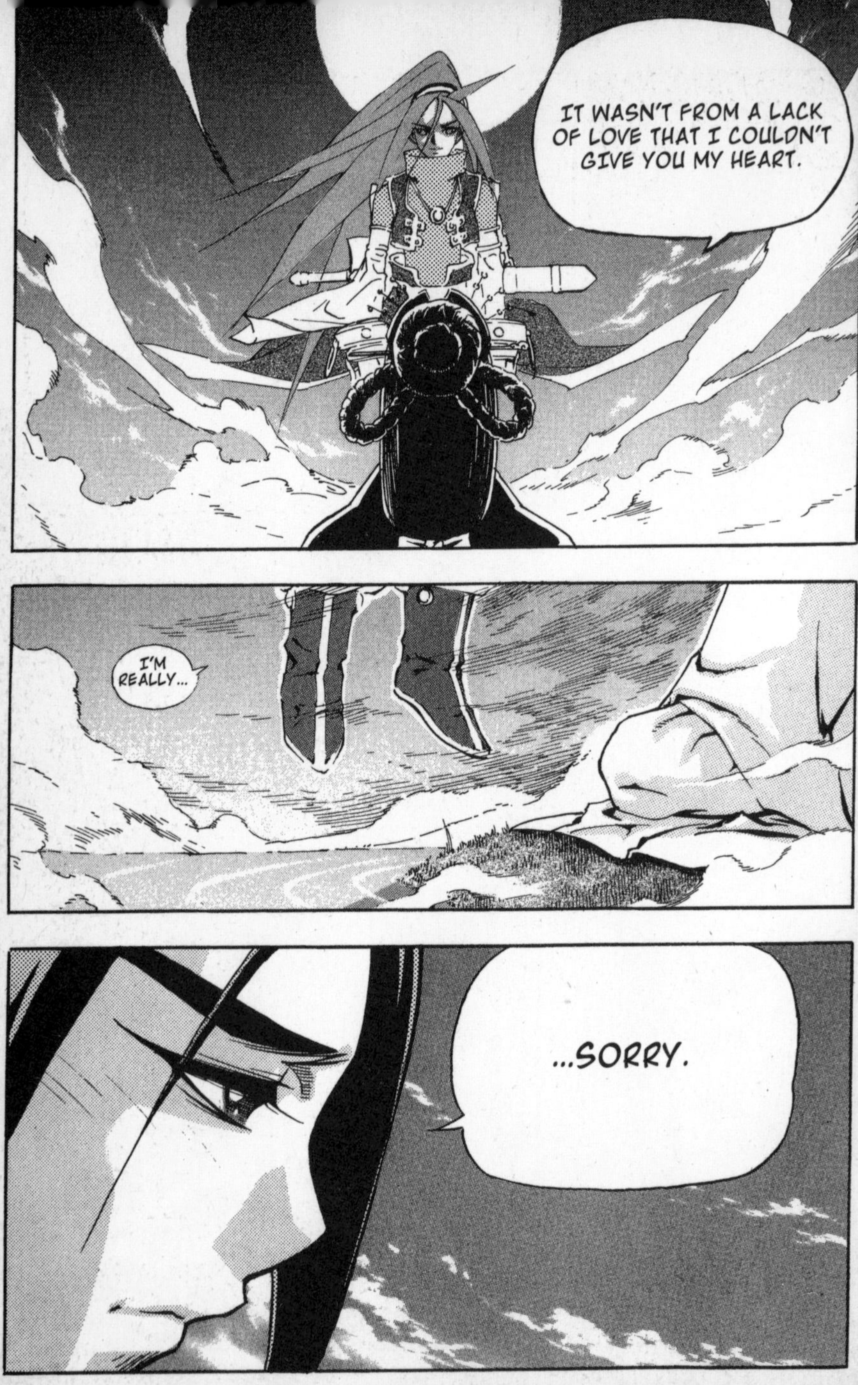
IT WASN'T FROM A LACK OF LOVE THAT I COULDN'T GIVE YOU MY HEART.
I'M REALLY...
...SORRY.

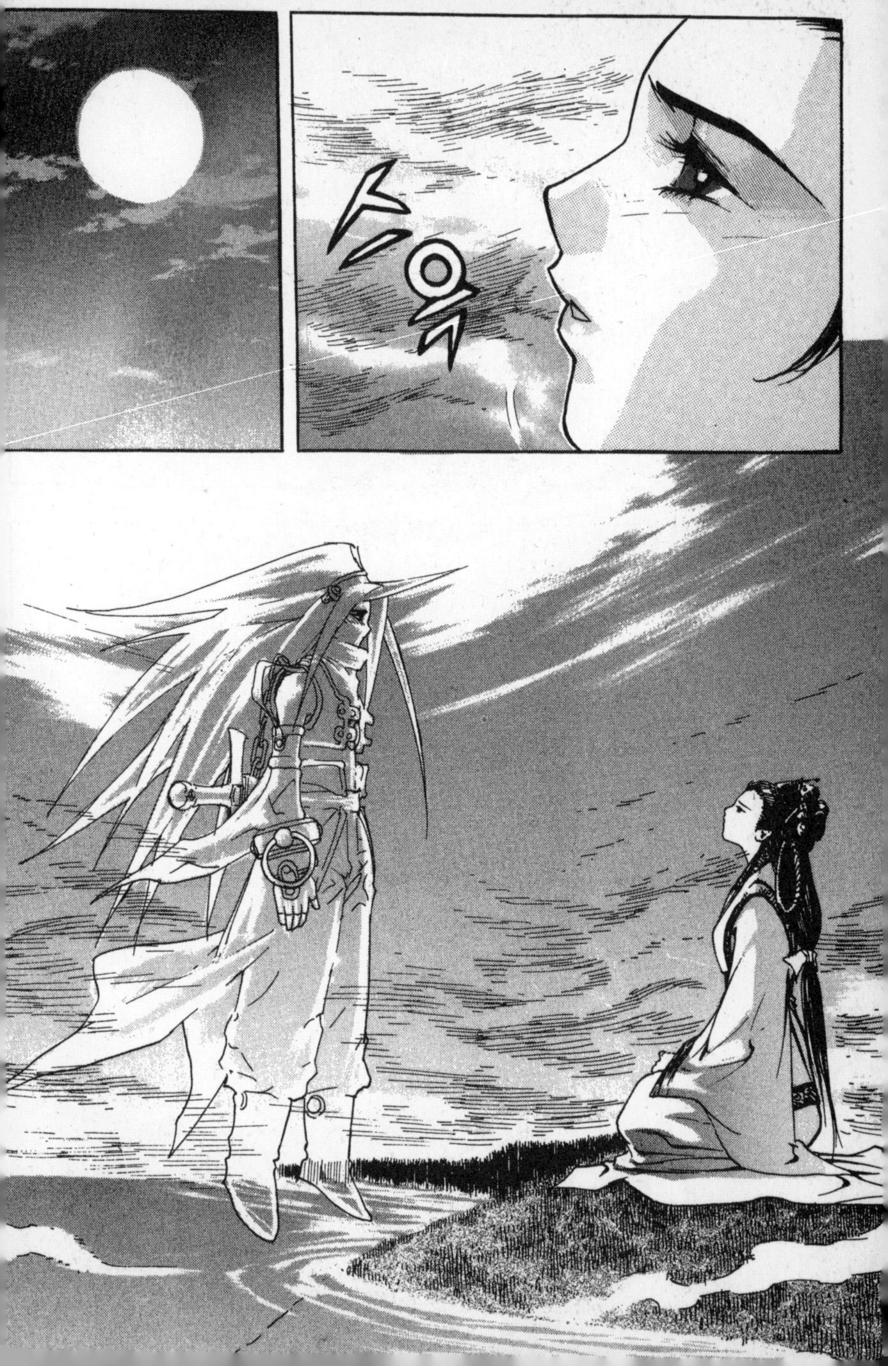

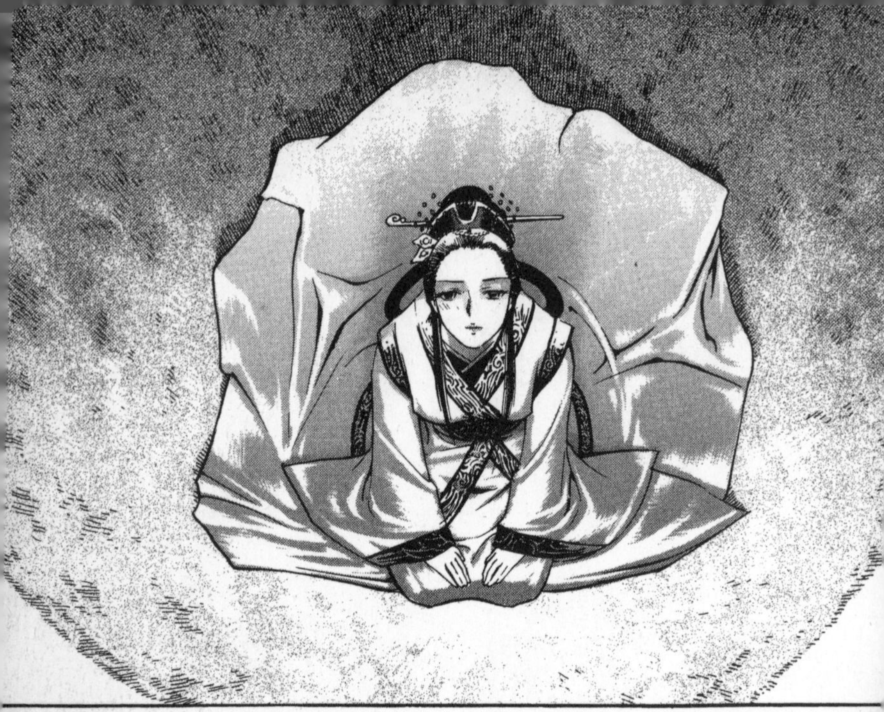
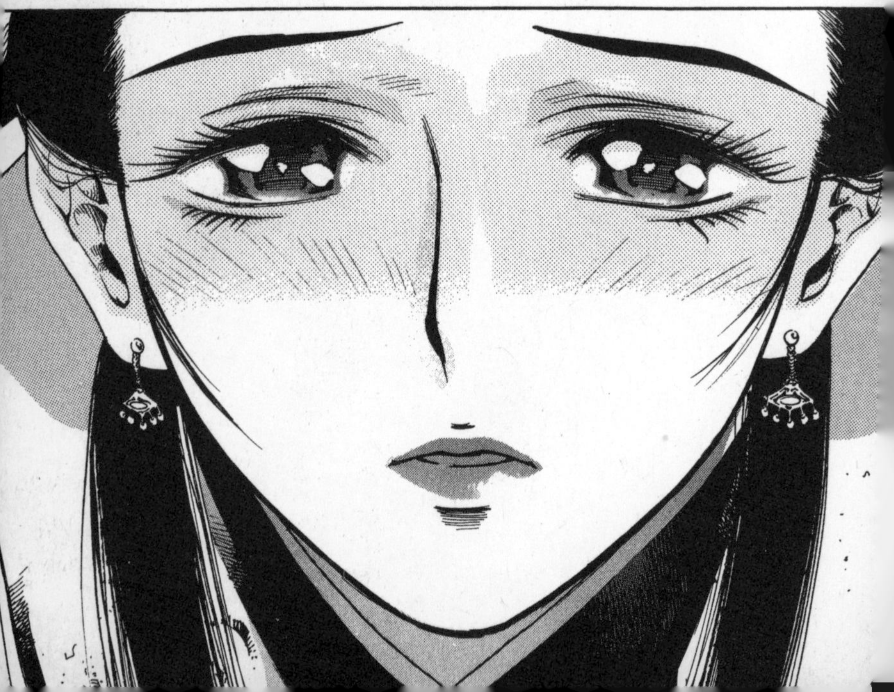

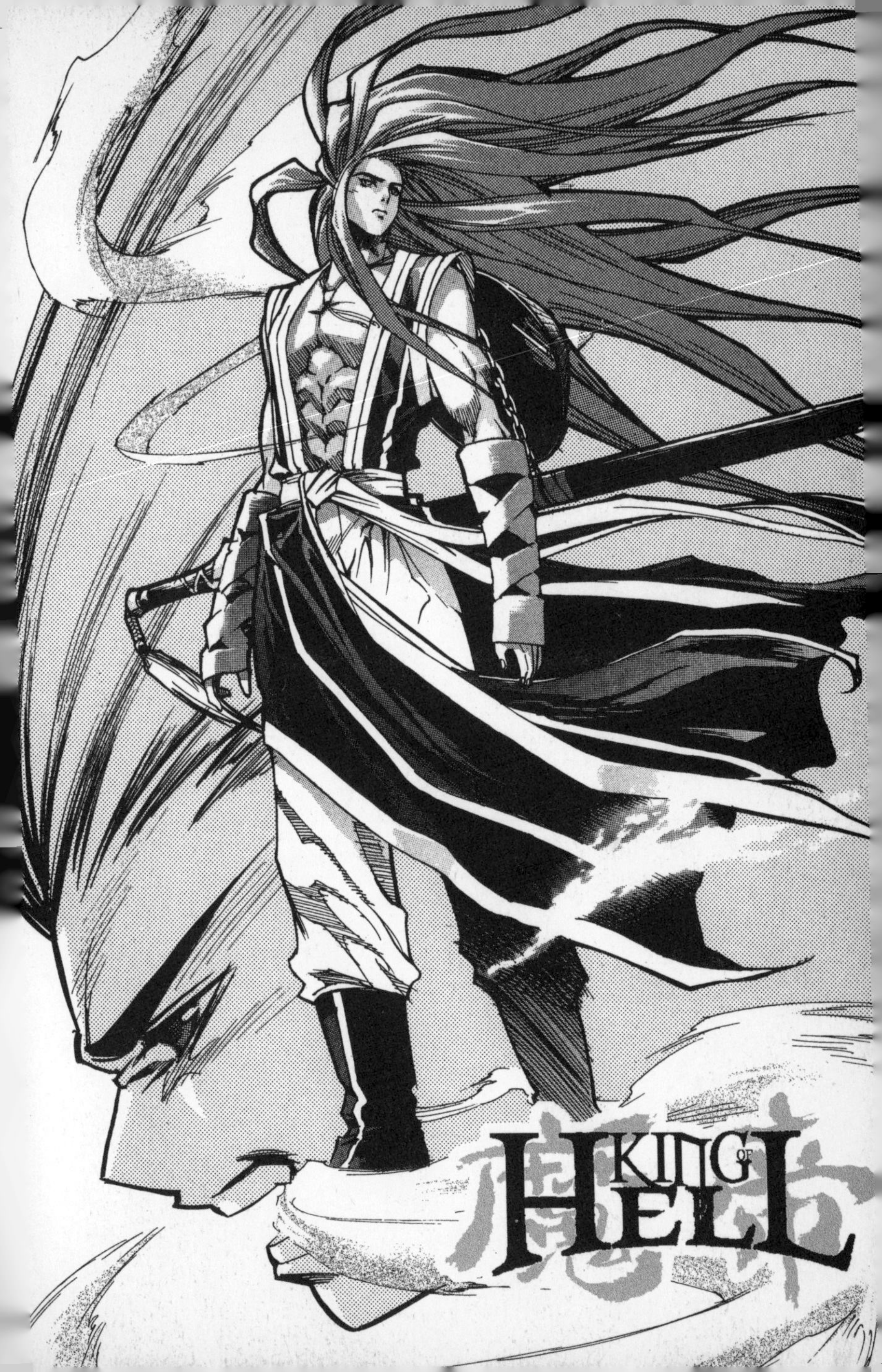
KING OF HELL

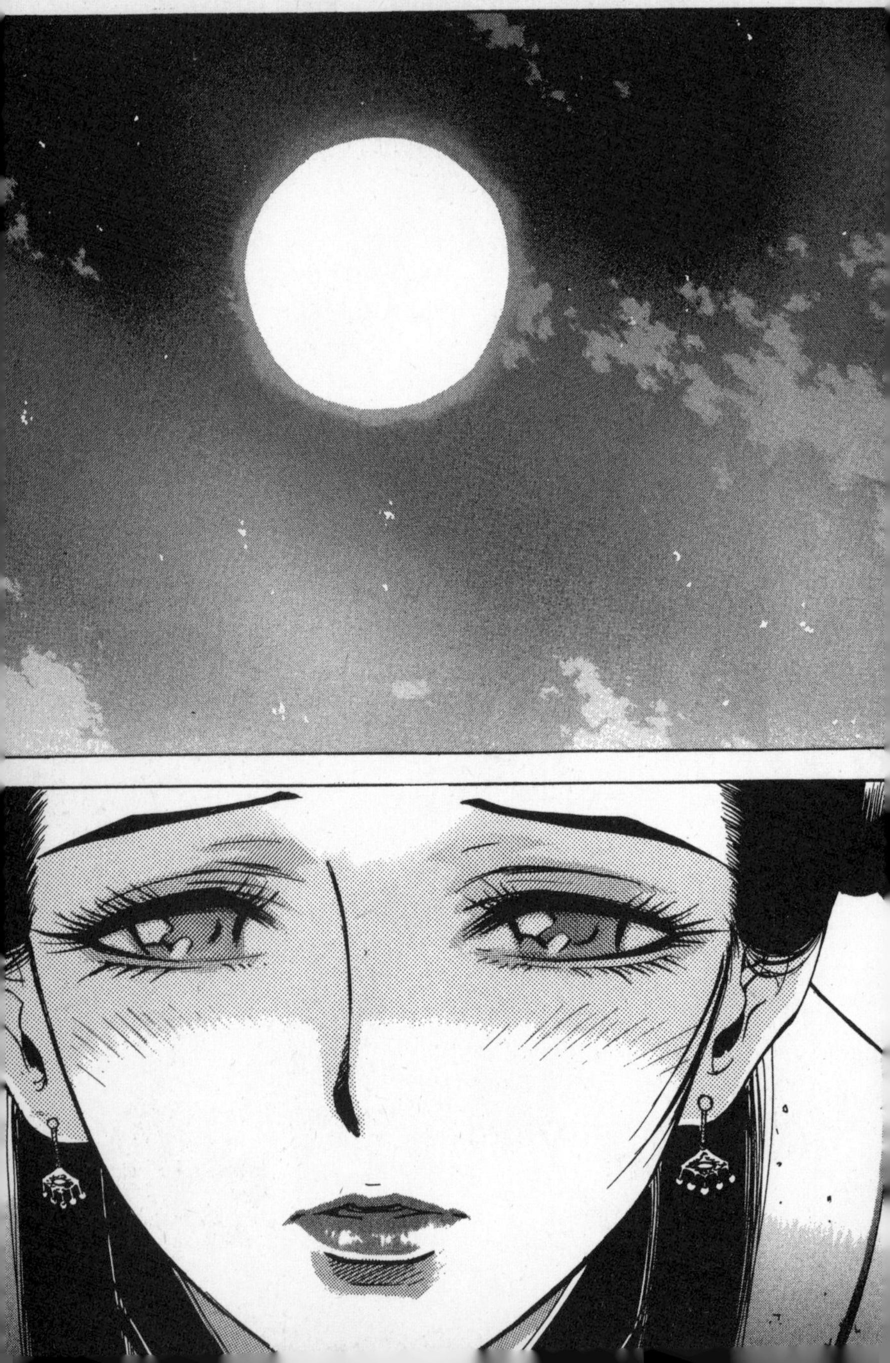

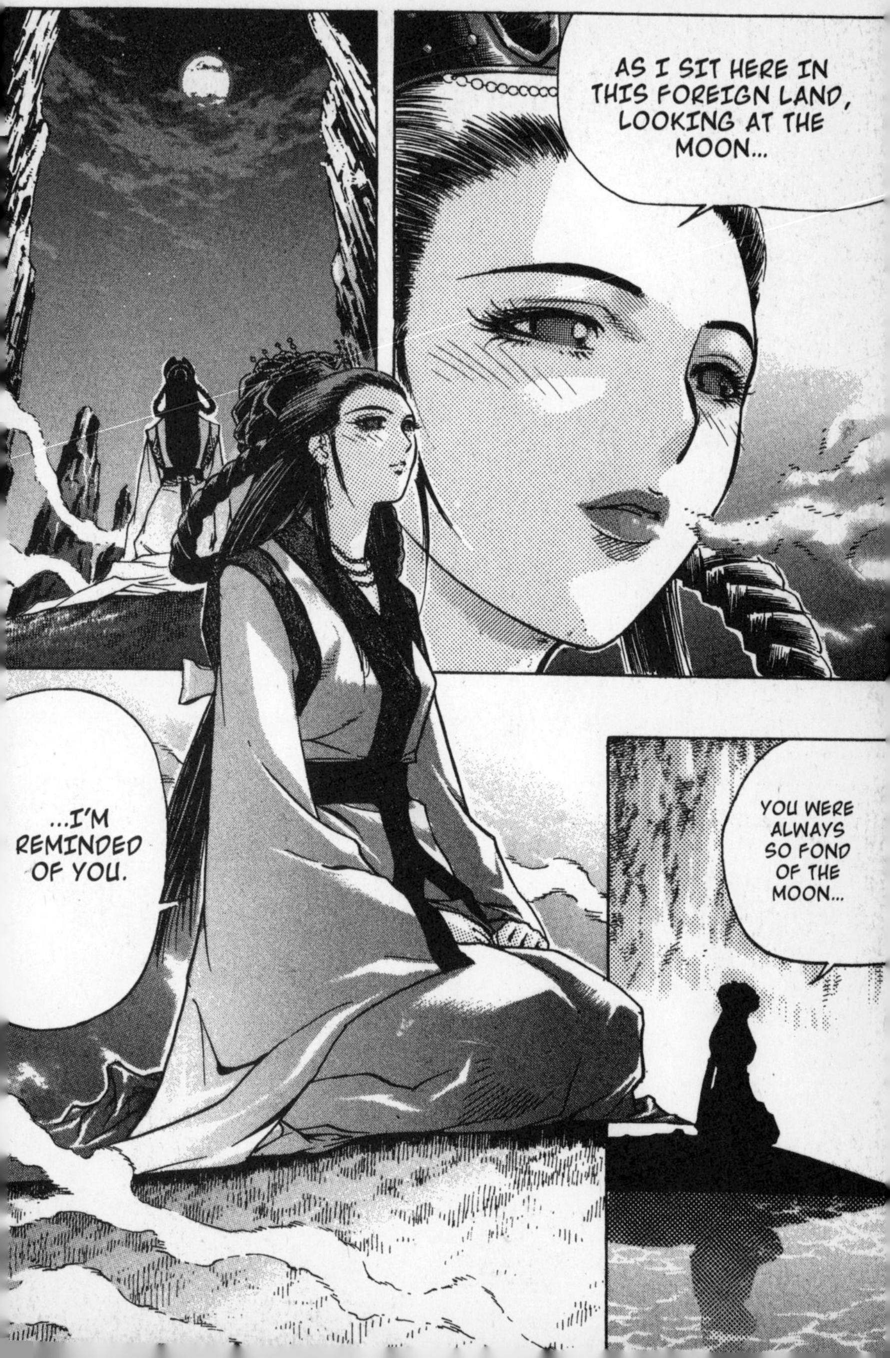
AS I SIT HERE IN THIS FOREIGN LAND, LOOKING AT THE MOON...
...I'M REMINDED OF YOU.
YOU WERE ALWAYS SO FOND OF THE MOON...

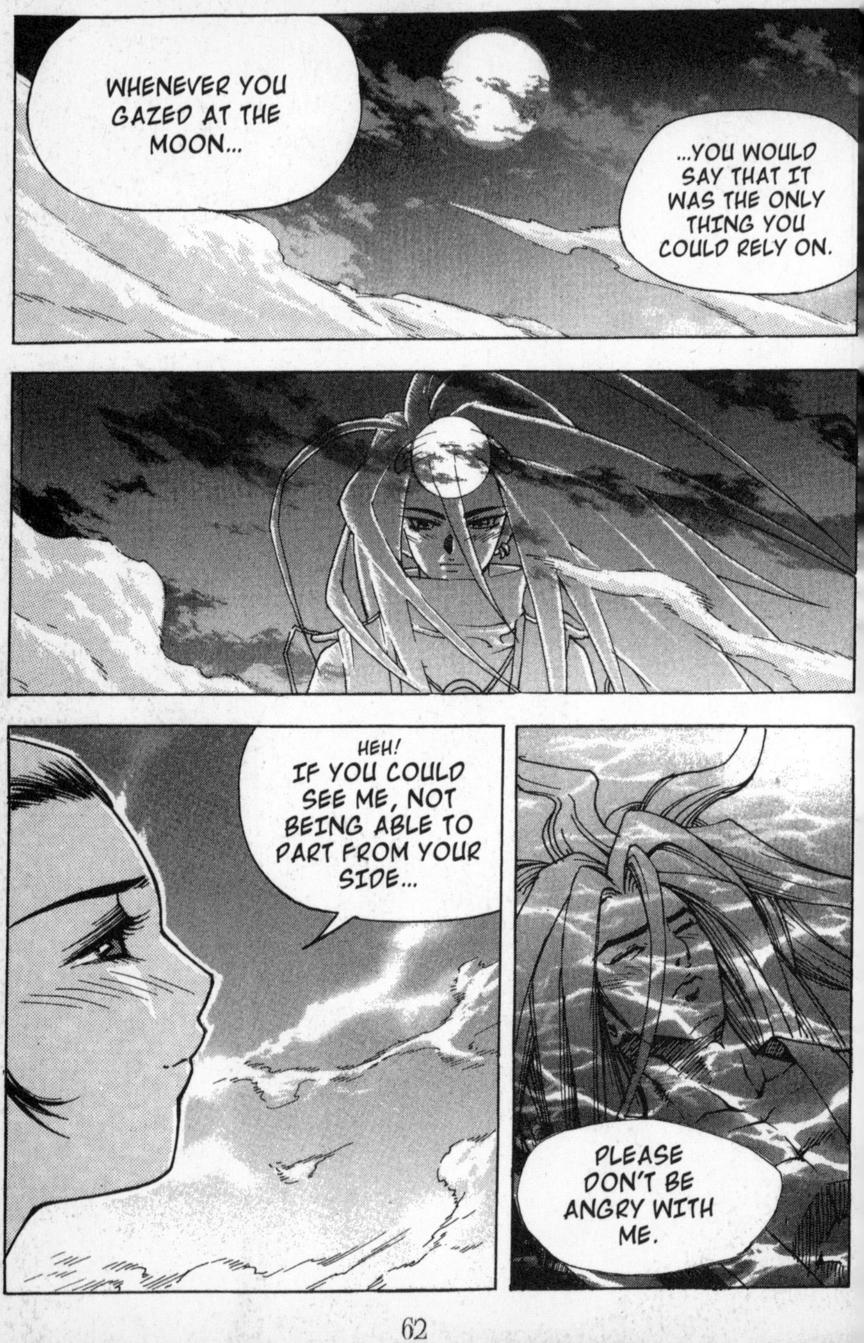
WHENEVER YOU GAZED AT THE MOON...
...YOU WOULD SAY THAT IT WAS THE ONLY THING YOU COULD RELY ON.
HEH! IF YOU COULD SEE ME, NOT BEING ABLE TO PART FROM YOUR SIDE...
PLEASE DON'T BE ANGRY WITH ME.

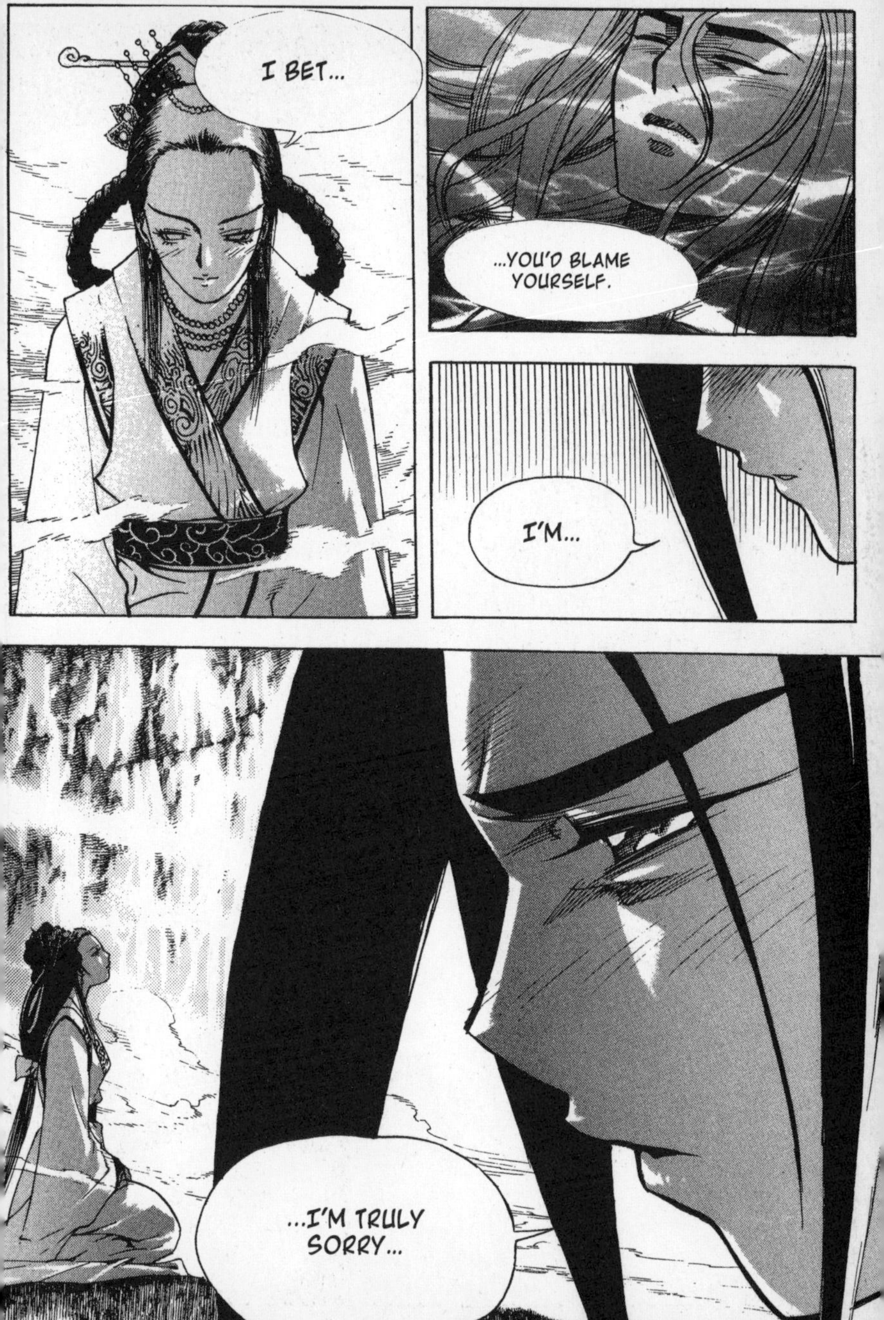
I BET...
...YOU'D BLAME YOURSELF.
I'M...
...I'M TRULY SORRY...

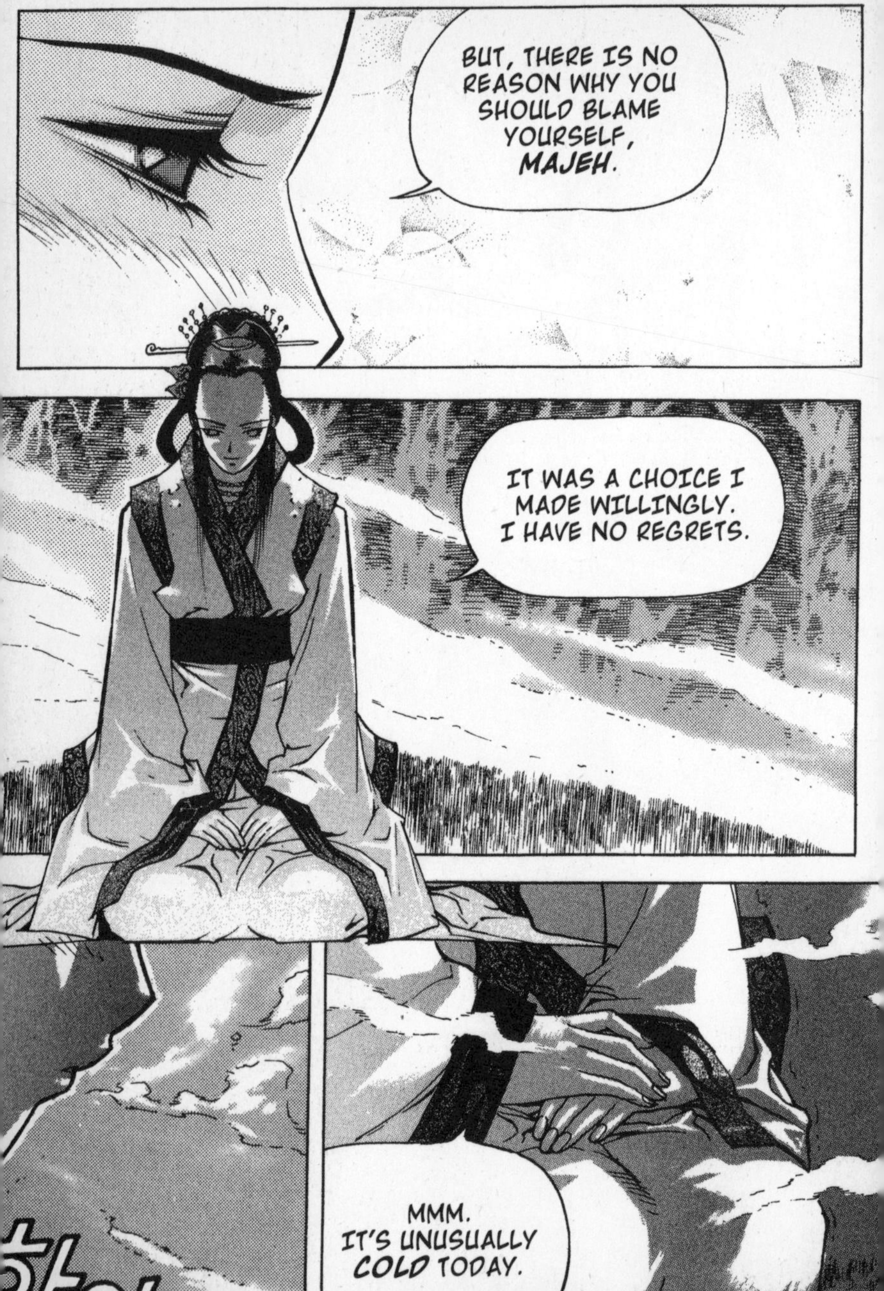
BUT, THERE IS NO REASON WHY YOU SHOULD BLAME YOURSELF, MAJEH.
IT WAS A CHOICE I MADE WILLINGLY. I HAVE NO REGRETS.
하아
MMM. IT'S UNUSUALLY COLD TODAY.

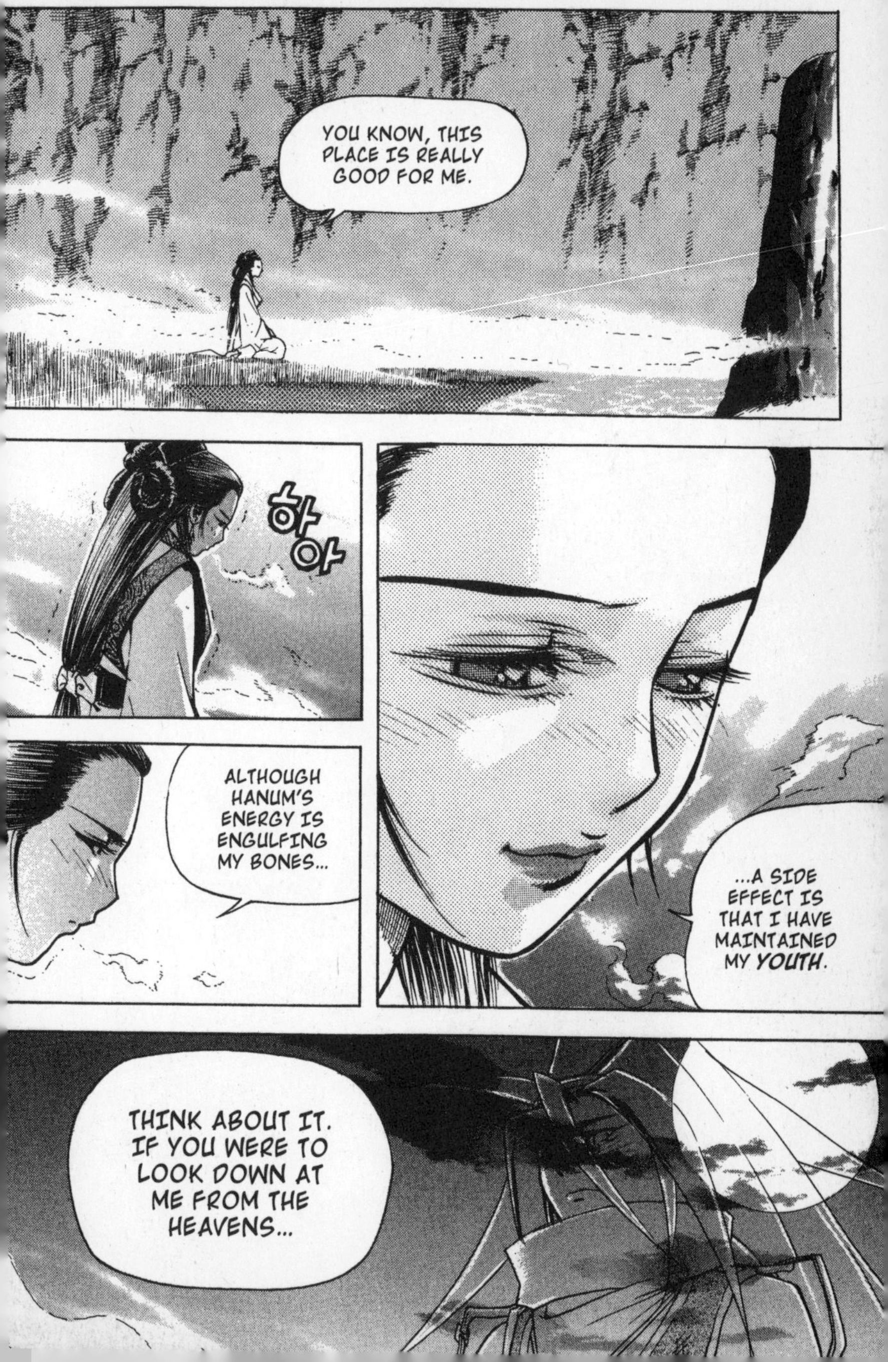
YOU KNOW, THIS PLACE IS REALLY GOOD FOR ME.
하아
ALTHOUGH HANUM'S ENERGY IS ENGULFING MY BONES...
...A SIDE EFFECT IS THAT I HAVE MAINTAINED MY *YOUTH*.
THINK ABOUT IT. IF YOU WERE TO LOOK DOWN AT ME FROM THE HEAVENS...

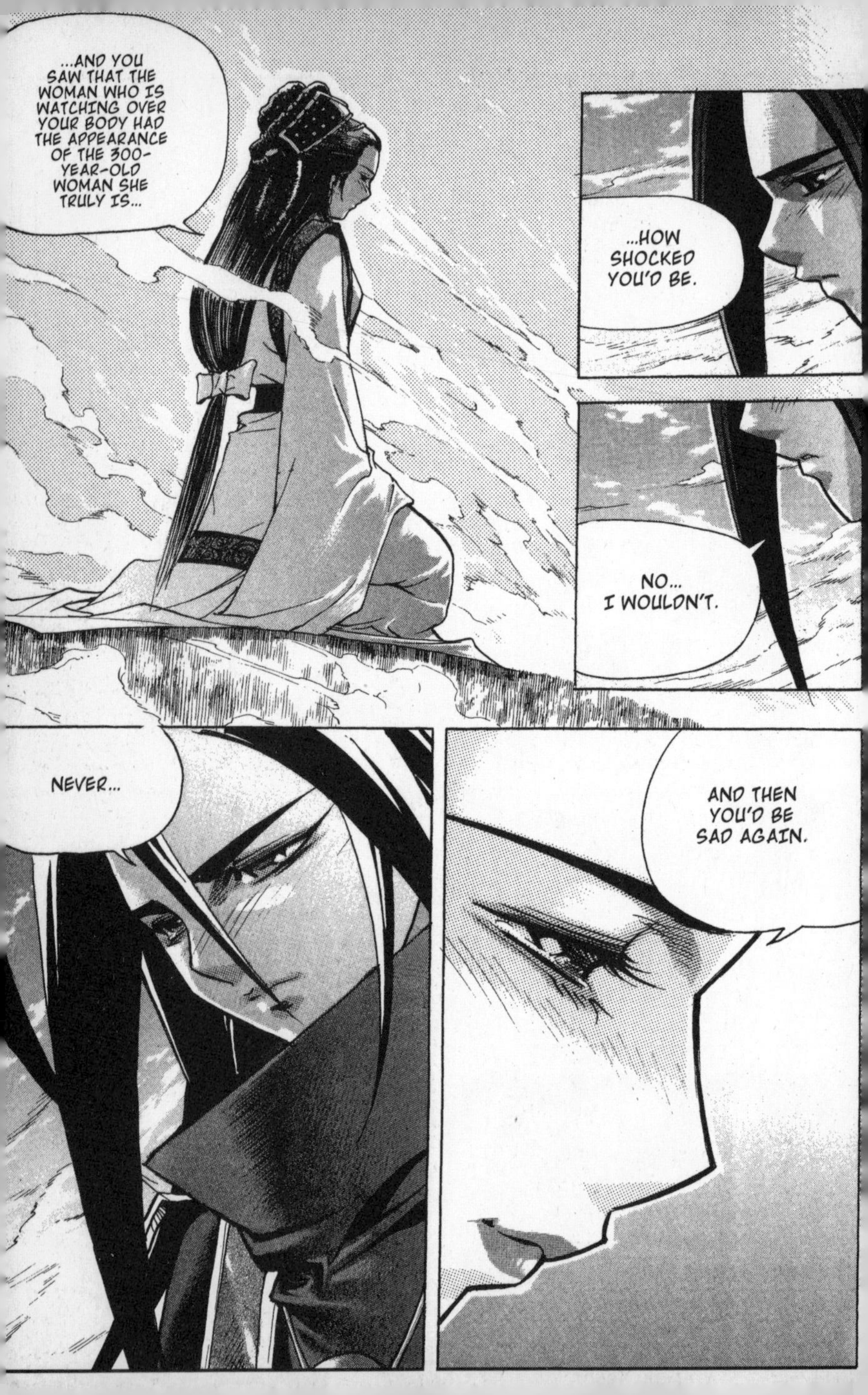
...AND YOU SAW THAT THE WOMAN WHO IS WATCHING OVER YOUR BODY HAD THE APPEARANCE OF THE 300-YEAR-OLD WOMAN SHE TRULY IS...
...HOW SHOCKED YOU'D BE.
NO... I WOULDN'T.
NEVER...
AND THEN YOU'D BE SAD AGAIN.

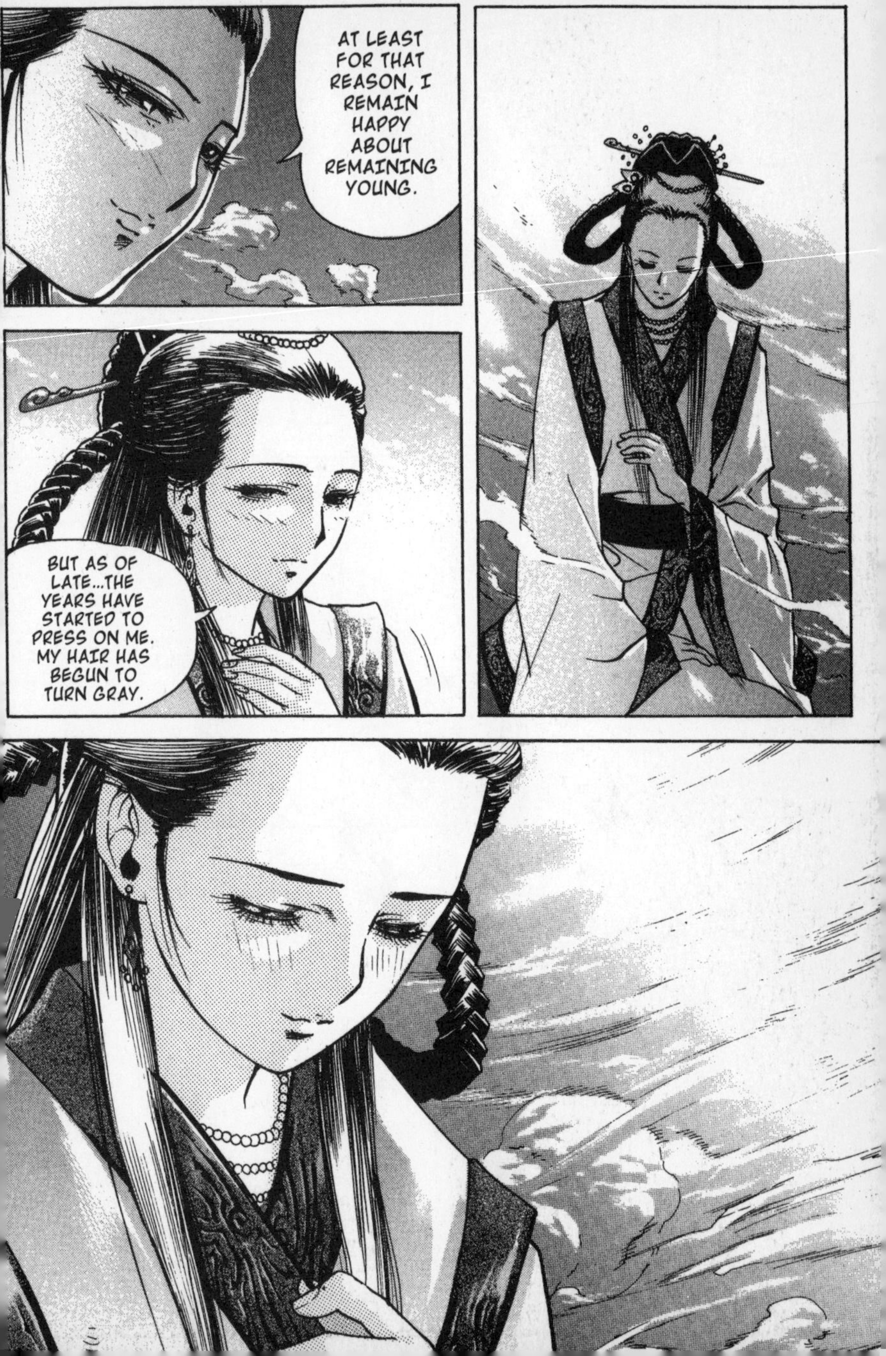
AT LEAST FOR THAT REASON, I REMAIN HAPPY ABOUT REMAINING YOUNG.
BUT AS OF LATE...THE YEARS HAVE STARTED TO PRESS ON ME. MY HAIR HAS BEGUN TO TURN GRAY.

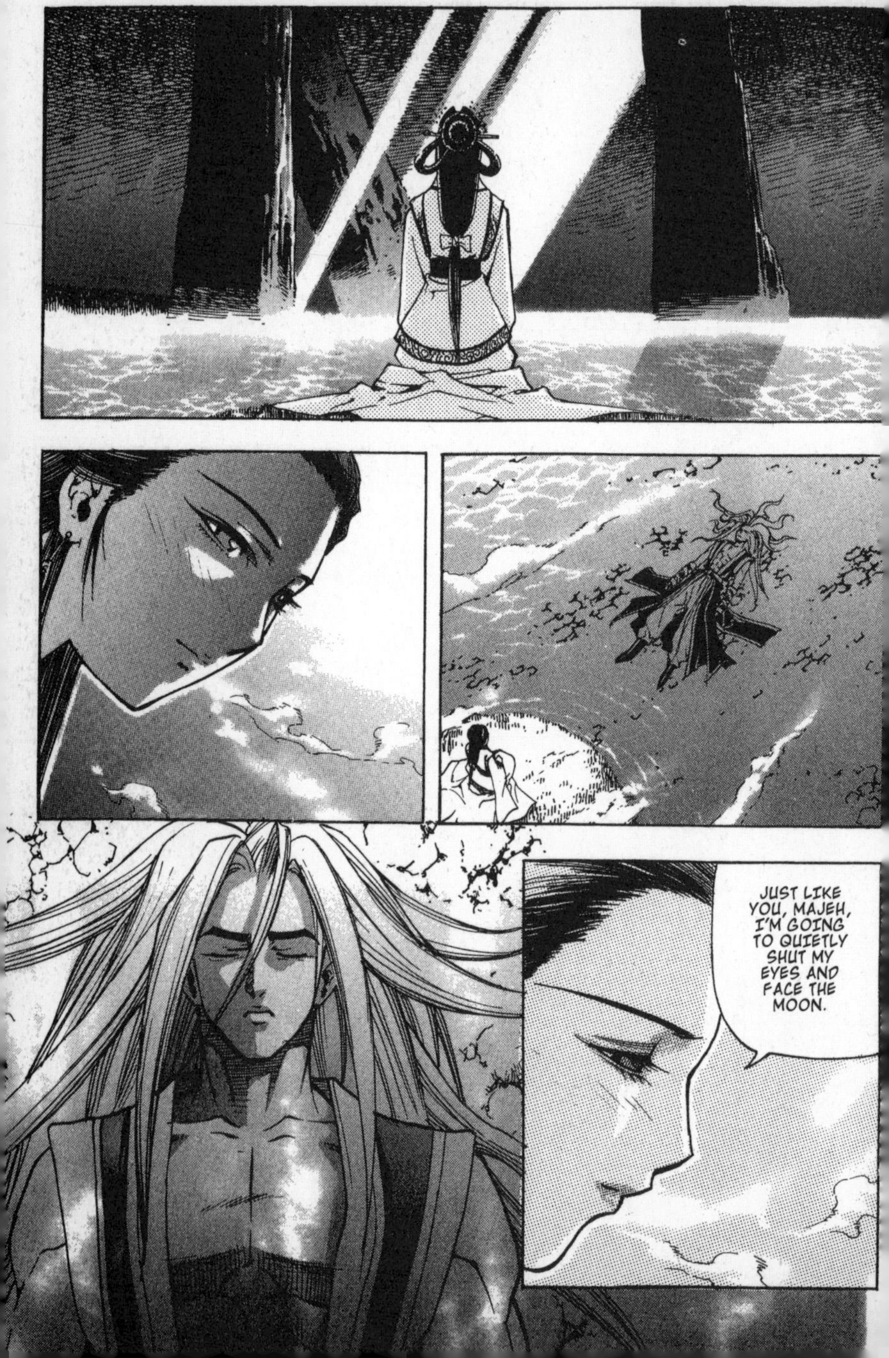
JUST LIKE YOU, MAJEH, I'M GOING TO QUIETLY SHUT MY EYES AND FACE THE MOON.

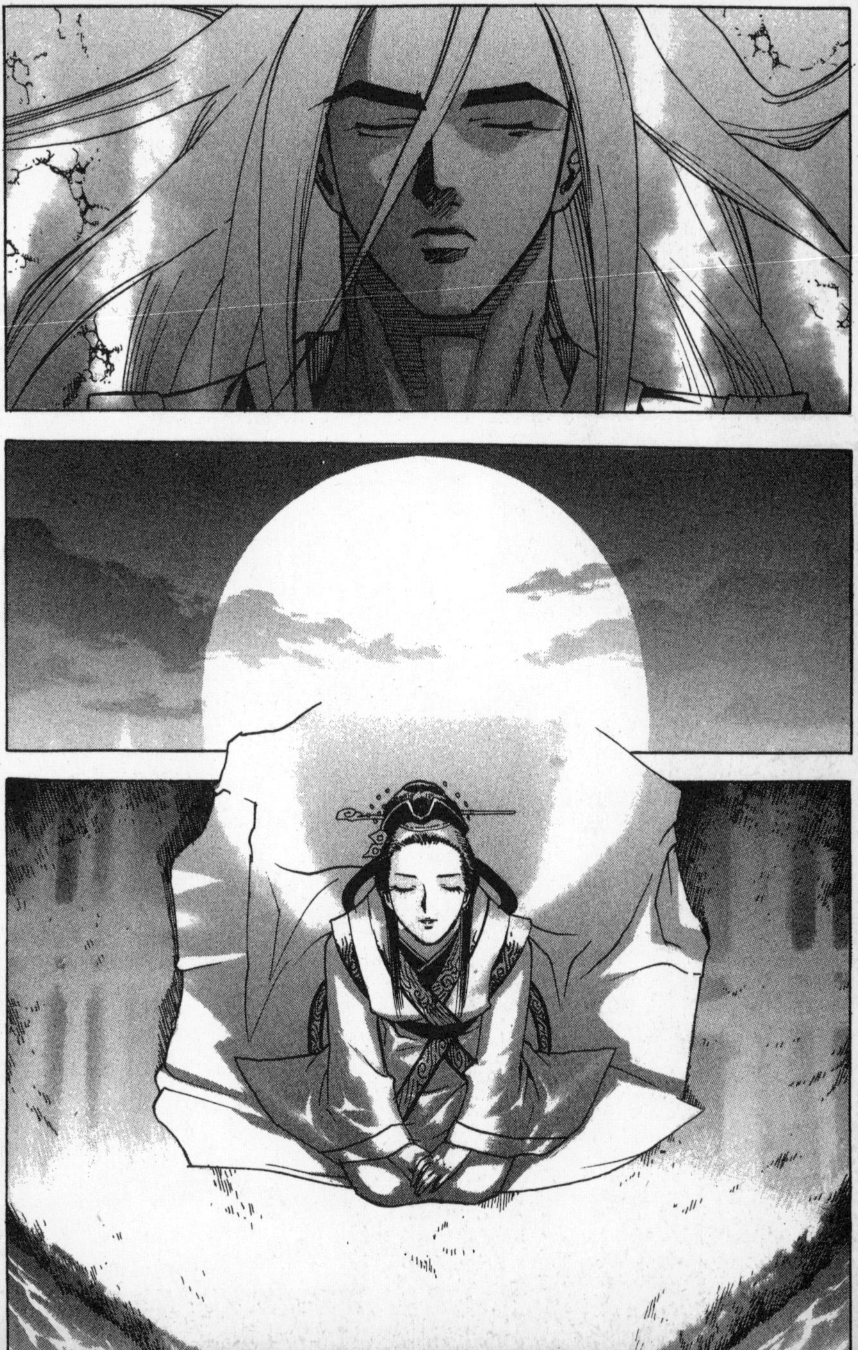

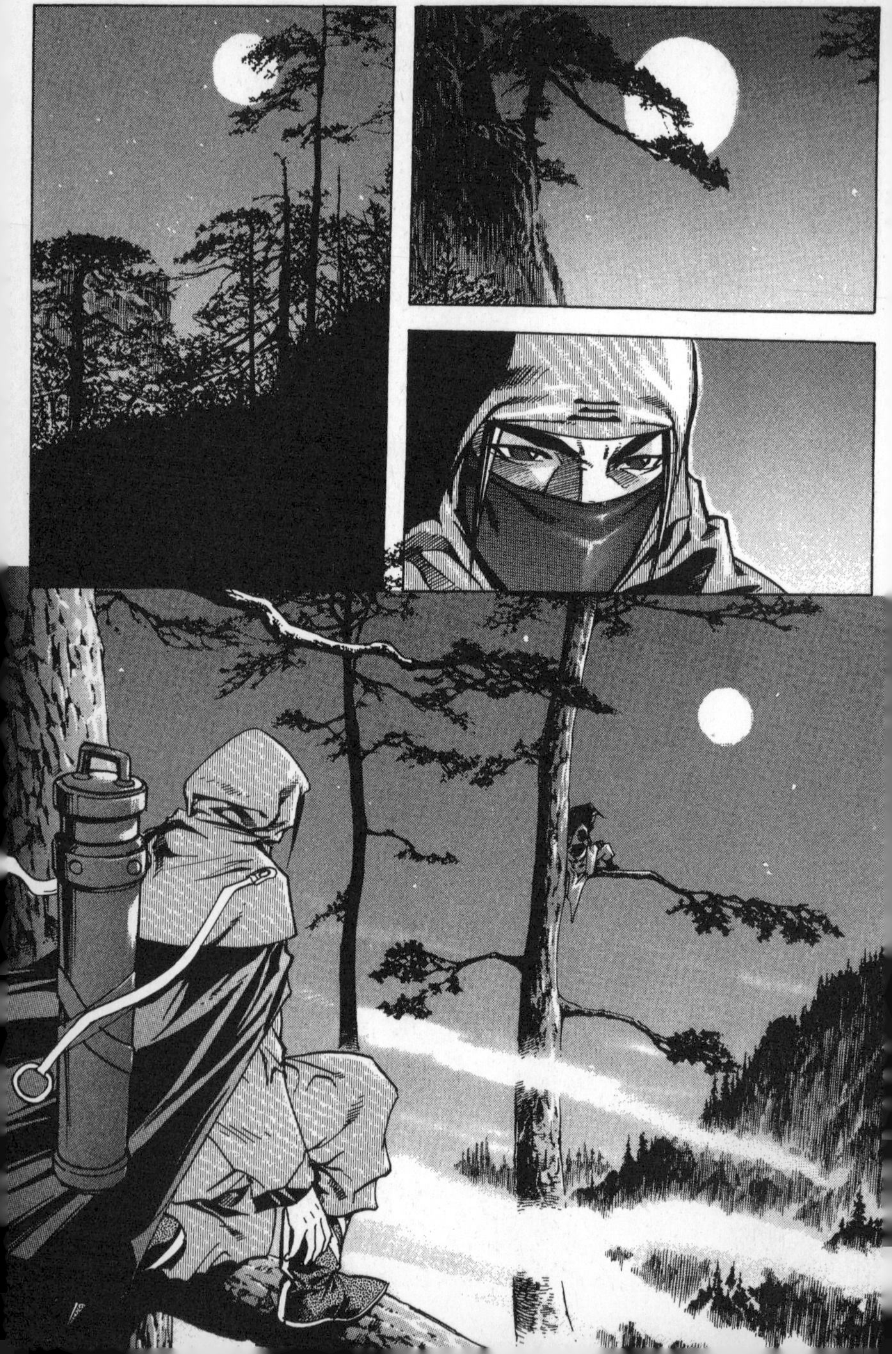

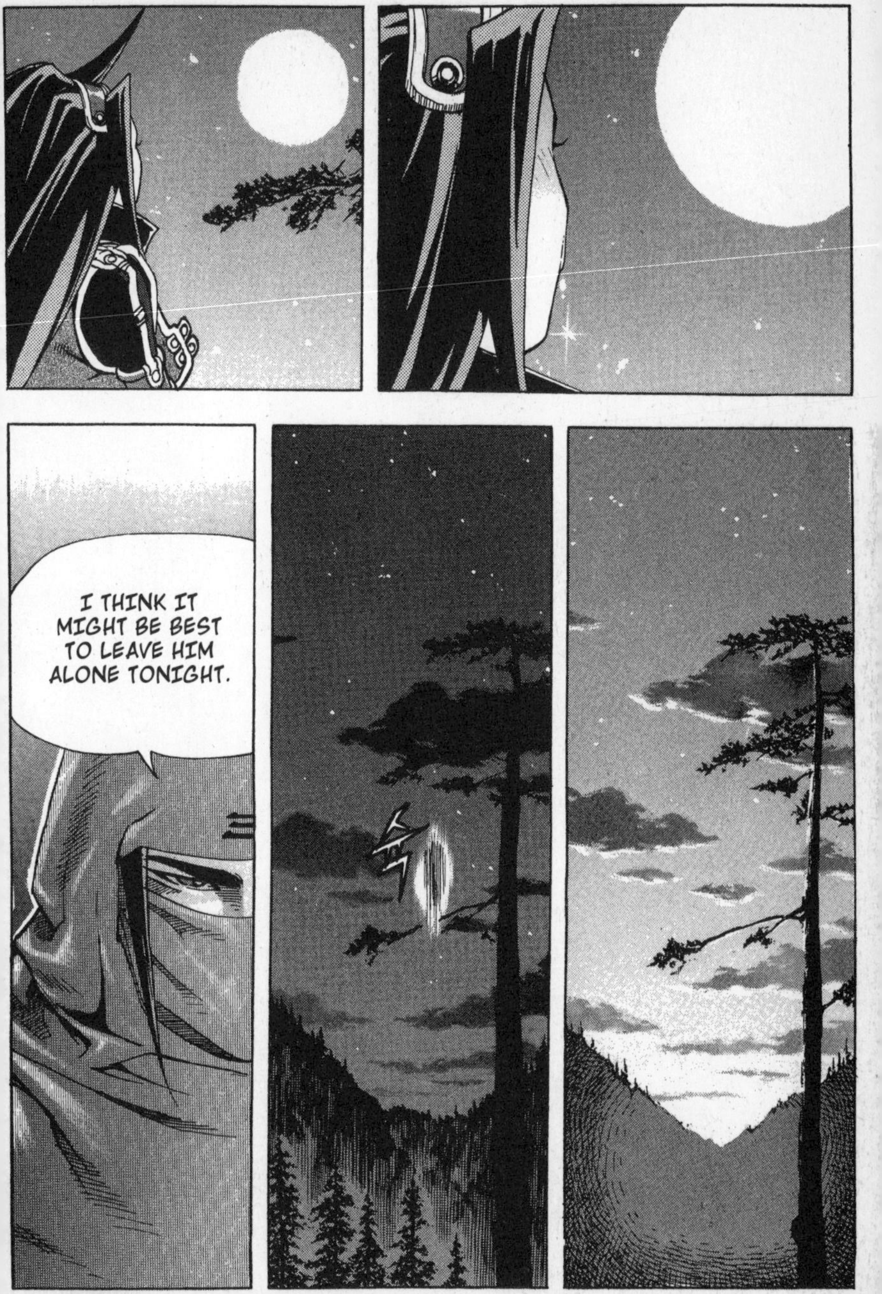
I THINK IT MIGHT BE BEST TO LEAVE HIM ALONE TONIGHT.

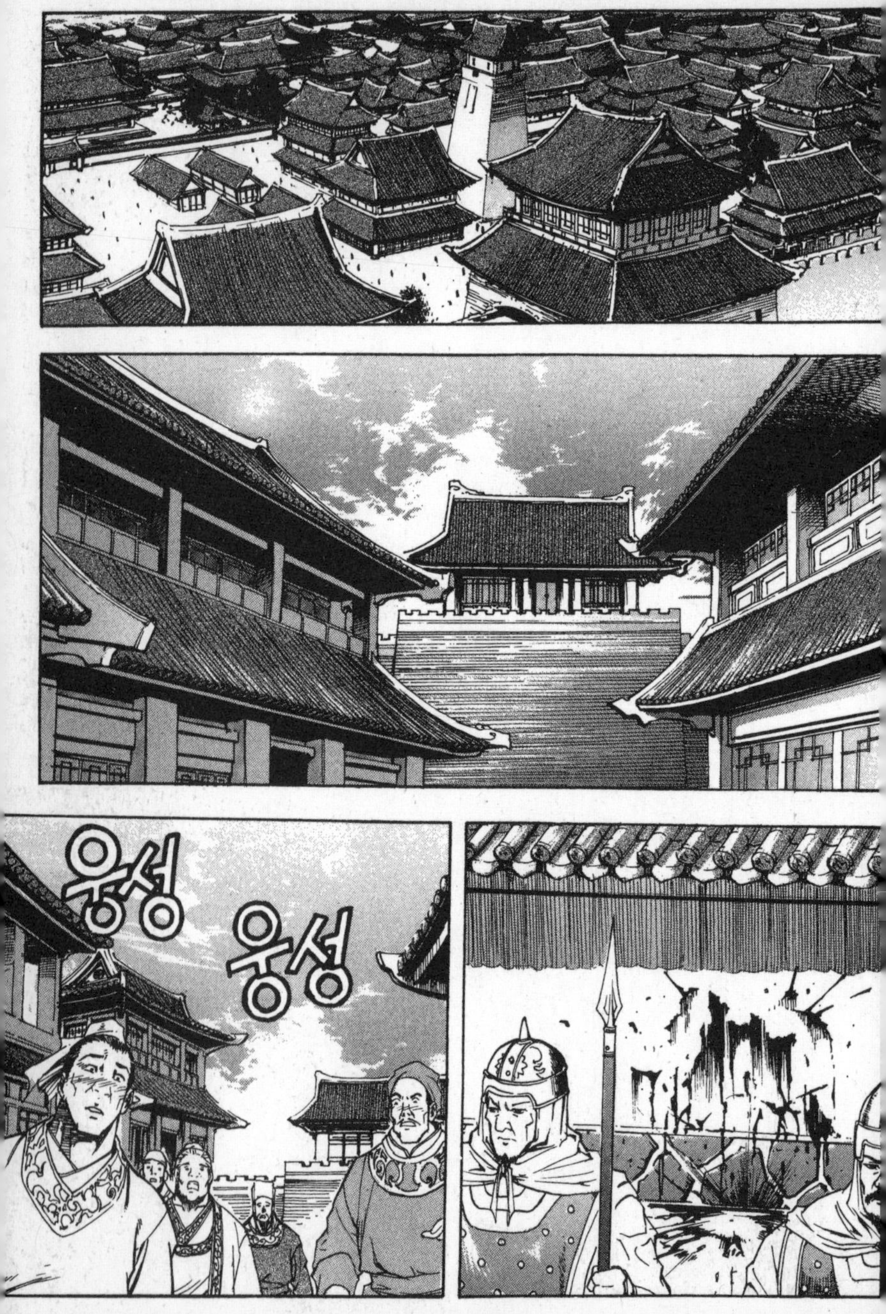
웅성
웅성

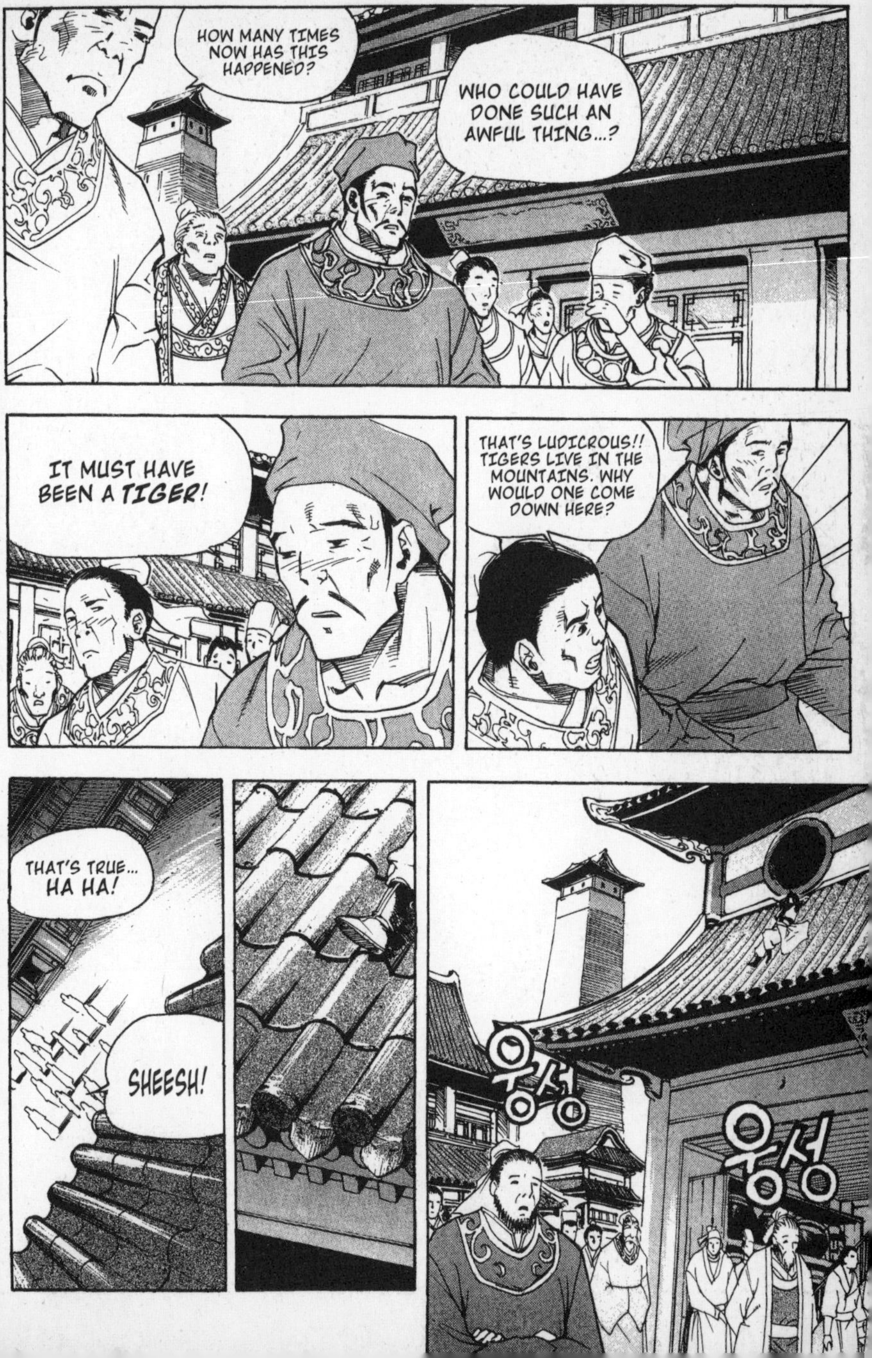
HOW MANY TIMES NOW HAS THIS HAPPENED?
WHO COULD HAVE DONE SUCH AN AWFUL THING...?
IT MUST HAVE BEEN A TIGER!
THAT'S LUDICROUS!! TIGERS LIVE IN THE MOUNTAINS. WHY WOULD ONE COME DOWN HERE?
THAT'S TRUE... HA HA!
SHEESH!
웅성
웅성

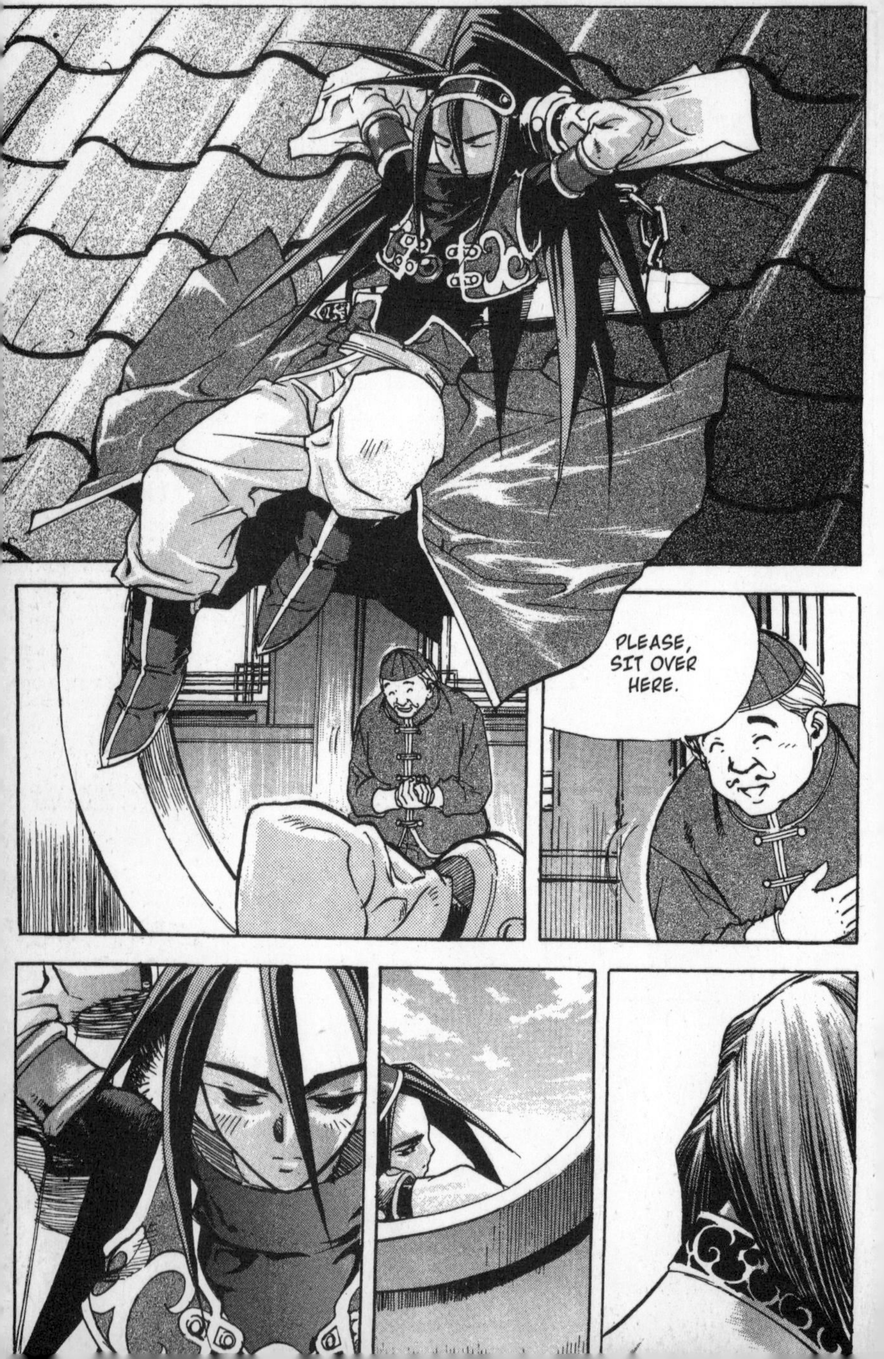
PLEASE, SIT OVER HERE.

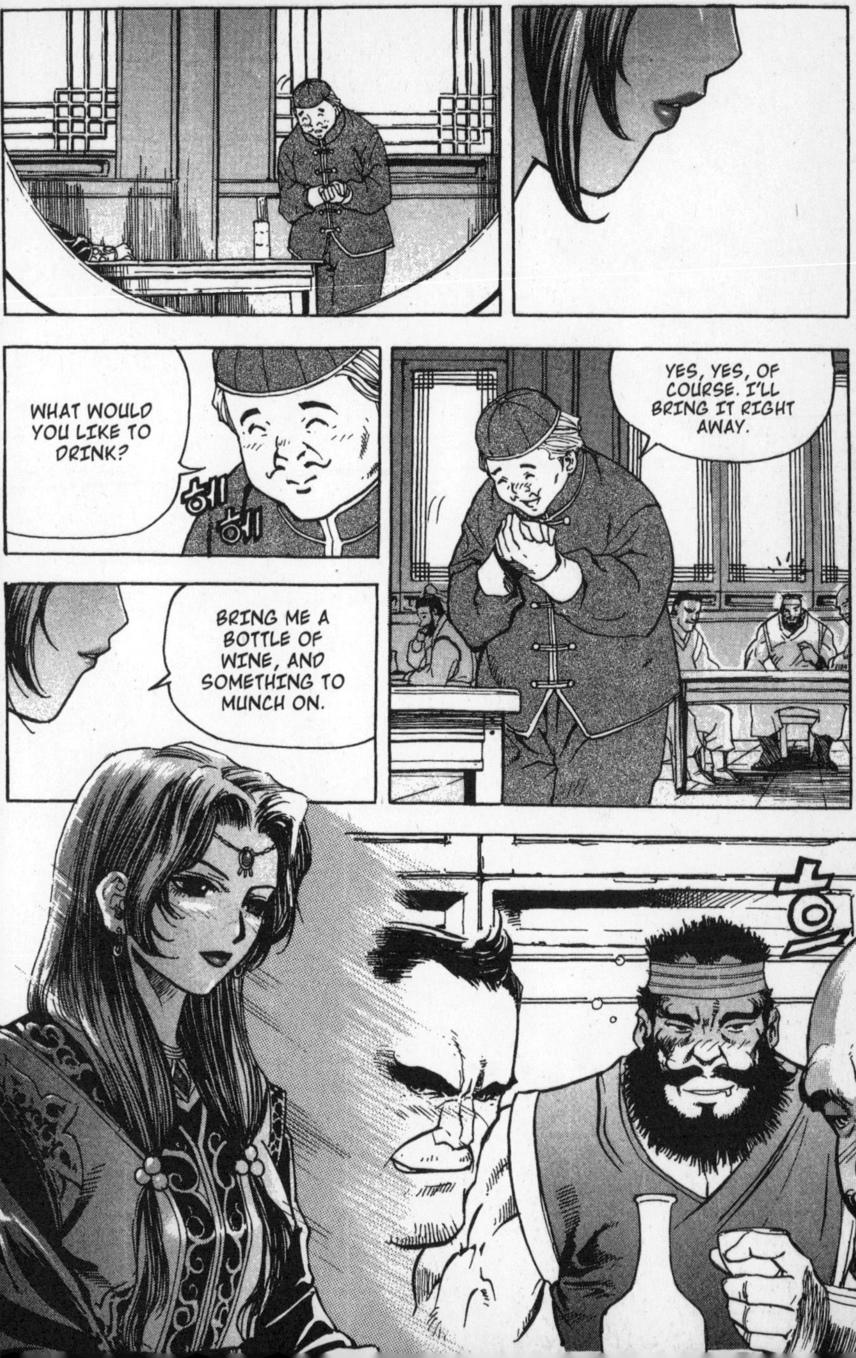
WHAT WOULD YOU LIKE TO DRINK?
헤 헤
BRING ME A BOTTLE OF WINE, AND SOMETHING TO MUNCH ON.
YES, YES, OF COURSE. I'LL BRING IT RIGHT AWAY.
흥

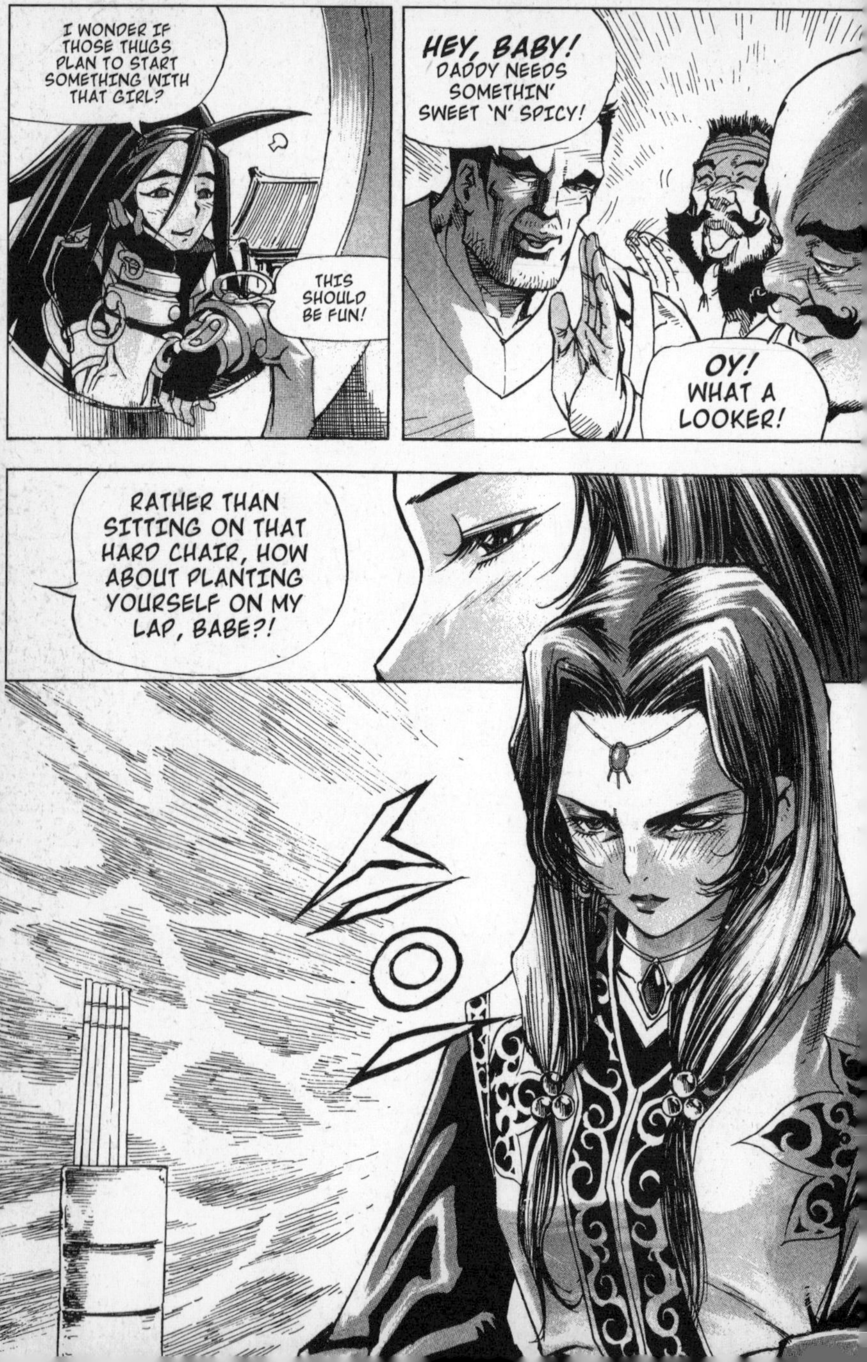
I WONDER IF THOSE THUGS PLAN TO START SOMETHING WITH THAT GIRL?
THIS SHOULD BE FUN!
HEY, BABY! DADDY NEEDS SOMETHIN' SWEET 'N' SPICY!
OY! WHAT A LOOKER!
RATHER THAN SITTING ON THAT HARD CHAIR, HOW ABOUT PLANTING YOURSELF ON MY LAP, BABE?!

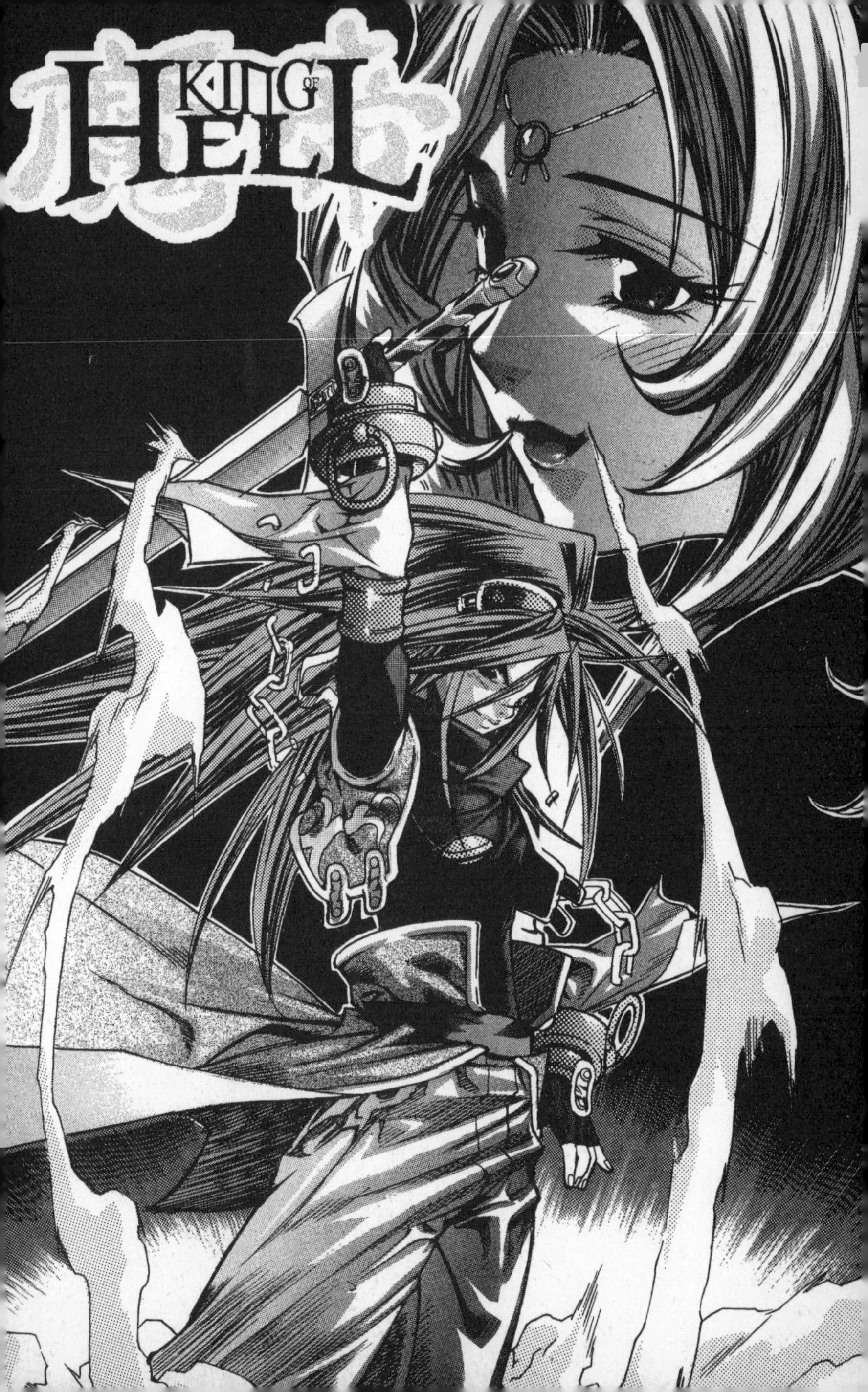
KING OF HELL

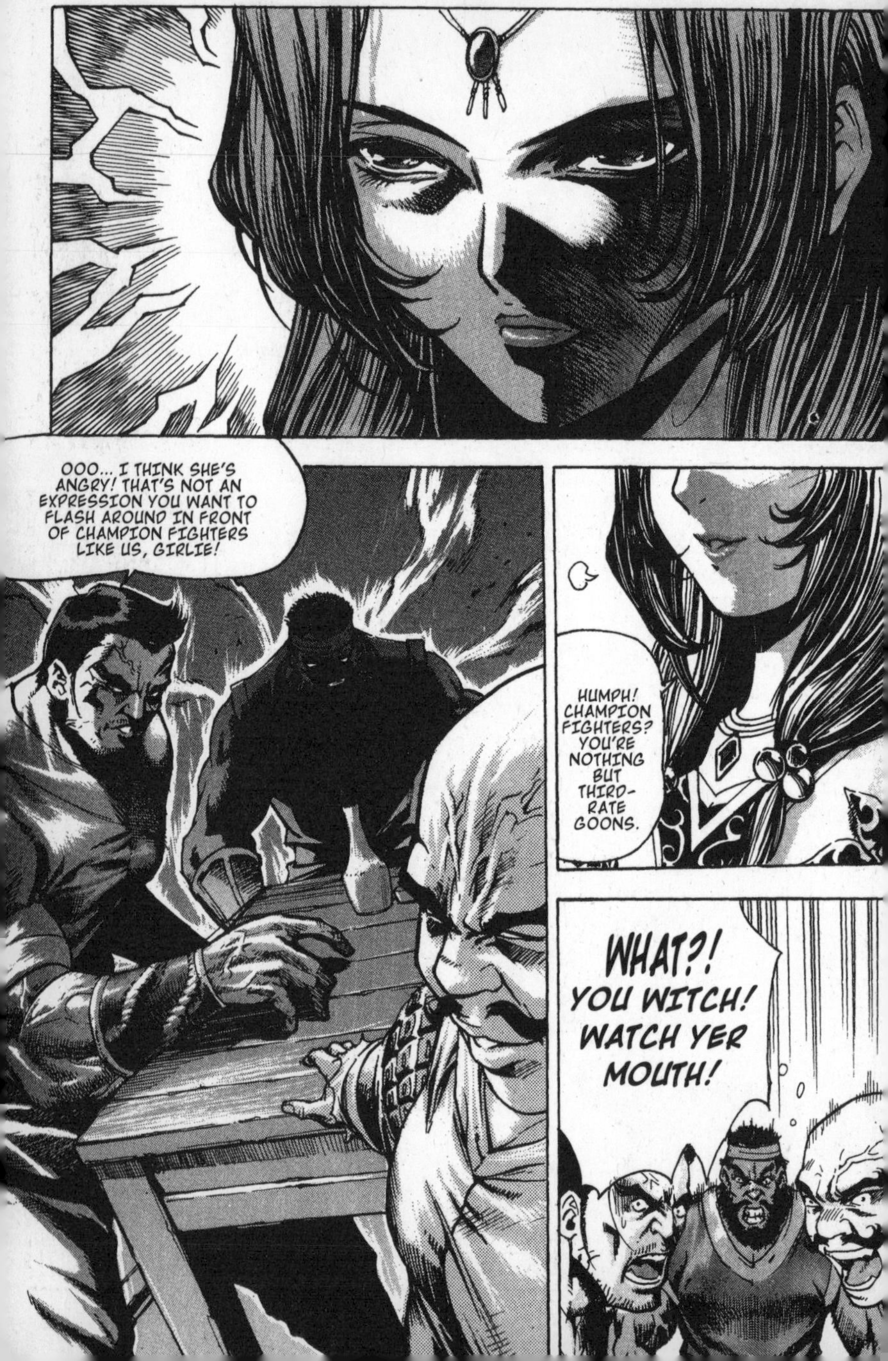
OOO... I THINK SHE'S ANGRY! THAT'S NOT AN EXPRESSION YOU WANT TO FLASH AROUND IN FRONT OF CHAMPION FIGHTERS LIKE US, GIRLIE!
HUMPH! CHAMPION FIGHTERS? YOU'RE NOTHING BUT THIRD-RATE GOONS.
WHAT?! YOU WITCH! WATCH YER MOUTH!

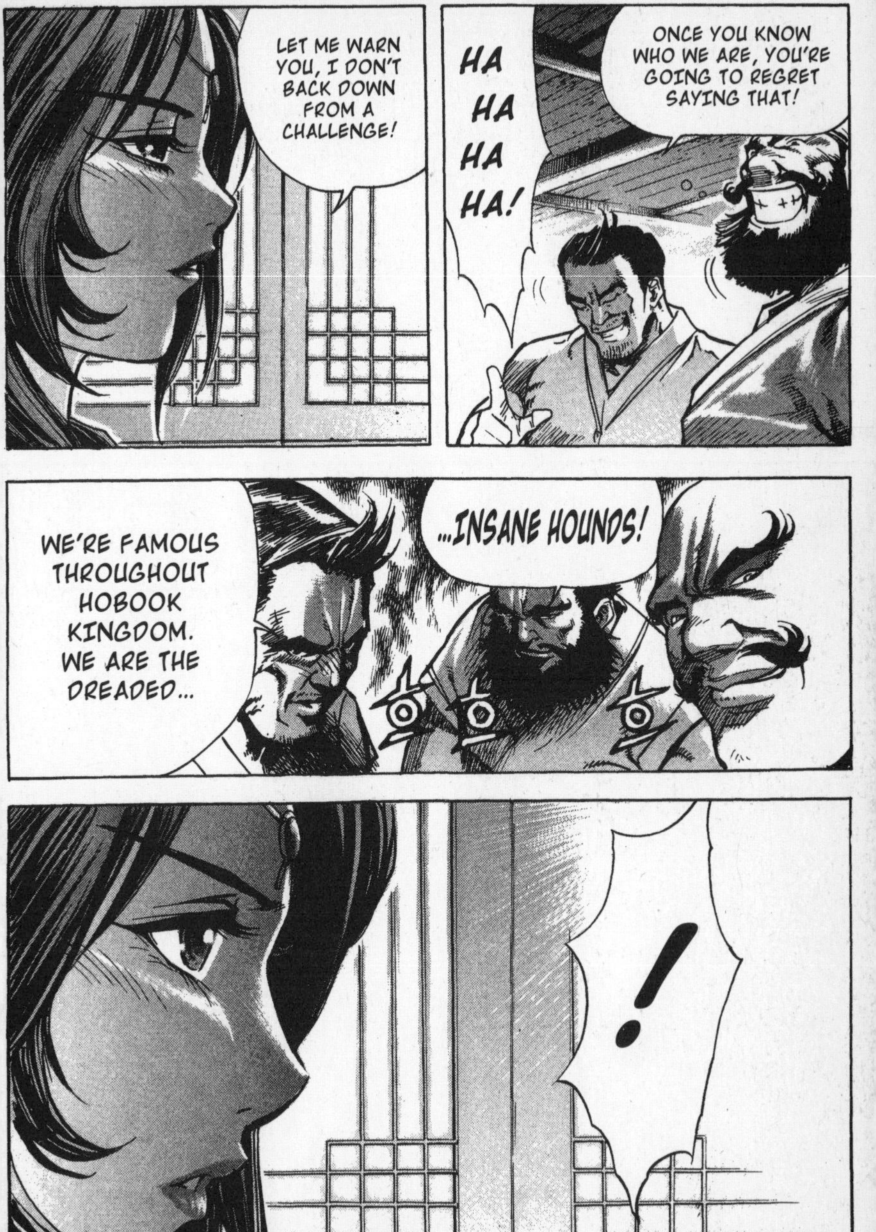
LET ME WARN YOU, I DON'T BACK DOWN FROM A CHALLENGE!
HA HA HA HA!
ONCE YOU KNOW WHO WE ARE, YOU'RE GOING TO REGRET SAYING THAT!
WE'RE FAMOUS THROUGHOUT HOBOOK KINGDOM. WE ARE THE DREADED...
...INSANE HOUNDS!
!

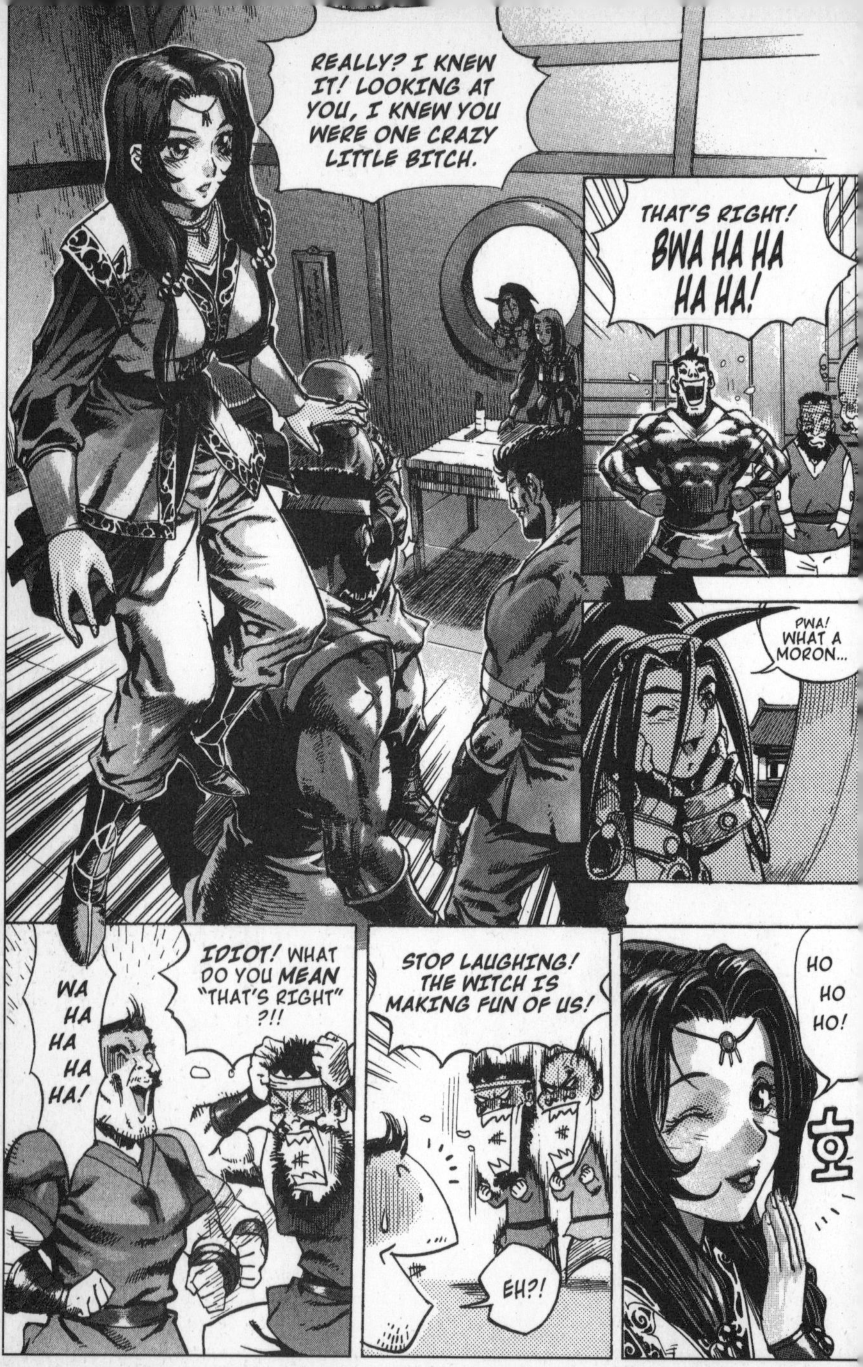
REALLY? I KNEW IT! LOOKING AT YOU, I KNEW YOU WERE ONE CRAZY LITTLE BITCH.
THAT'S RIGHT! BWA HA HA HA HA!
PWA! WHAT A MORON...
WA HA HA HA HA HA!
IDIOT! WHAT DO YOU MEAN "THAT'S RIGHT" ?!!
STOP LAUGHING! THE WITCH IS MAKING FUN OF US!
EH?!
HO HO HO!
호

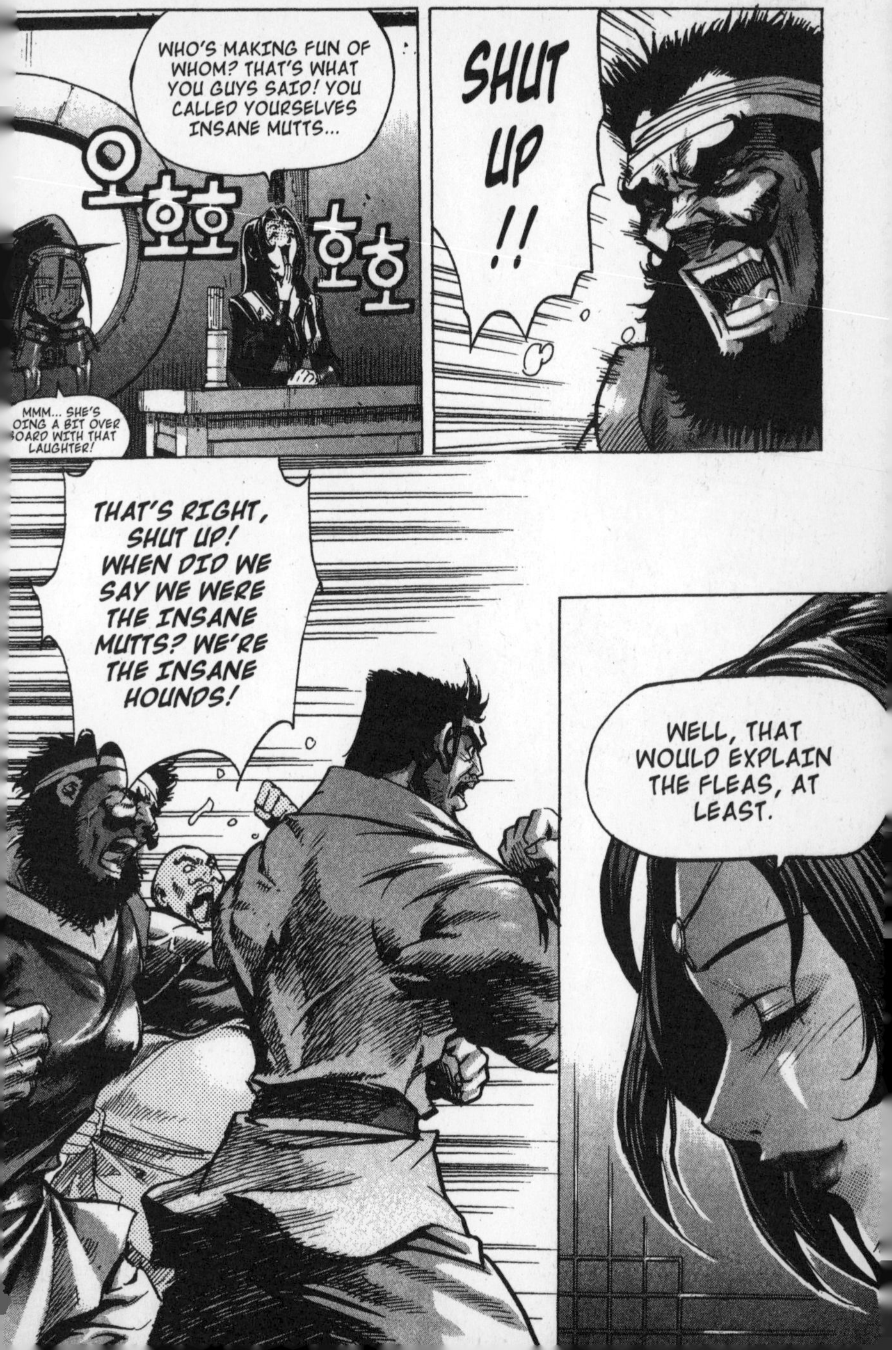

WHO'S MAKING FUN OF WHOM? THAT'S WHAT YOU GUYS SAID! YOU CALLED YOURSELVES INSANE MUTTS...
오호호 호호
MMM... SHE'S OING A BIT OVER OARD WITH THAT LAUGHTER!
SHUT UP!!
THAT'S RIGHT, SHUT UP! WHEN DID WE SAY WE WERE THE INSANE MUTTS? WE'RE THE INSANE HOUNDS!
WELL, THAT WOULD EXPLAIN THE FLEAS, AT LEAST.

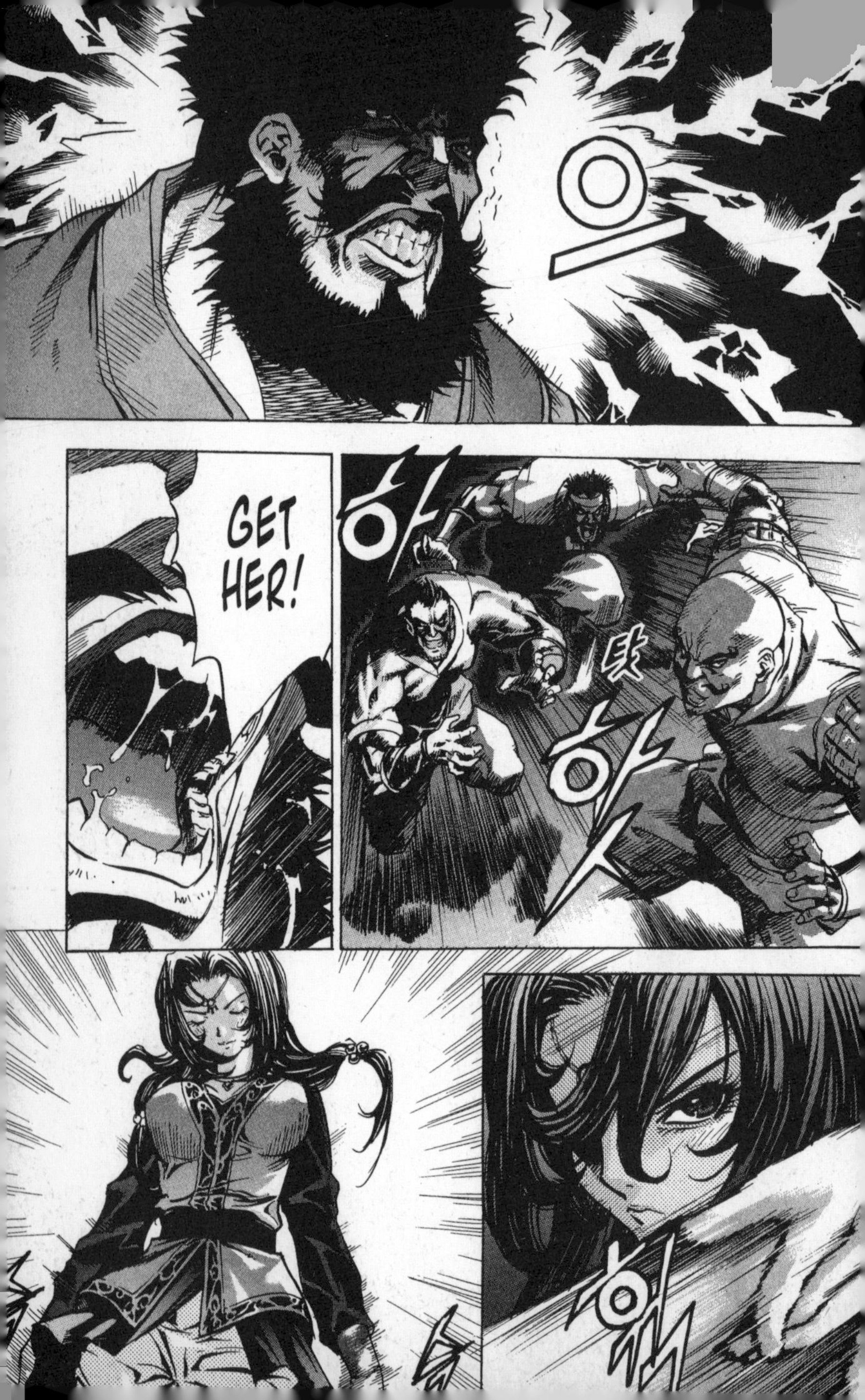
GET HER!

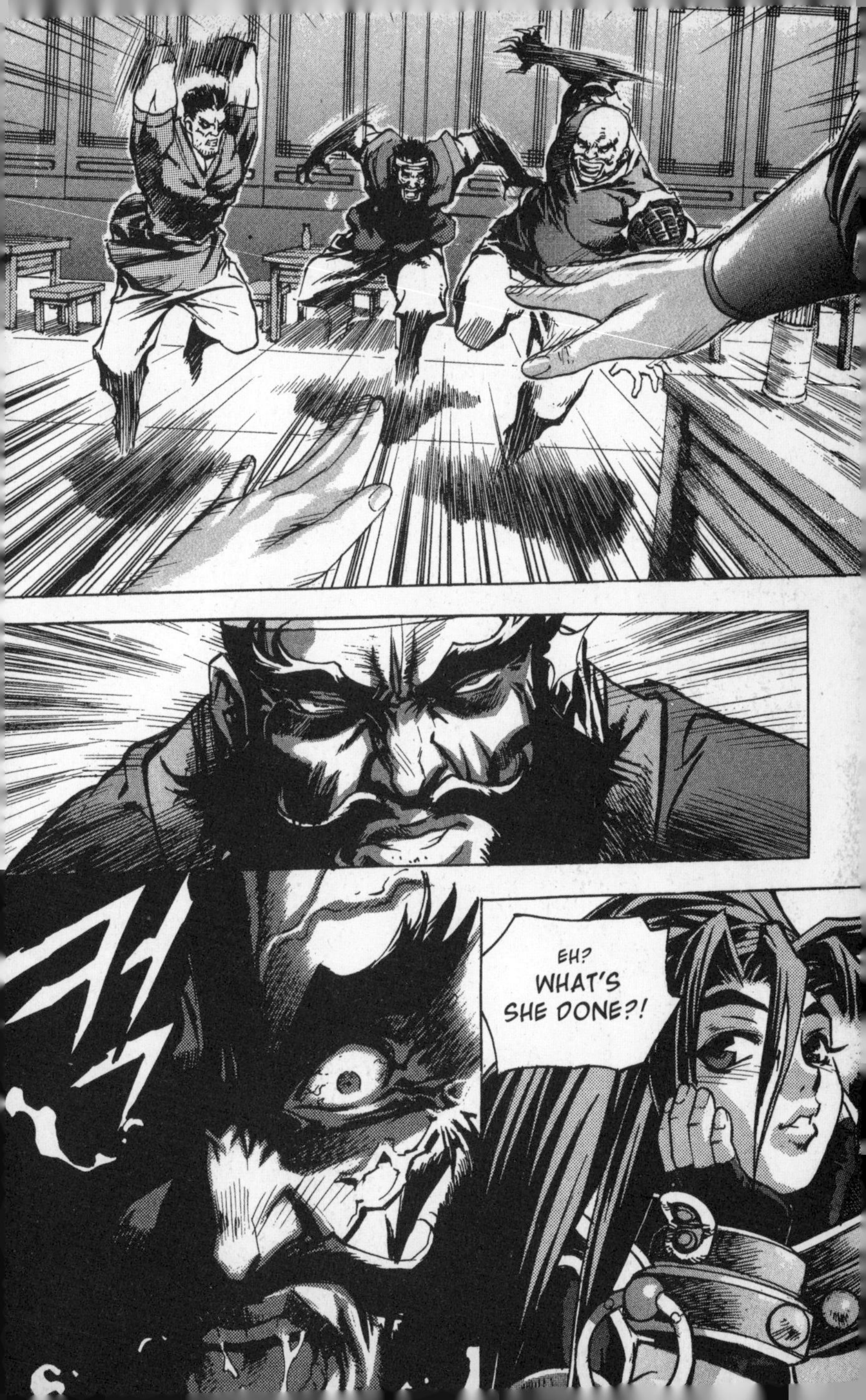
EH? WHAT'S SHE DONE?!

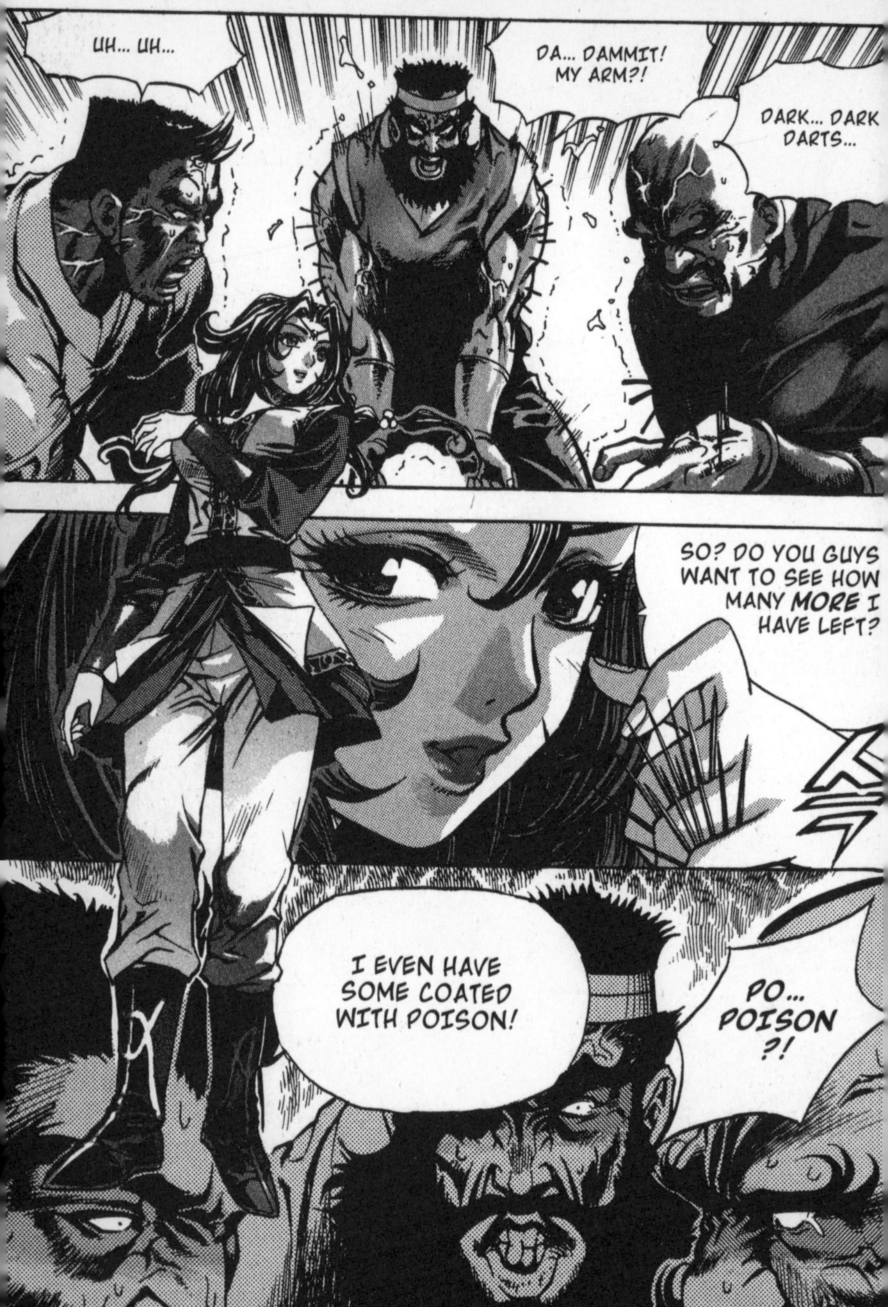
UH... UH...
DA... DAMMIT! MY ARM?!
DARK... DARK DARTS...
SO? DO YOU GUYS WANT TO SEE HOW MANY MORE I HAVE LEFT?
I EVEN HAVE SOME COATED WITH POISON!
PO... POISON ?!

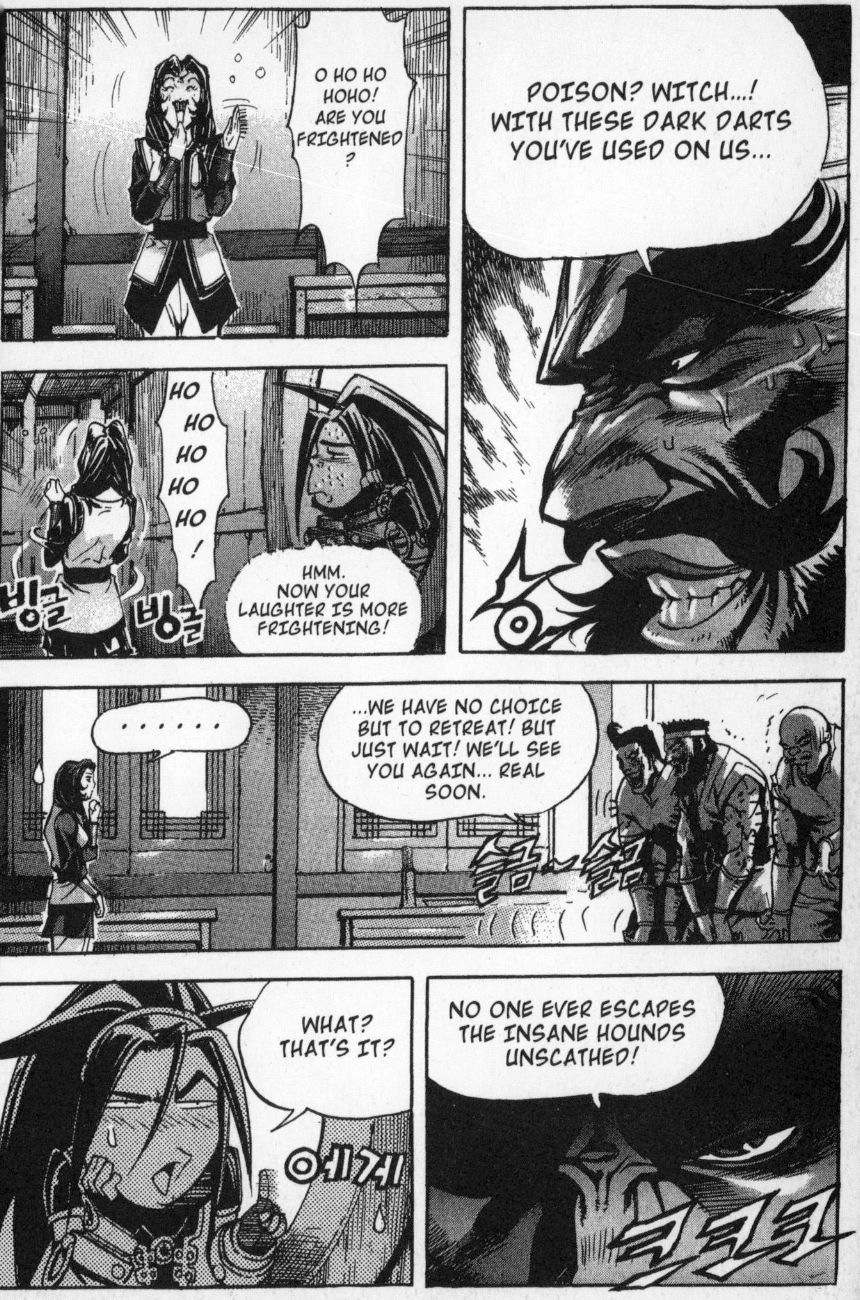
O HO HO HOHO! ARE YOU FRIGHTENED?
HO HO HO HO HO!
빙글 빙글
HMM. NOW YOUR LAUGHTER IS MORE FRIGHTENING!
POISON? WITCH...! WITH THESE DARK DARTS YOU'VE USED ON US...
......
...WE HAVE NO CHOICE BUT TO RETREAT! BUT JUST WAIT! WE'LL SEE YOU AGAIN... REAL SOON.
WHAT? THAT'S IT?
에게
NO ONE EVER ESCAPES THE INSANE HOUNDS UNSCATHED!

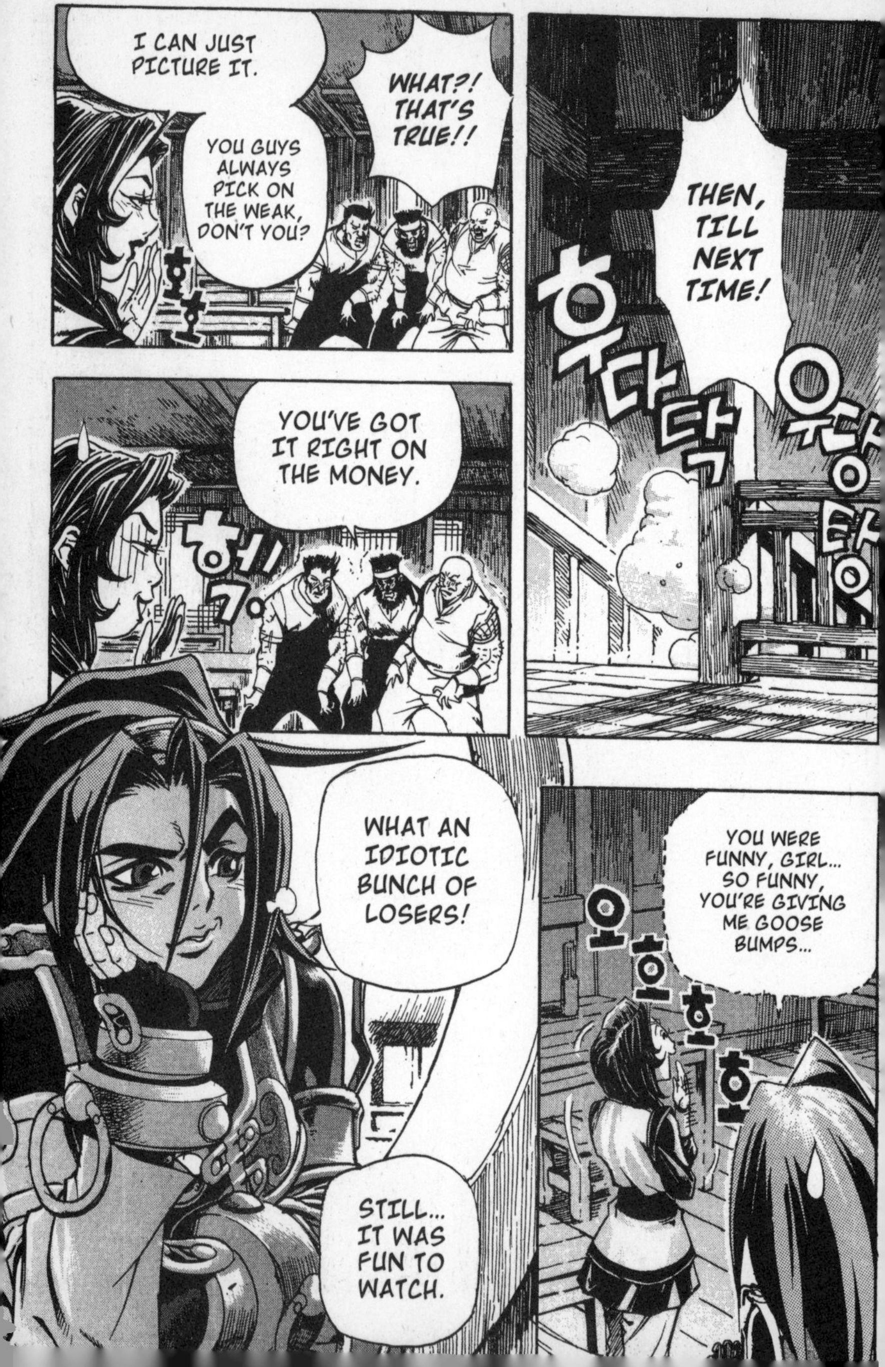
I CAN JUST PICTURE IT.
YOU GUYS ALWAYS PICK ON THE WEAK, DON'T YOU?
호호
WHAT?! THAT'S TRUE!!
YOU'VE GOT IT RIGHT ON THE MONEY.
THEN, TILL NEXT TIME!
후다닥
우당탕
WHAT AN IDIOTIC BUNCH OF LOSERS!
STILL... IT WAS FUN TO WATCH.
YOU WERE FUNNY, GIRL... SO FUNNY, YOU'RE GIVING ME GOOSE BUMPS...
오호호호

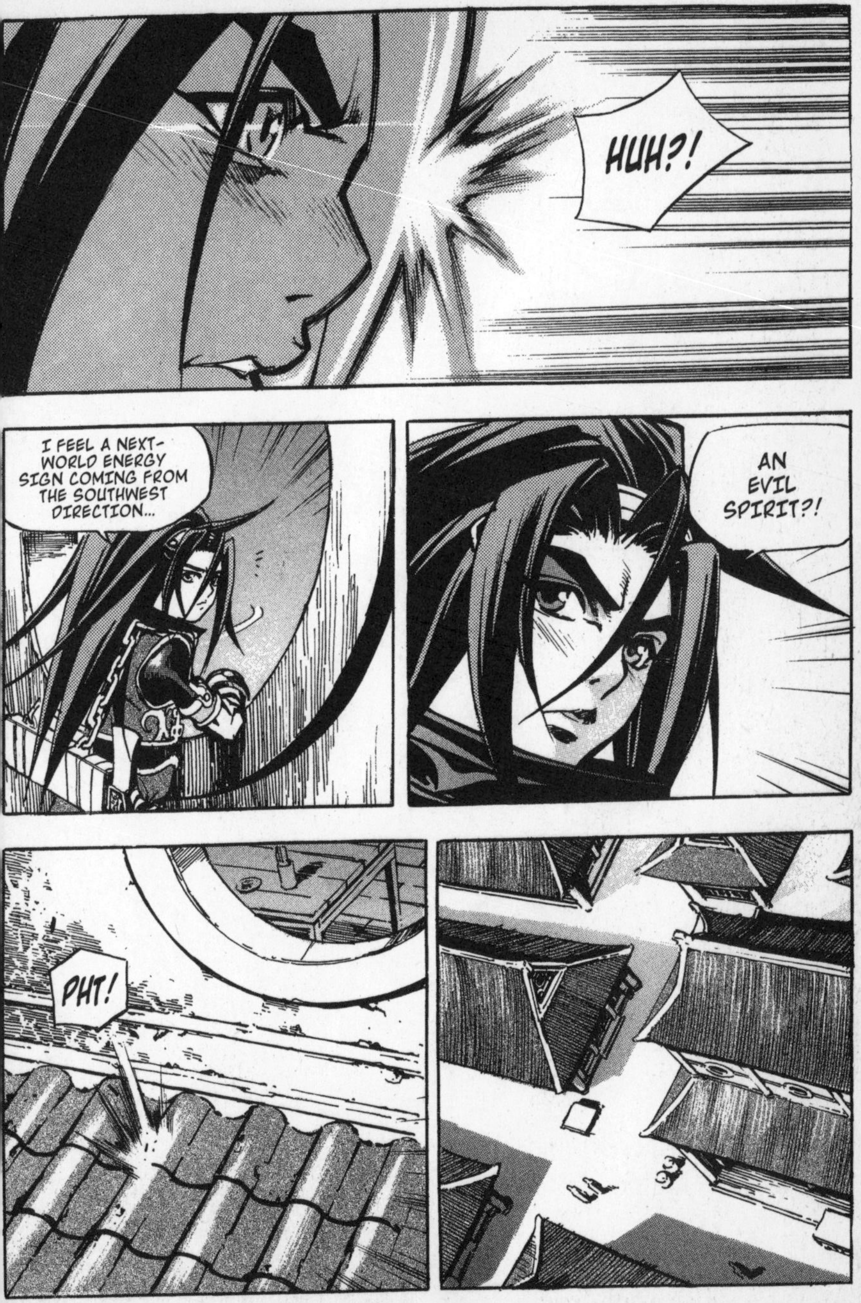
HUH?!
I FEEL A NEXT-WORLD ENERGY SIGN COMING FROM THE SOUTHWEST DIRECTION...
AN EVIL SPIRIT?!
PHT!

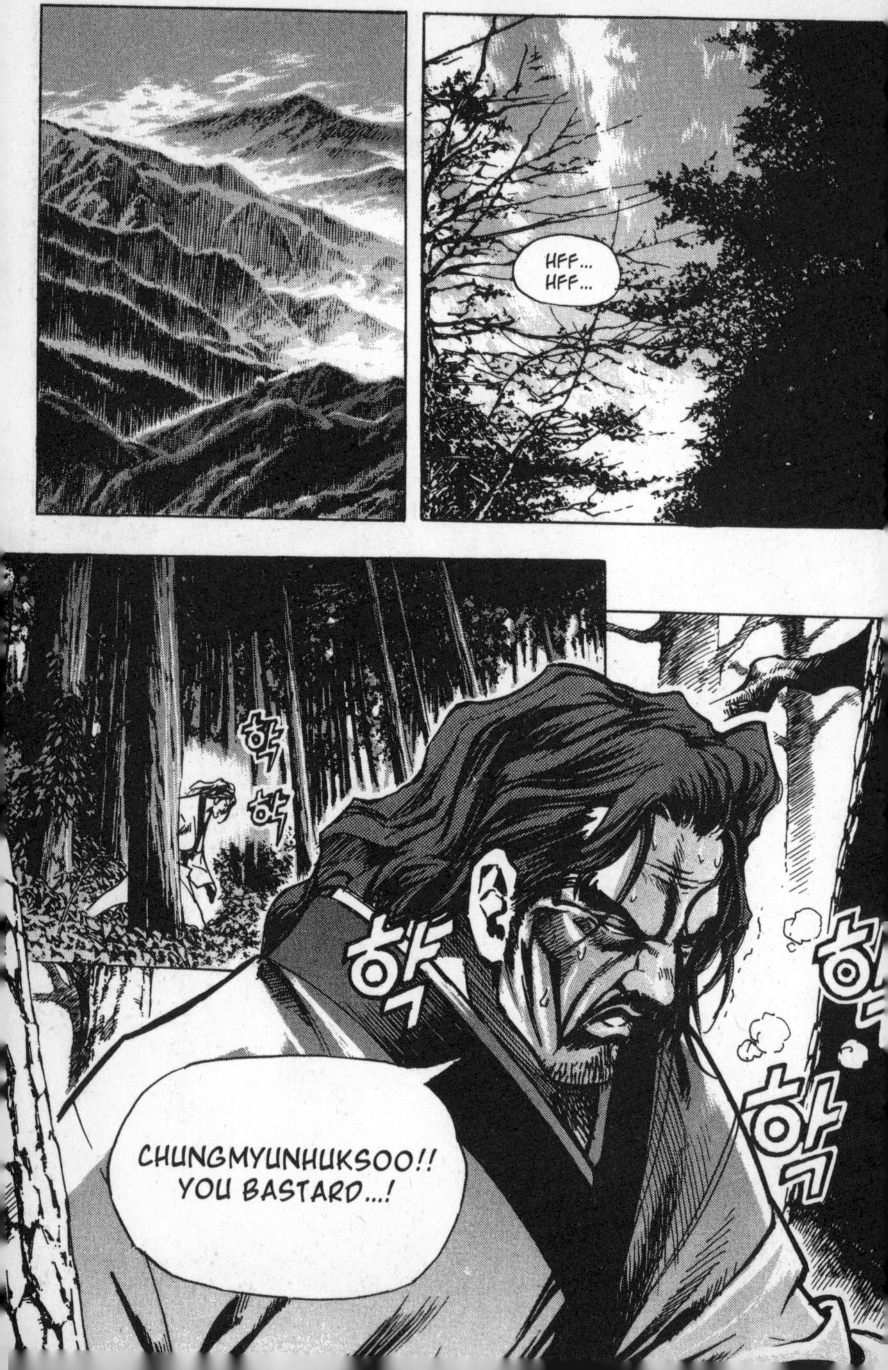
HFF... HFF...
헉 헉
헉
헉 헉
CHUNGMYUNHUKSOO!! YOU BASTARD...!

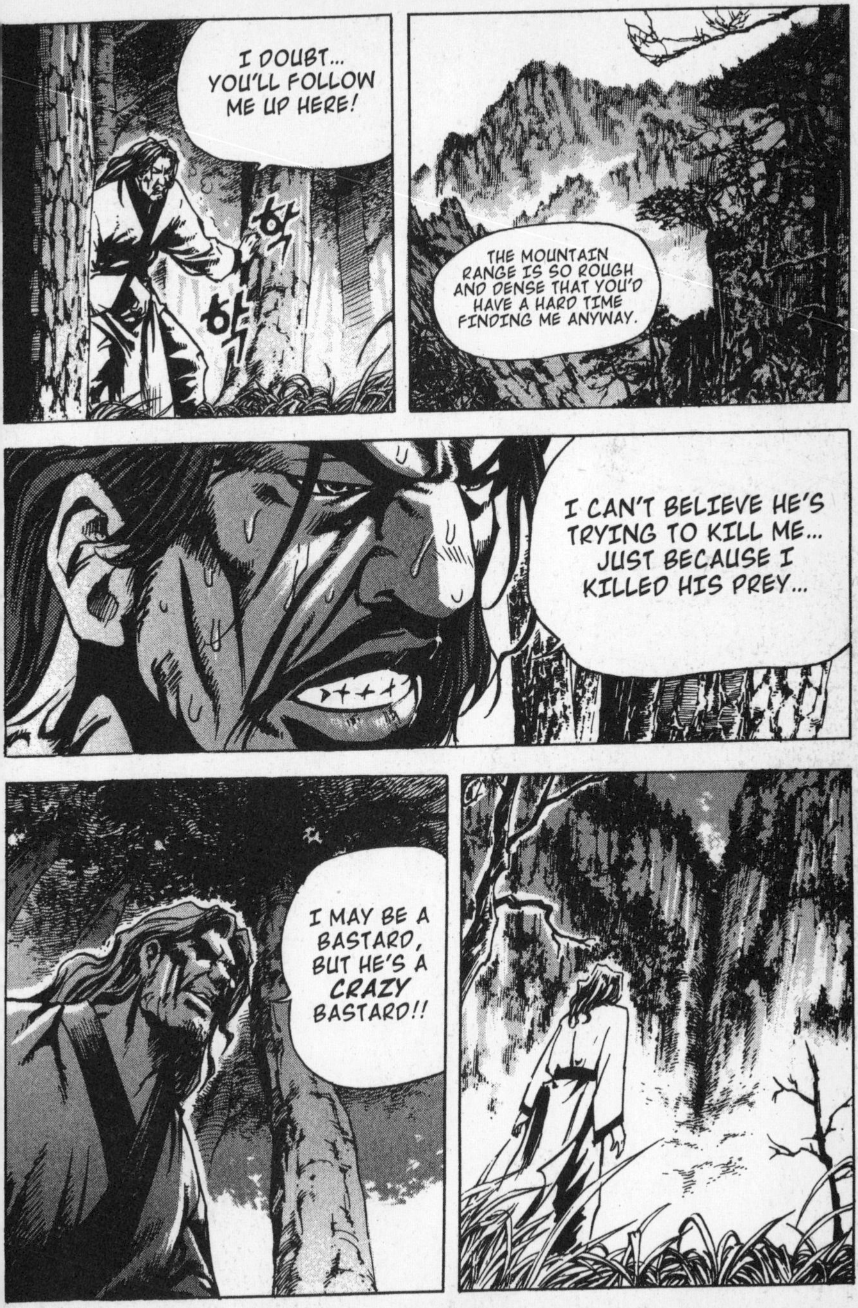
I DOUBT... YOU'LL FOLLOW ME UP HERE!
학
학
THE MOUNTAIN RANGE IS SO ROUGH AND DENSE THAT YOU'D HAVE A HARD TIME FINDING ME ANYWAY.
I CAN'T BELIEVE HE'S TRYING TO KILL ME... JUST BECAUSE I KILLED HIS PREY...
I MAY BE A BASTARD, BUT HE'S A *CRAZY* BASTARD!!

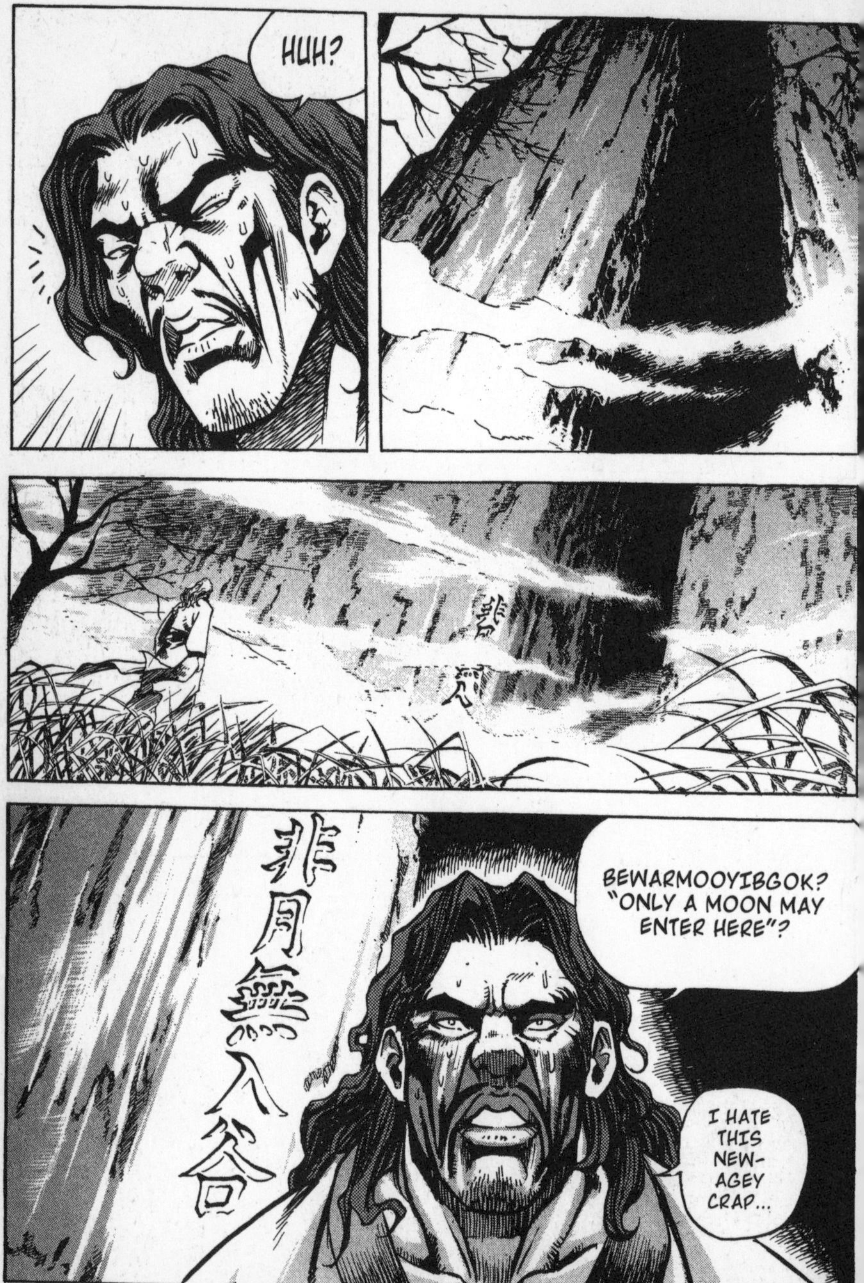
HUH?
非月無入谷
BEWARMOOYIBGOK? "ONLY A MOON MAY ENTER HERE"?
I HATE THIS NEW-AGEY CRAP...

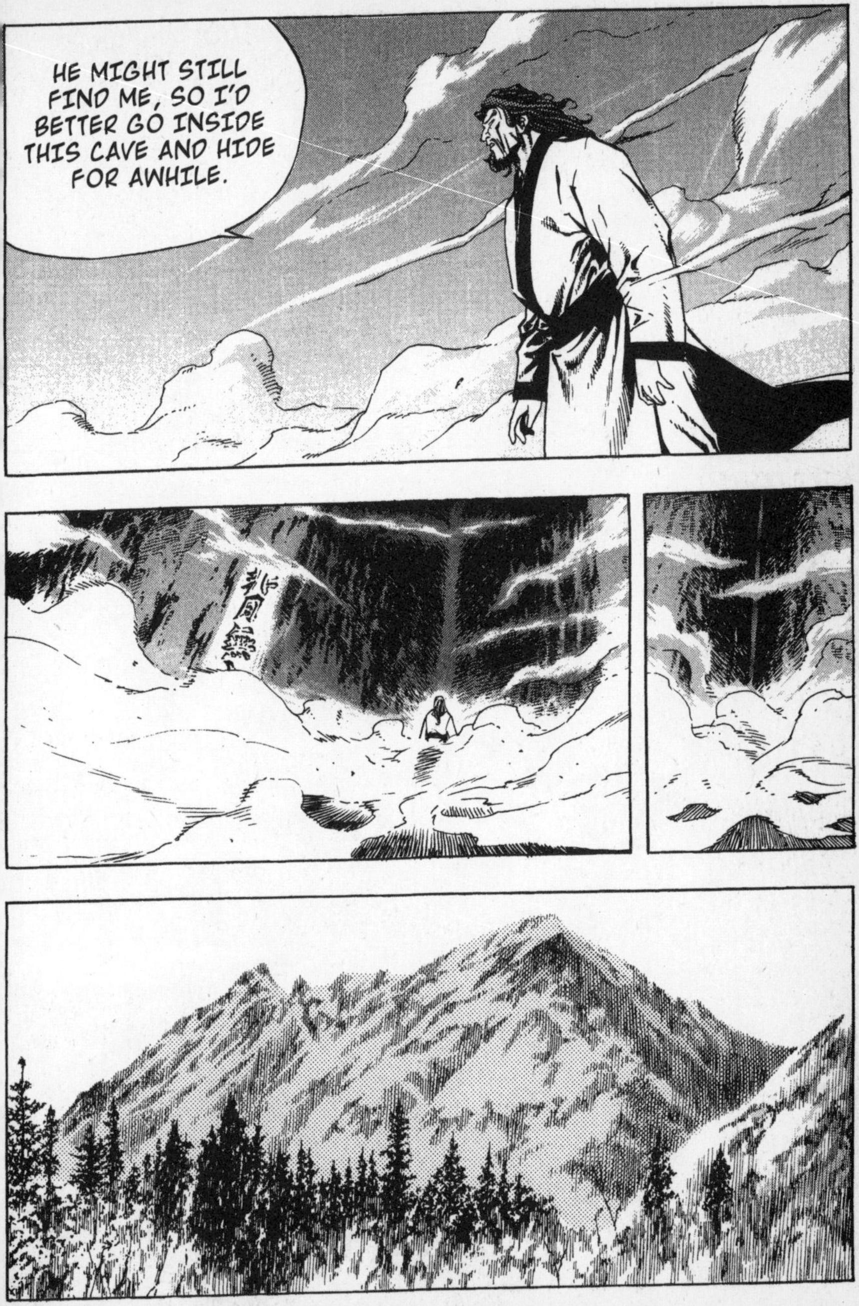
HE MIGHT STILL FIND ME, SO I'D BETTER GO INSIDE THIS CAVE AND HIDE FOR AWHILE.

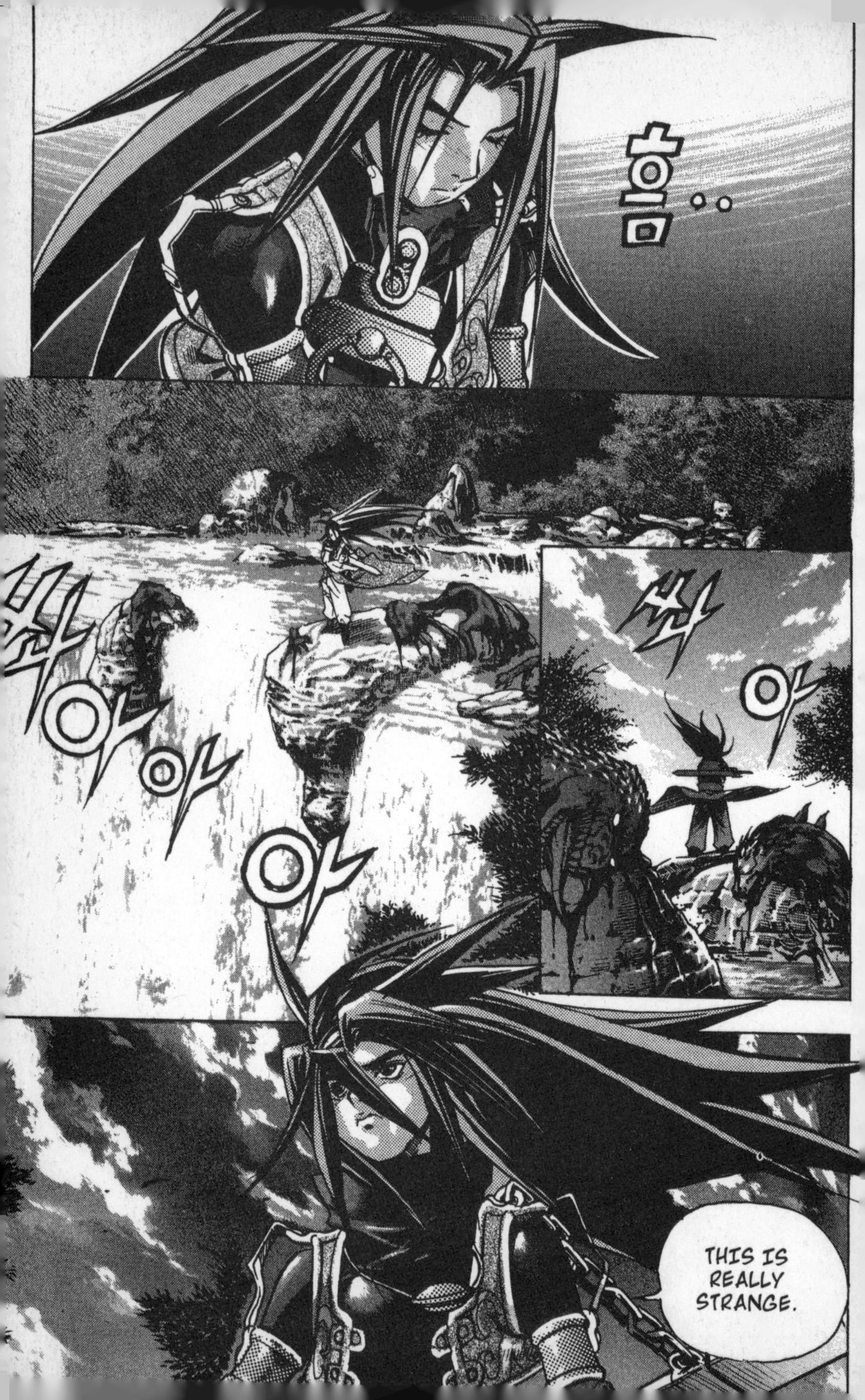
흠..
쏴아아아
쏴아
THIS IS REALLY STRANGE.

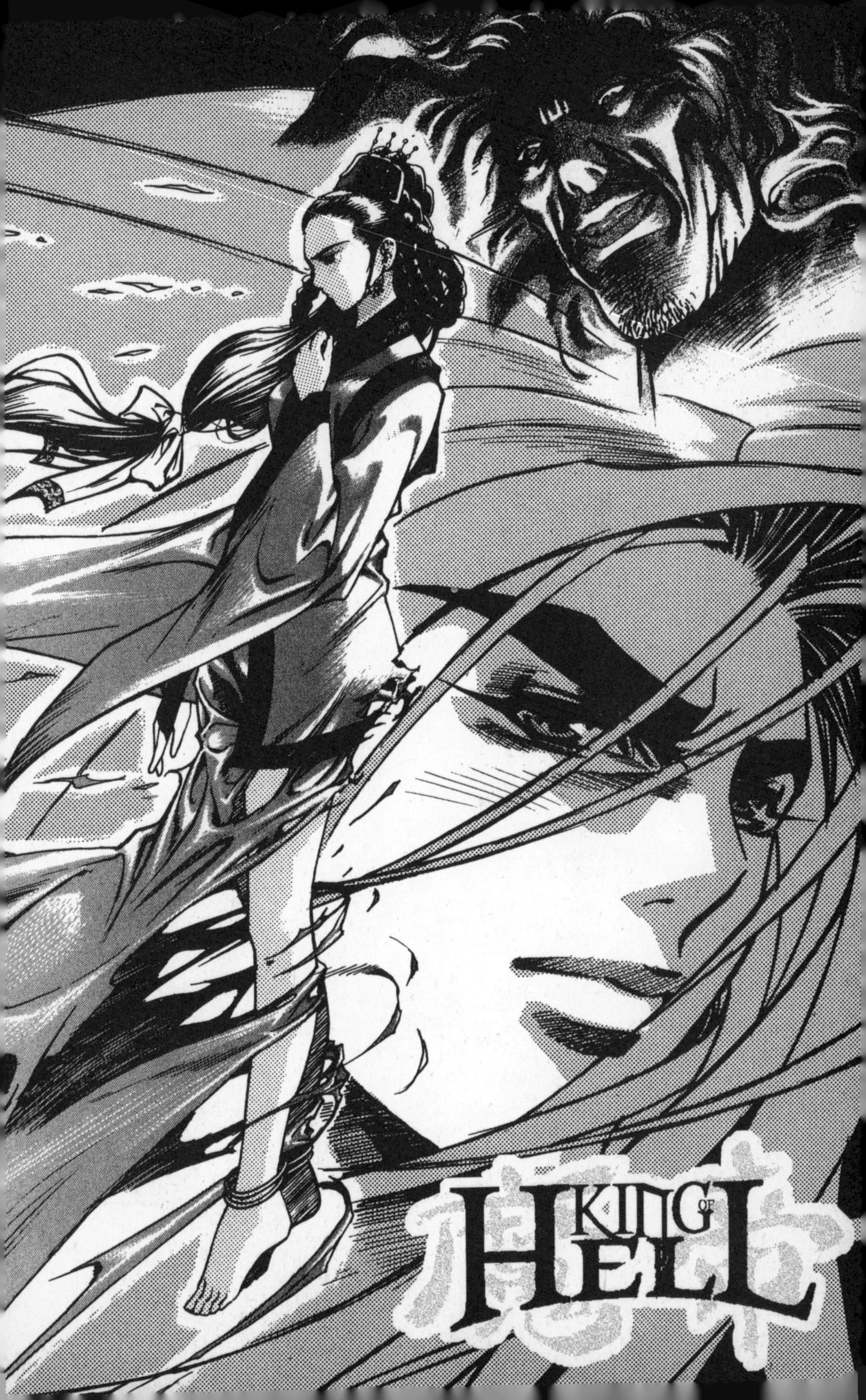
KING OF HELL

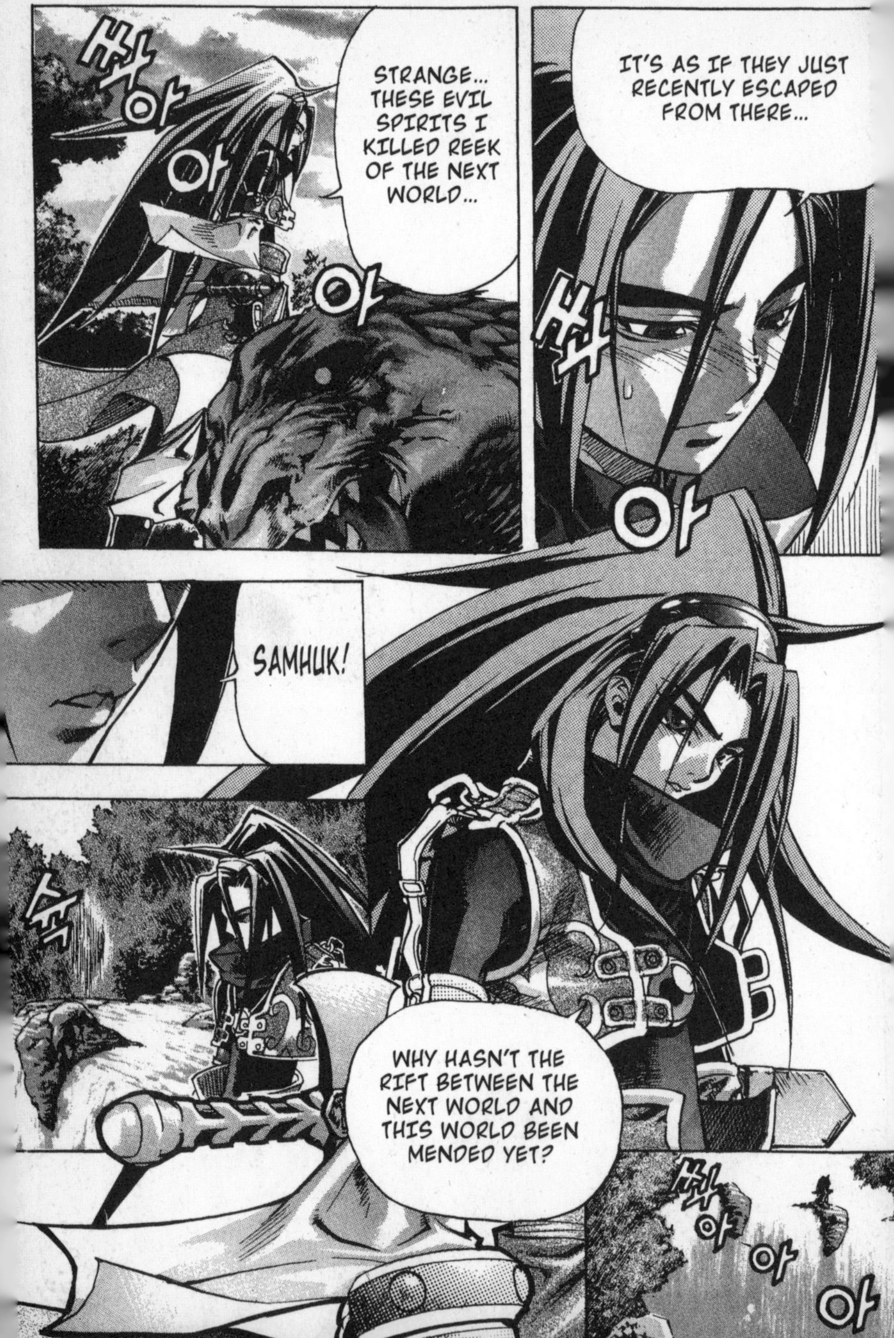
STRANGE... THESE EVIL SPIRITS I KILLED REEK OF THE NEXT WORLD...
IT'S AS IF THEY JUST RECENTLY ESCAPED FROM THERE...
SAMHUK!
WHY HASN'T THE RIFT BETWEEN THE NEXT WORLD AND THIS WORLD BEEN MENDED YET?

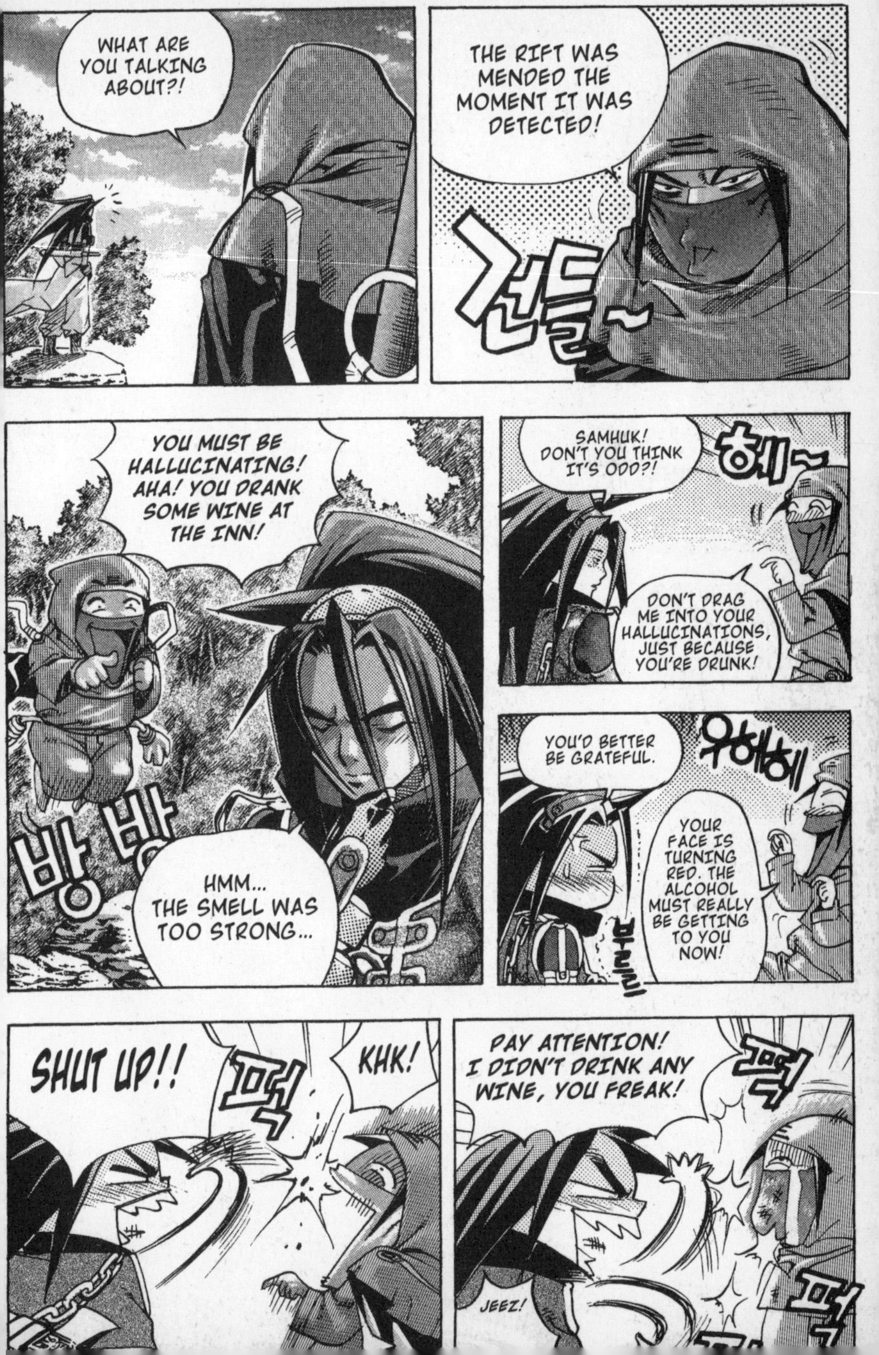
WHAT ARE YOU TALKING ABOUT?!
THE RIFT WAS MENDED THE MOMENT IT WAS DETECTED!
건들~
YOU MUST BE HALLUCINATING! AHA! YOU DRANK SOME WINE AT THE INN!
방 방
HMM... THE SMELL WAS TOO STRONG...
SAMHUK! DON'T YOU THINK IT'S ODD?!
헤~
DON'T DRAG ME INTO YOUR HALLUCINATIONS, JUST BECAUSE YOU'RE DRUNK!
YOU'D BETTER BE GRATEFUL.
우헤헤
YOUR FACE IS TURNING RED. THE ALCOHOL MUST REALLY BE GETTING TO YOU NOW!
SHUT UP!!
퍽
KHK!
PAY ATTENTION! I DIDN'T DRINK ANY WINE, YOU FREAK!
퍽
JEEZ!
퍽

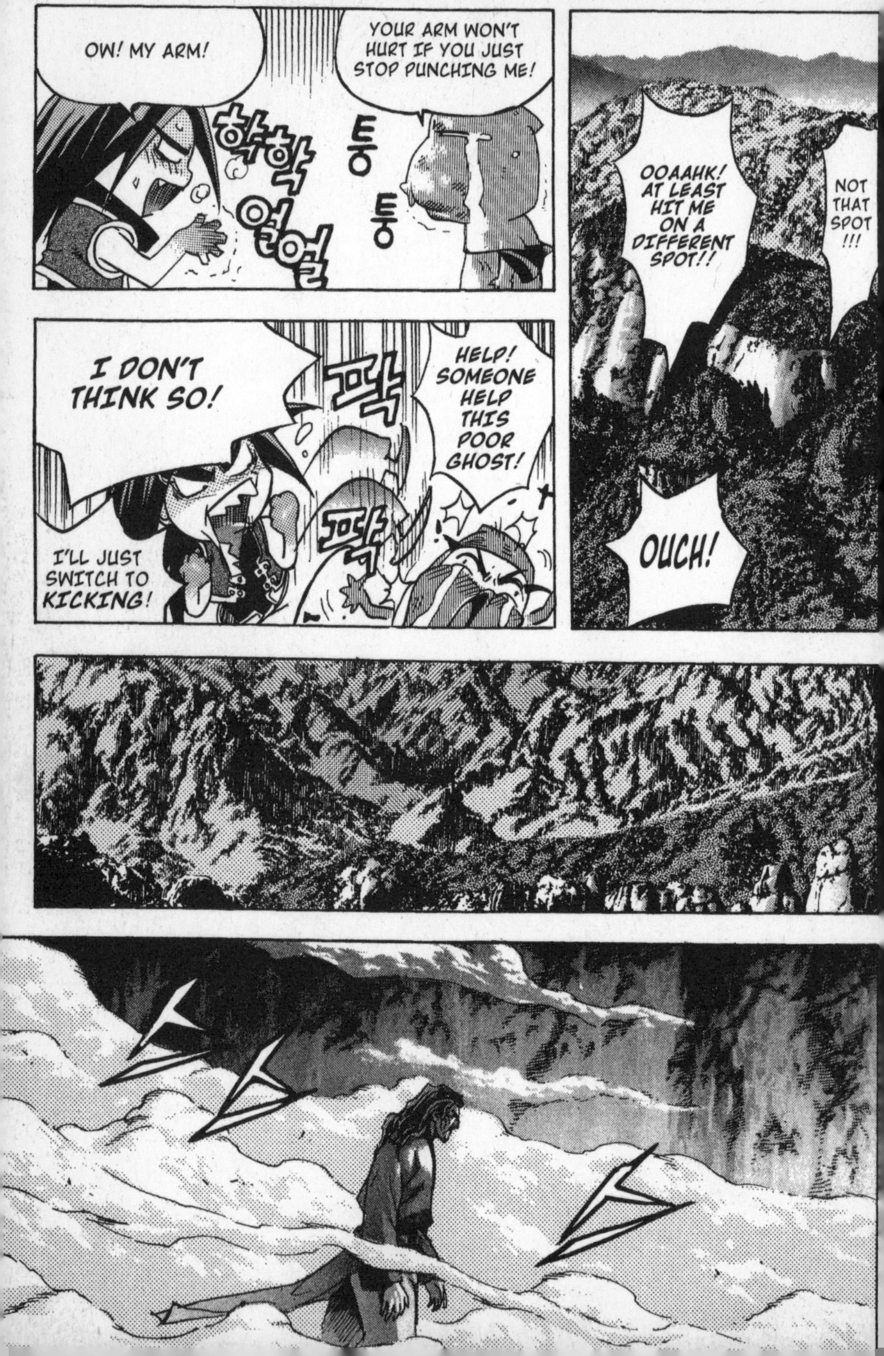
OW! MY ARM!
YOUR ARM WON'T HURT IF YOU JUST STOP PUNCHING ME!
I DON'T THINK SO!
HELP! SOMEONE HELP THIS POOR GHOST!
I'LL JUST SWITCH TO KICKING!
OOAAHK! AT LEAST HIT ME ON A DIFFERENT SPOT!!
NOT THAT SPOT!!!
OUCH!

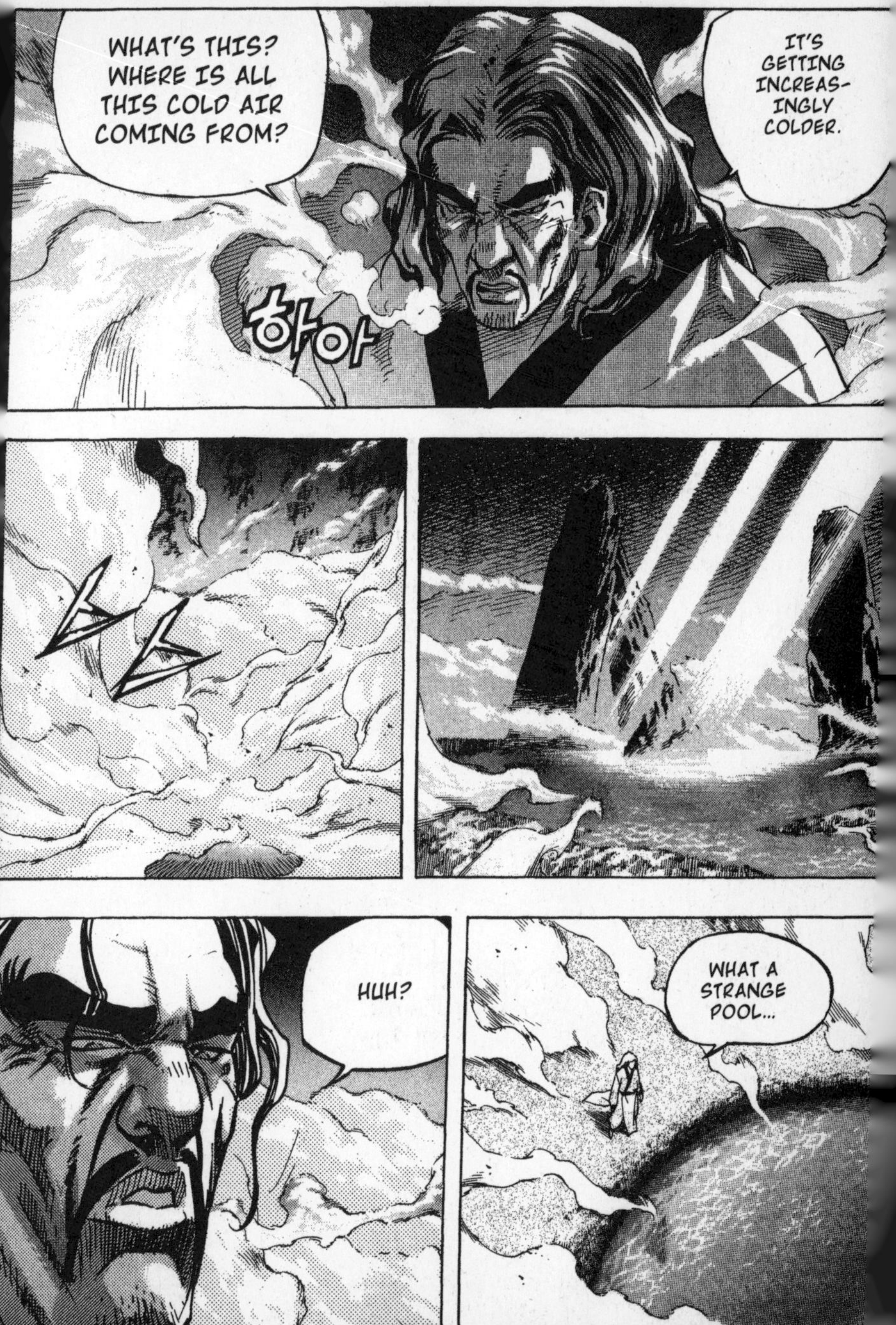
WHAT'S THIS? WHERE IS ALL THIS COLD AIR COMING FROM?
하아
IT'S GETTING INCREAS-INGLY COLDER.
HUH?
WHAT A STRANGE POOL...

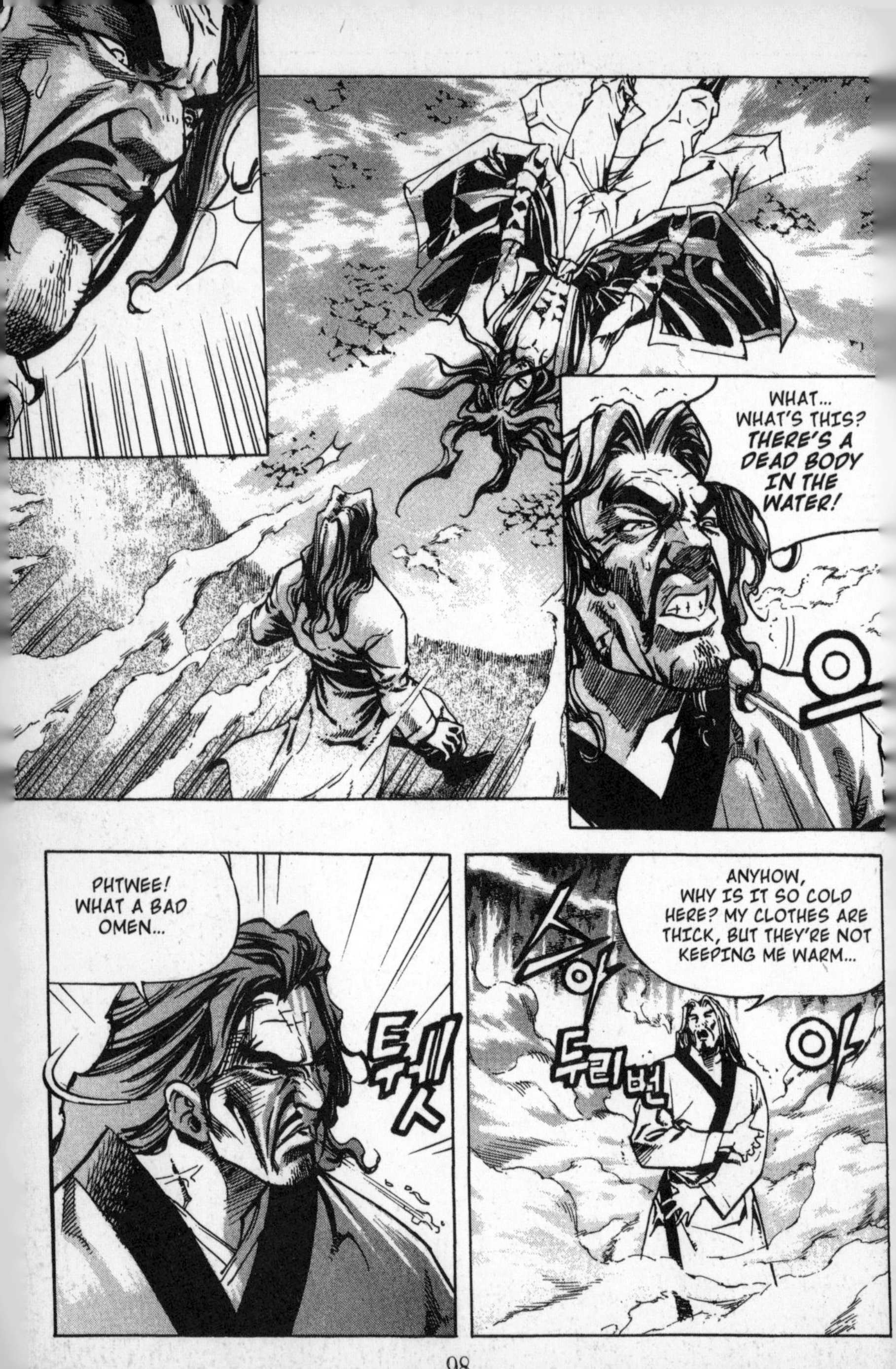
WHAT... WHAT'S THIS? THERE'S A DEAD BODY IN THE WATER!
PHTWEE! WHAT A BAD OMEN...
ANYHOW, WHY IS IT SO COLD HERE? MY CLOTHES ARE THICK, BUT THEY'RE NOT KEEPING ME WARM...
두리번

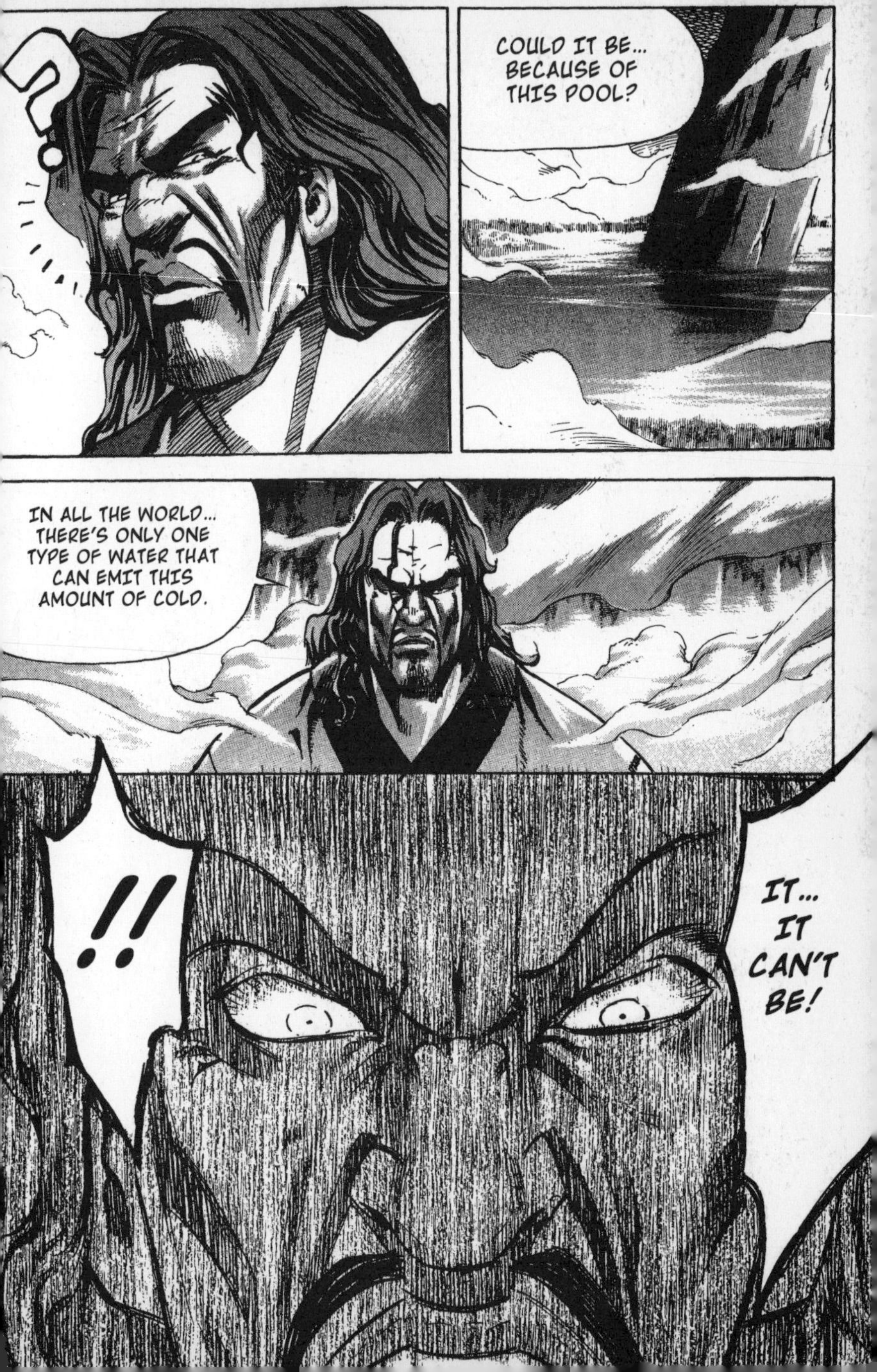
COULD IT BE... BECAUSE OF THIS POOL?
?
IN ALL THE WORLD... THERE'S ONLY ONE TYPE OF WATER THAT CAN EMIT THIS AMOUNT OF COLD.
IT... IT CAN'T BE!
!!

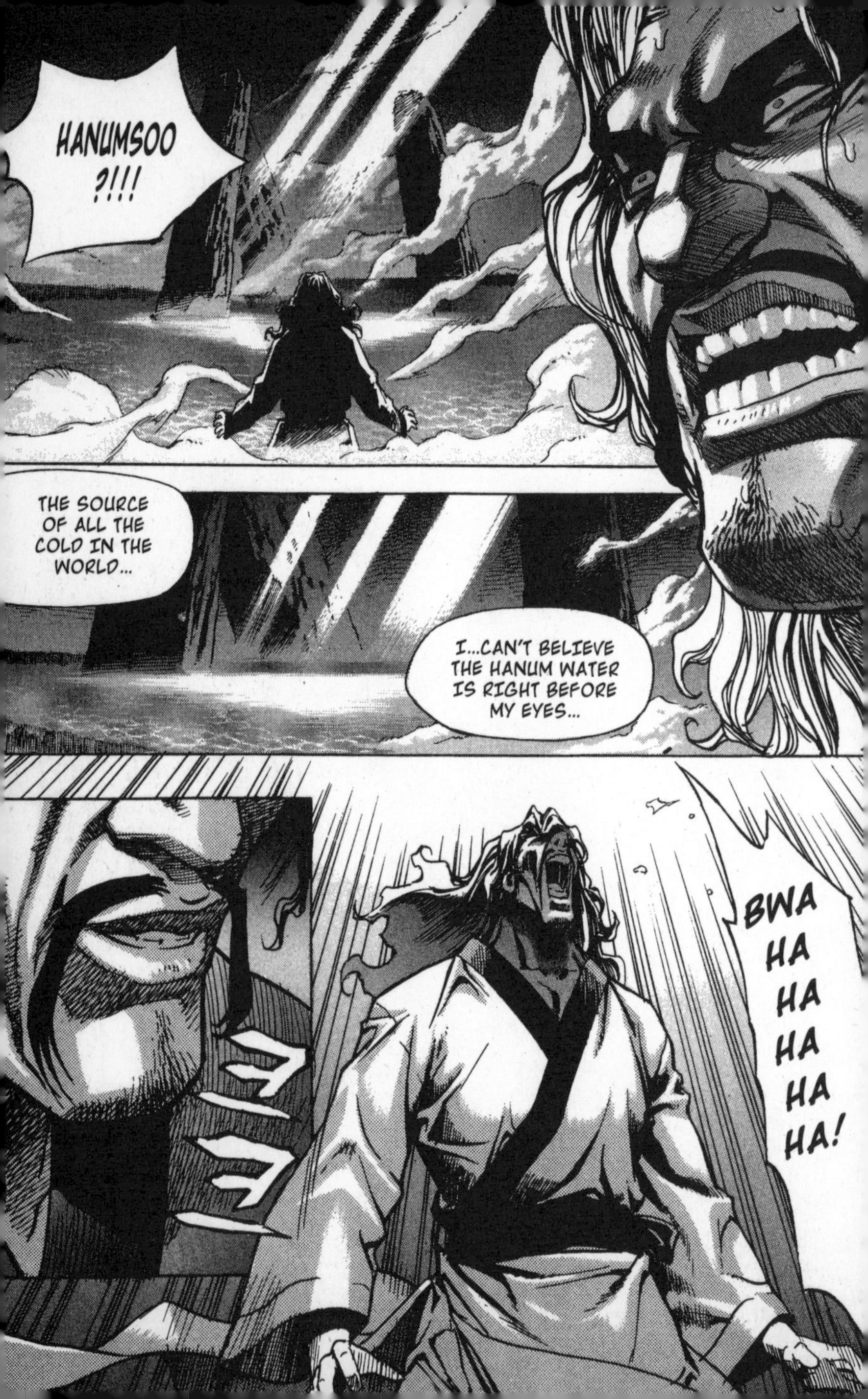
HANUMSOO ?!!!
THE SOURCE OF ALL THE COLD IN THE WORLD...
I...CAN'T BELIEVE THE HANUM WATER IS RIGHT BEFORE MY EYES...
BWA HA HA HA HA HA HA!

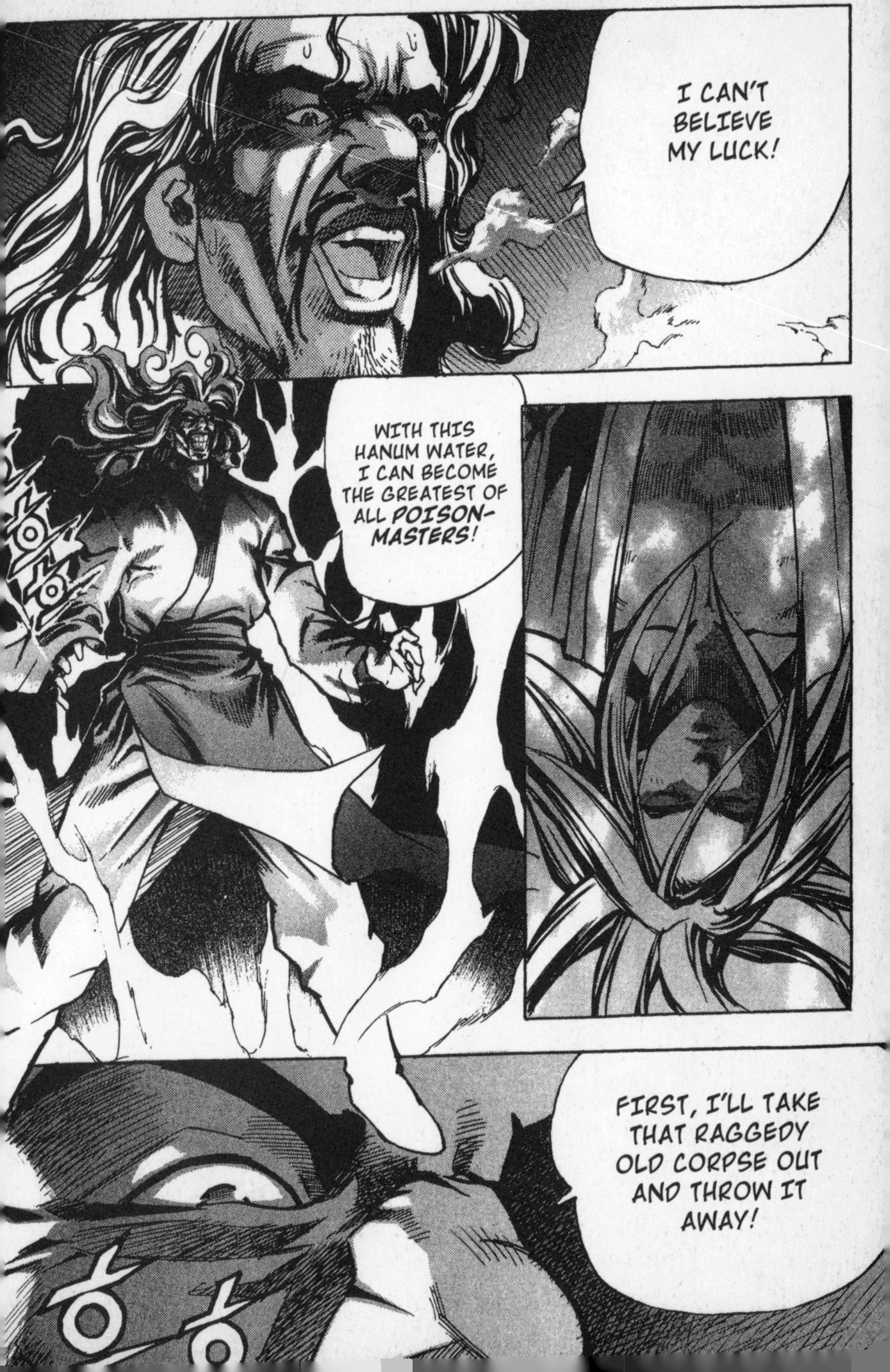
I CAN'T BELIEVE MY LUCK!
WITH THIS HANUM WATER, I CAN BECOME THE GREATEST OF ALL POISON-MASTERS!
FIRST, I'LL TAKE THAT RAGGEDY OLD CORPSE OUT AND THROW IT AWAY!

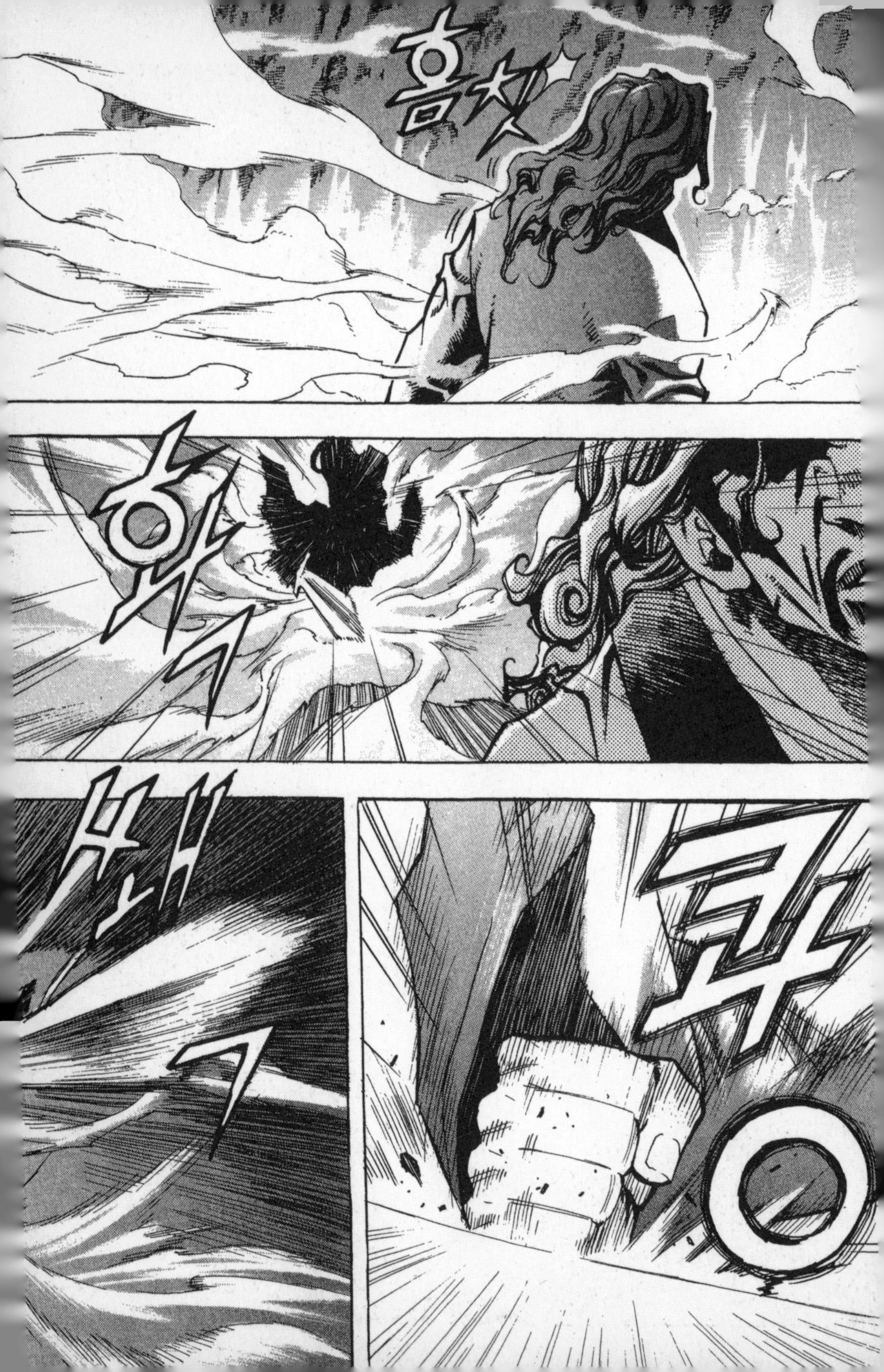
흠칫
쾅

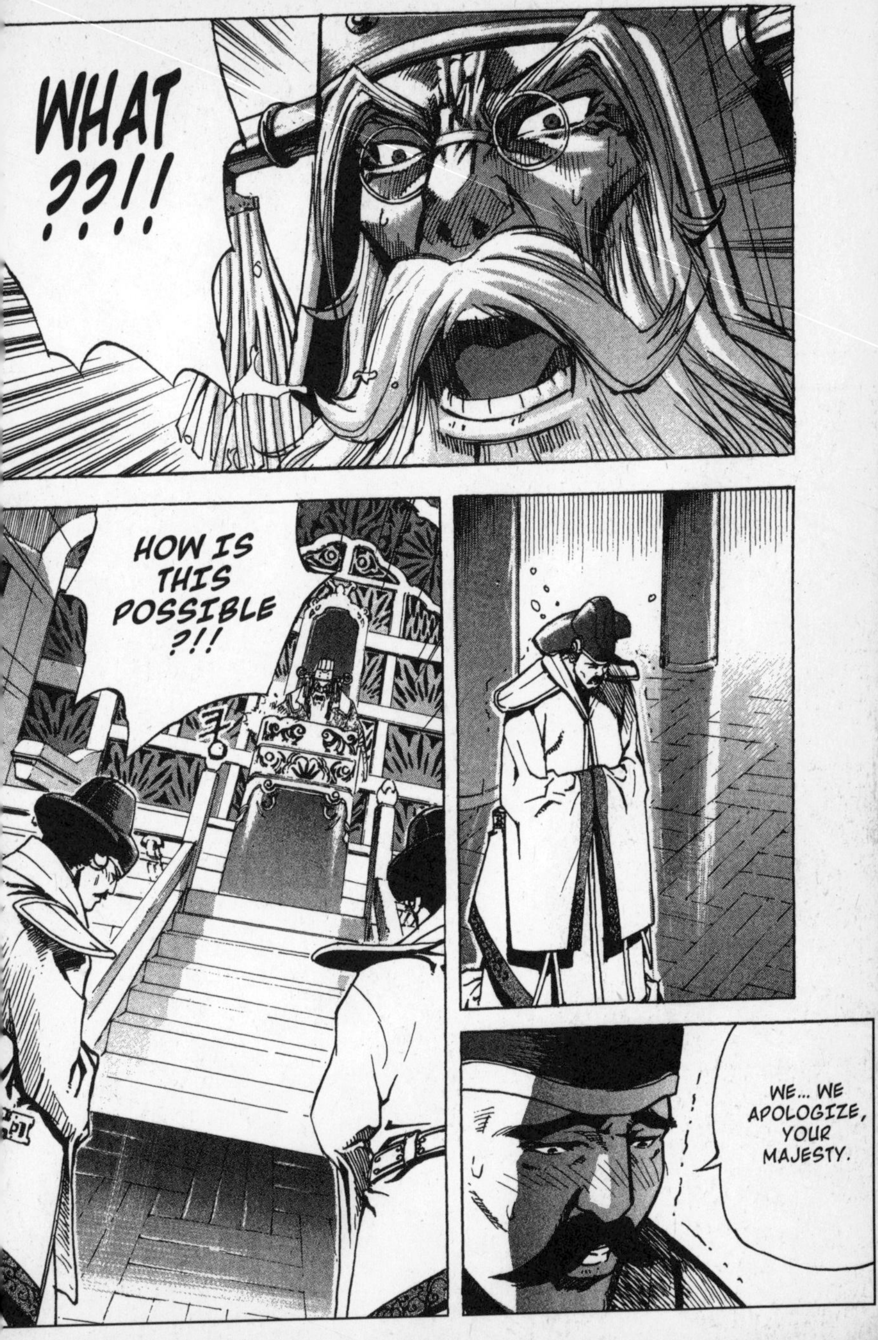
WHAT ??!!
HOW IS THIS POSSIBLE ?!!
WE... WE APOLOGIZE, YOUR MAJESTY.

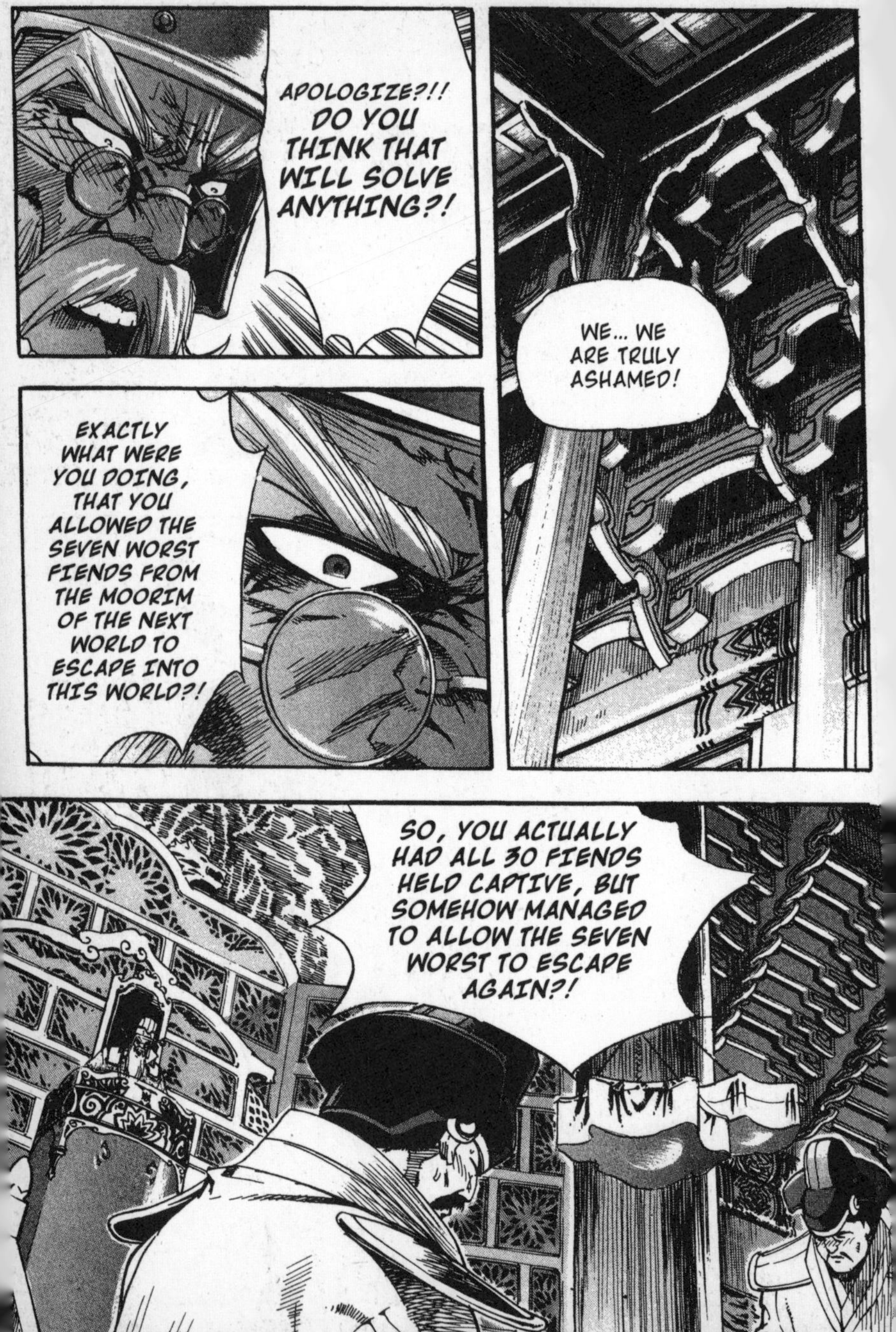
APOLOGIZE?!! DO YOU THINK THAT WILL SOLVE ANYTHING?!
WE... WE ARE TRULY ASHAMED!
EXACTLY WHAT WERE YOU DOING, THAT YOU ALLOWED THE SEVEN WORST FIENDS FROM THE MOORIM OF THE NEXT WORLD TO ESCAPE INTO THIS WORLD?!
SO, YOU ACTUALLY HAD ALL 30 FIENDS HELD CAPTIVE, BUT SOMEHOW MANAGED TO ALLOW THE SEVEN WORST TO ESCAPE AGAIN?!

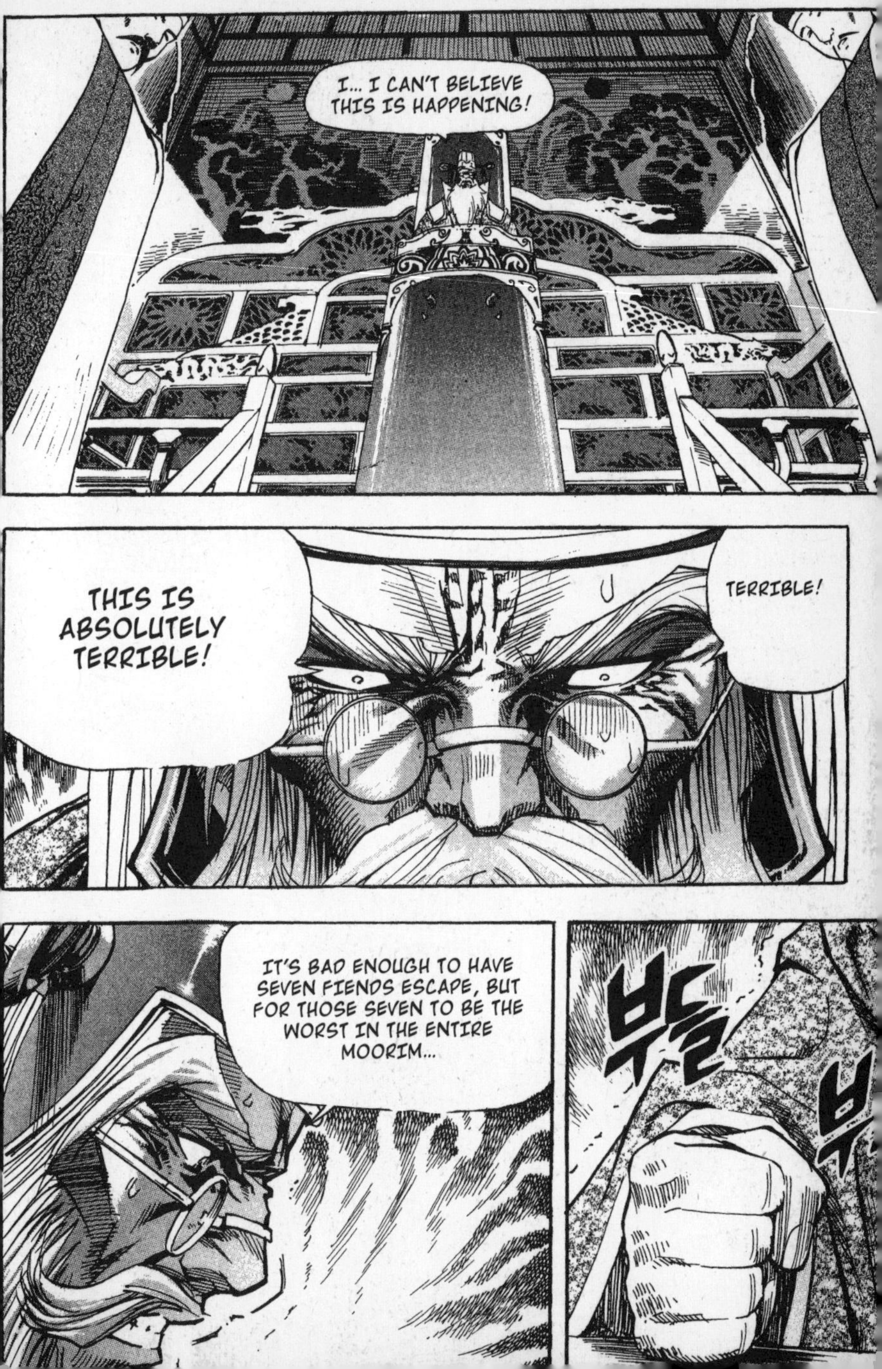
I... I CAN'T BELIEVE THIS IS HAPPENING!
THIS IS ABSOLUTELY TERRIBLE!
TERRIBLE!
IT'S BAD ENOUGH TO HAVE SEVEN FIENDS ESCAPE, BUT FOR THOSE SEVEN TO BE THE WORST IN THE ENTIRE MOORIM...
부들
부

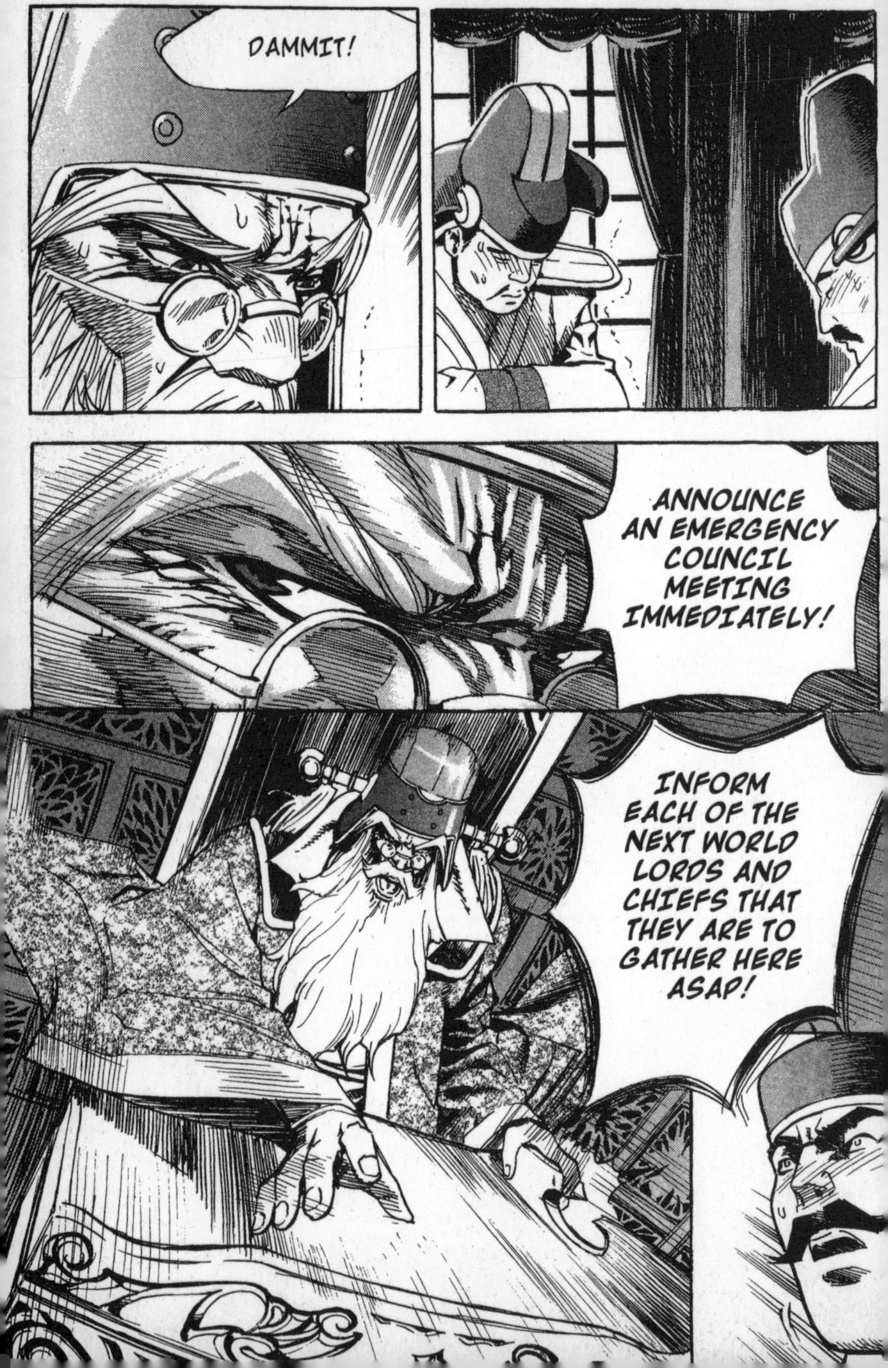
DAMMIT!
ANNOUNCE AN EMERGENCY COUNCIL MEETING IMMEDIATELY!
INFORM EACH OF THE NEXT WORLD LORDS AND CHIEFS THAT THEY ARE TO GATHER HERE ASAP!

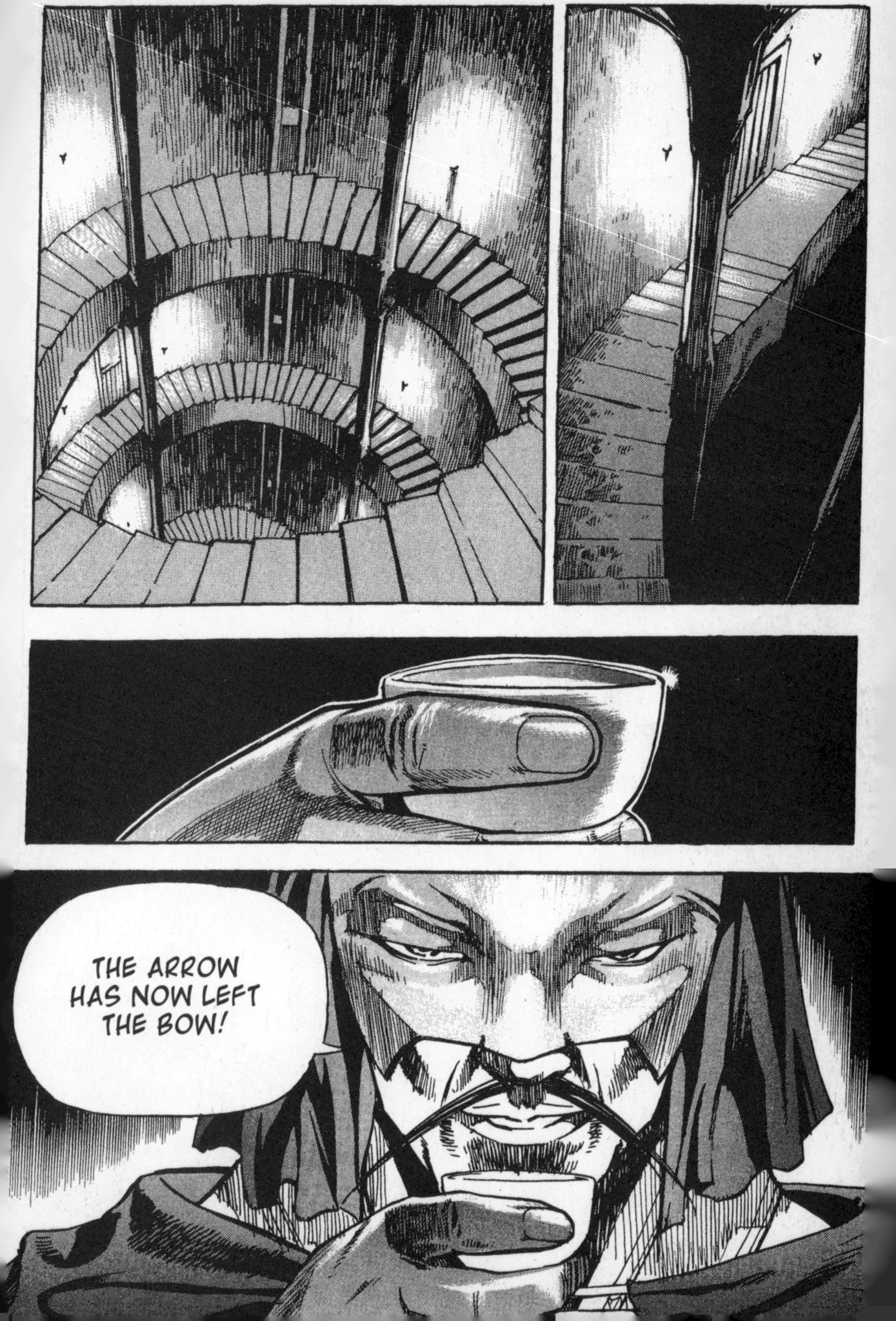
THE ARROW HAS NOW LEFT THE BOW!

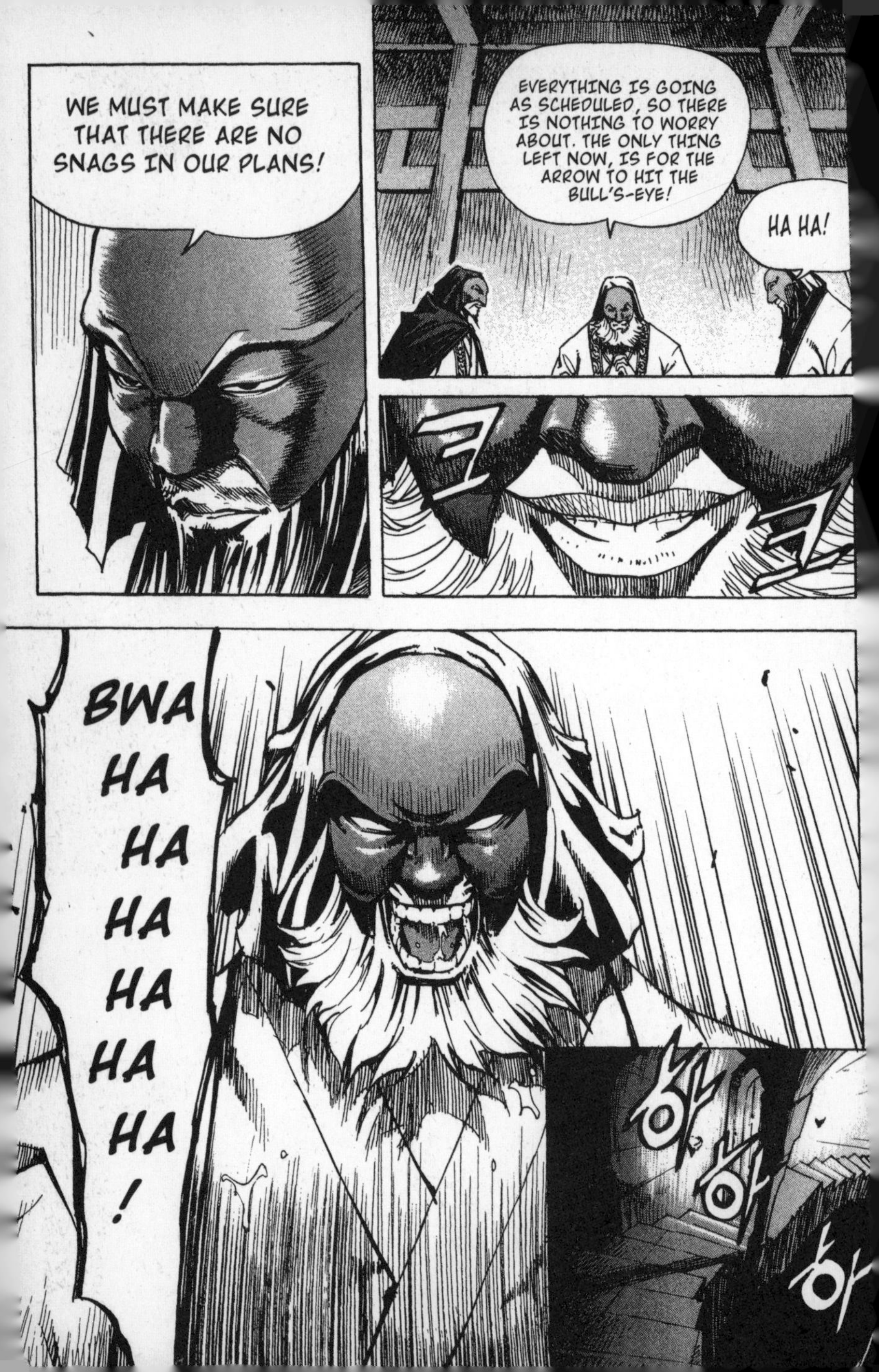
WE MUST MAKE SURE THAT THERE ARE NO SNAGS IN OUR PLANS!
EVERYTHING IS GOING AS SCHEDULED, SO THERE IS NOTHING TO WORRY ABOUT. THE ONLY THING LEFT NOW, IS FOR THE ARROW TO HIT THE BULL'S-EYE!
HA HA!
BWA HA HA HA HA HA HA!

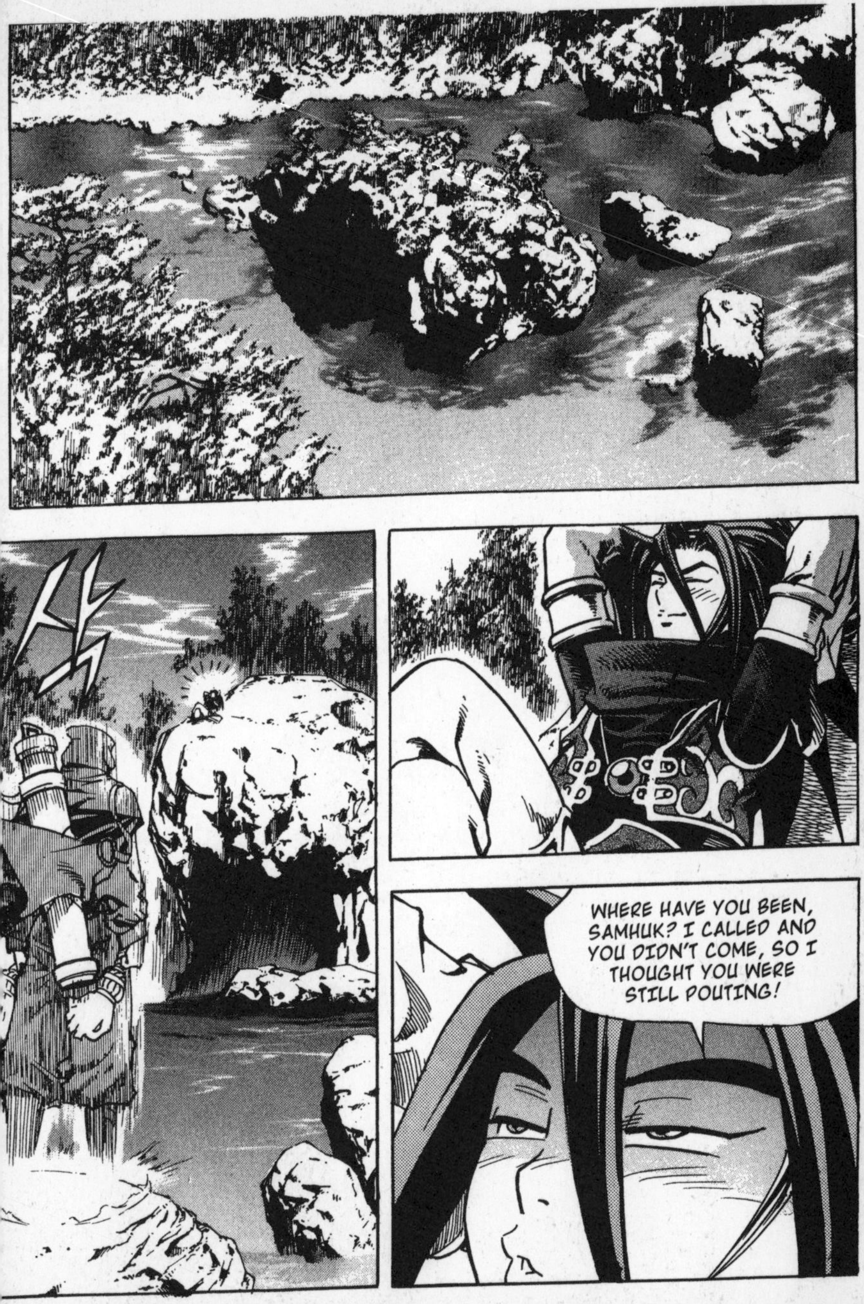
WHERE HAVE YOU BEEN, SAMHUK? I CALLED AND YOU DIDN'T COME, SO I THOUGHT YOU WERE STILL POUTING!

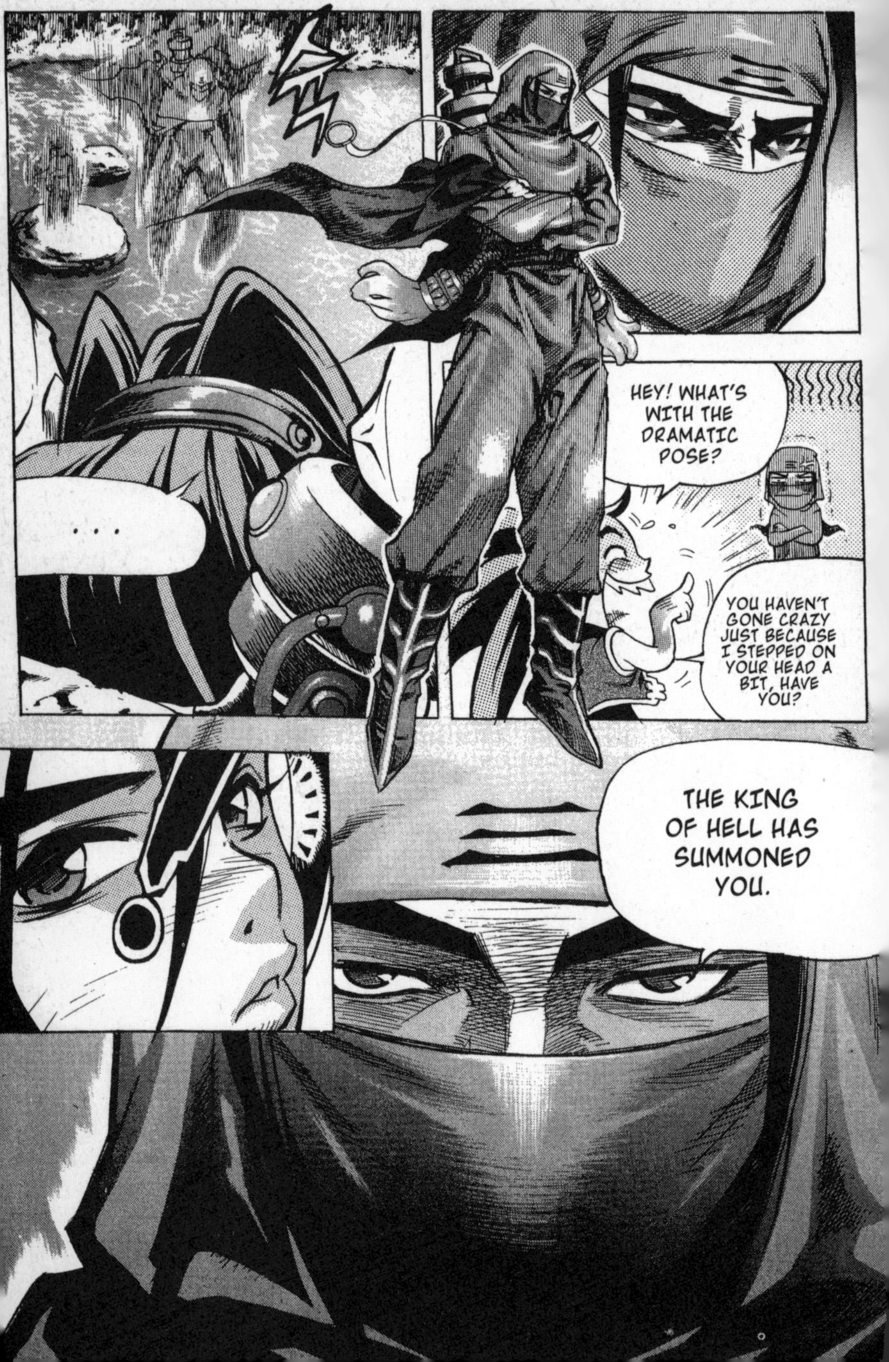
...
HEY! WHAT'S WITH THE DRAMATIC POSE?
YOU HAVEN'T GONE CRAZY JUST BECAUSE I STEPPED ON YOUR HEAD A BIT, HAVE YOU?
THE KING OF HELL HAS SUMMONED YOU.

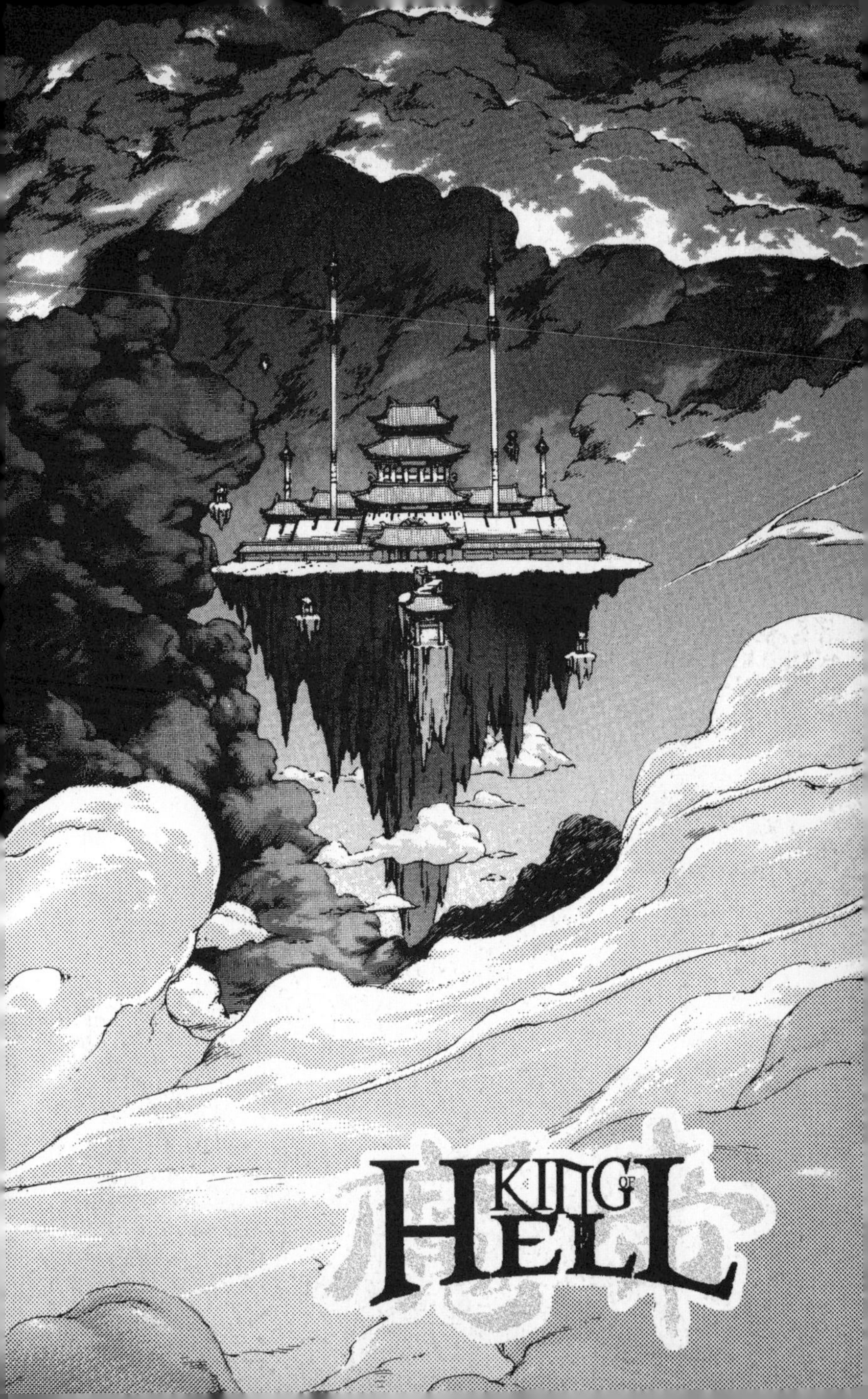
KING OF HELL

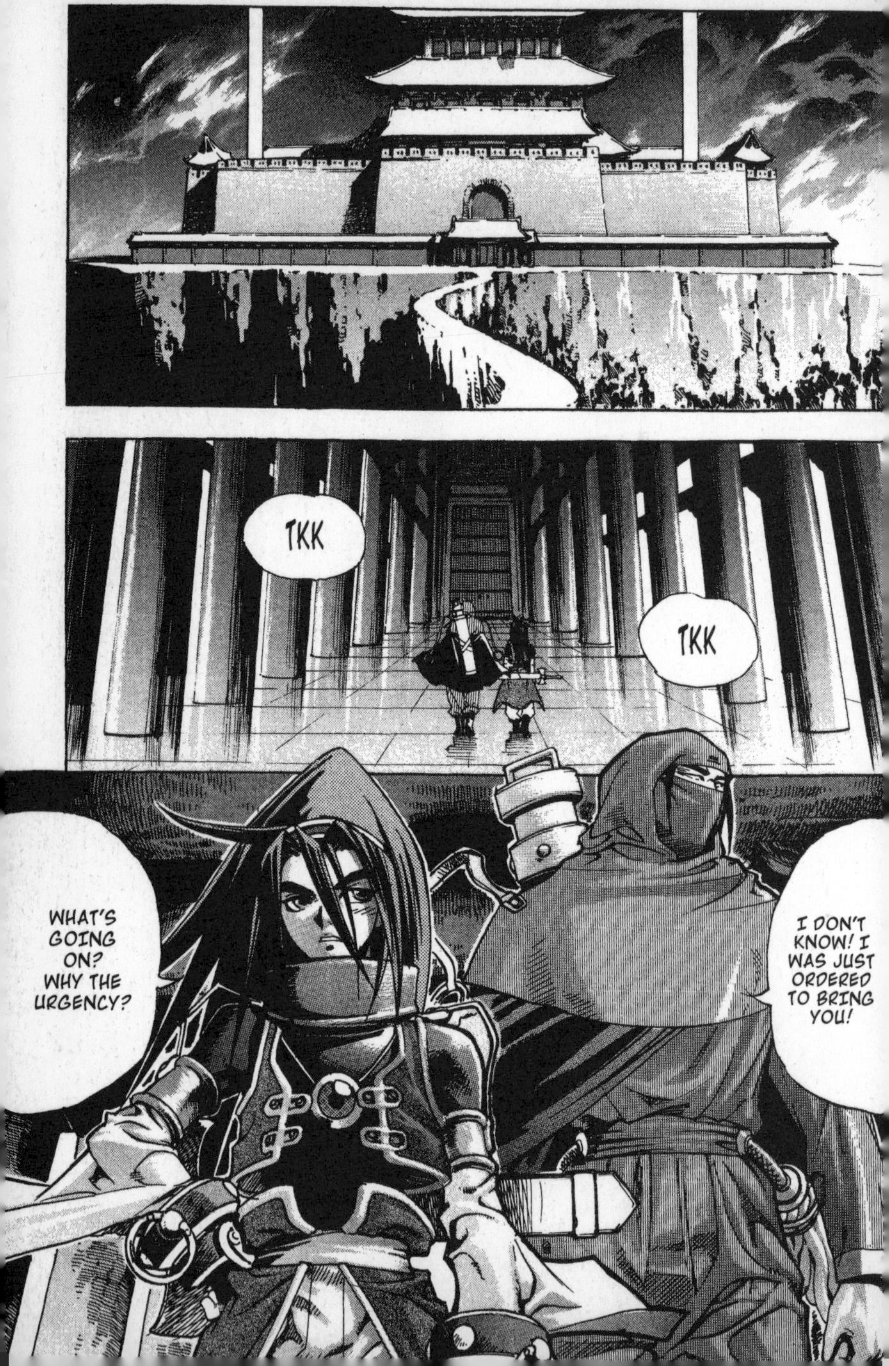
TKK
TKK
I DON'T KNOW! I WAS JUST ORDERED TO BRING YOU!
WHAT'S GOING ON? WHY THE URGENCY?

SAMHUK! ARE YOU STILL POUTING?

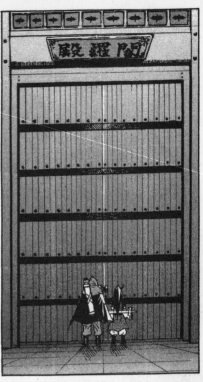

HUMPH!

PLEASE, GO INSIDE. I'LL BE TAKING MY LEAVE OF YOU FOR NOW.

?!

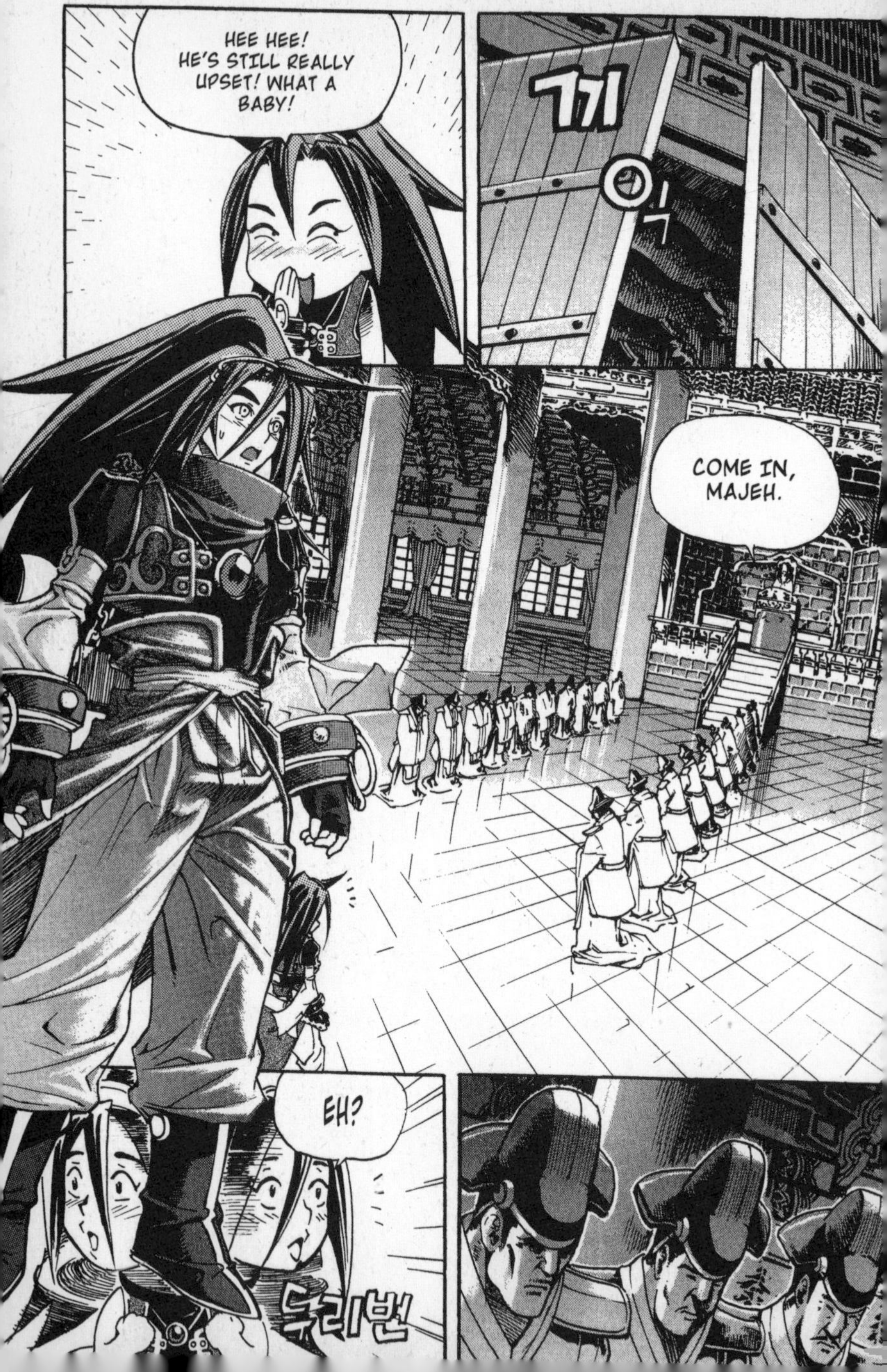
HEE HEE! HE'S STILL REALLY UPSET! WHAT A BABY!
끼
COME IN, MAJEH.
EH?
두리번

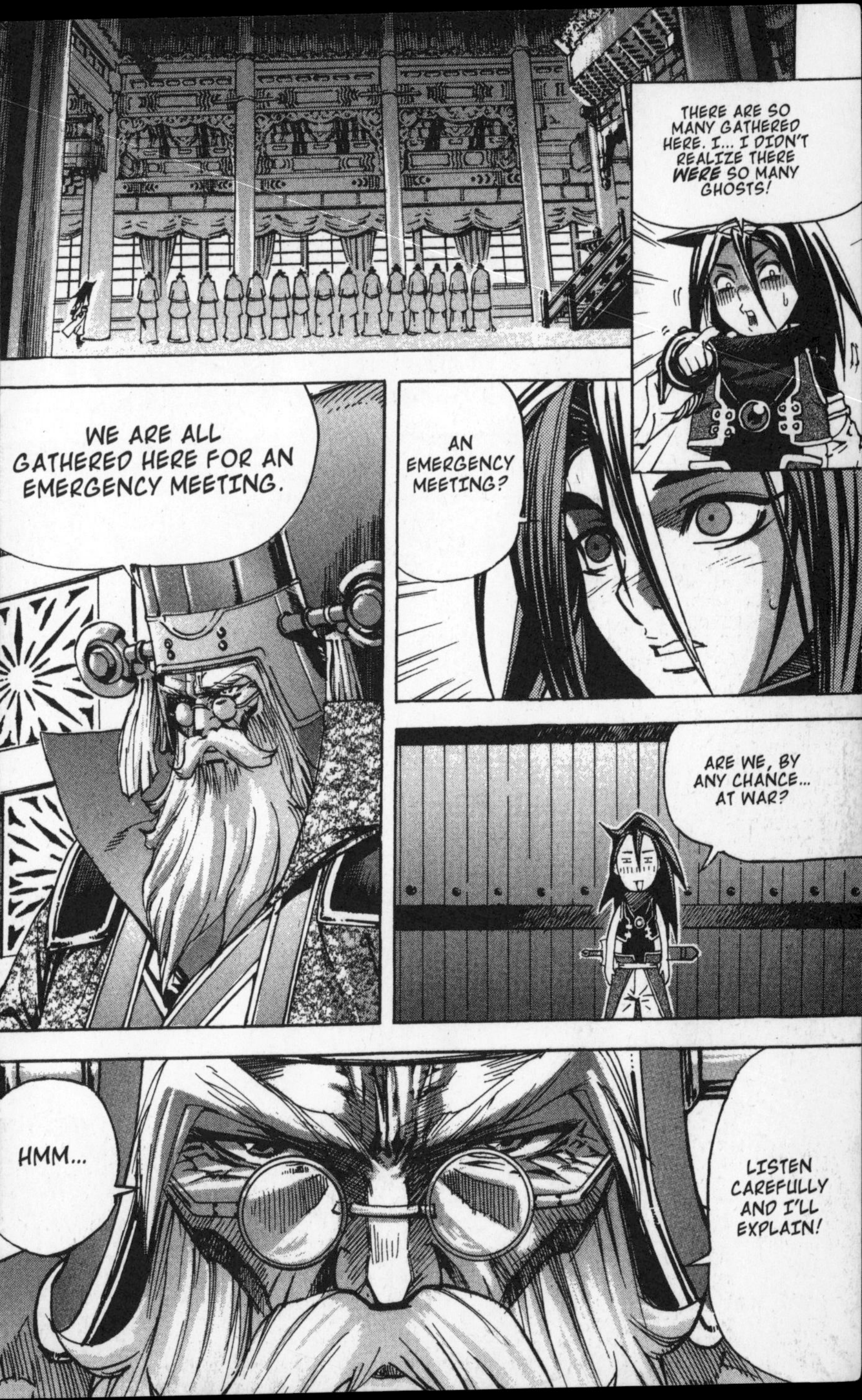
THERE ARE SO MANY GATHERED HERE. I... I DIDN'T REALIZE THERE *WERE* SO MANY GHOSTS!
WE ARE ALL GATHERED HERE FOR AN EMERGENCY MEETING.
AN EMERGENCY MEETING?
ARE WE, BY ANY CHANCE... AT WAR?
HMM...
LISTEN CAREFULLY AND I'LL EXPLAIN!

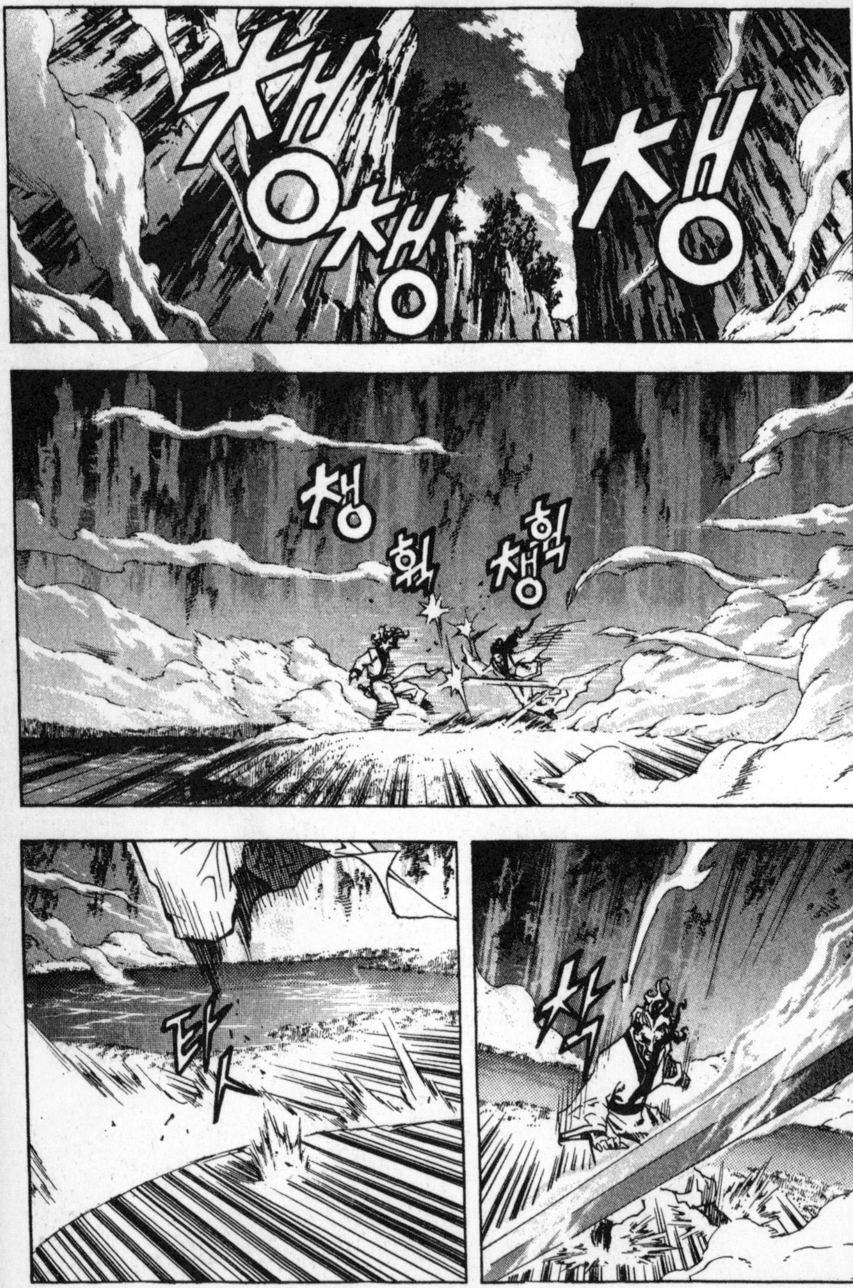
챙
챙
챙
챙
휙
챙
휙
탁
착

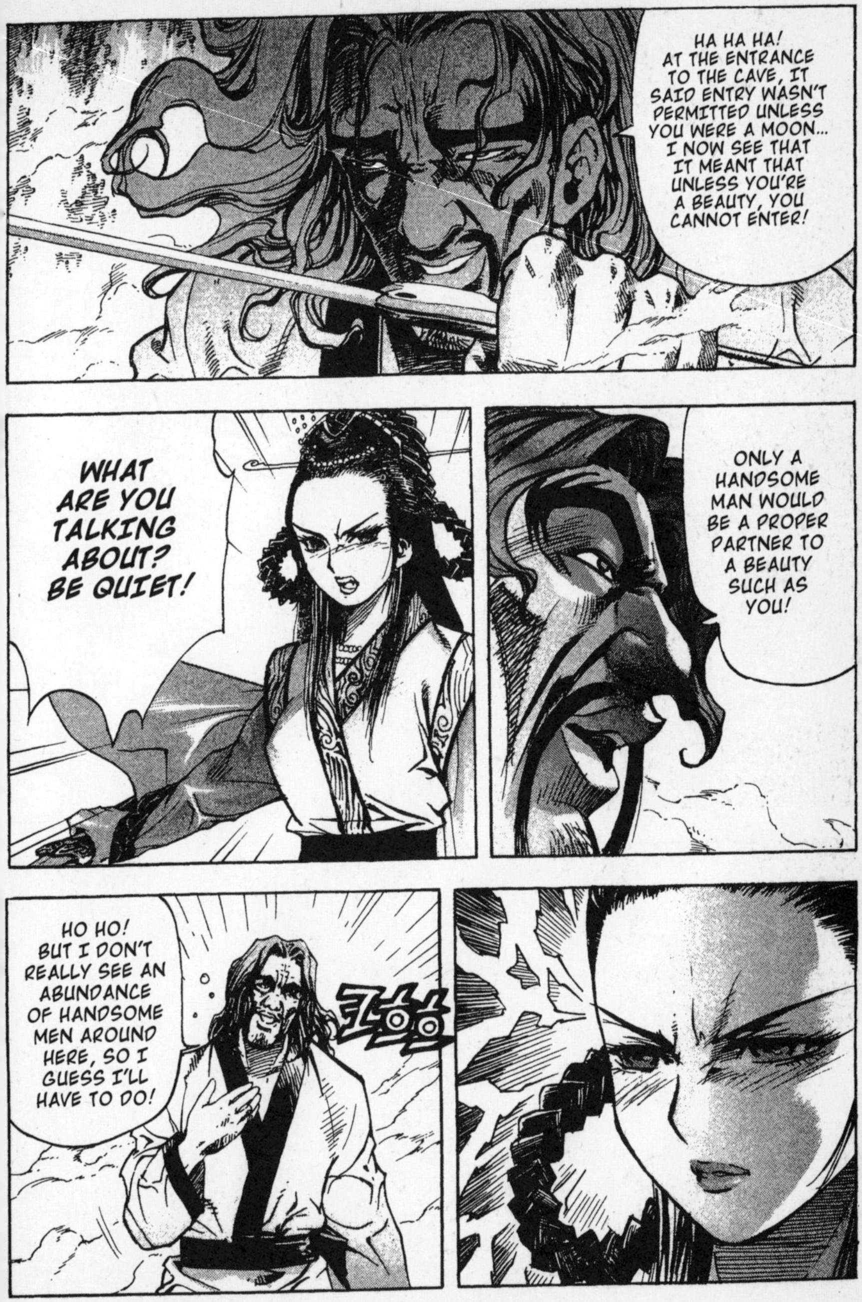
HA HA HA! AT THE ENTRANCE TO THE CAVE, IT SAID ENTRY WASN'T PERMITTED UNLESS YOU WERE A MOON... I NOW SEE THAT IT MEANT THAT UNLESS YOU'RE A BEAUTY, YOU CANNOT ENTER!
WHAT ARE YOU TALKING ABOUT? BE QUIET!
ONLY A HANDSOME MAN WOULD BE A PROPER PARTNER TO A BEAUTY SUCH AS YOU!
HO HO! BUT I DON'T REALLY SEE AN ABUNDANCE OF HANDSOME MEN AROUND HERE, SO I GUESS I'LL HAVE TO DO!

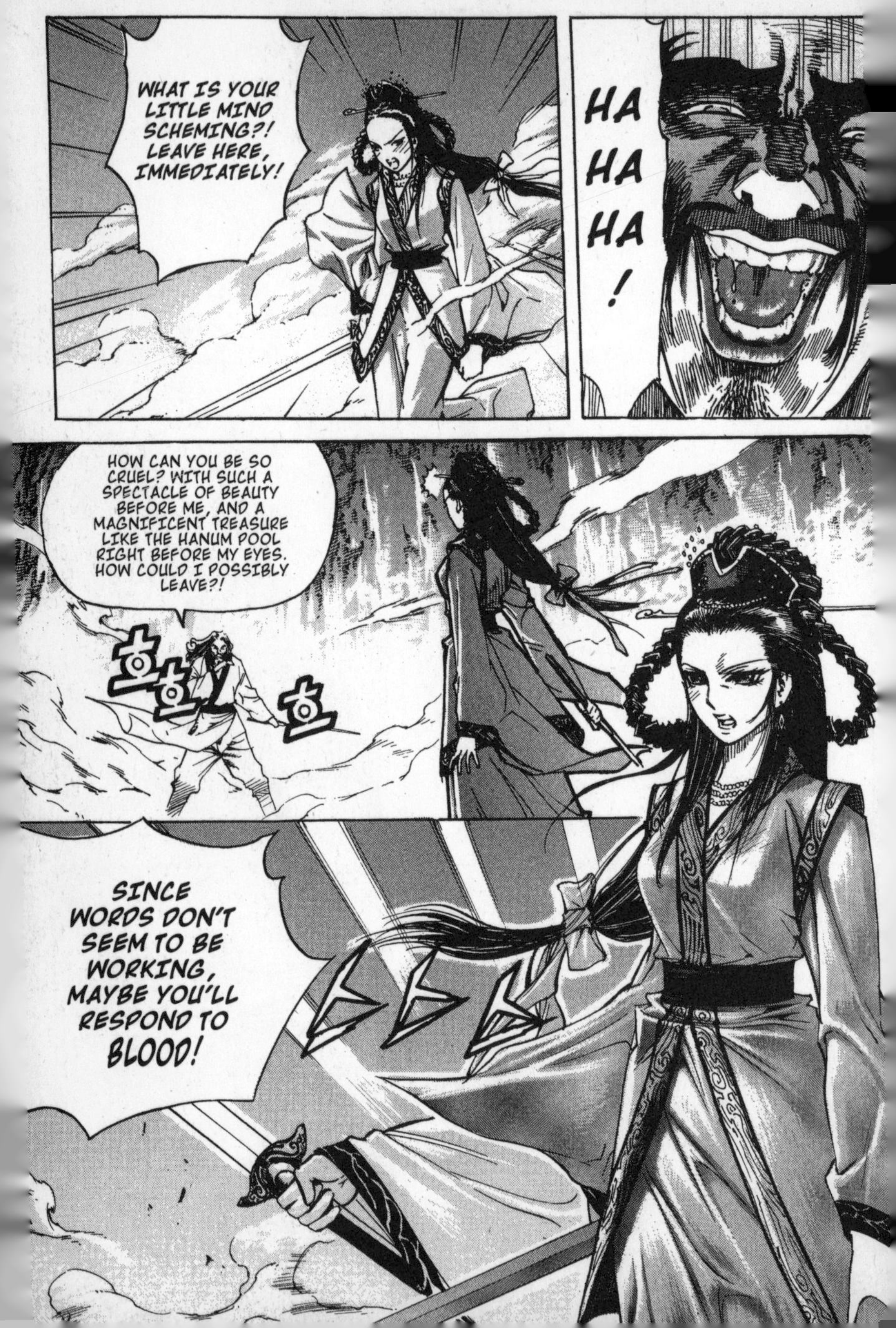
WHAT IS YOUR LITTLE MIND SCHEMING?! LEAVE HERE, IMMEDIATELY!
HA HA HA !
HOW CAN YOU BE SO CRUEL? WITH SUCH A SPECTACLE OF BEAUTY BEFORE ME, AND A MAGNIFICENT TREASURE LIKE THE HANUM POOL RIGHT BEFORE MY EYES. HOW COULD I POSSIBLY LEAVE?!
흐흐흐
SINCE WORDS DON'T SEEM TO BE WORKING, MAYBE YOU'LL RESPOND TO BLOOD!

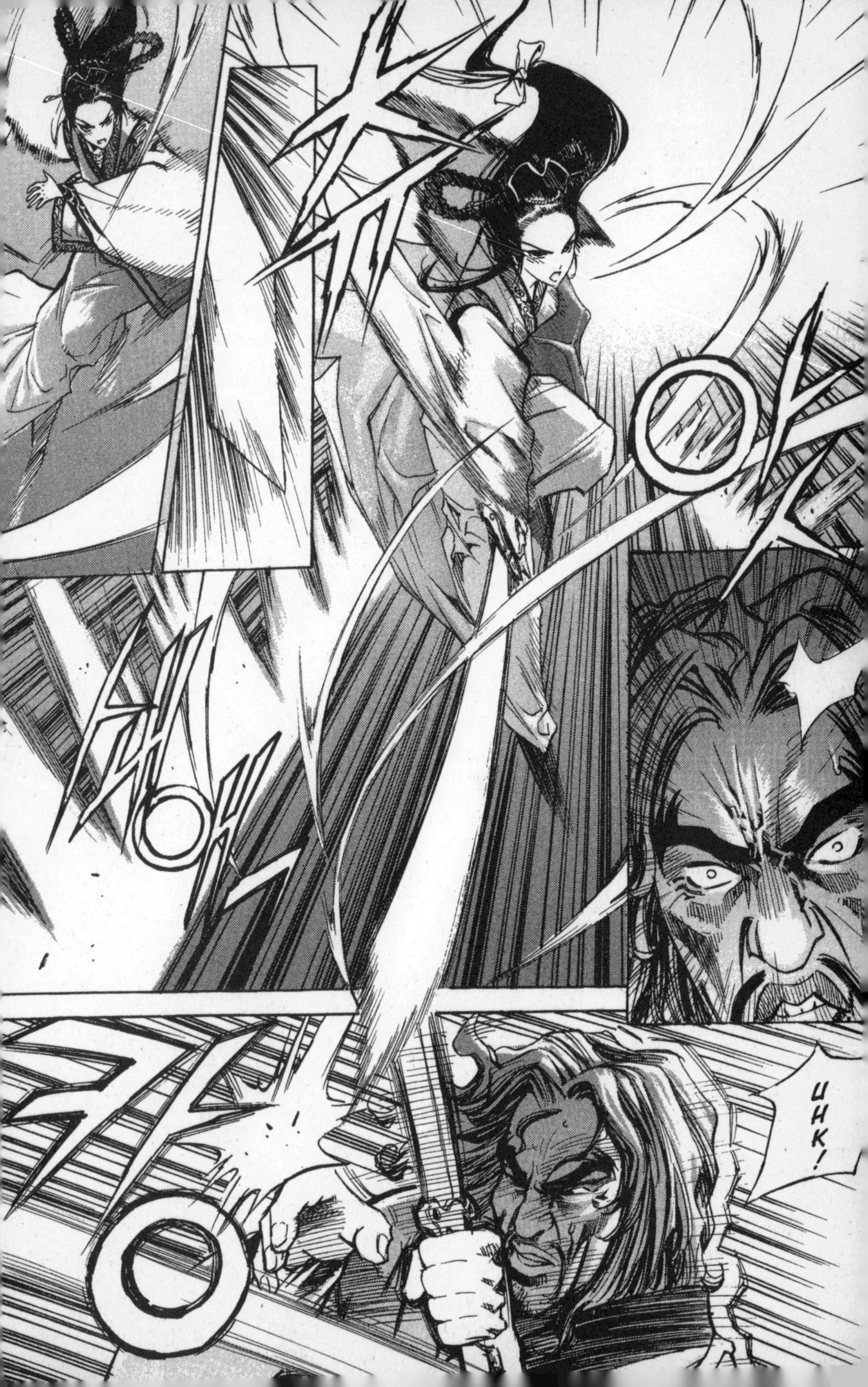
UHK!

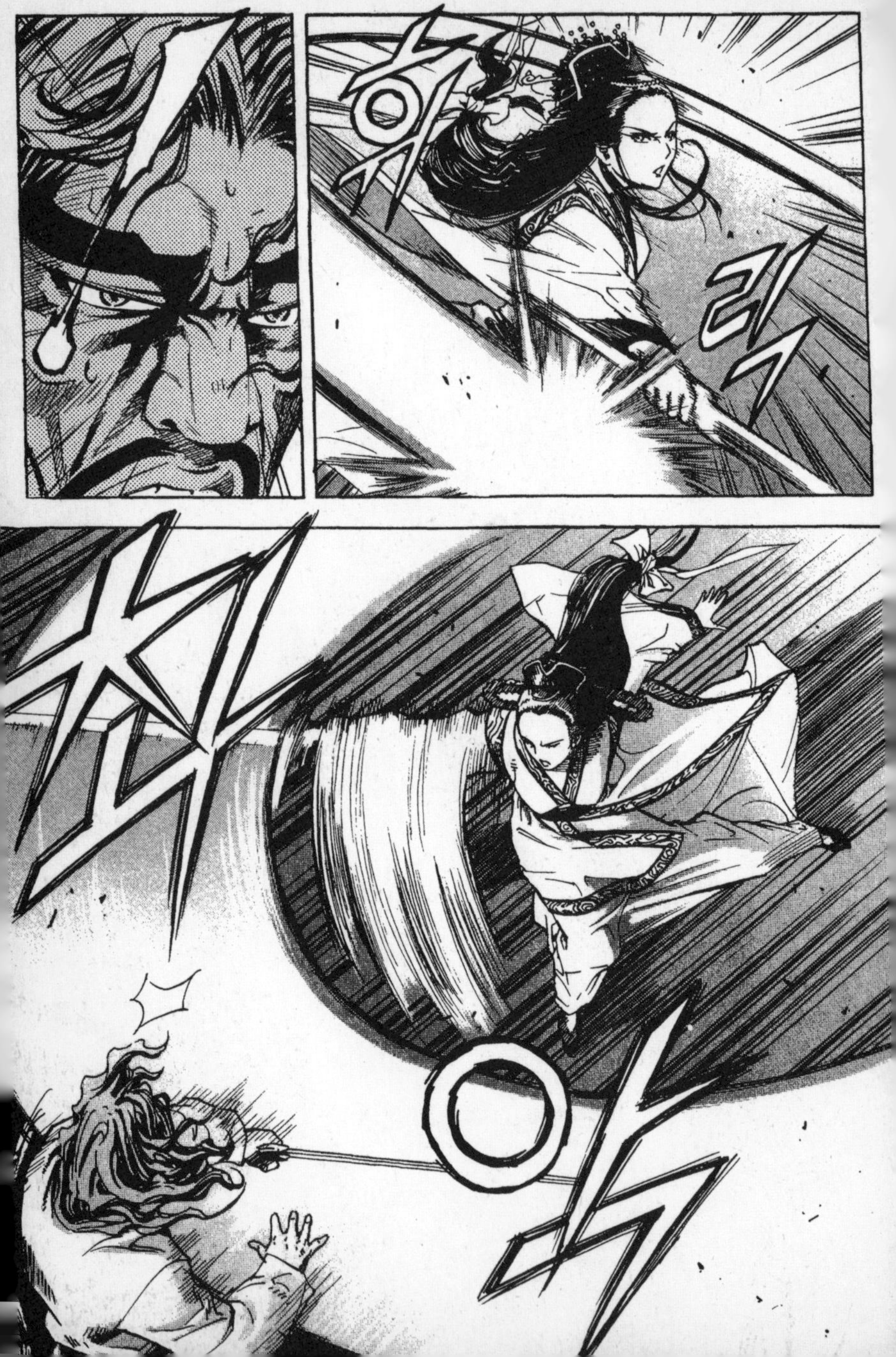

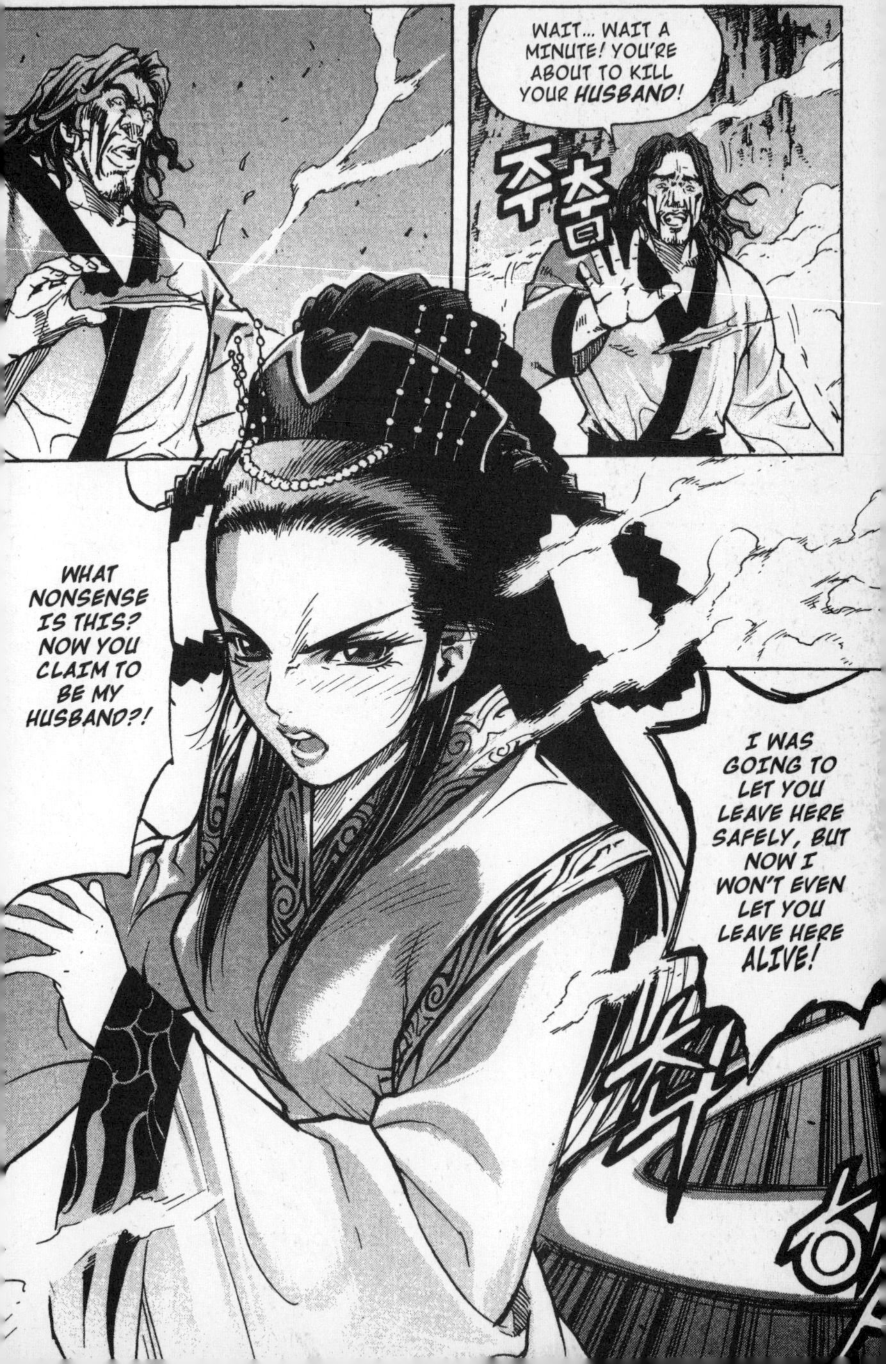
WAIT... WAIT A MINUTE! YOU'RE ABOUT TO KILL YOUR HUSBAND!
WHAT NONSENSE IS THIS? NOW YOU CLAIM TO BE MY HUSBAND?!
I WAS GOING TO LET YOU LEAVE HERE SAFELY, BUT NOW I WON'T EVEN LET YOU LEAVE HERE ALIVE!

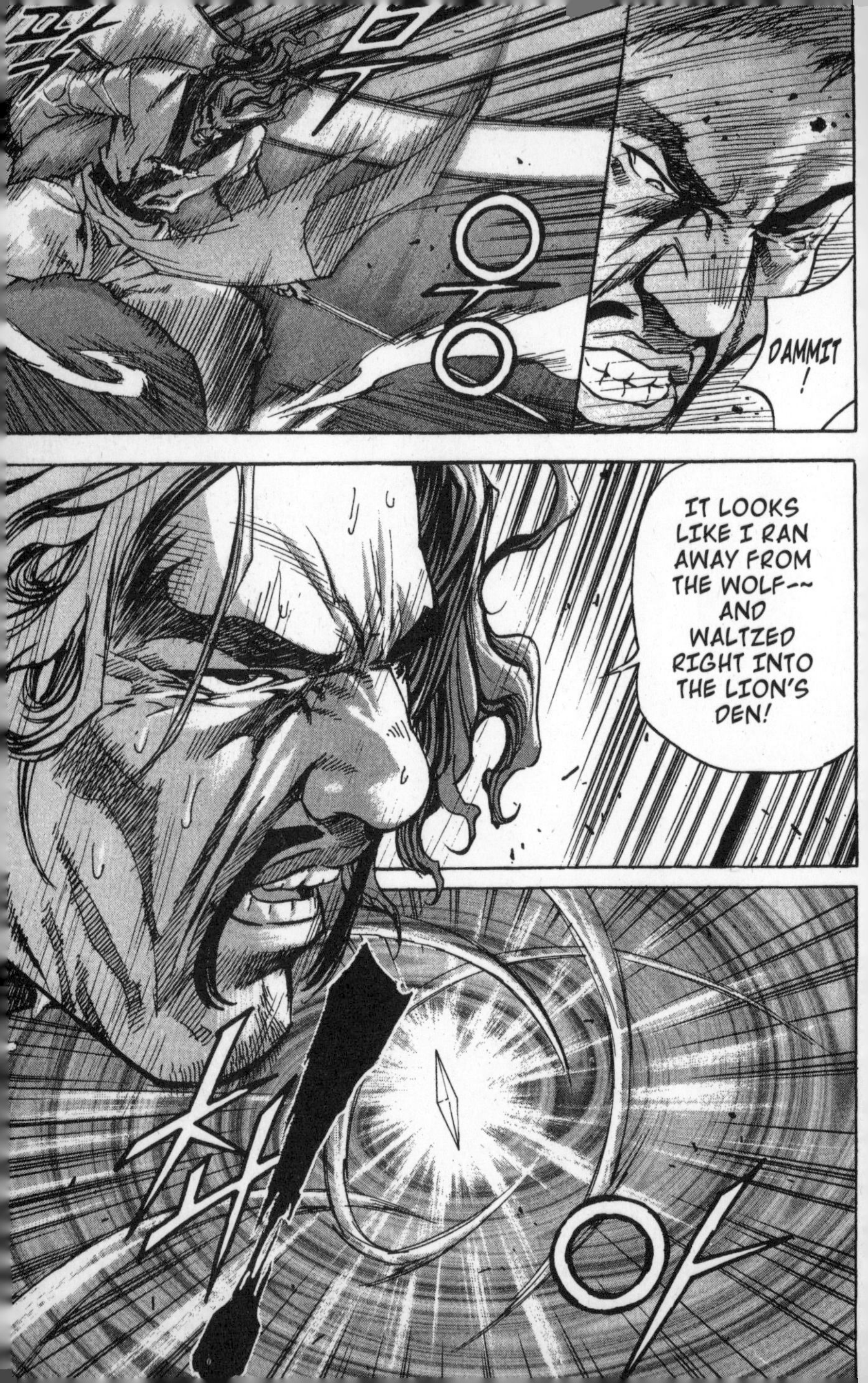
DAMMIT!
IT LOOKS LIKE I RAN AWAY FROM THE WOLF-- AND WALTZED RIGHT INTO THE LION'S DEN!

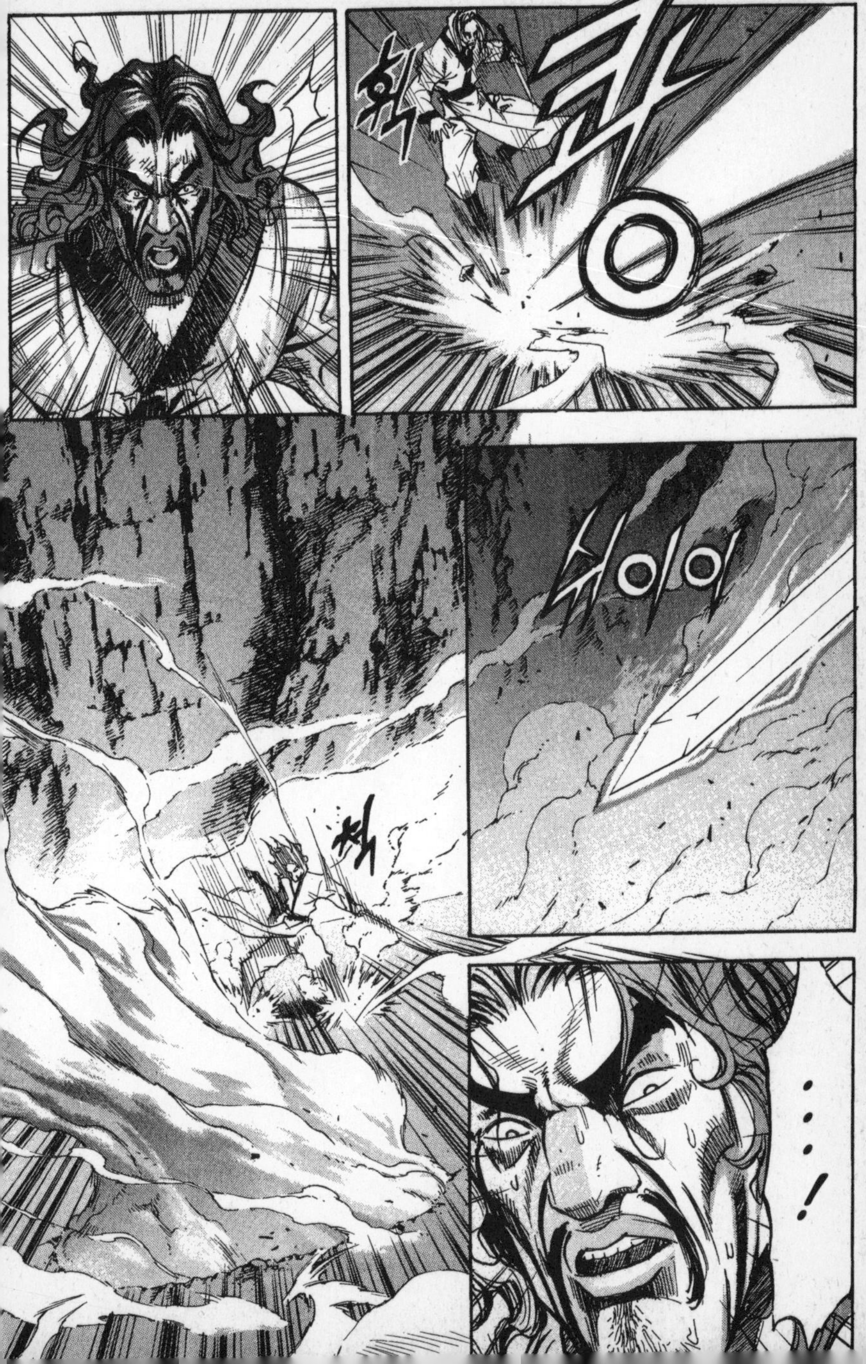

휙
쾅
샤아아
....!

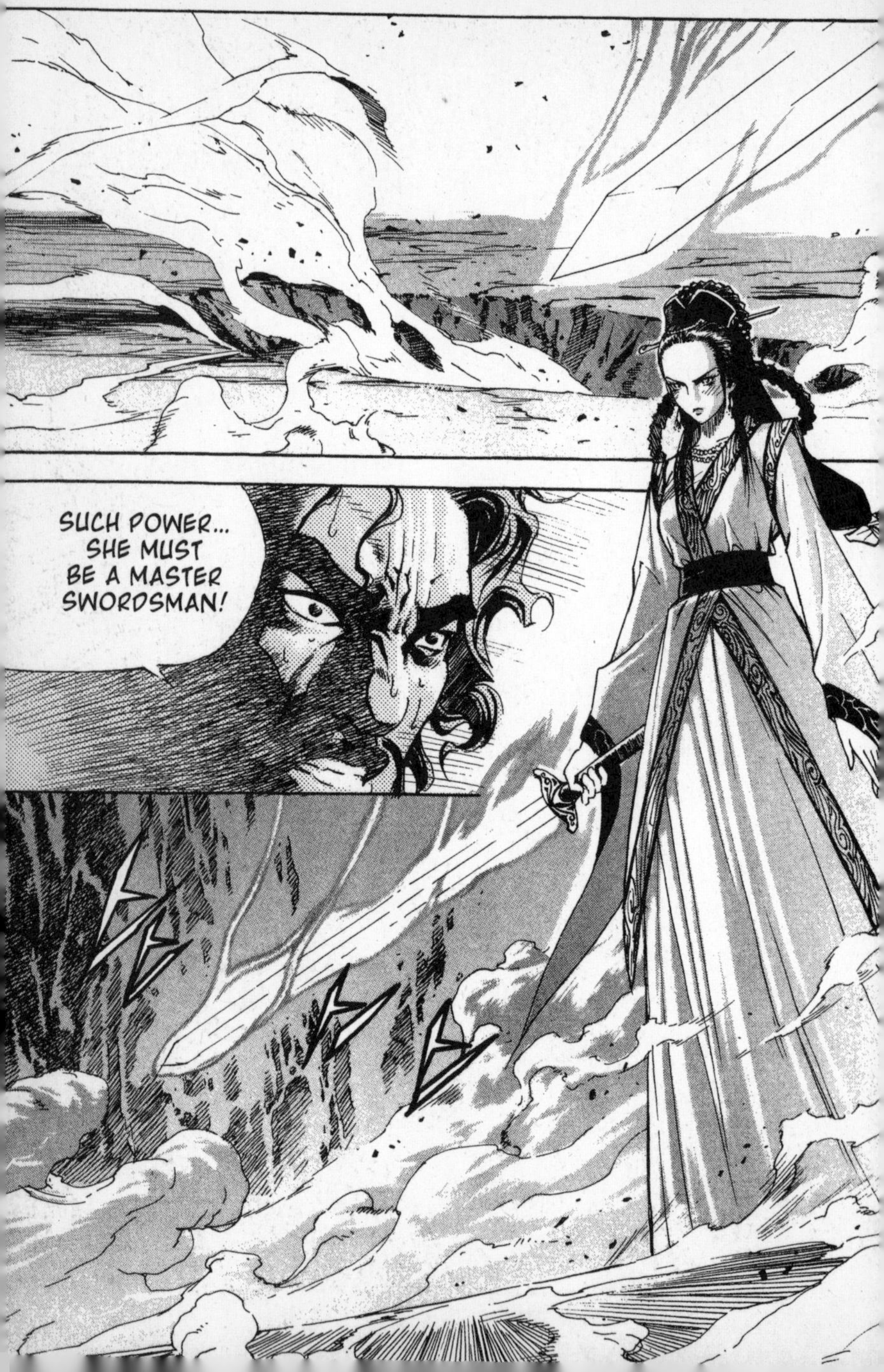
SUCH POWER...
SHE MUST
BE A MASTER
SWORDSMAN!

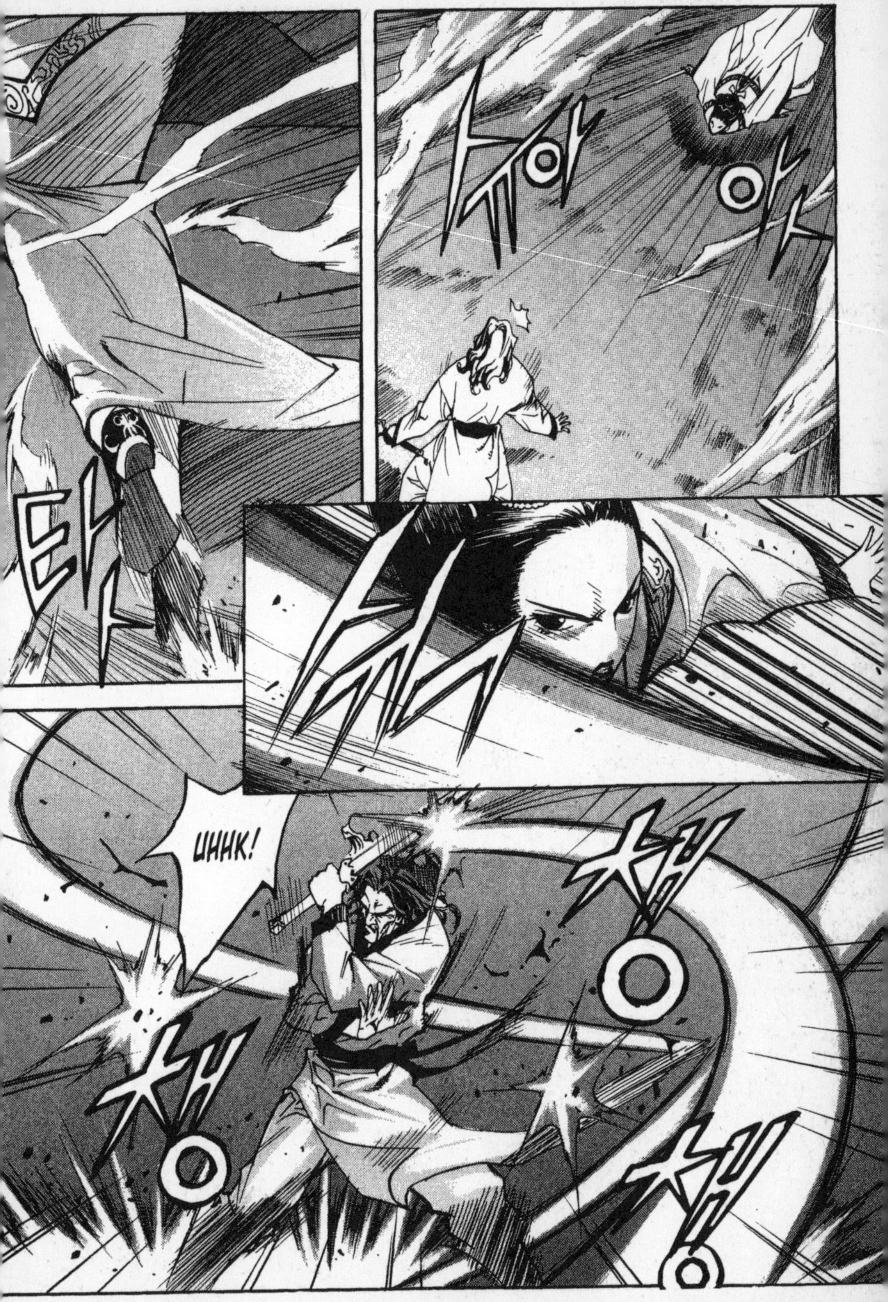
UHHK!

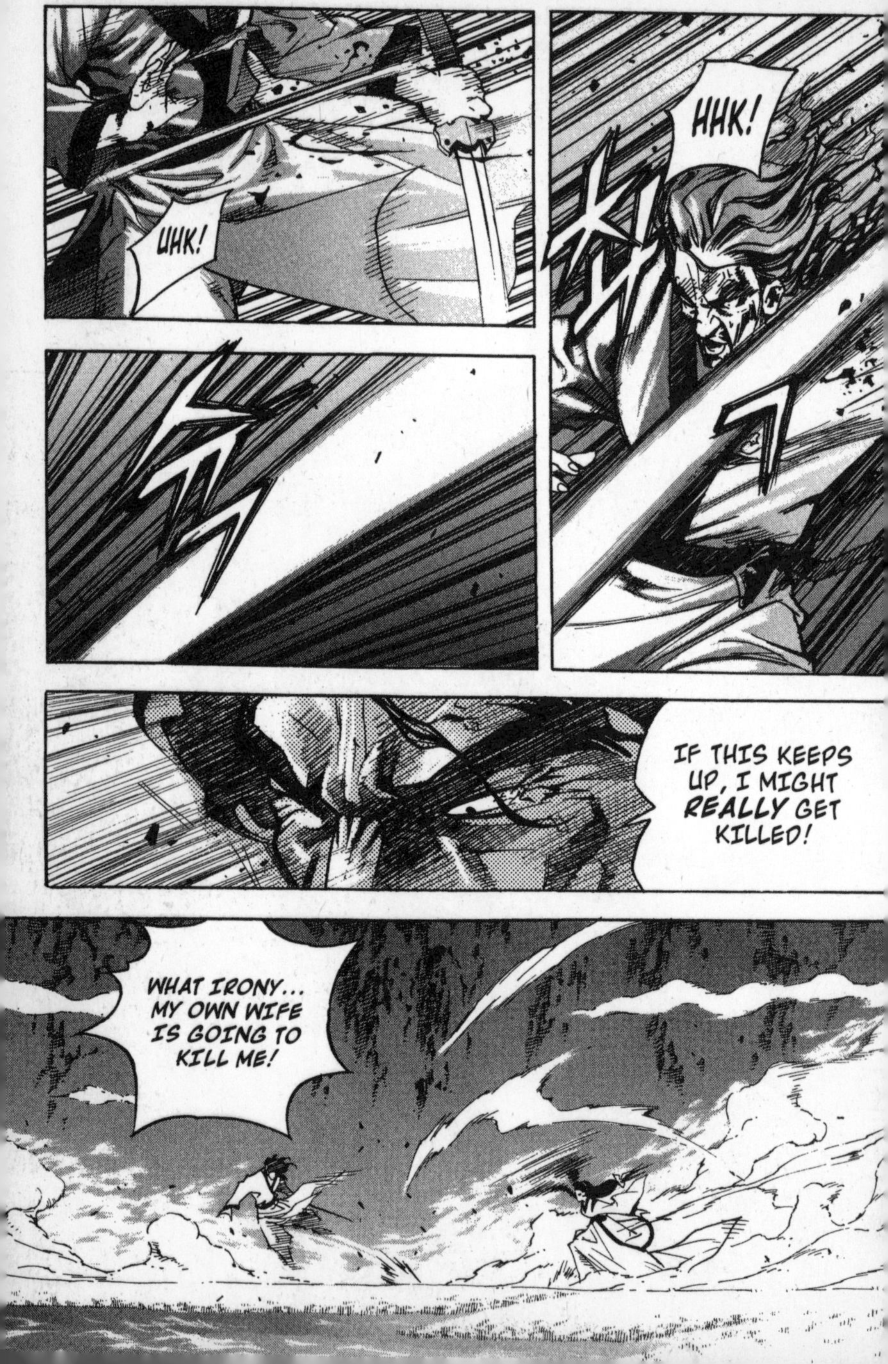
UHK!
HHK!
IF THIS KEEPS UP, I MIGHT REALLY GET KILLED!
WHAT IRONY... MY OWN WIFE IS GOING TO KILL ME!

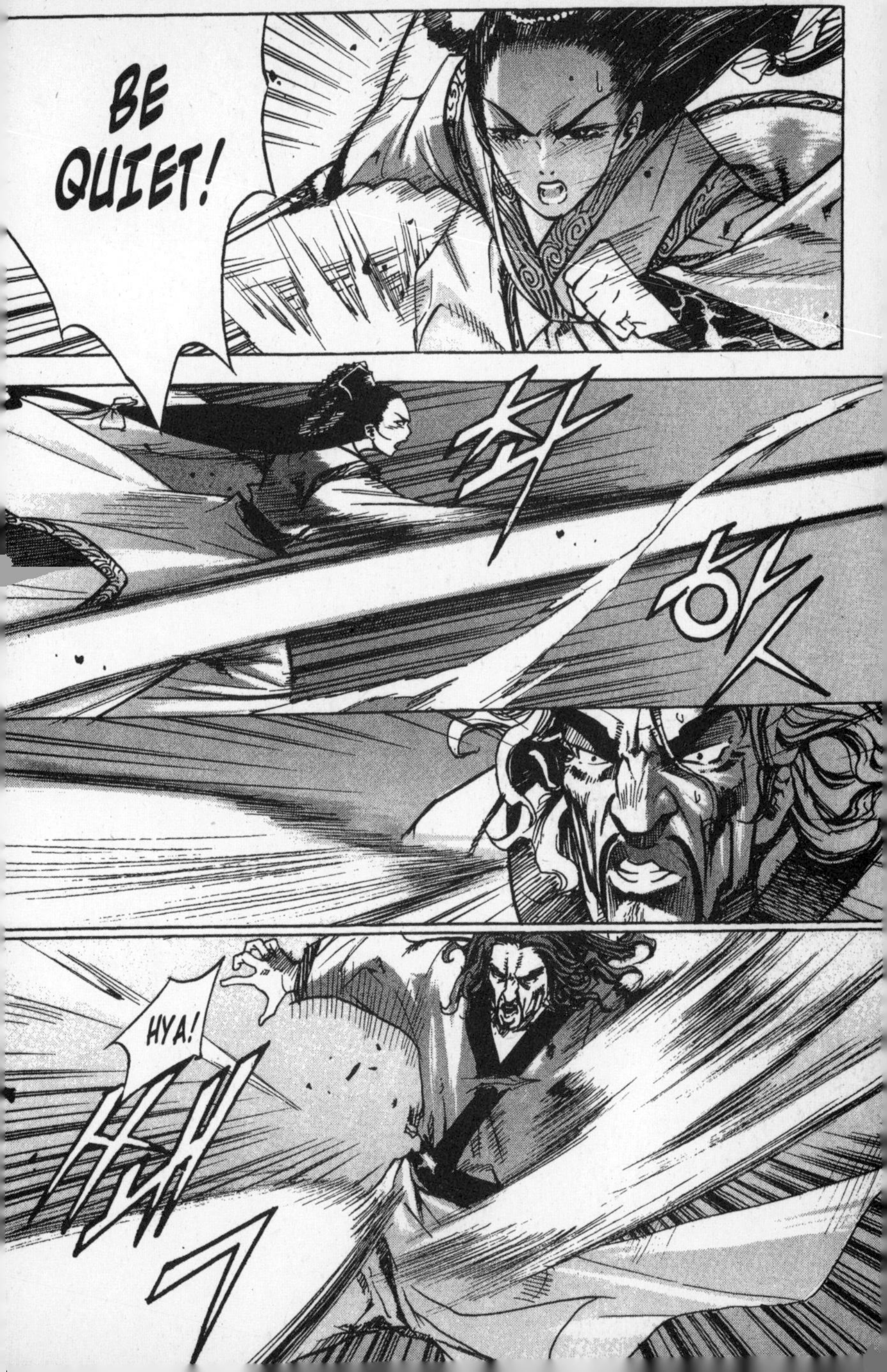
BE QUIET!
HYA!

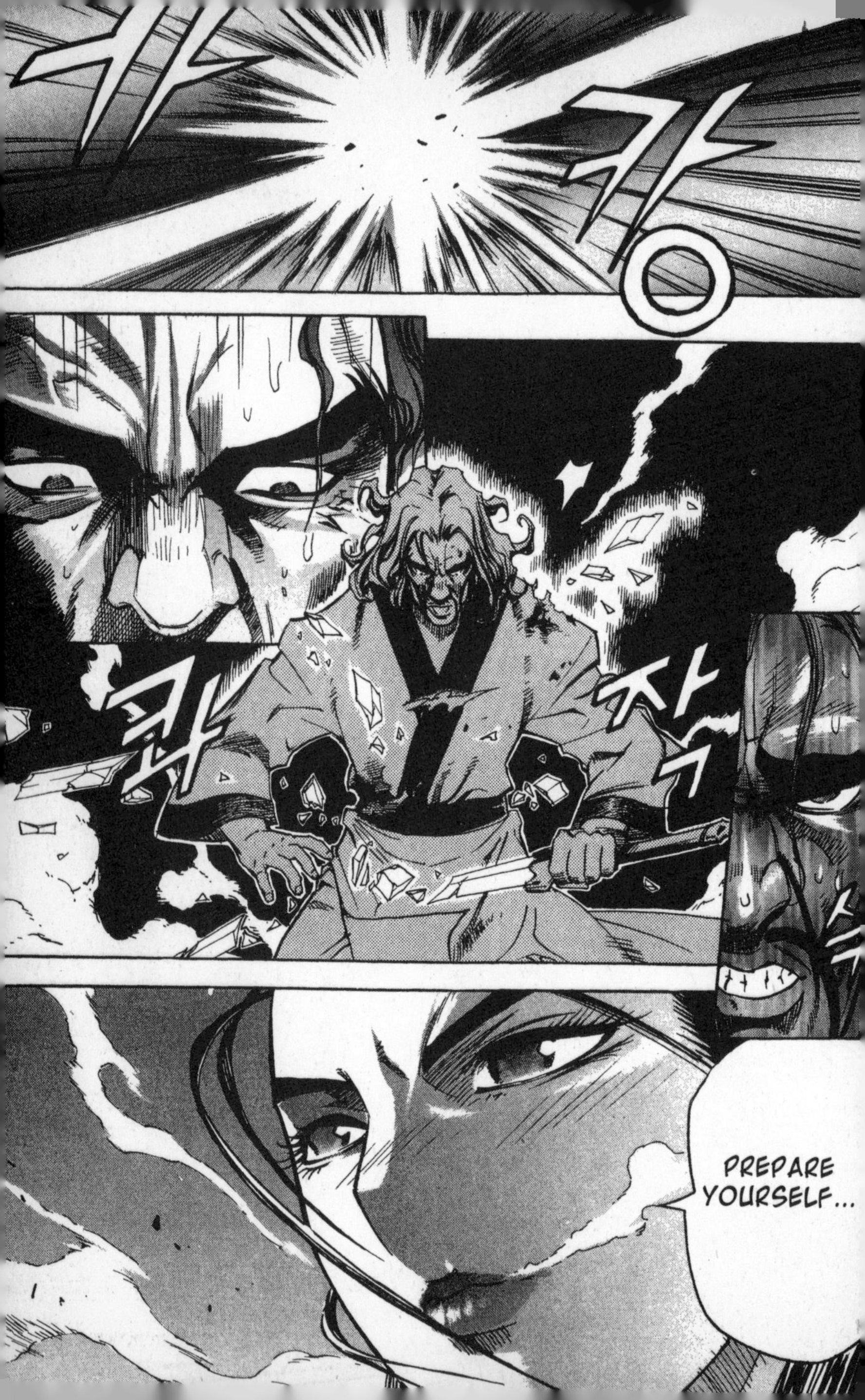
PREPARE YOURSELF...

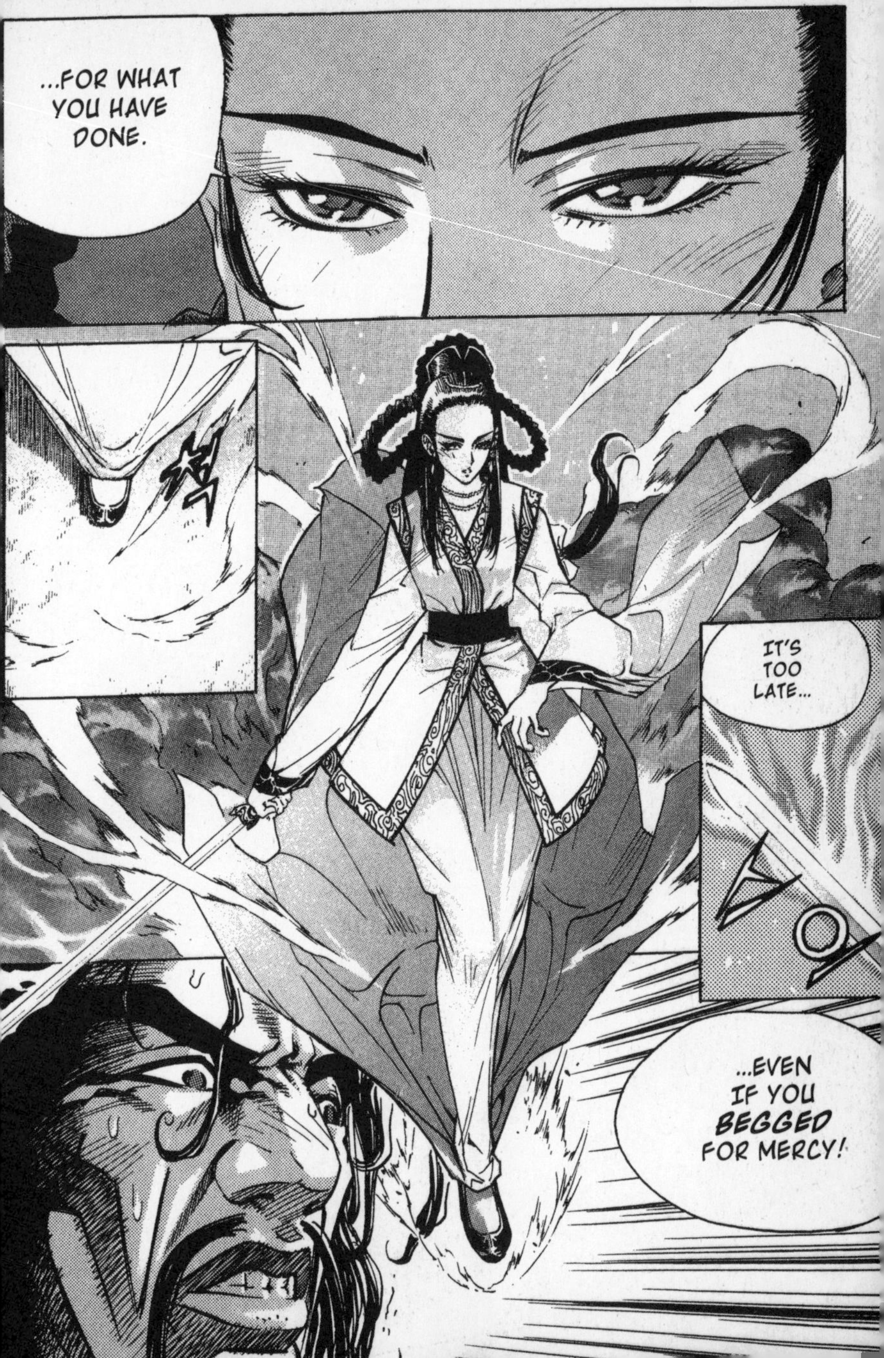
...FOR WHAT YOU HAVE DONE.
IT'S TOO LATE...
...EVEN IF YOU BEGGED FOR MERCY!

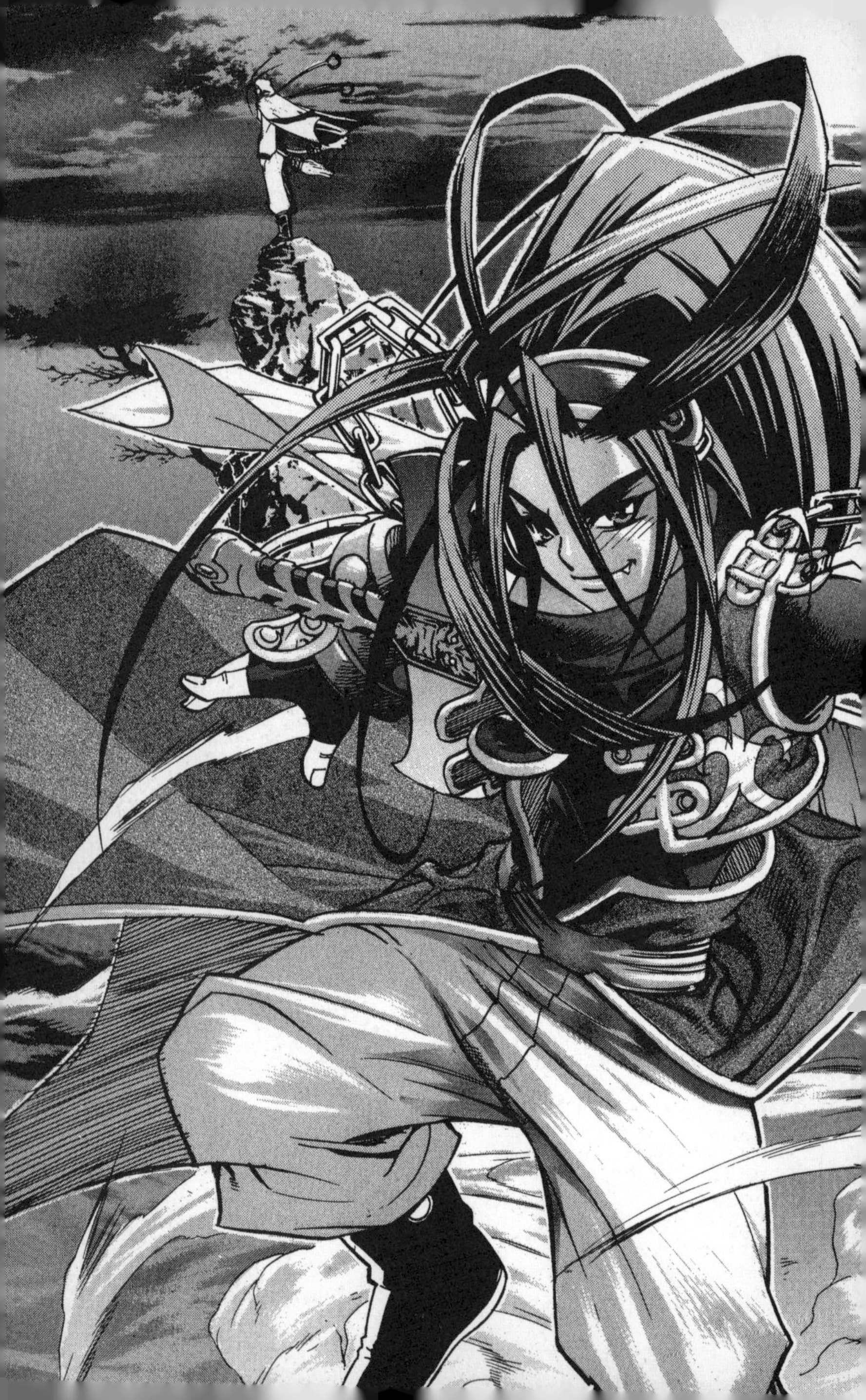

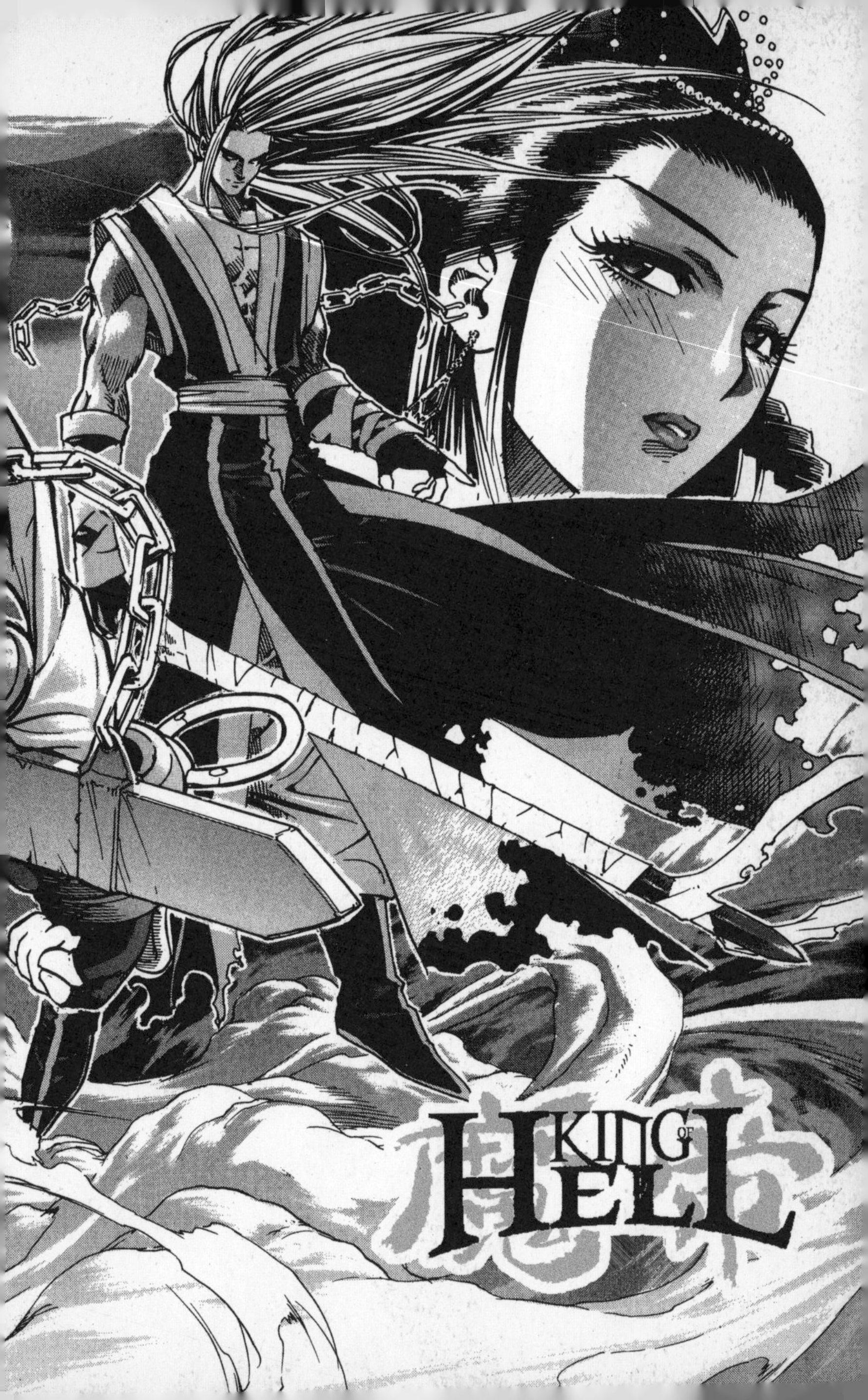
KING OF HELL

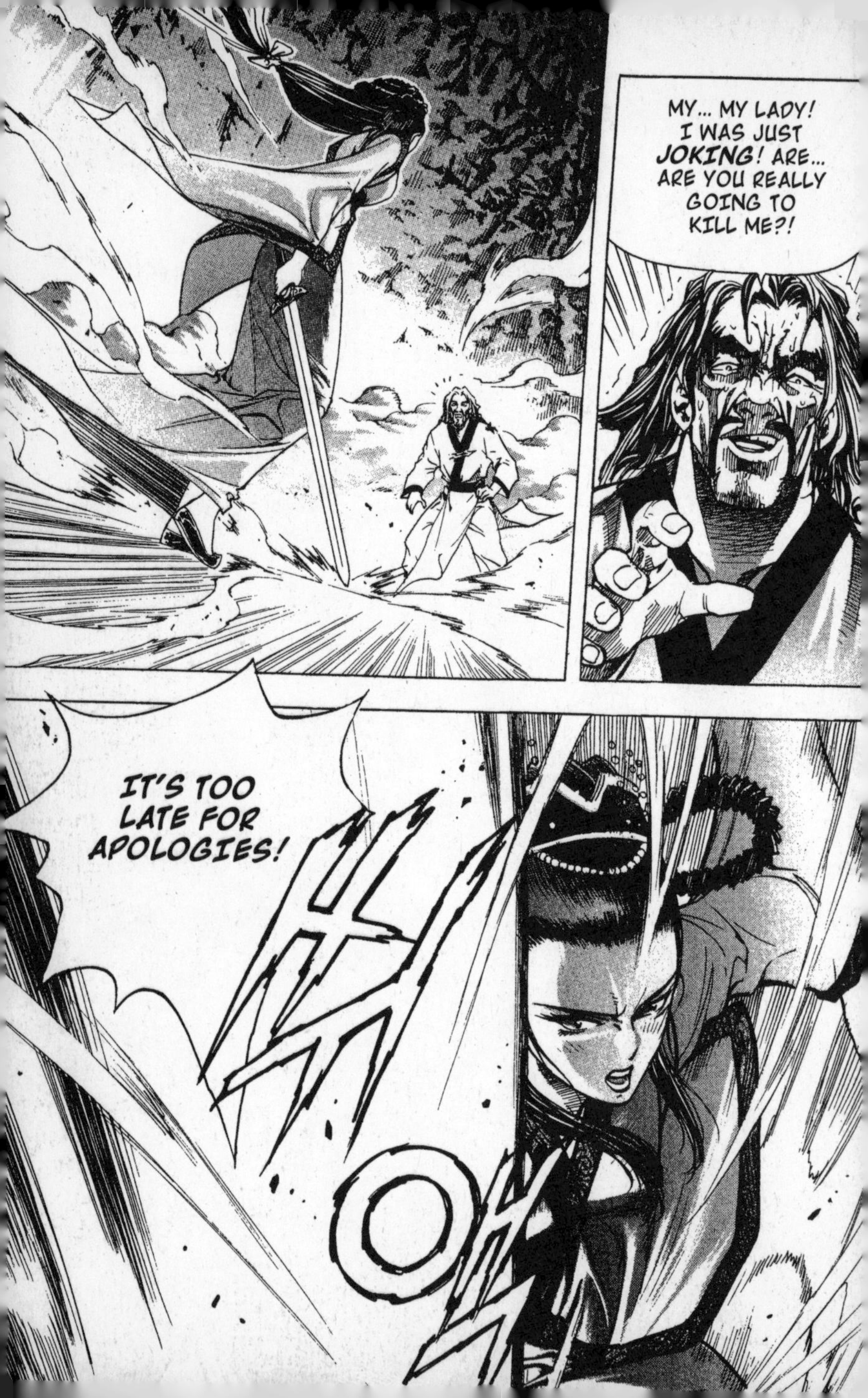
MY... MY LADY! I WAS JUST JOKING! ARE... ARE YOU REALLY GOING TO KILL ME?!
IT'S TOO LATE FOR APOLOGIES!

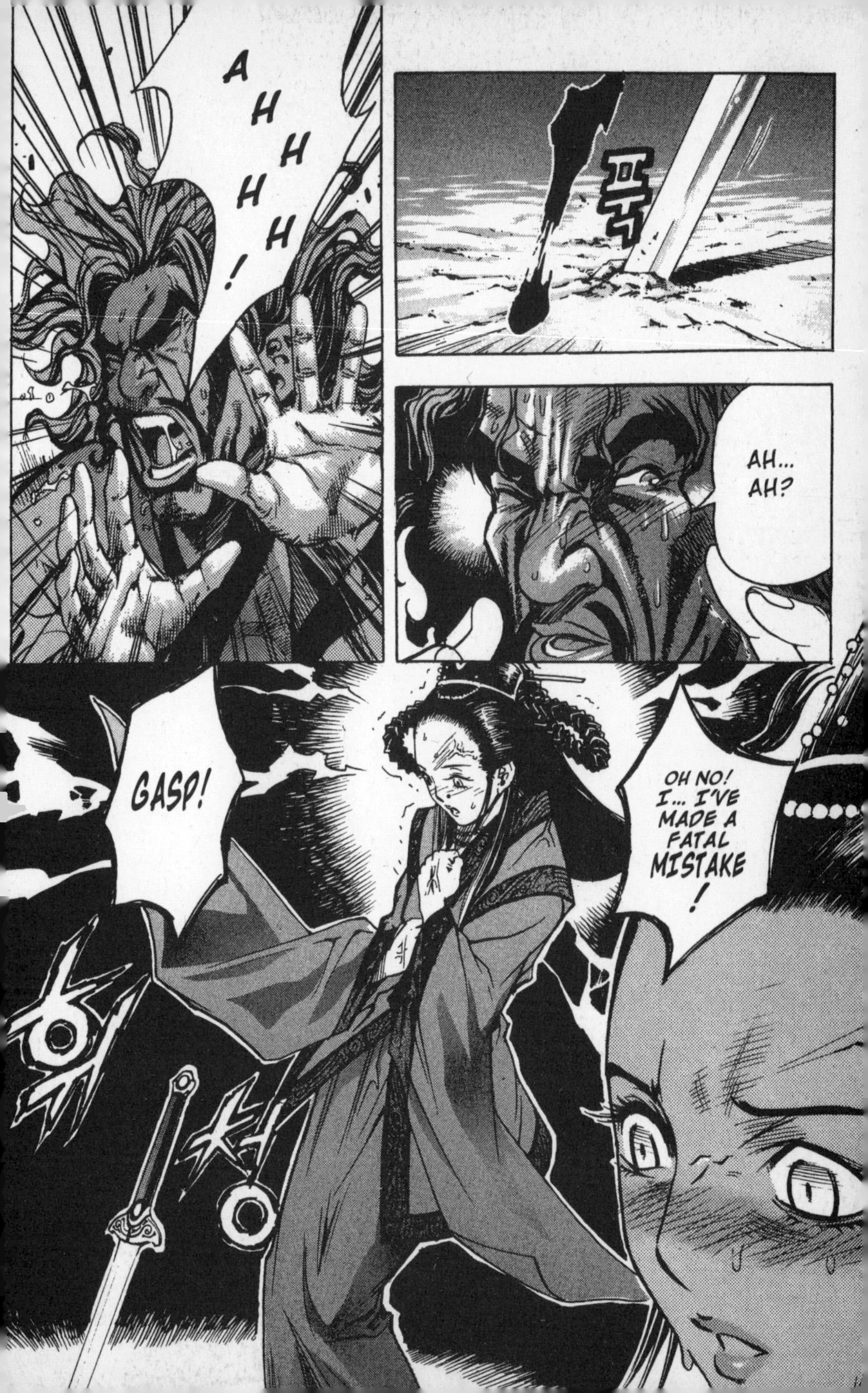
AHHHH!
AH... AH?
GASP!
OH NO! I... I'VE MADE A FATAL MISTAKE!

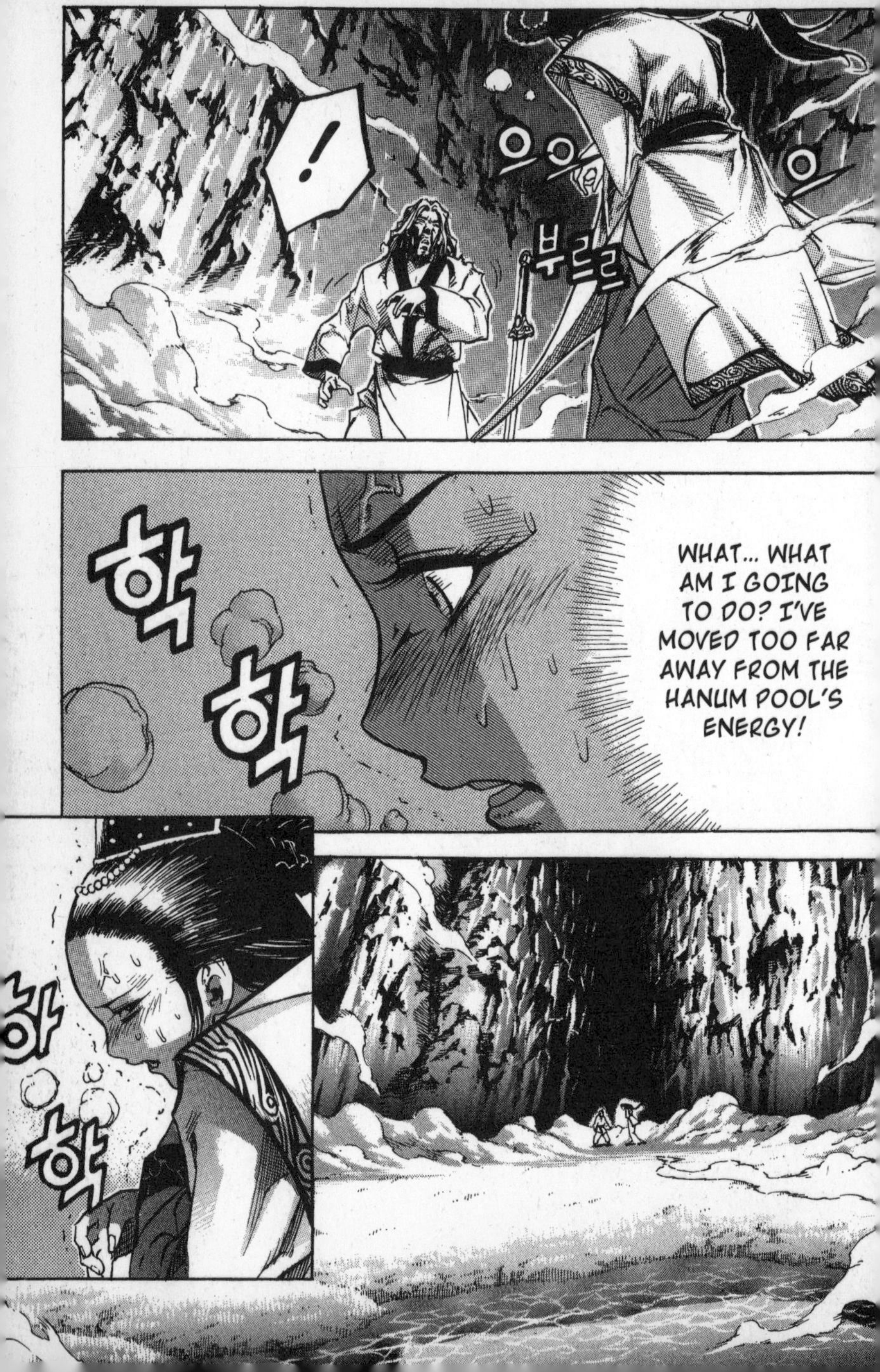
!
으으
으
부르르
학
학
WHAT... WHAT AM I GOING TO DO? I'VE MOVED TOO FAR AWAY FROM THE HANUM POOL'S ENERGY!
하
학

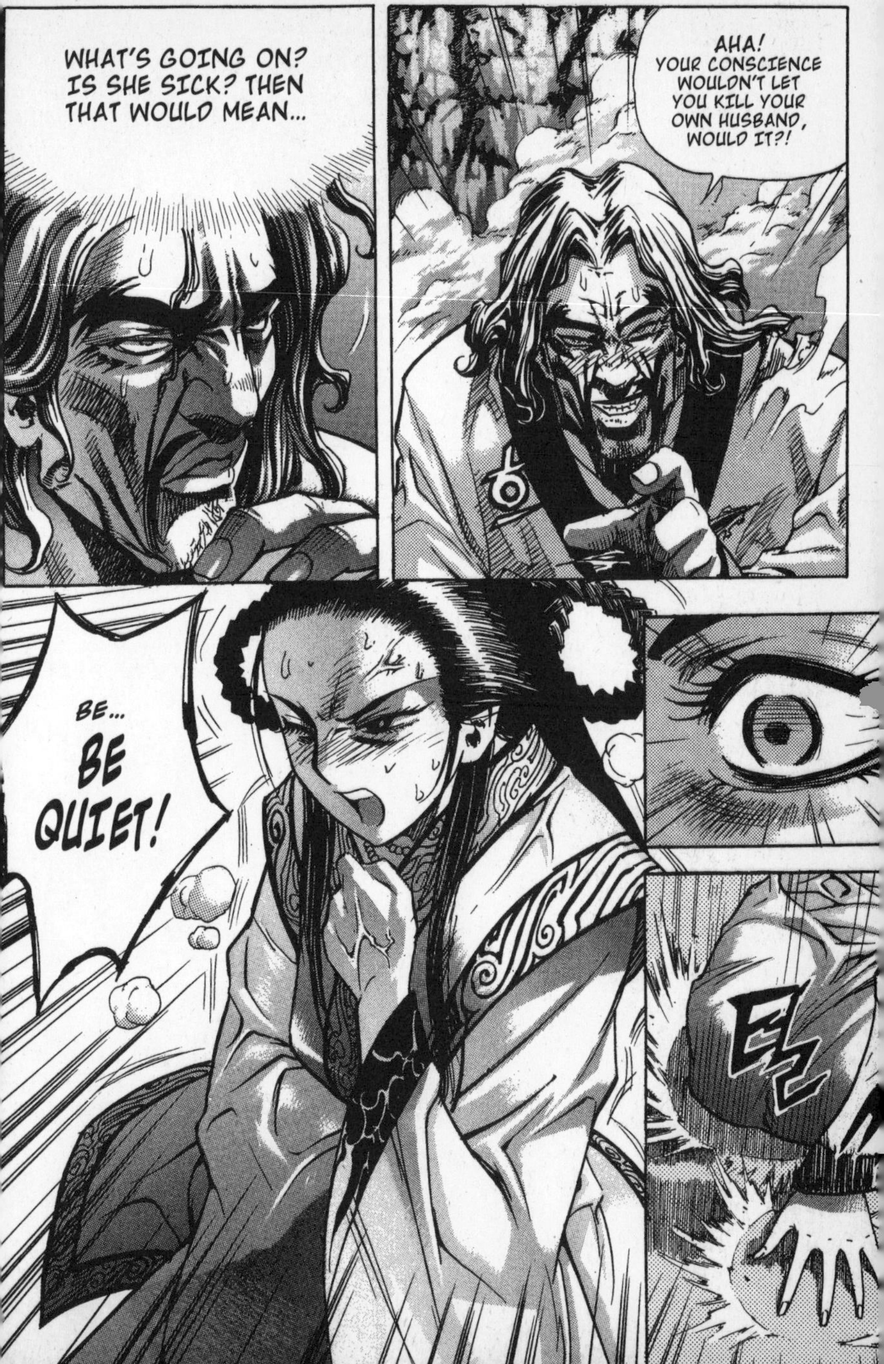
WHAT'S GOING ON? IS SHE SICK? THEN THAT WOULD MEAN...
AHA! YOUR CONSCIENCE WOULDN'T LET YOU KILL YOUR OWN HUSBAND, WOULD IT?!
BE... BE QUIET!

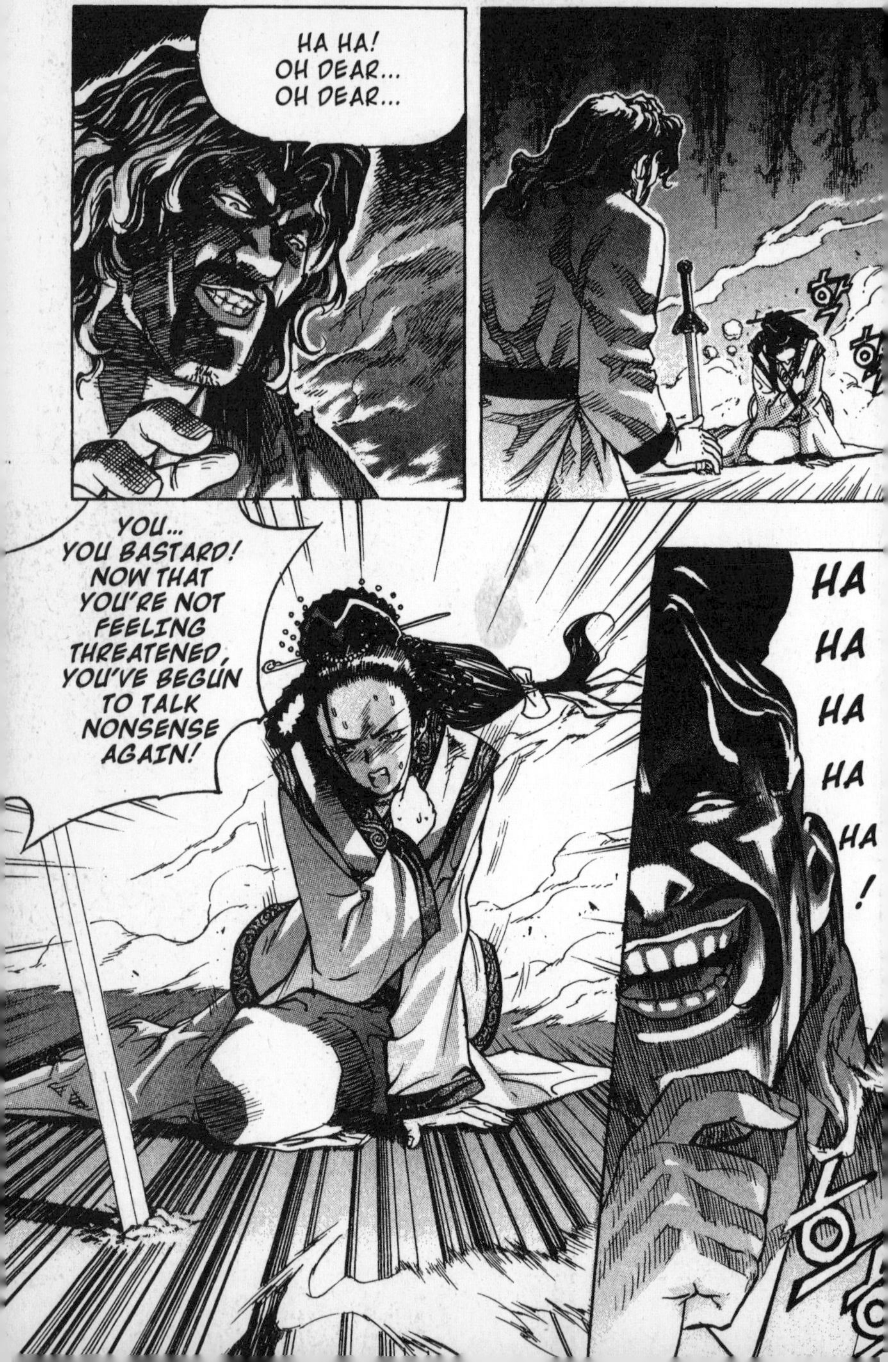
HA HA! OH DEAR... OH DEAR...
YOU... YOU BASTARD! NOW THAT YOU'RE NOT FEELING THREATENED, YOU'VE BEGUN TO TALK NONSENSE AGAIN!
HA HA HA HA HA!

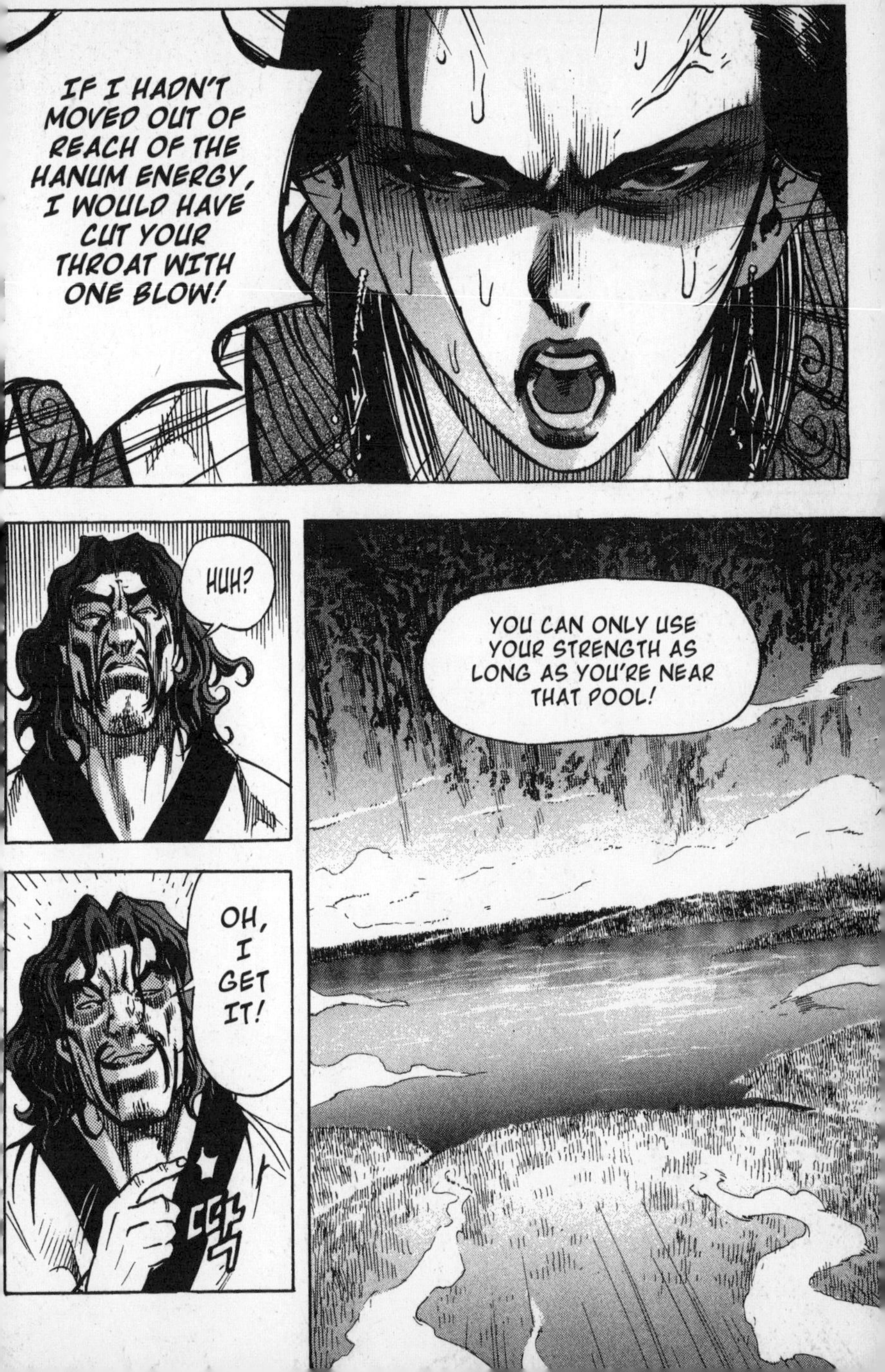
IF I HADN'T MOVED OUT OF REACH OF THE HANUM ENERGY, I WOULD HAVE CUT YOUR THROAT WITH ONE BLOW!
HUH?
OH, I GET IT!
YOU CAN ONLY USE YOUR STRENGTH AS LONG AS YOU'RE NEAR THAT POOL!

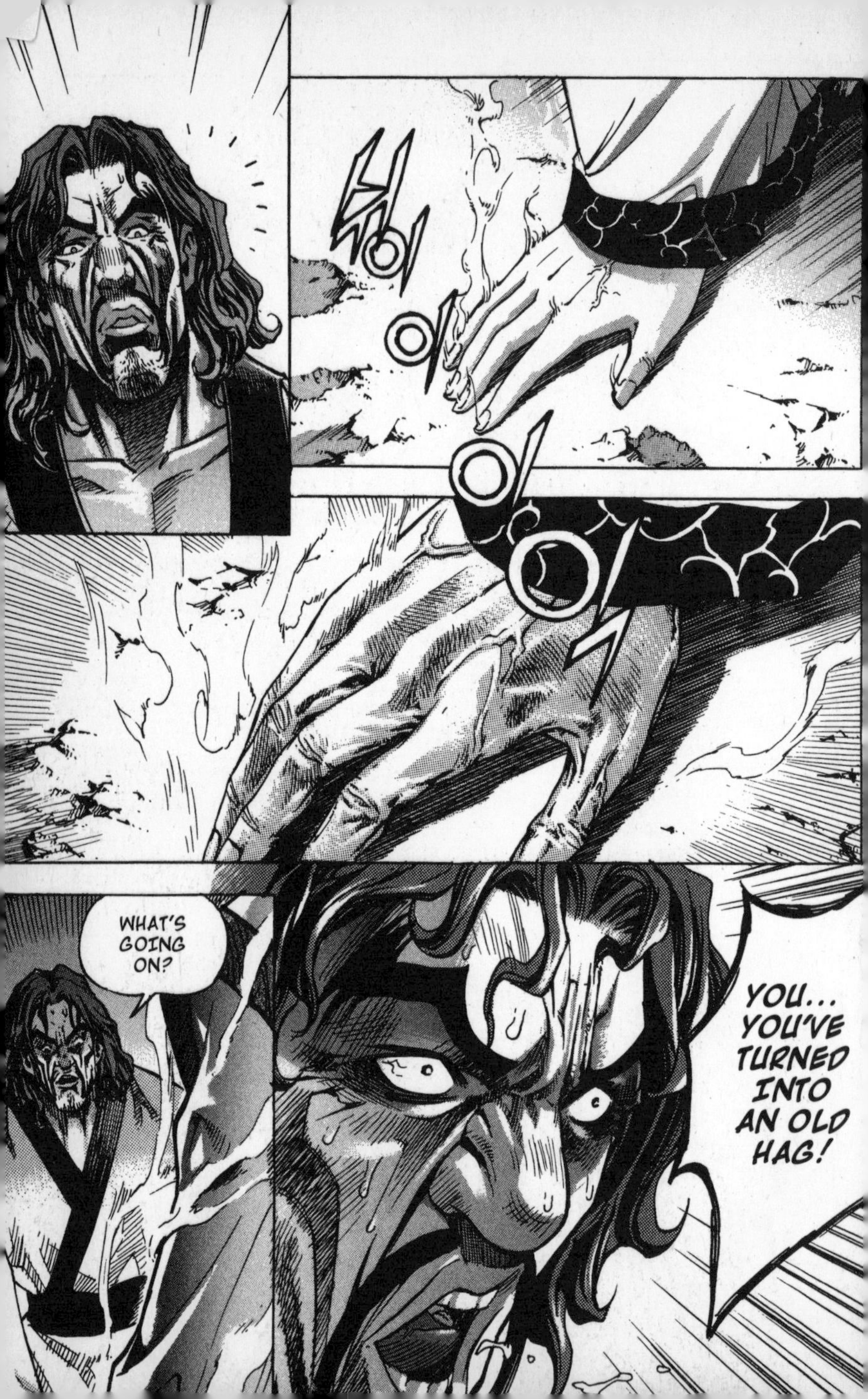
WHAT'S GOING ON?
YOU... YOU'VE TURNED INTO AN OLD HAG!

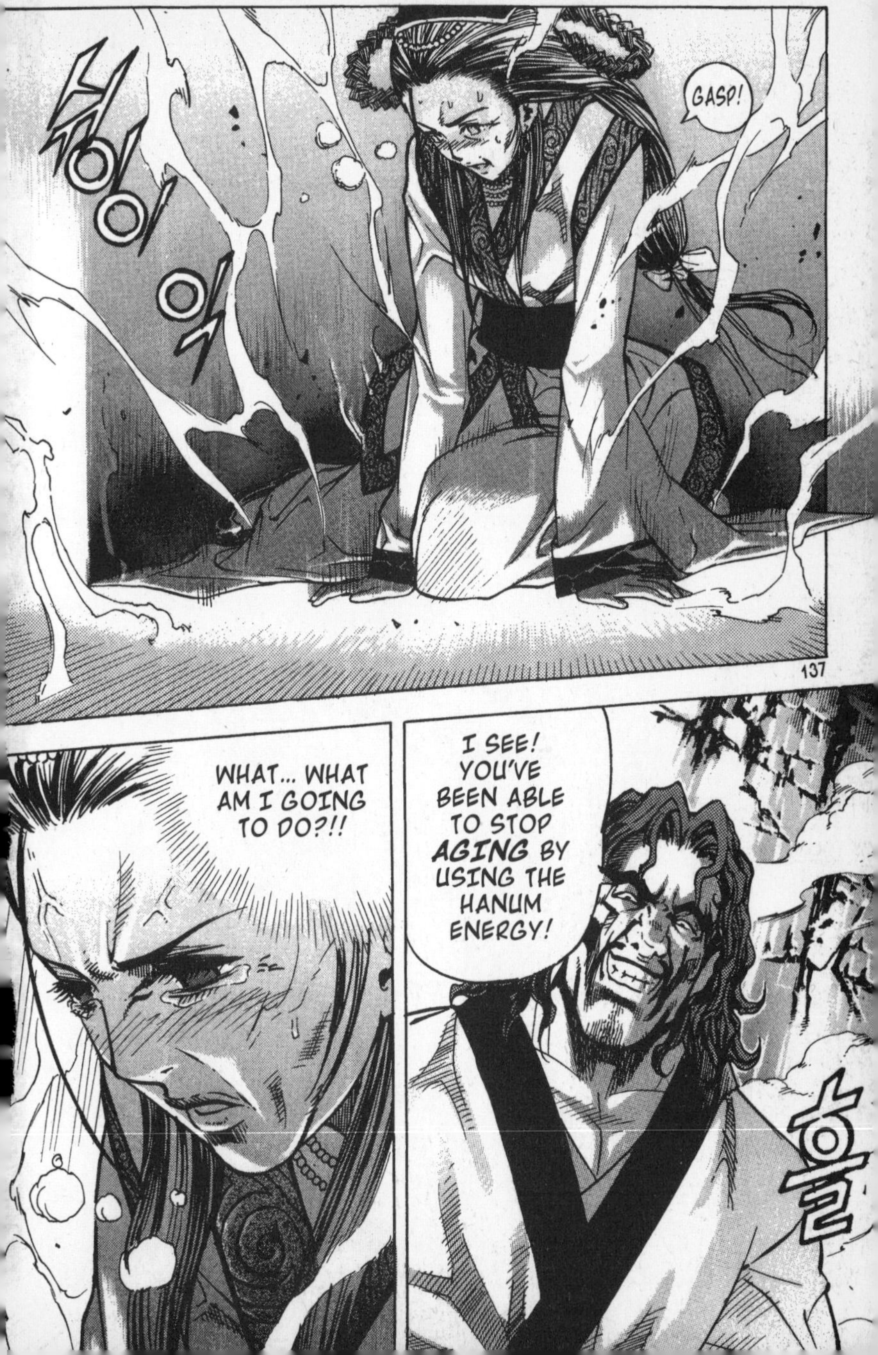
GASP!
WHAT... WHAT AM I GOING TO DO?!!
I SEE! YOU'VE BEEN ABLE TO STOP AGING BY USING THE HANUM ENERGY!

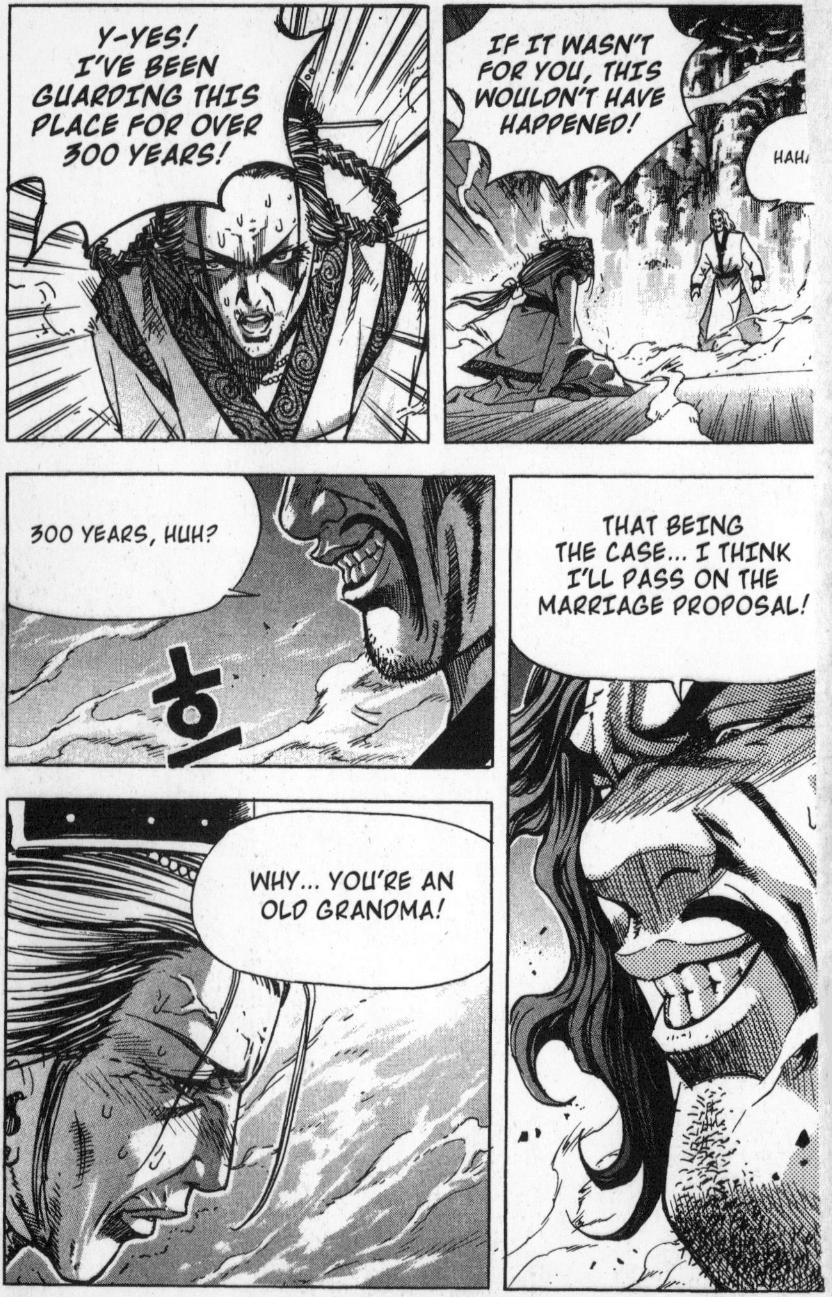
Y-YES! I'VE BEEN GUARDING THIS PLACE FOR OVER 300 YEARS!
IF IT WASN'T FOR YOU, THIS WOULDN'T HAVE HAPPENED!
HAH
300 YEARS, HUH?
THAT BEING THE CASE... I THINK I'LL PASS ON THE MARRIAGE PROPOSAL!
WHY... YOU'RE AN OLD GRANDMA!

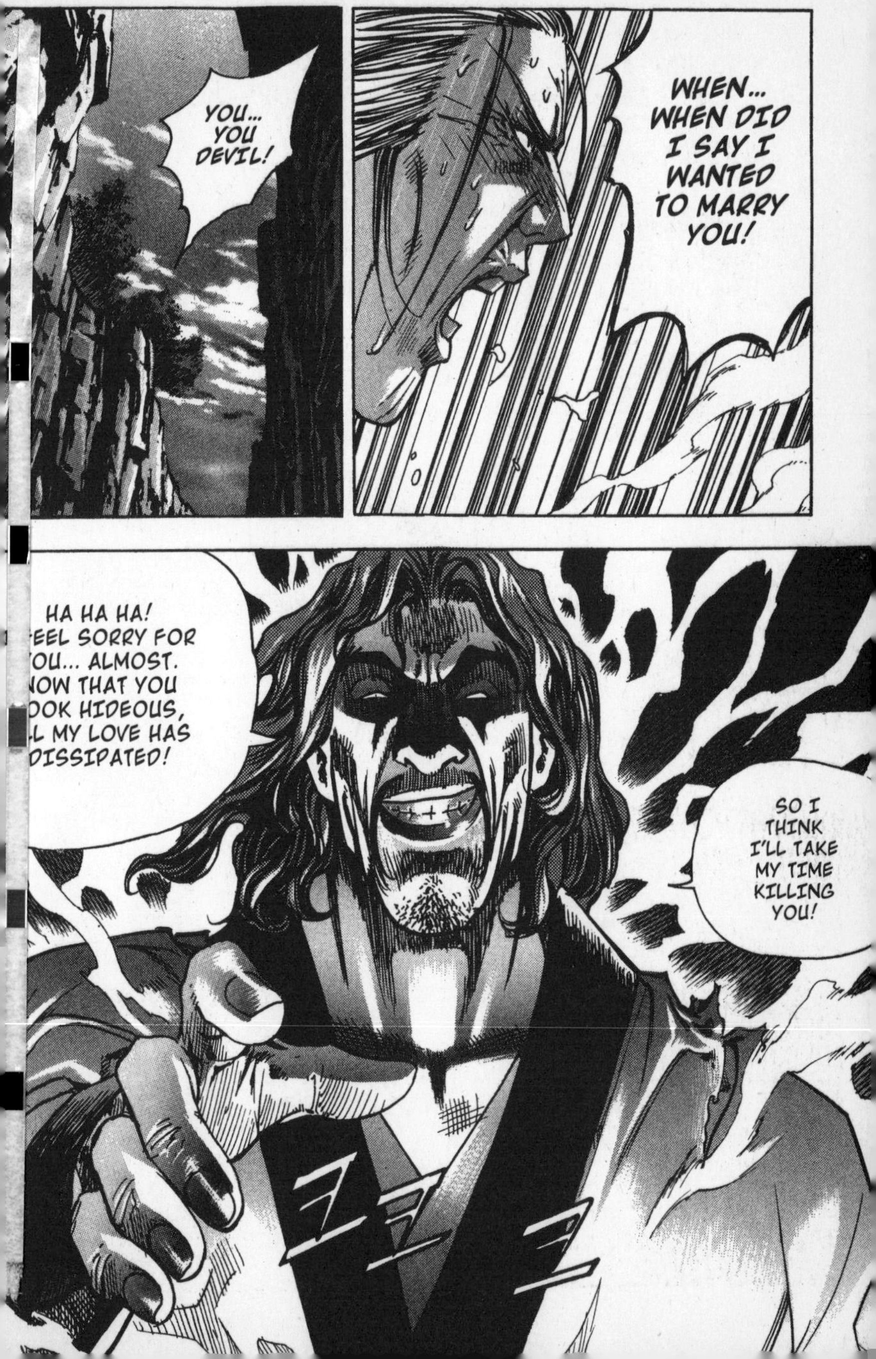
YOU... YOU DEVIL!
WHEN... WHEN DID I SAY I WANTED TO MARRY YOU!
HA HA HA! EEL SORRY FOR OU... ALMOST. NOW THAT YOU OOK HIDEOUS, L MY LOVE HAS DISSIPATED!
SO I THINK I'LL TAKE MY TIME KILLING YOU!

NO!
WHAT... WHAT DID YOU SAY??!!
I SAID NO!

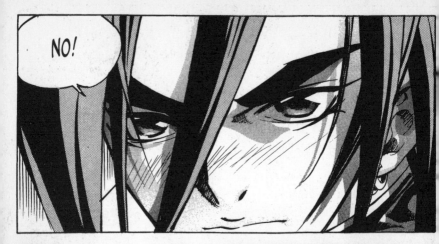

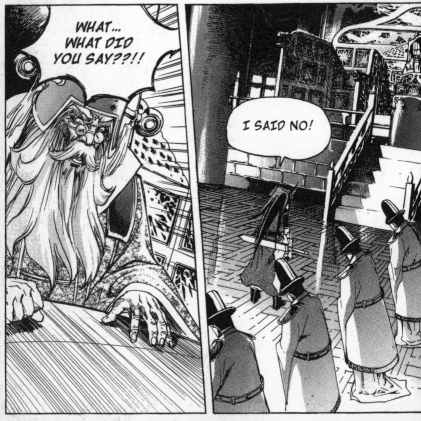

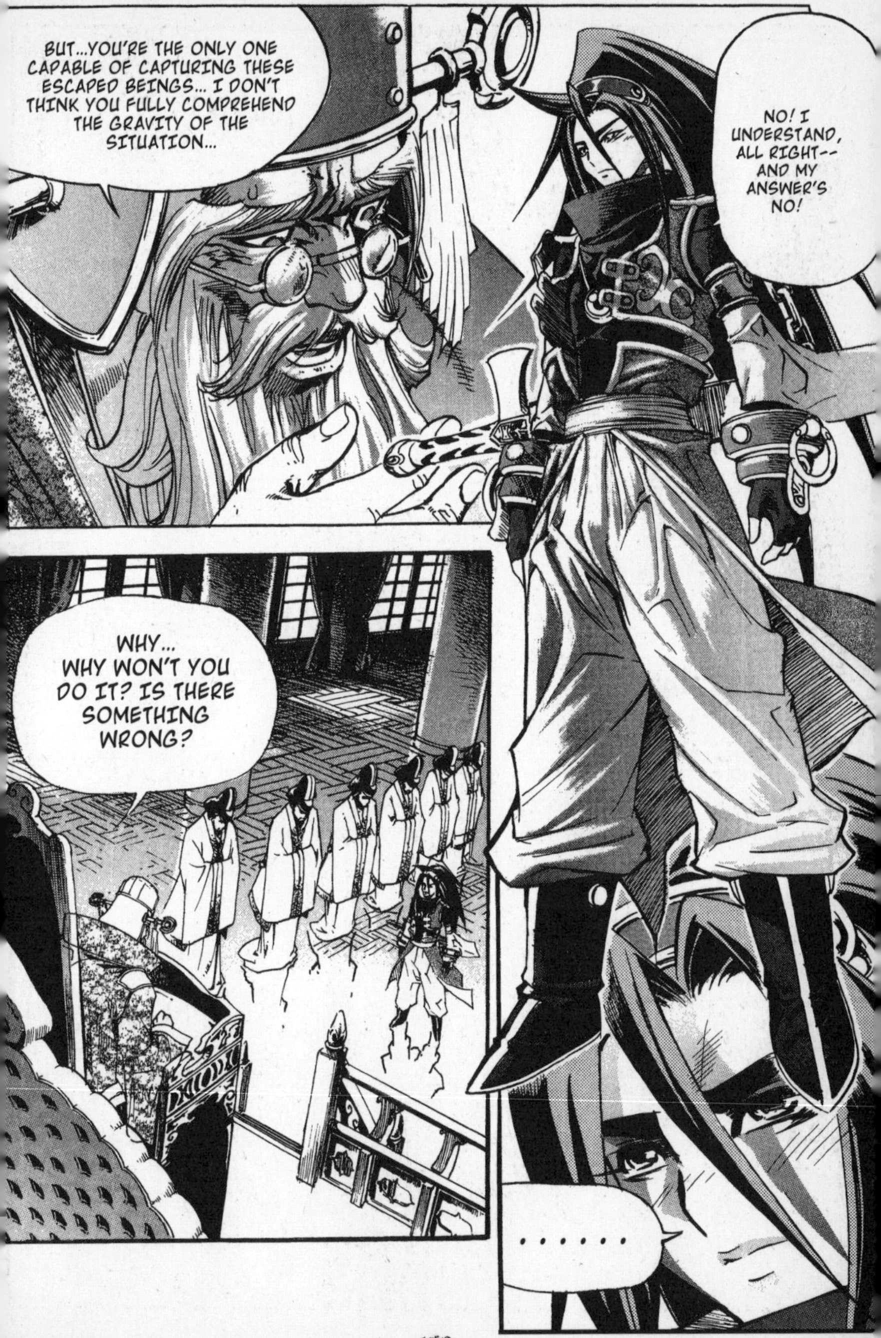
BUT...YOU'RE THE ONLY ONE CAPABLE OF CAPTURING THESE ESCAPED BEINGS... I DON'T THINK YOU FULLY COMPREHEND THE GRAVITY OF THE SITUATION...
NO! I UNDERSTAND, ALL RIGHT-- AND MY ANSWER'S NO!
WHY... WHY WON'T YOU DO IT? IS THERE SOMETHING WRONG?
......

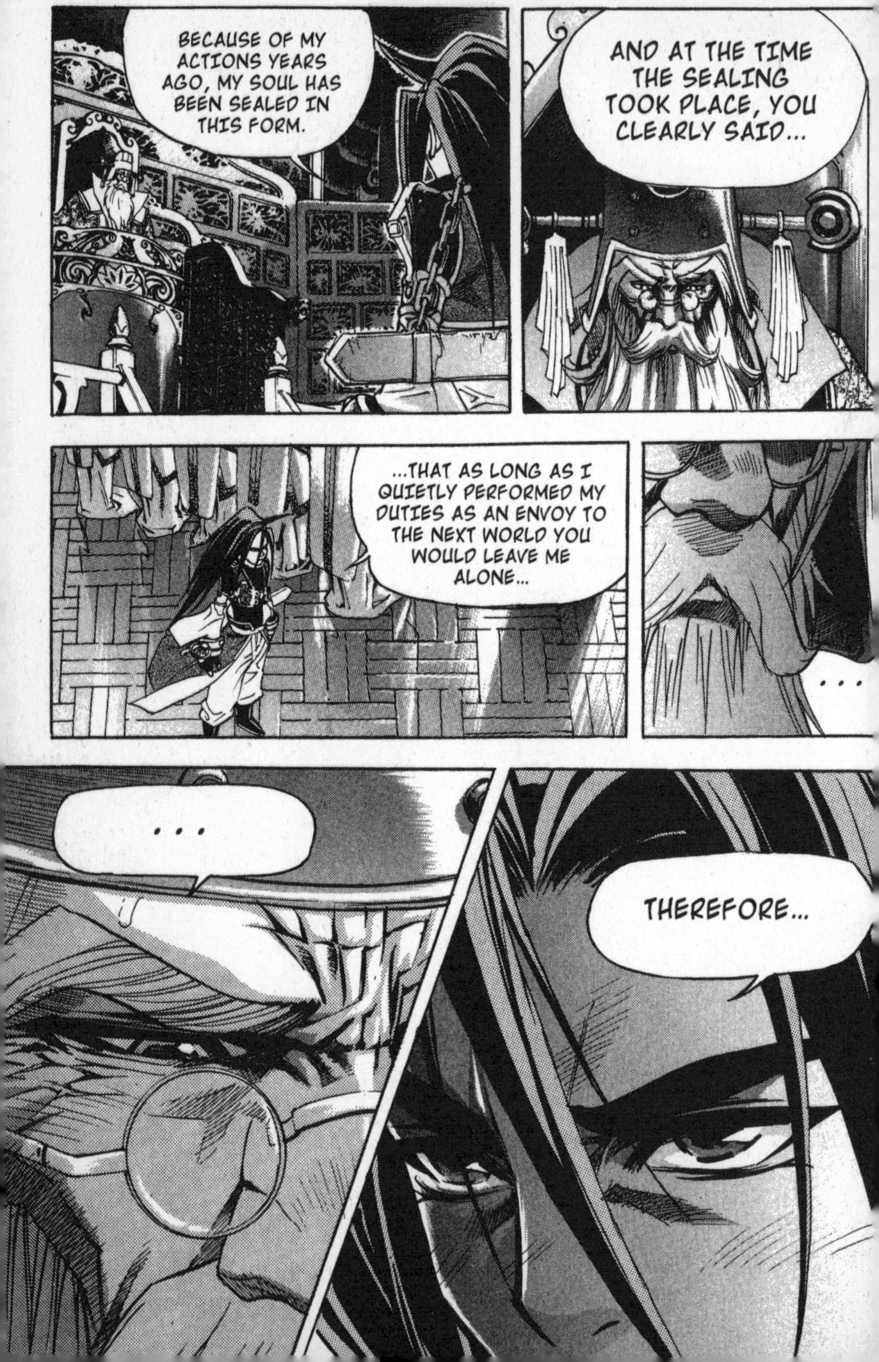
BECAUSE OF MY ACTIONS YEARS AGO, MY SOUL HAS BEEN SEALED IN THIS FORM.
AND AT THE TIME THE SEALING TOOK PLACE, YOU CLEARLY SAID...
...THAT AS LONG AS I QUIETLY PERFORMED MY DUTIES AS AN ENVOY TO THE NEXT WORLD YOU WOULD LEAVE ME ALONE...
...
...
THEREFORE...

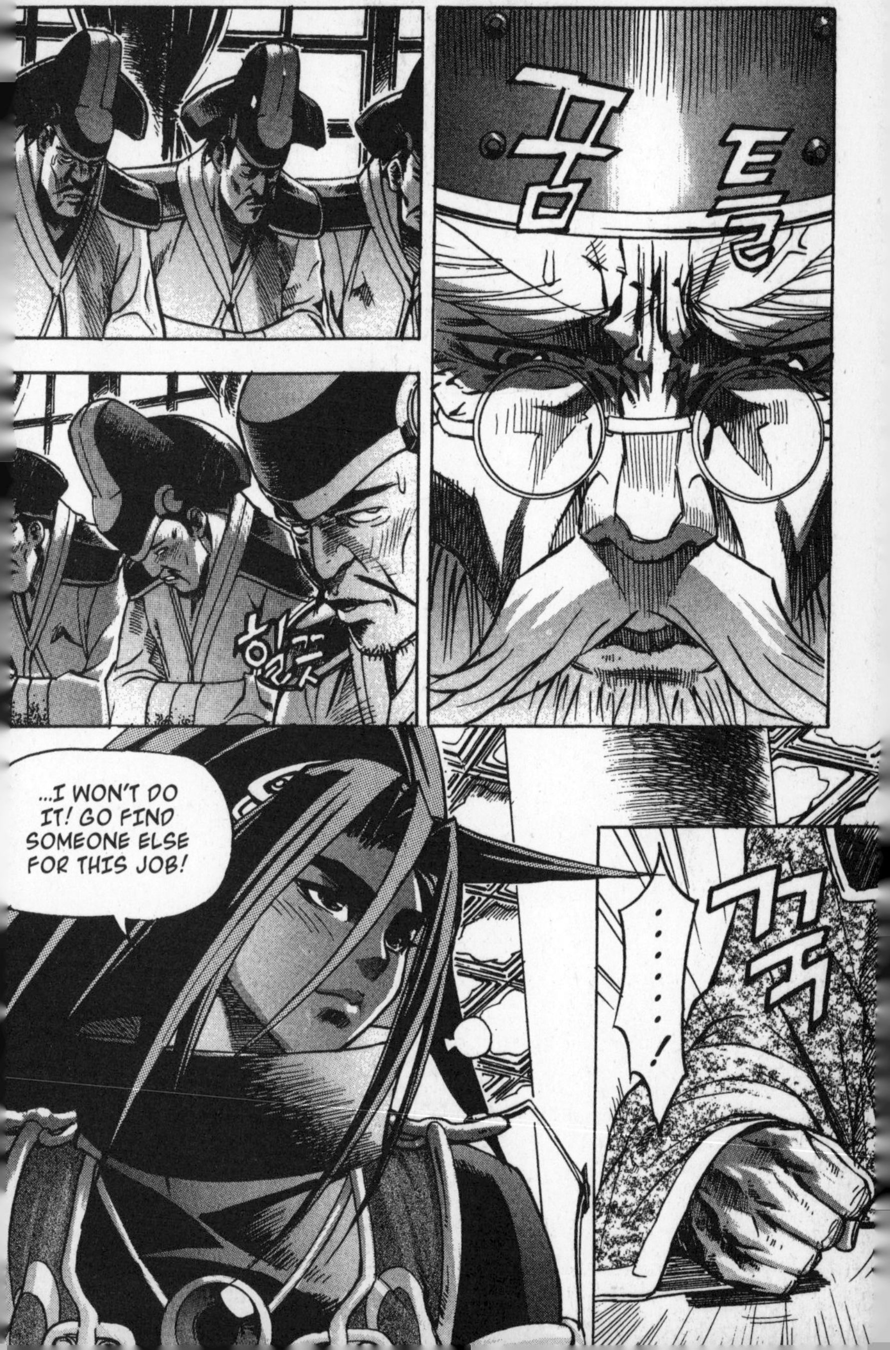
...I WON'T DO IT! GO FIND SOMEONE ELSE FOR THIS JOB!
……!

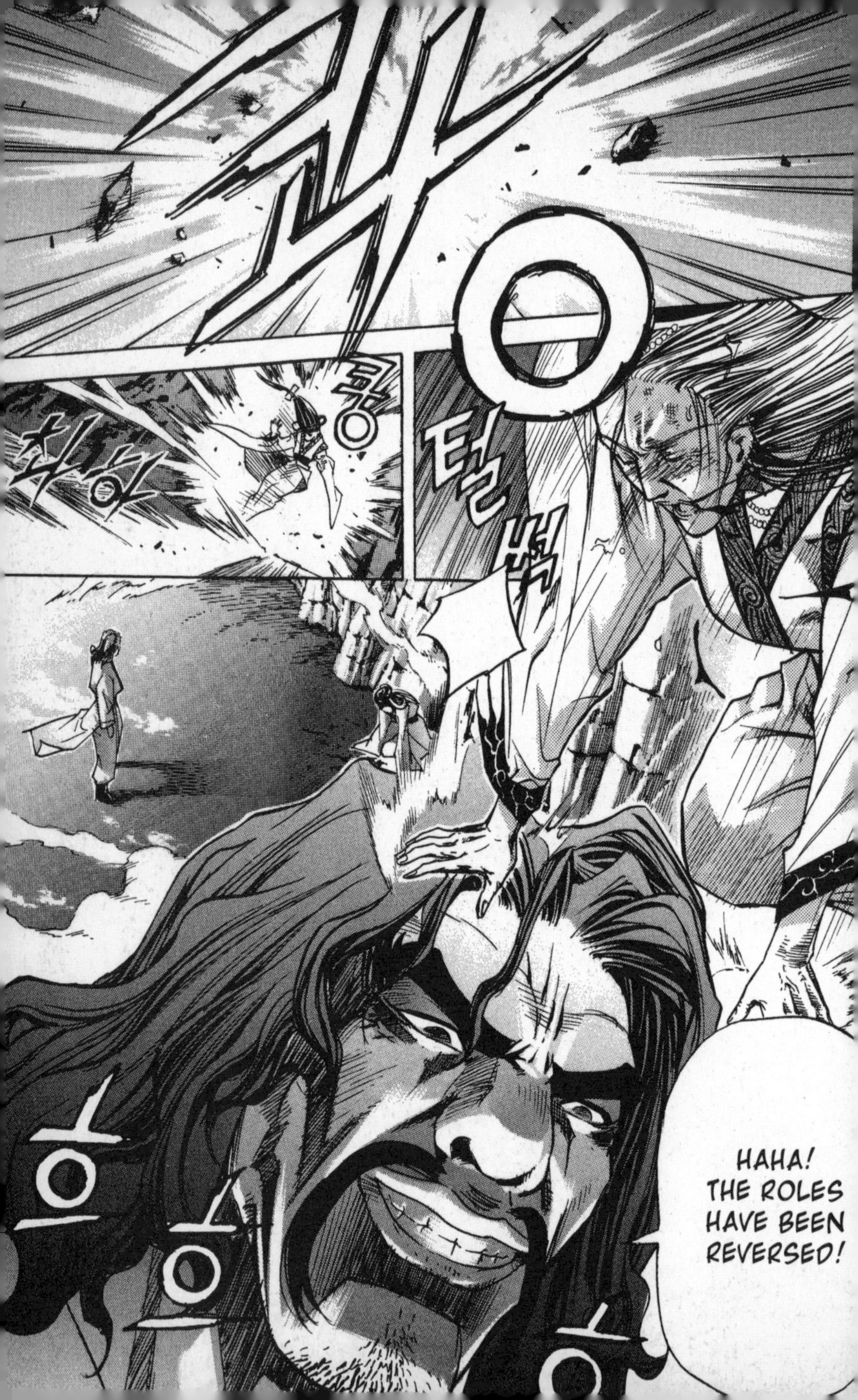
HAHA! THE ROLES HAVE BEEN REVERSED!

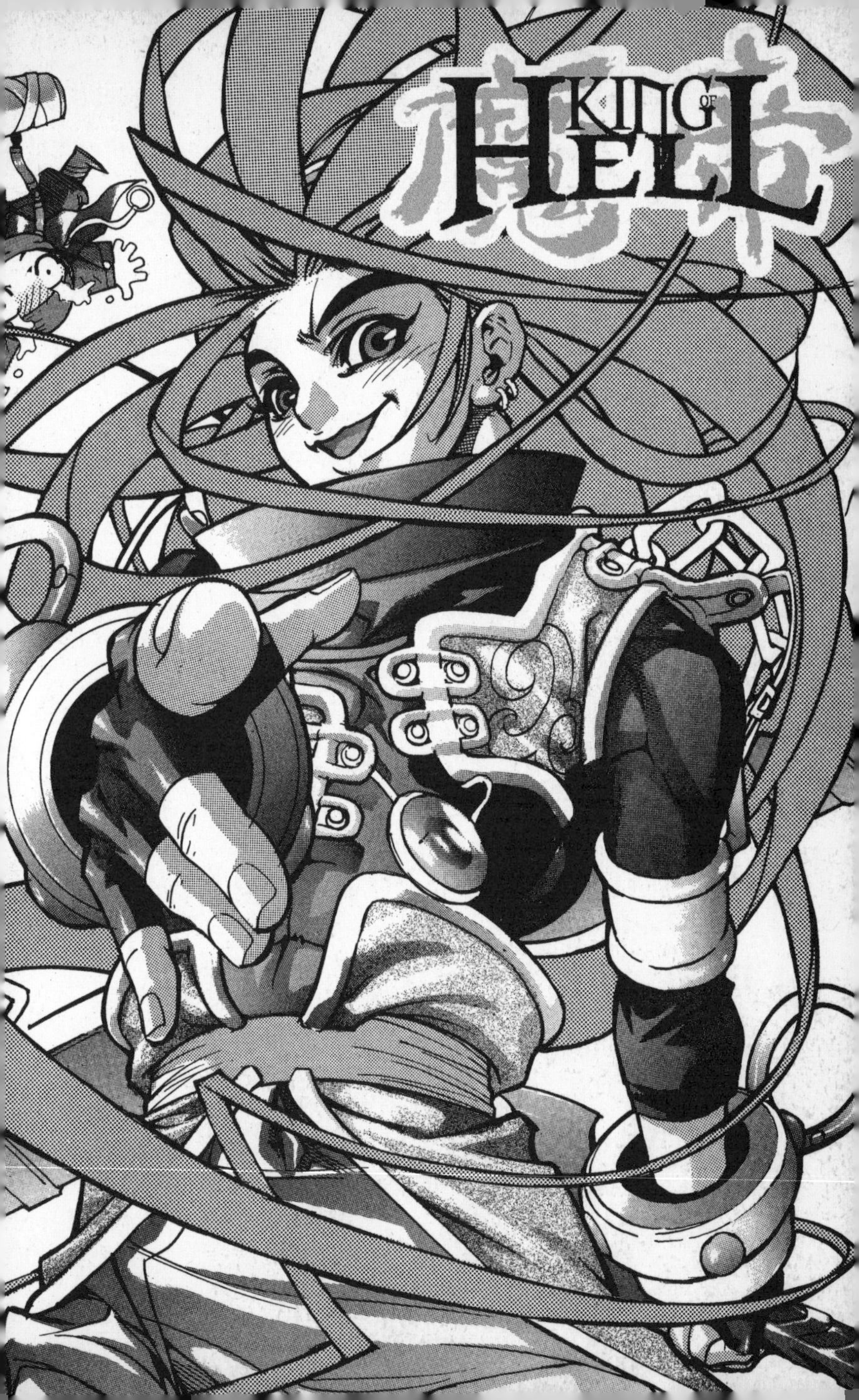
KING OF HELL

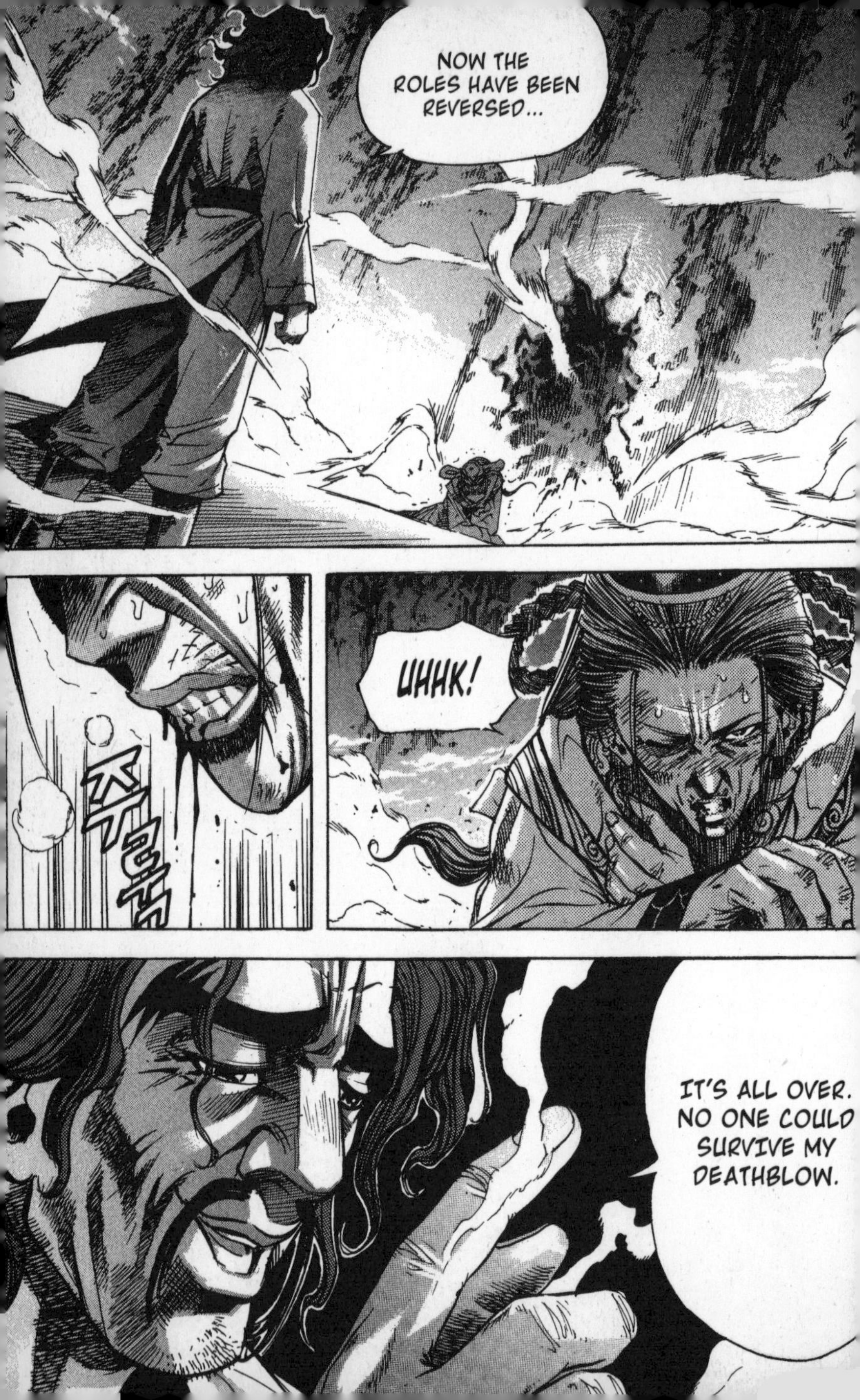
NOW THE ROLES HAVE BEEN REVERSED...
UHHK!
IT'S ALL OVER. NO ONE COULD SURVIVE MY DEATHBLOW.

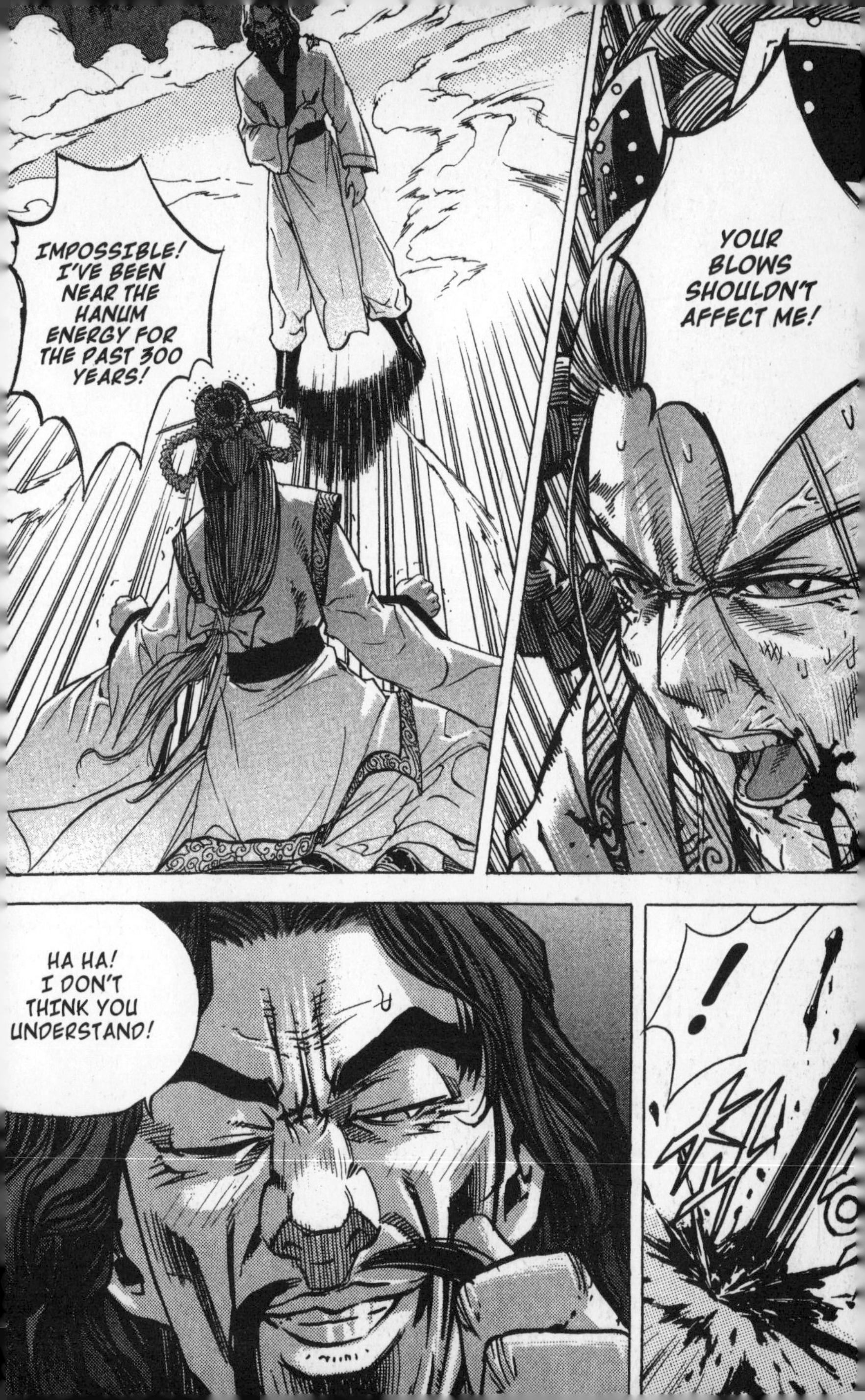
IMPOSSIBLE! I'VE BEEN NEAR THE HANUM ENERGY FOR THE PAST 300 YEARS!
YOUR BLOWS SHOULDN'T AFFECT ME!
HA HA! I DON'T THINK YOU UNDERSTAND!
!

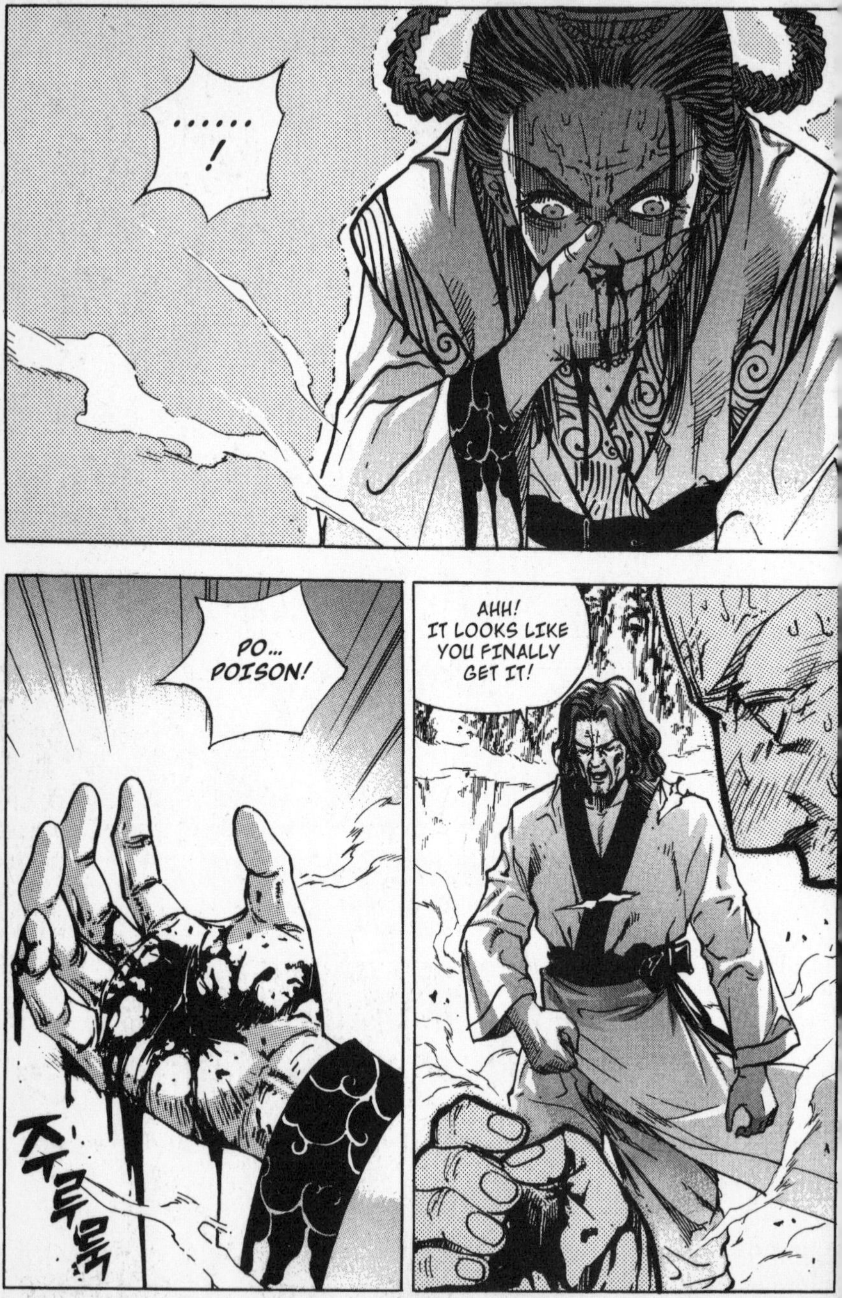
......!
PO... POISON!
주르륵
AHH! IT LOOKS LIKE YOU FINALLY GET IT!

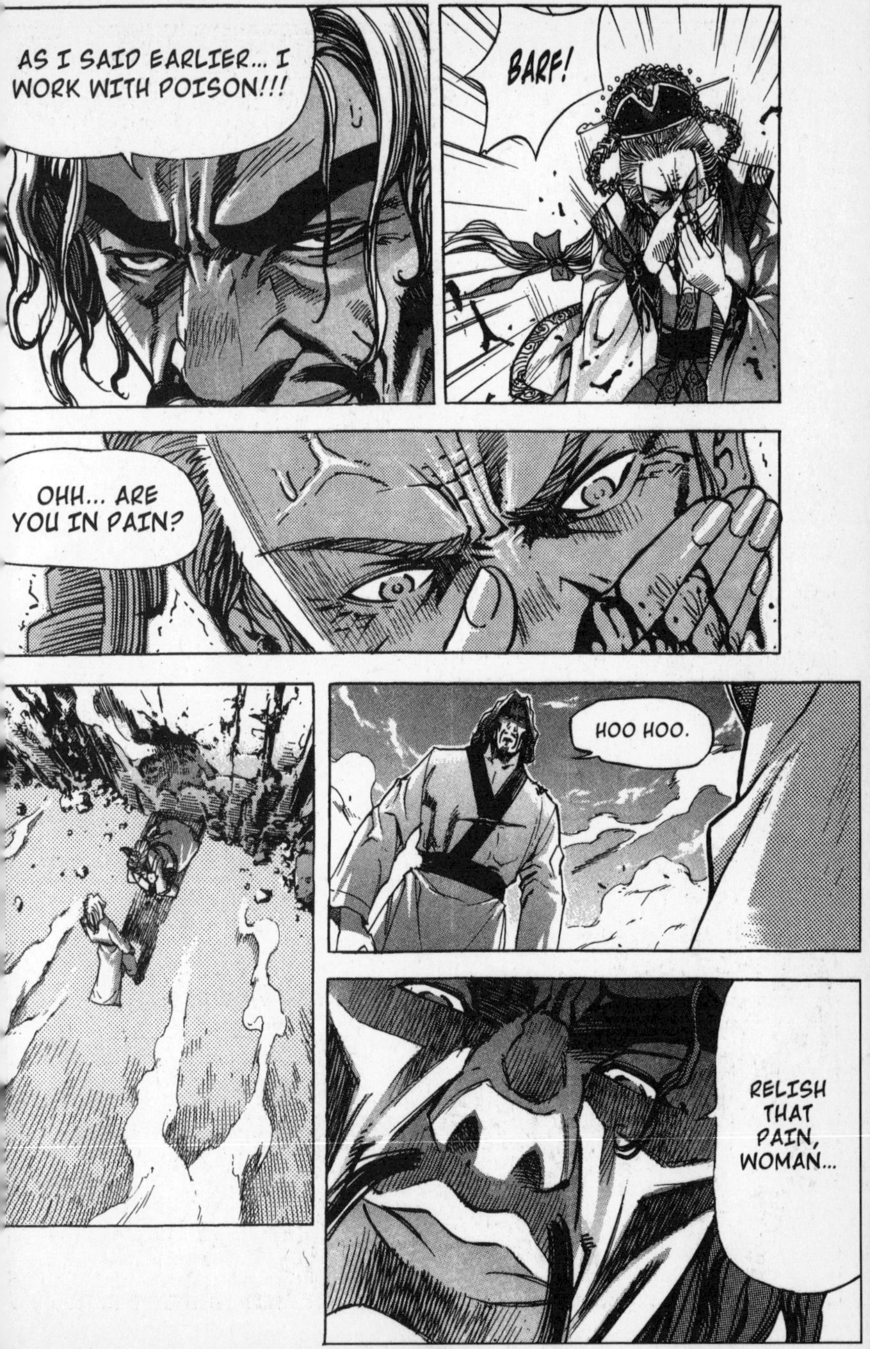
AS I SAID EARLIER... I WORK WITH POISON!!!
BARF!
OHH... ARE YOU IN PAIN?
HOO HOO.
RELISH THAT PAIN, WOMAN...

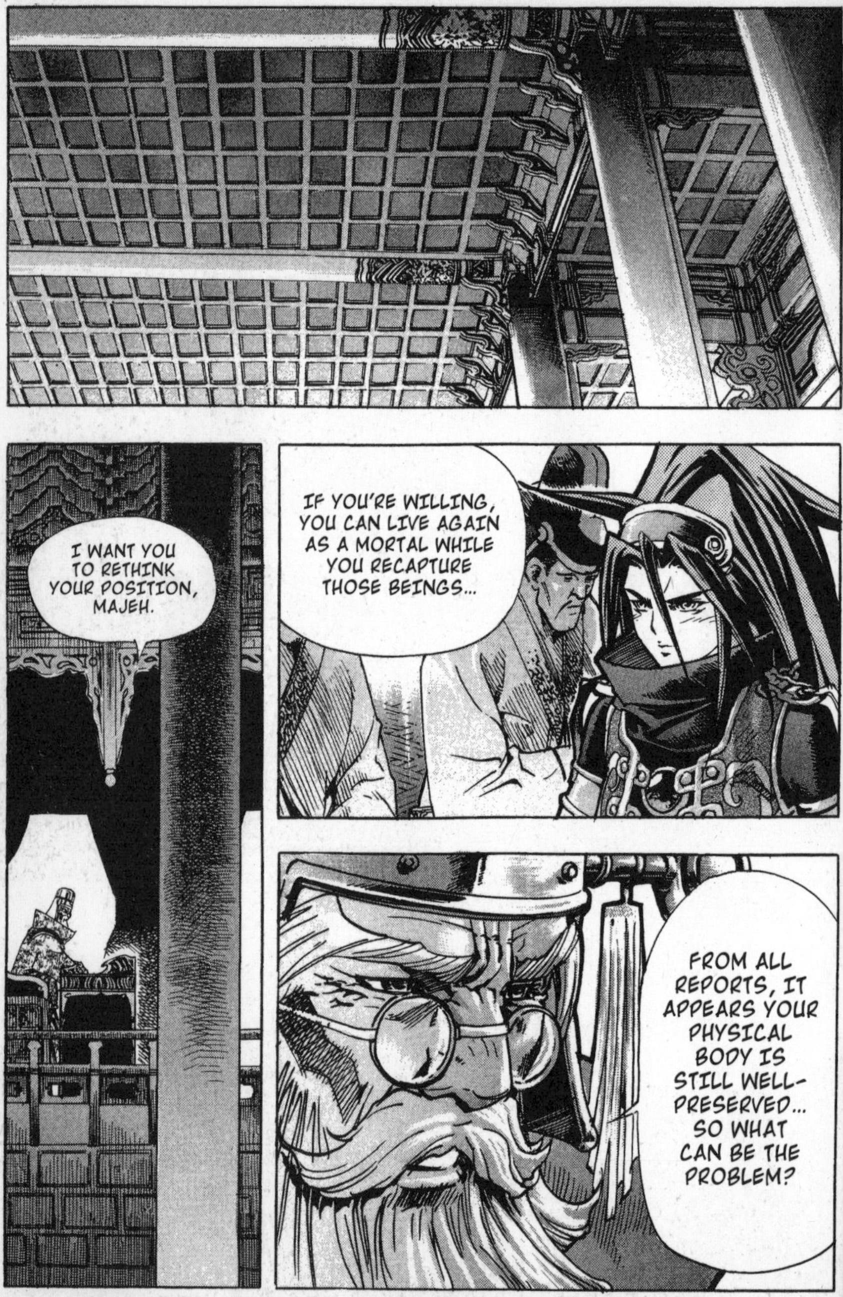
I WANT YOU TO RETHINK YOUR POSITION, MAJEH.
IF YOU'RE WILLING, YOU CAN LIVE AGAIN AS A MORTAL WHILE YOU RECAPTURE THOSE BEINGS...
FROM ALL REPORTS, IT APPEARS YOUR PHYSICAL BODY IS STILL WELL-PRESERVED... SO WHAT CAN BE THE PROBLEM?

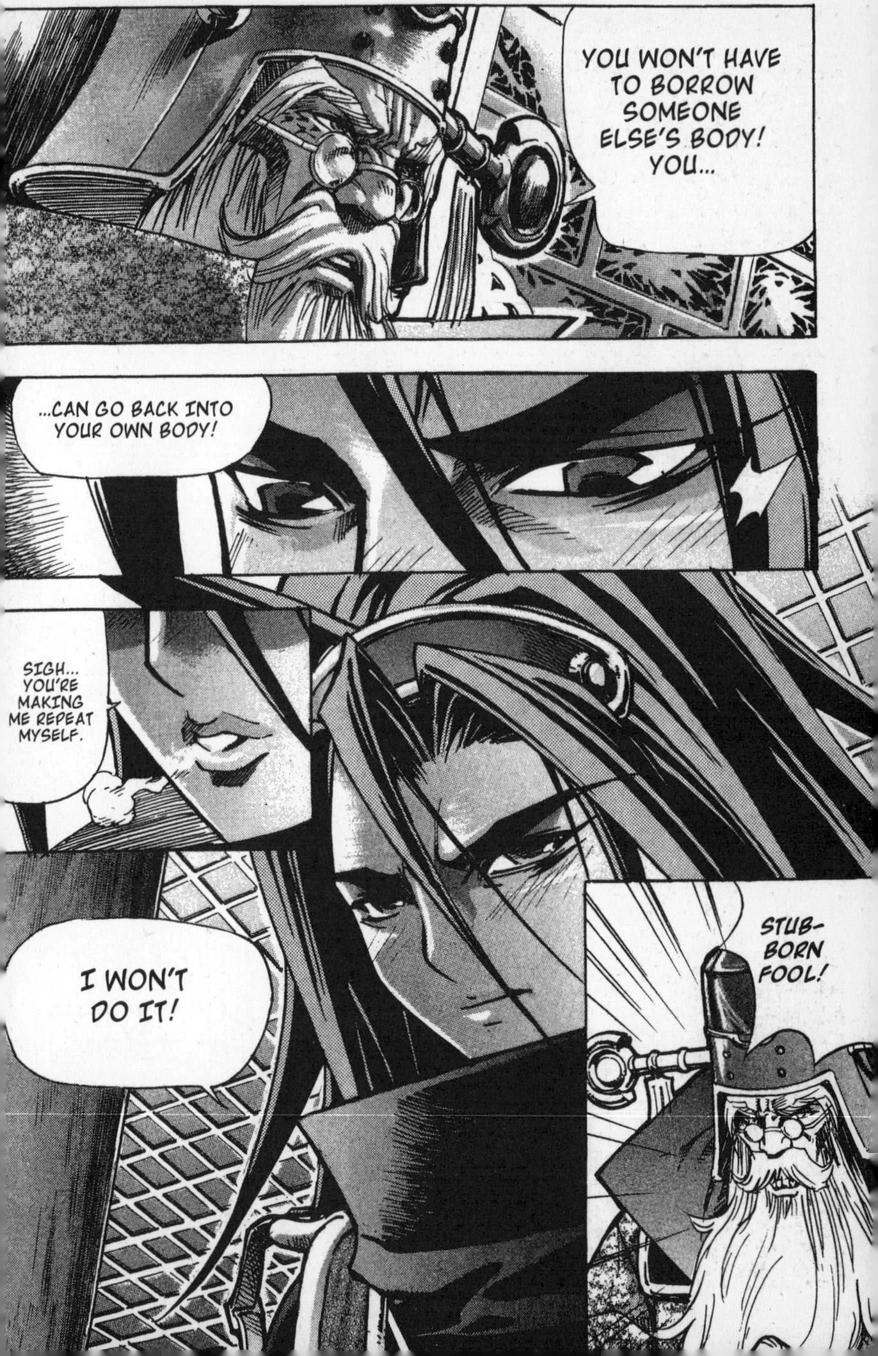
YOU WON'T HAVE TO BORROW SOMEONE ELSE'S BODY! YOU...
...CAN GO BACK INTO YOUR OWN BODY!
SIGH... YOU'RE MAKING ME REPEAT MYSELF.
I WON'T DO IT!
STUB-BORN FOOL!

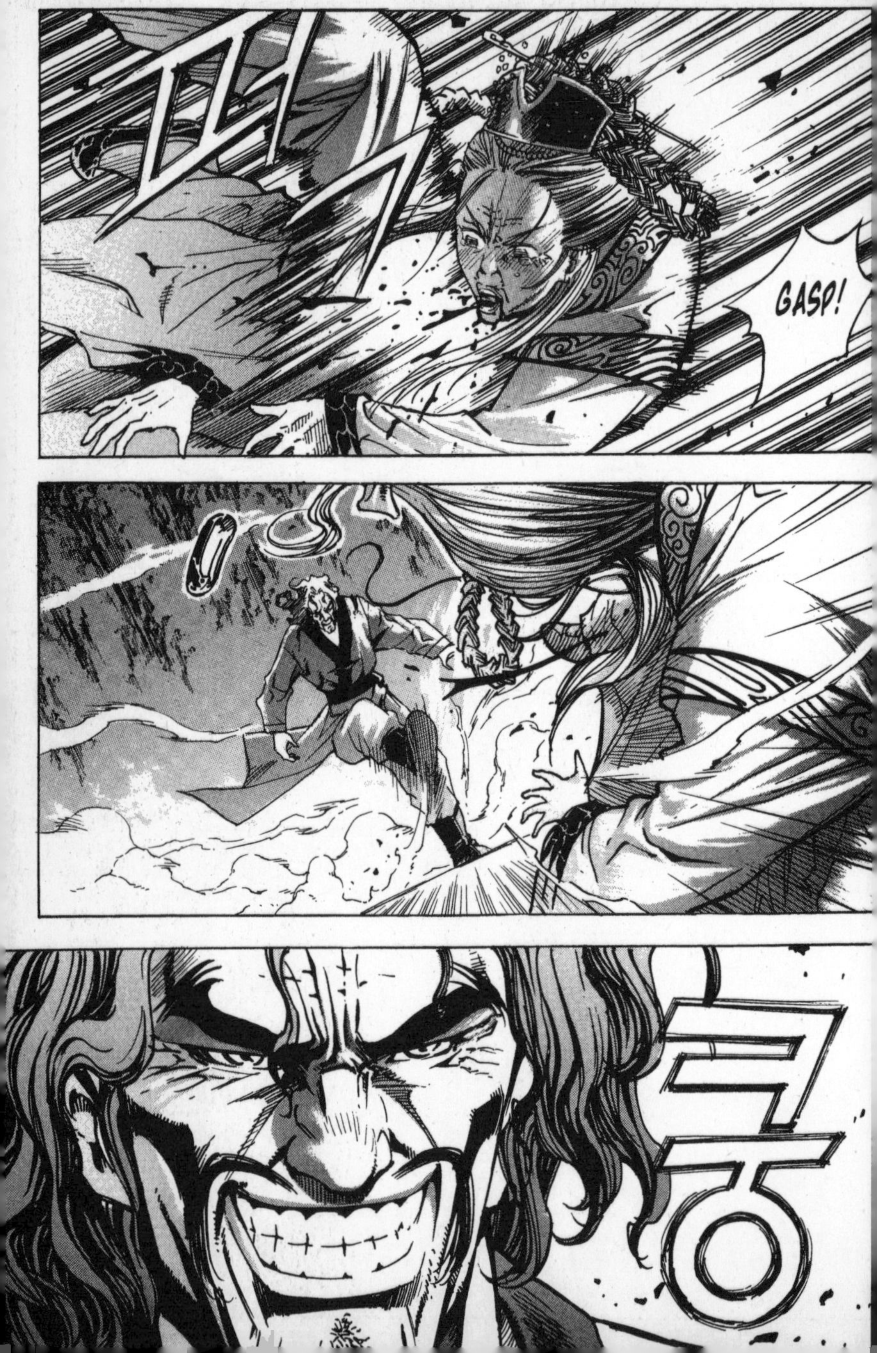
GASP!

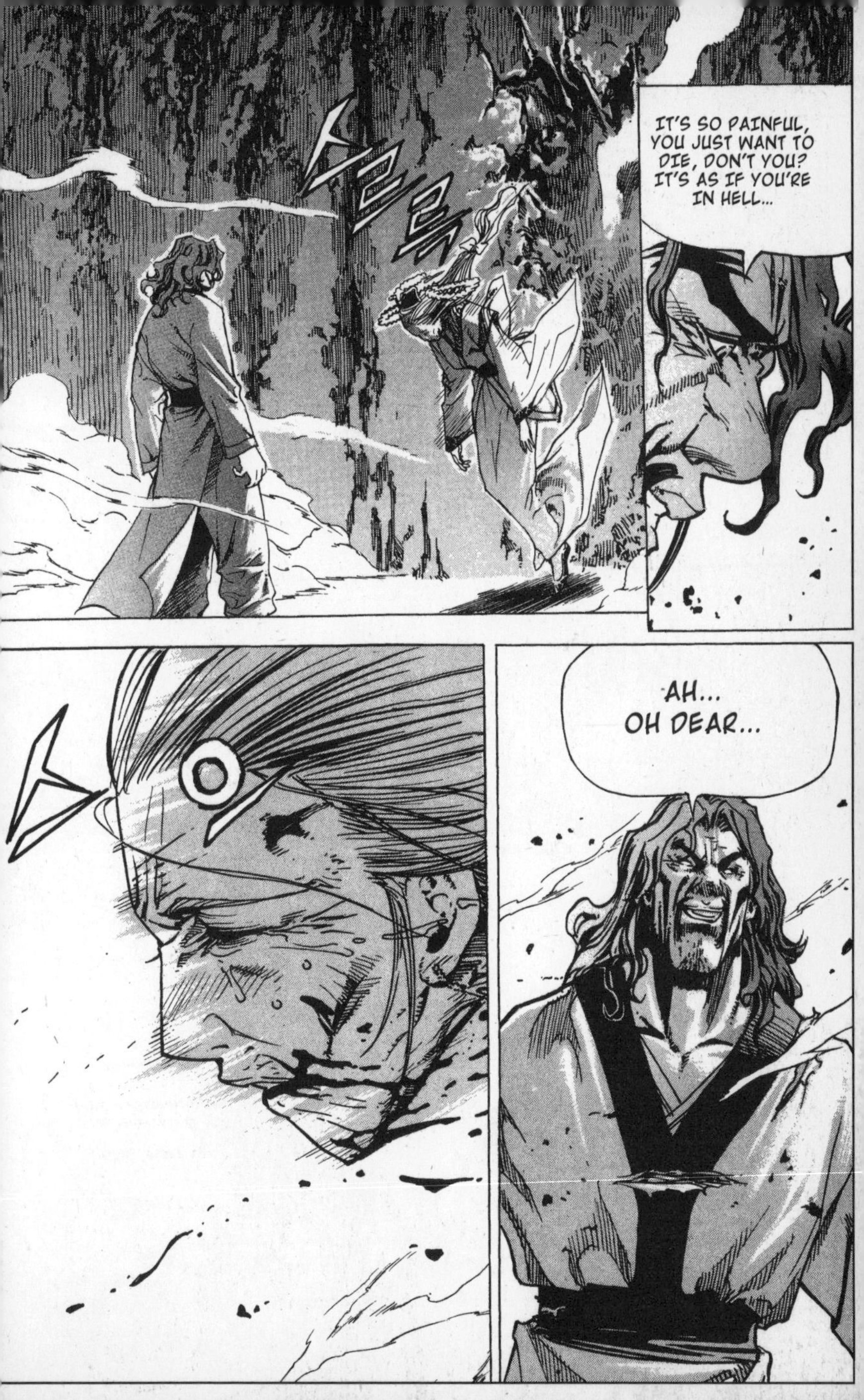
IT'S SO PAINFUL, YOU JUST WANT TO DIE, DON'T YOU? IT'S AS IF YOU'RE IN HELL...
AH... OH DEAR...

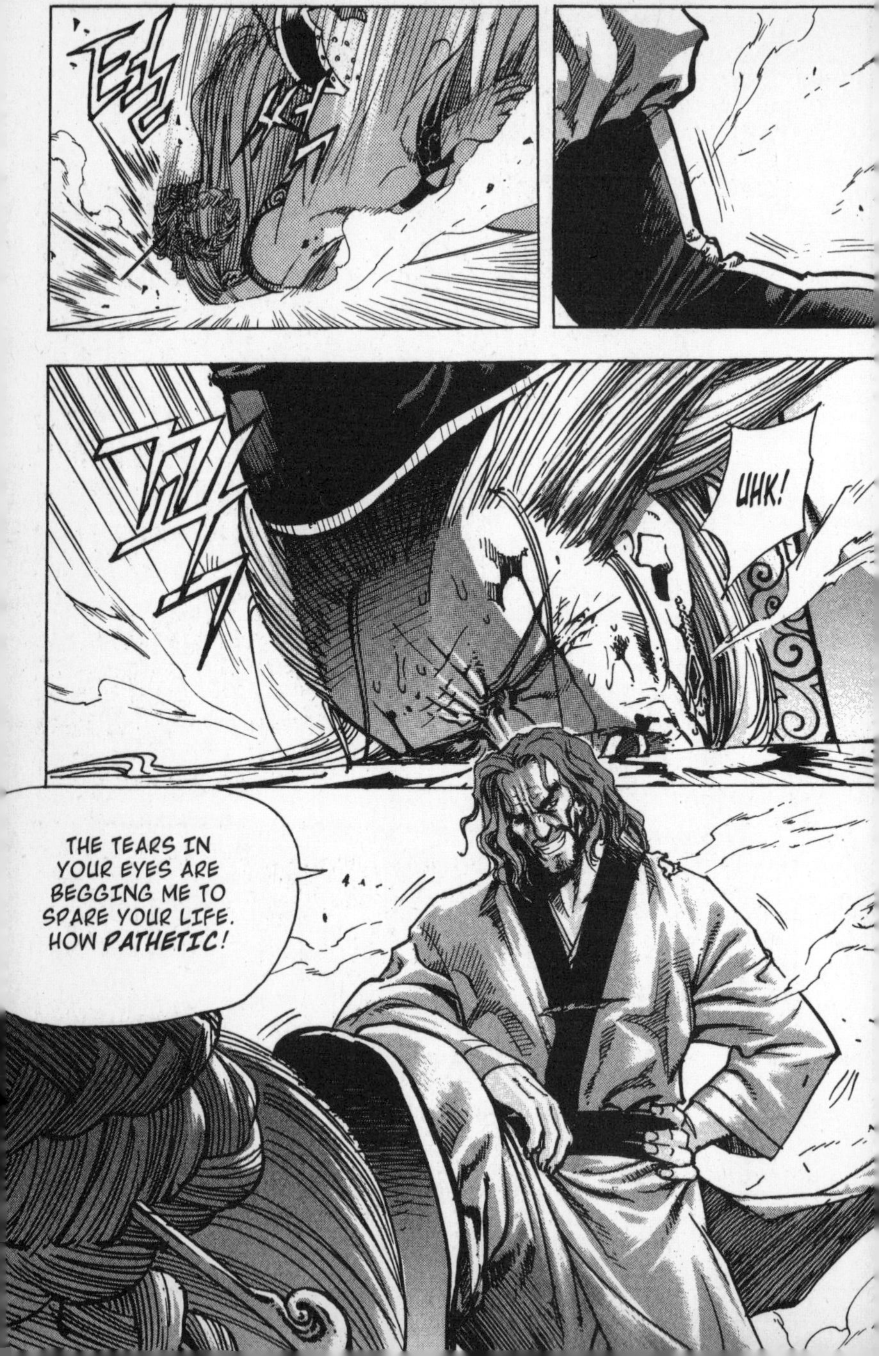
UHK!
THE TEARS IN YOUR EYES ARE BEGGING ME TO SPARE YOUR LIFE. HOW PATHETIC!

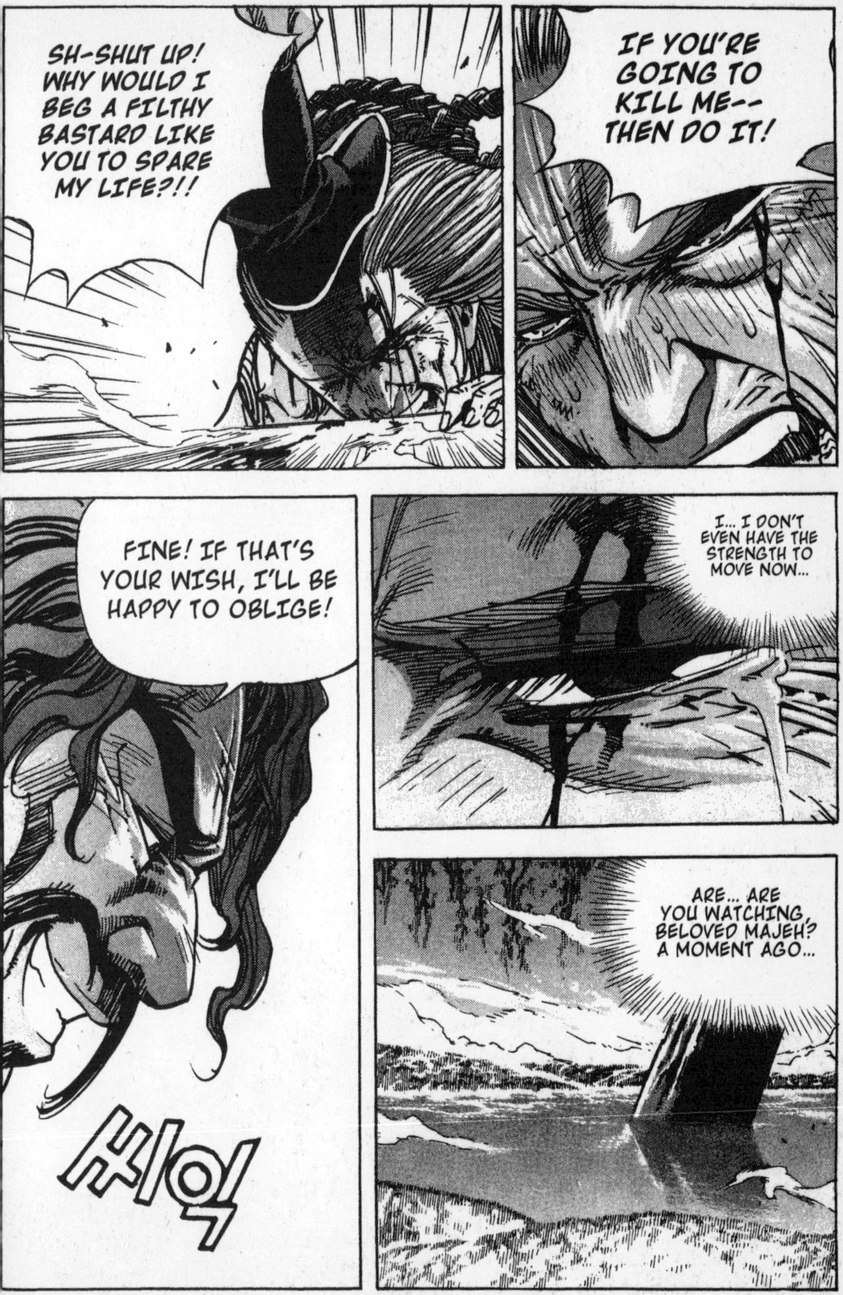
SH-SHUT UP! WHY WOULD I BEG A FILTHY BASTARD LIKE YOU TO SPARE MY LIFE?!!
IF YOU'RE GOING TO KILL ME-- THEN DO IT!
FINE! IF THAT'S YOUR WISH, I'LL BE HAPPY TO OBLIGE!
I... I DON'T EVEN HAVE THE STRENGTH TO MOVE NOW...
ARE... ARE YOU WATCHING, BELOVED MAJEH? A MOMENT AGO...

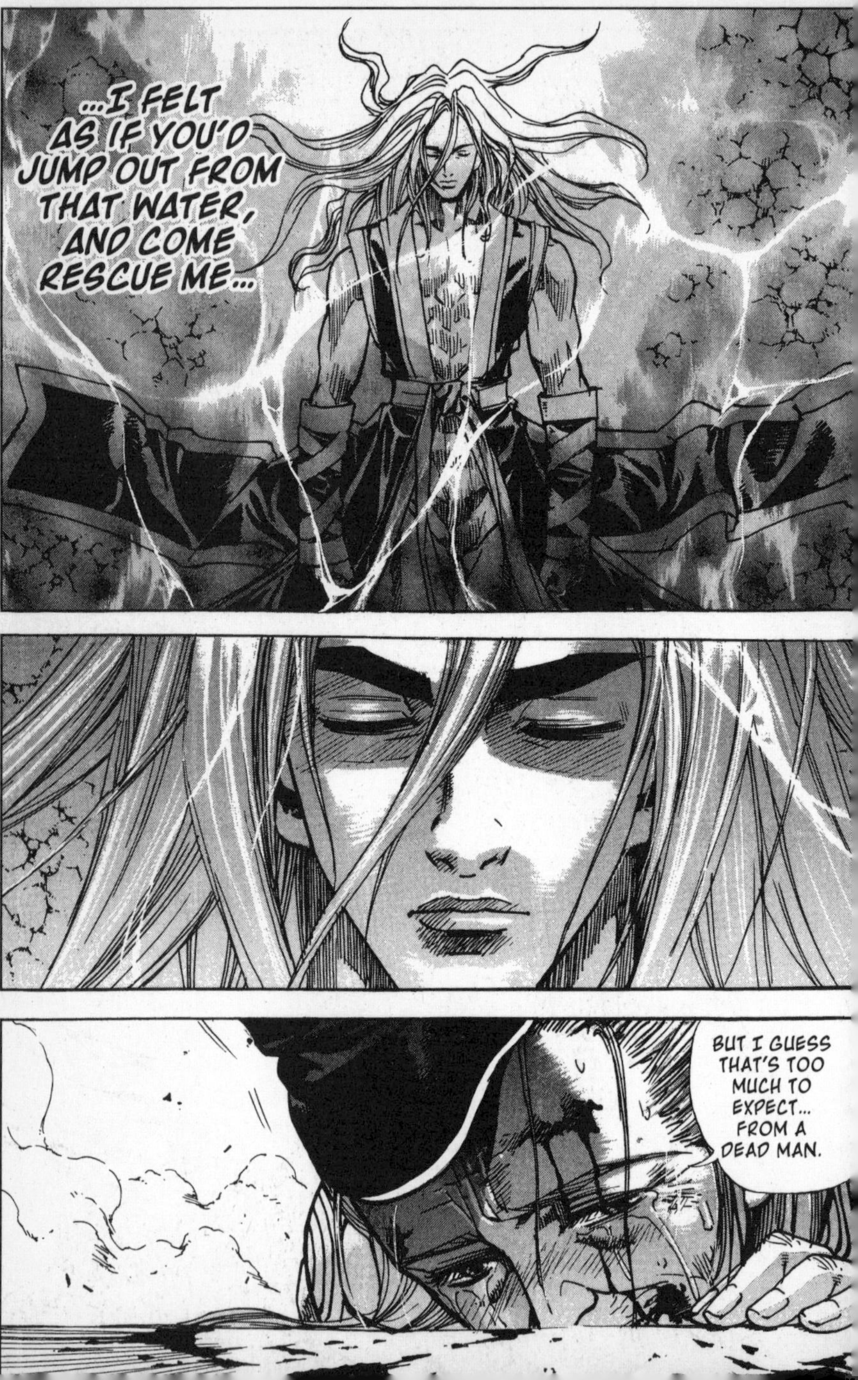
...I FELT AS IF YOU'D JUMP OUT FROM THAT WATER, AND COME RESCUE ME...
BUT I GUESS THAT'S TOO MUCH TO EXPECT... FROM A DEAD MAN.

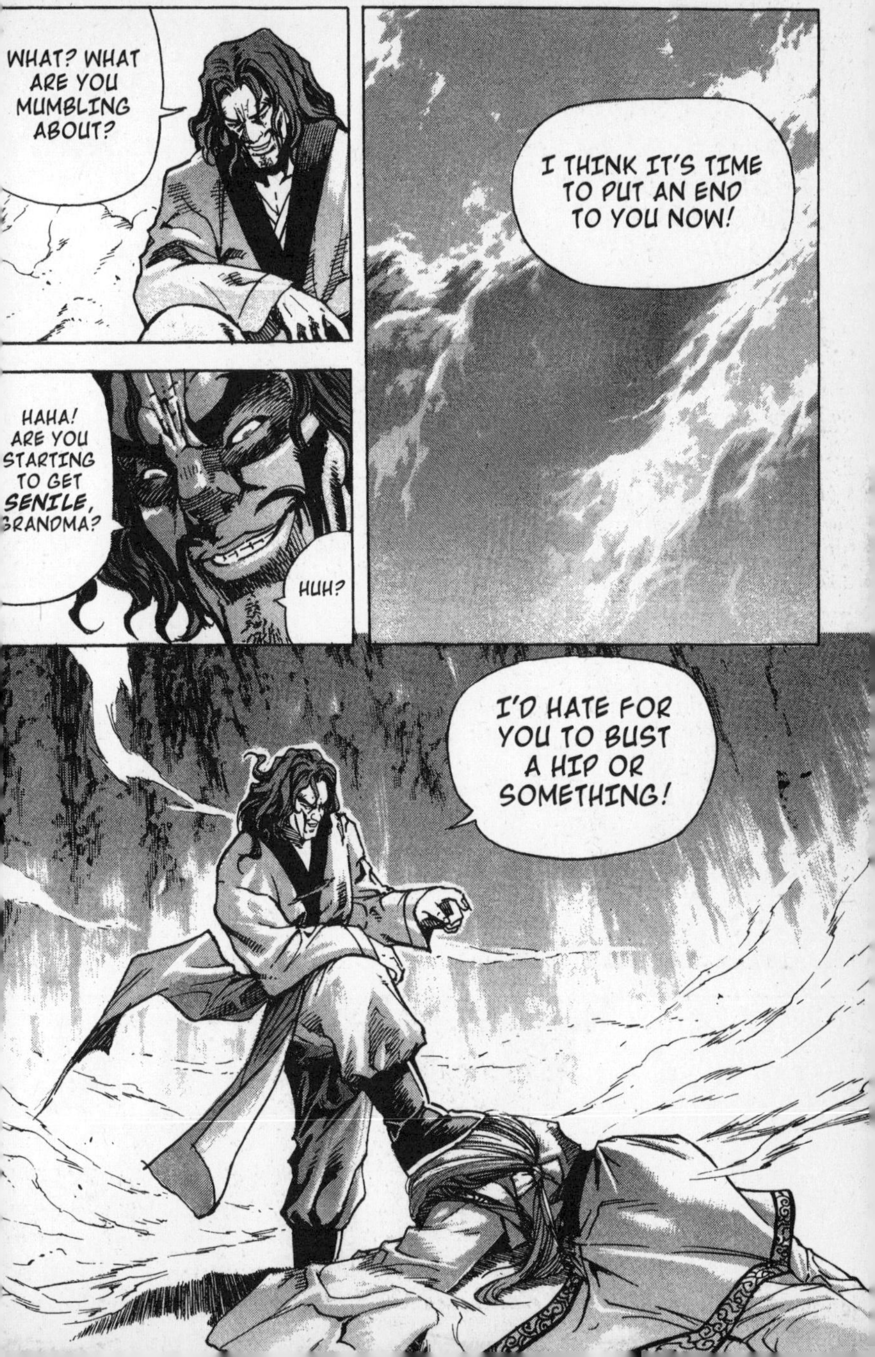
WHAT? WHAT ARE YOU MUMBLING ABOUT?
HAHA! ARE YOU STARTING TO GET SENILE, GRANDMA?
HUH?
I THINK IT'S TIME TO PUT AN END TO YOU NOW!
I'D HATE FOR YOU TO BUST A HIP OR SOMETHING!

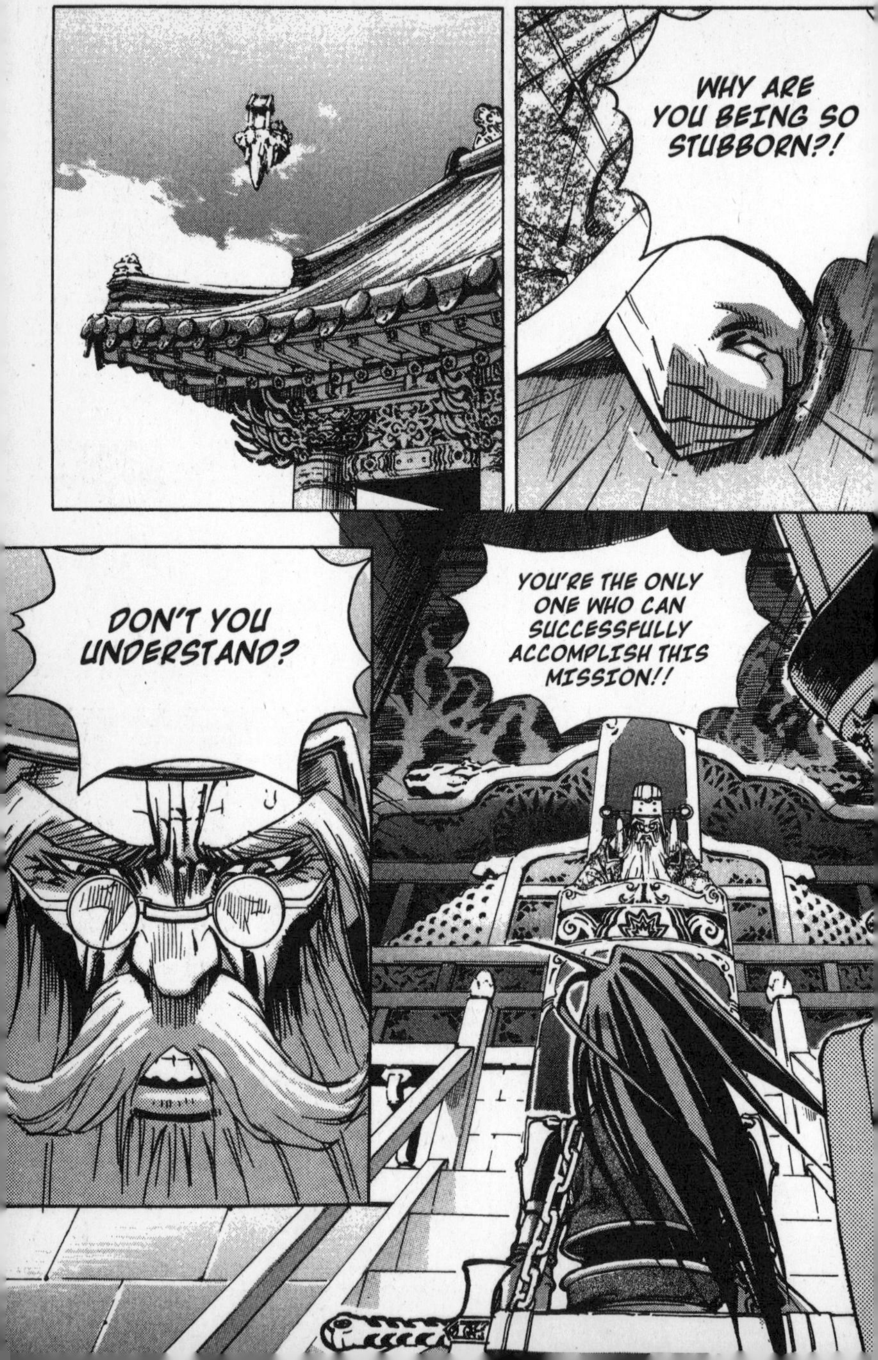
WHY ARE YOU BEING SO STUBBORN?!
DON'T YOU UNDERSTAND?
YOU'RE THE ONLY ONE WHO CAN SUCCESSFULLY ACCOMPLISH THIS MISSION!!

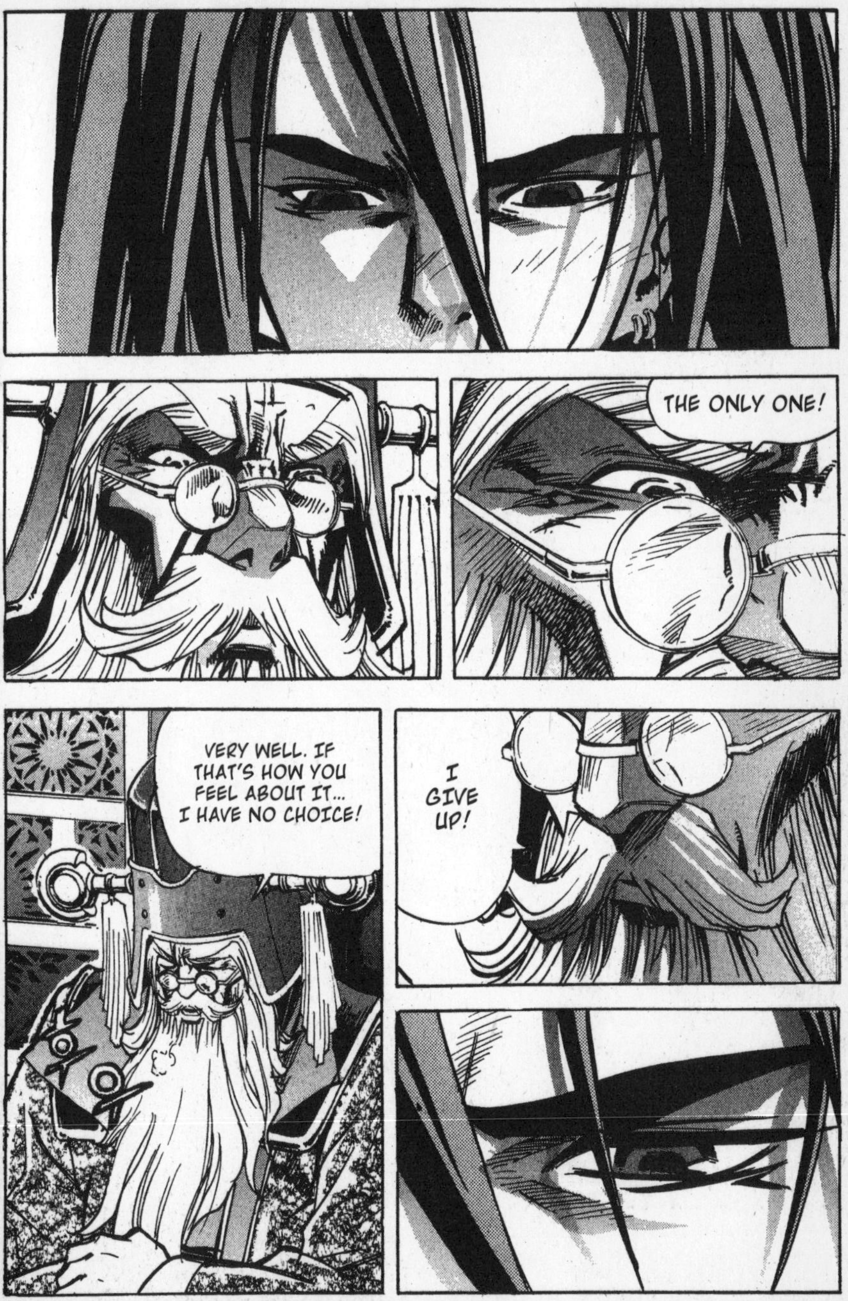
THE ONLY ONE!
VERY WELL. IF THAT'S HOW YOU FEEL ABOUT IT... I HAVE NO CHOICE!
I GIVE UP!

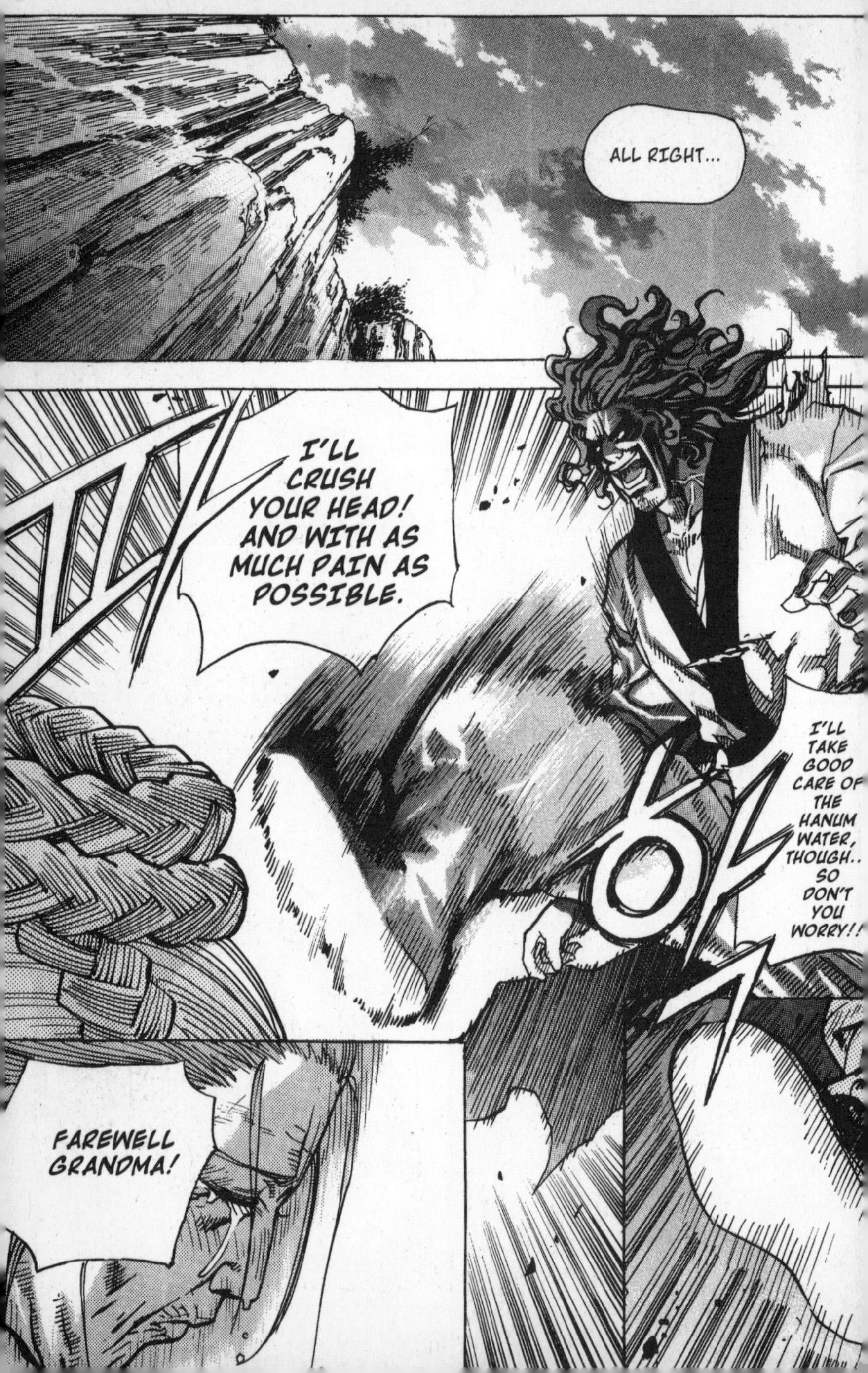
ALL RIGHT...
I'LL CRUSH YOUR HEAD! AND WITH AS MUCH PAIN AS POSSIBLE.
I'LL TAKE GOOD CARE OF THE HANUM WATER, THOUGH.. SO DON'T YOU WORRY!!
FAREWELL GRANDMA!

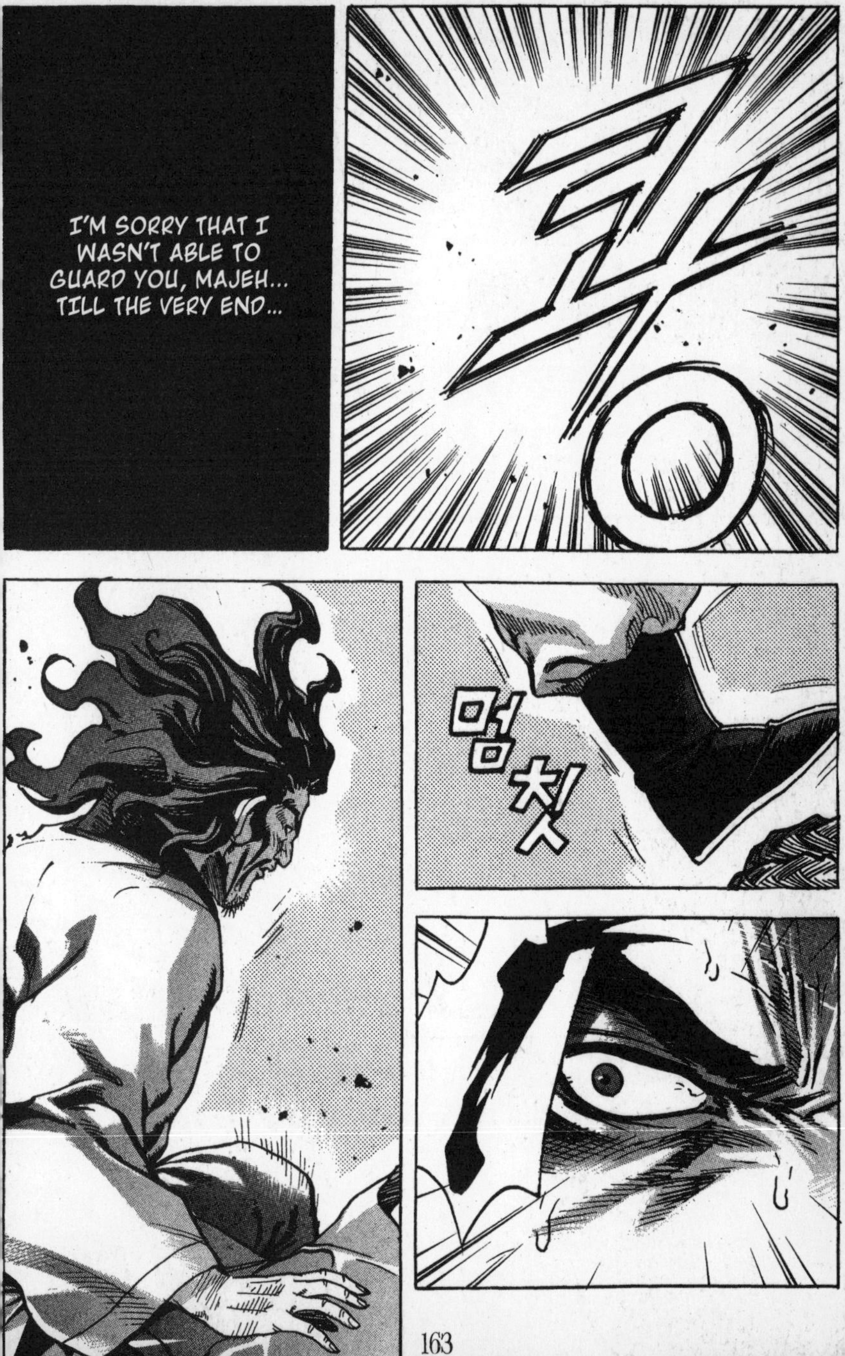
I'M SORRY THAT I WASN'T ABLE TO GUARD YOU, MAJEH... TILL THE VERY END...
멈칫

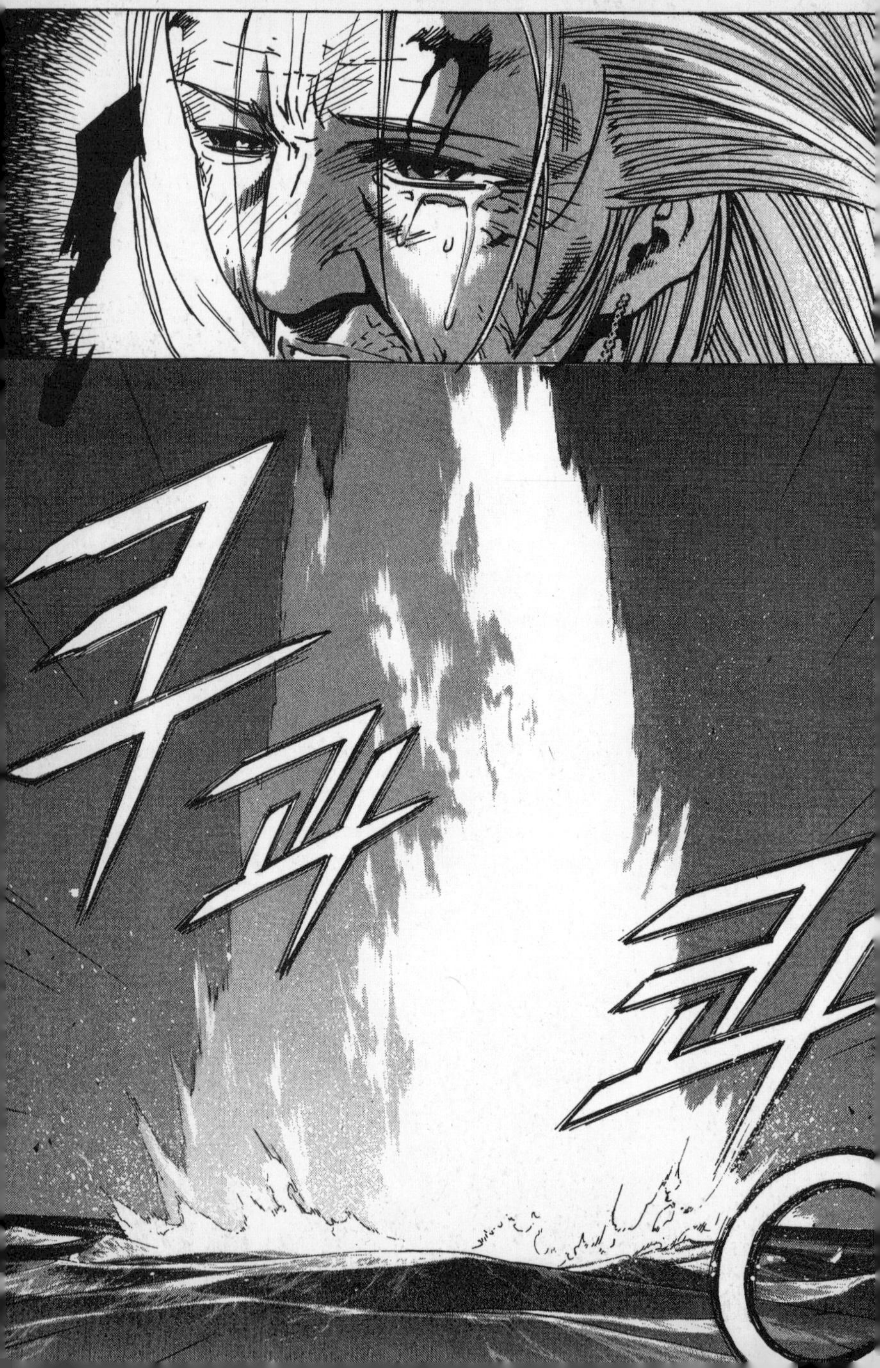

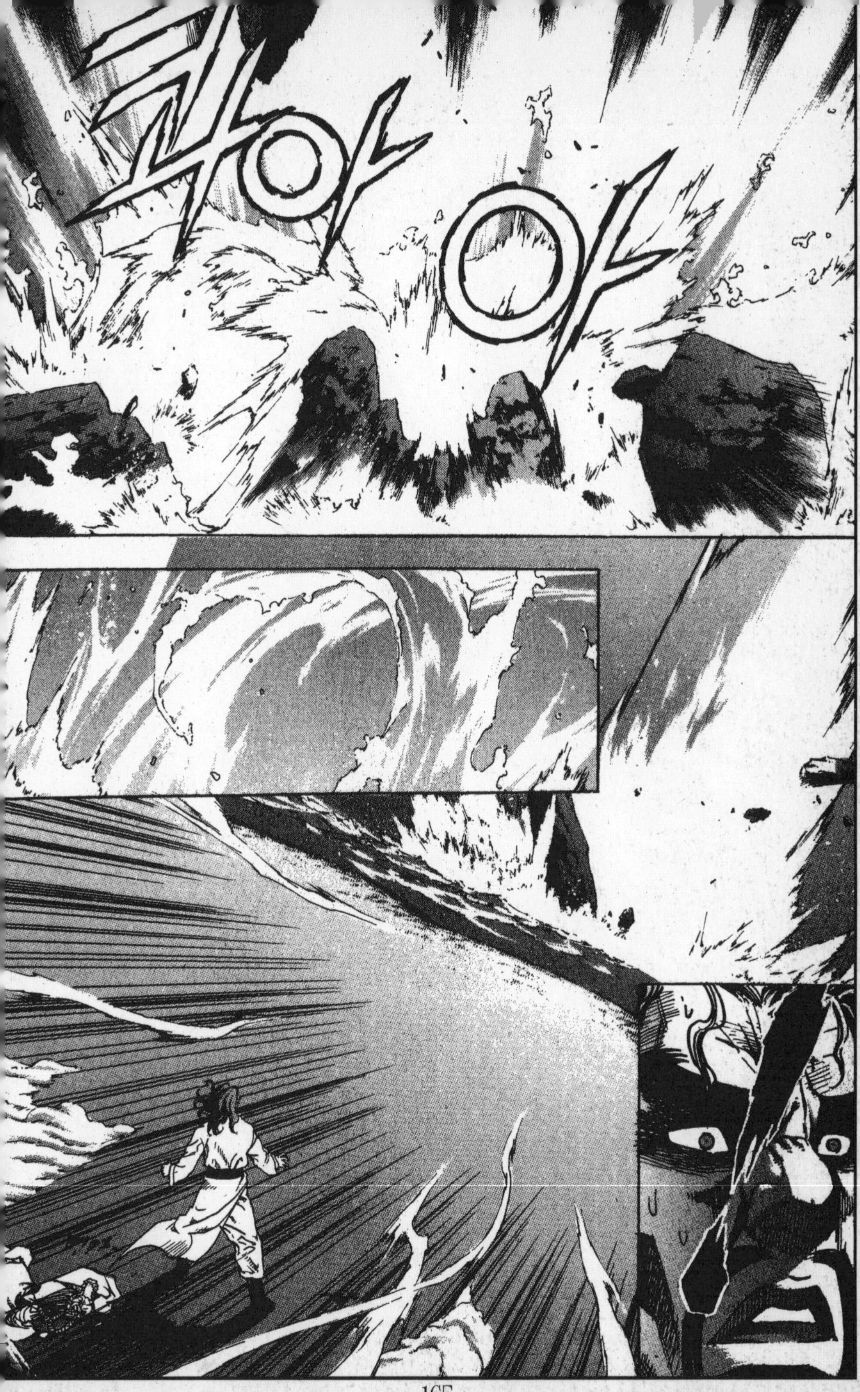

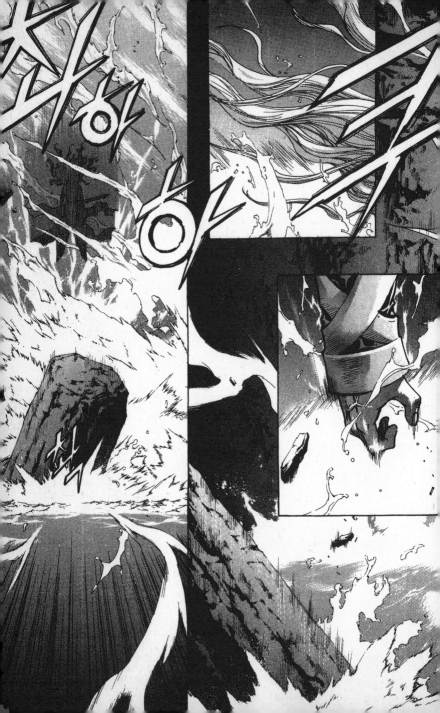

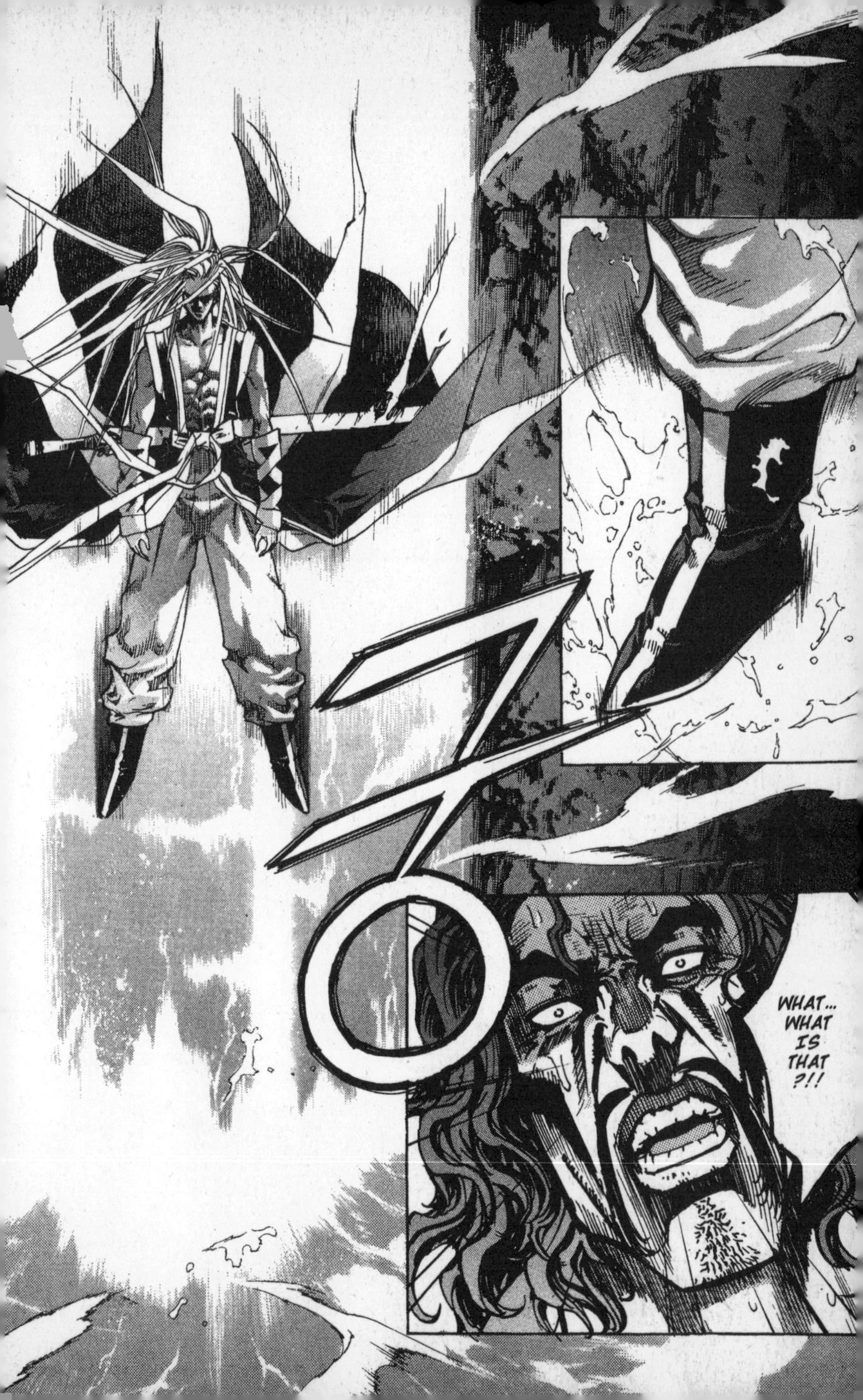
WHAT... WHAT IS THAT ?!!

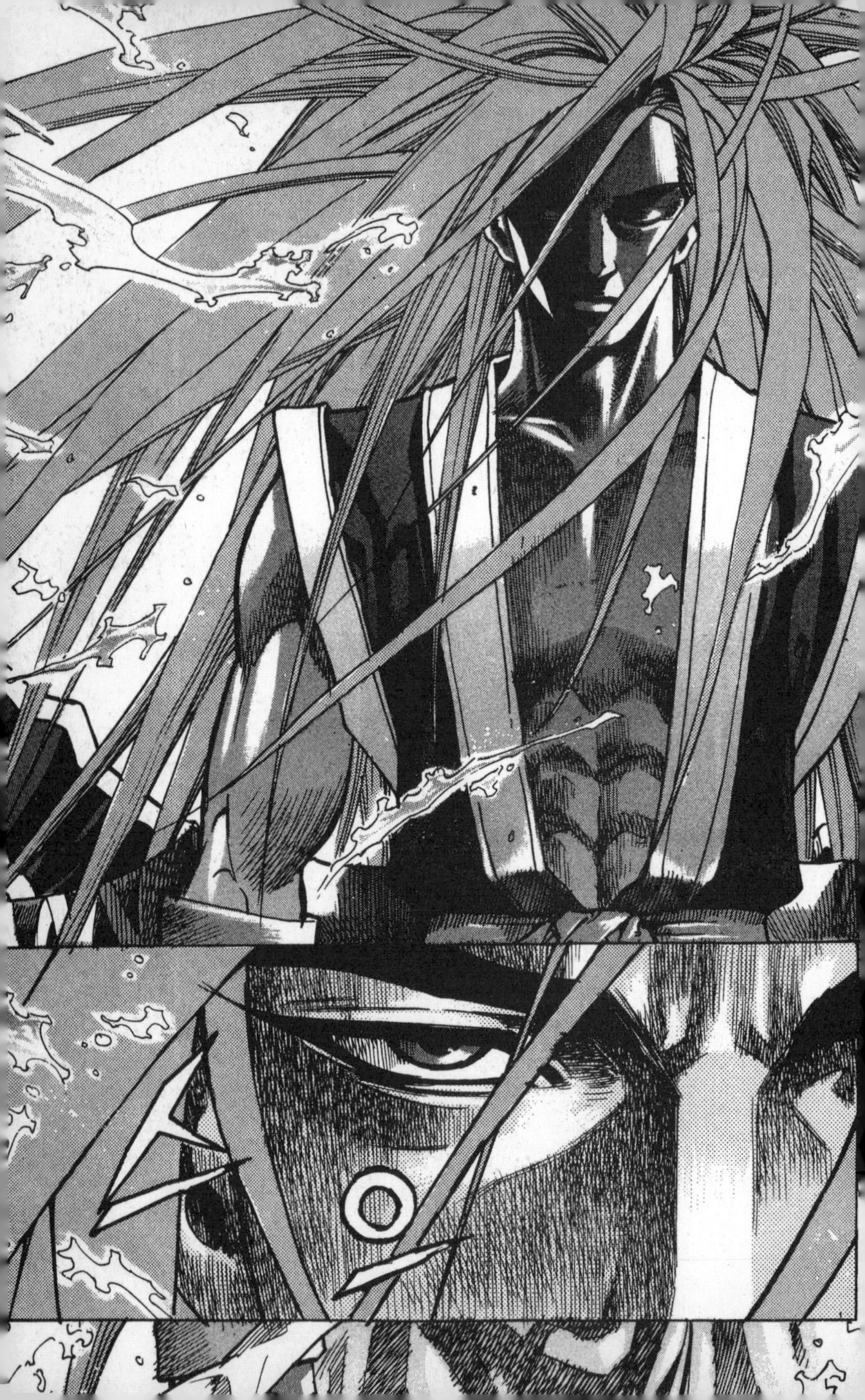

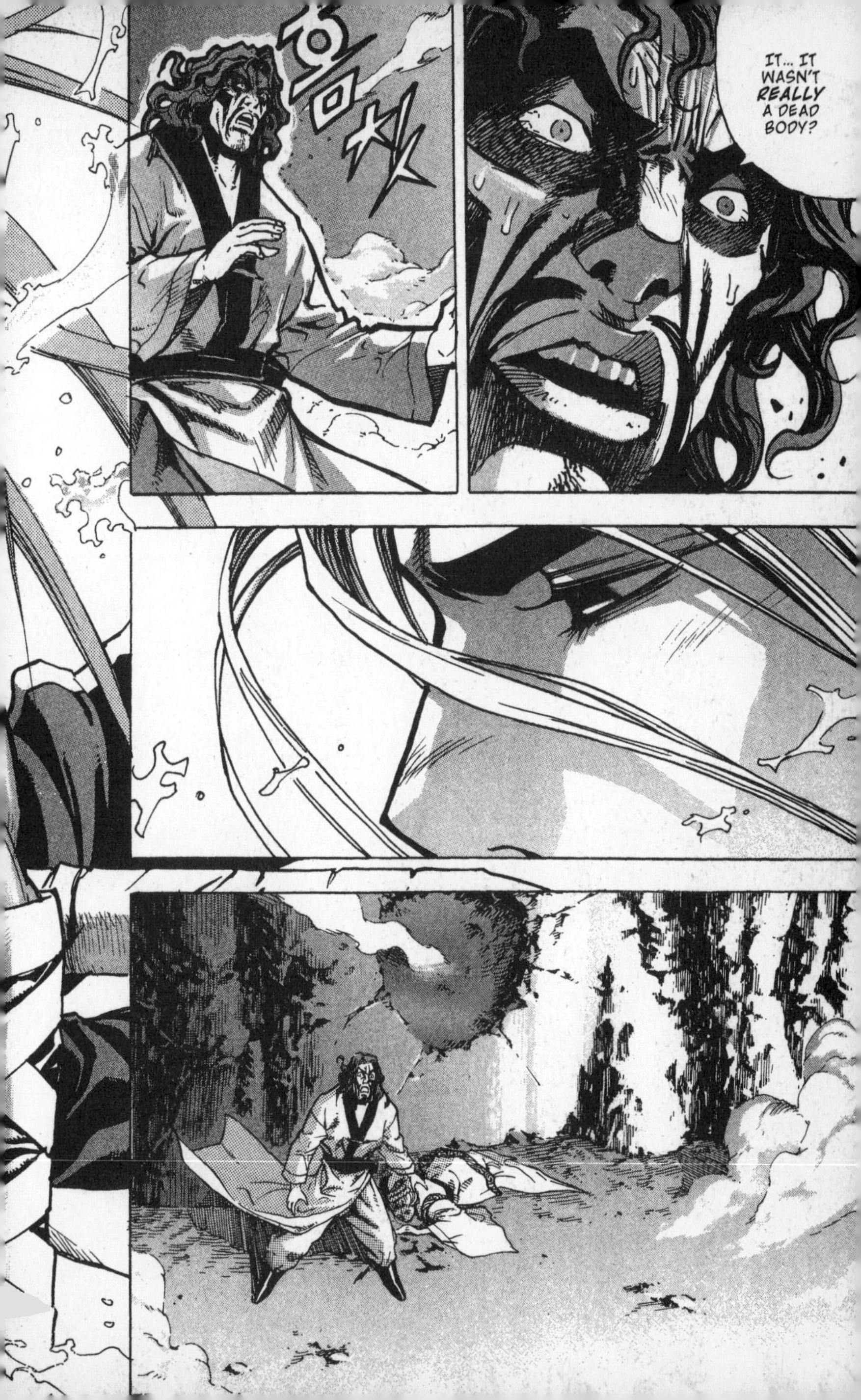
흠칫
IT... IT WASN'T *REALLY* A DEAD BODY?

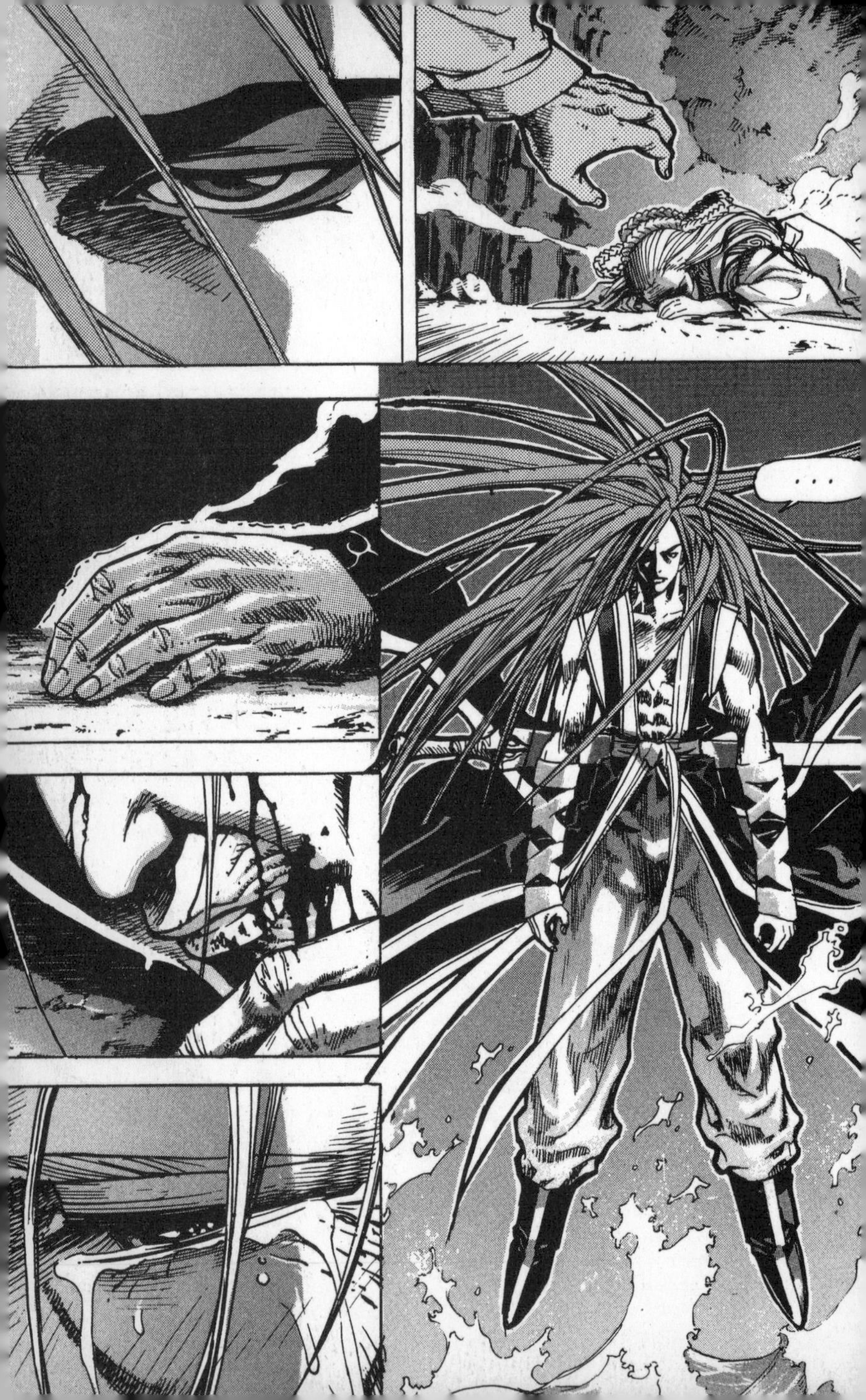
...

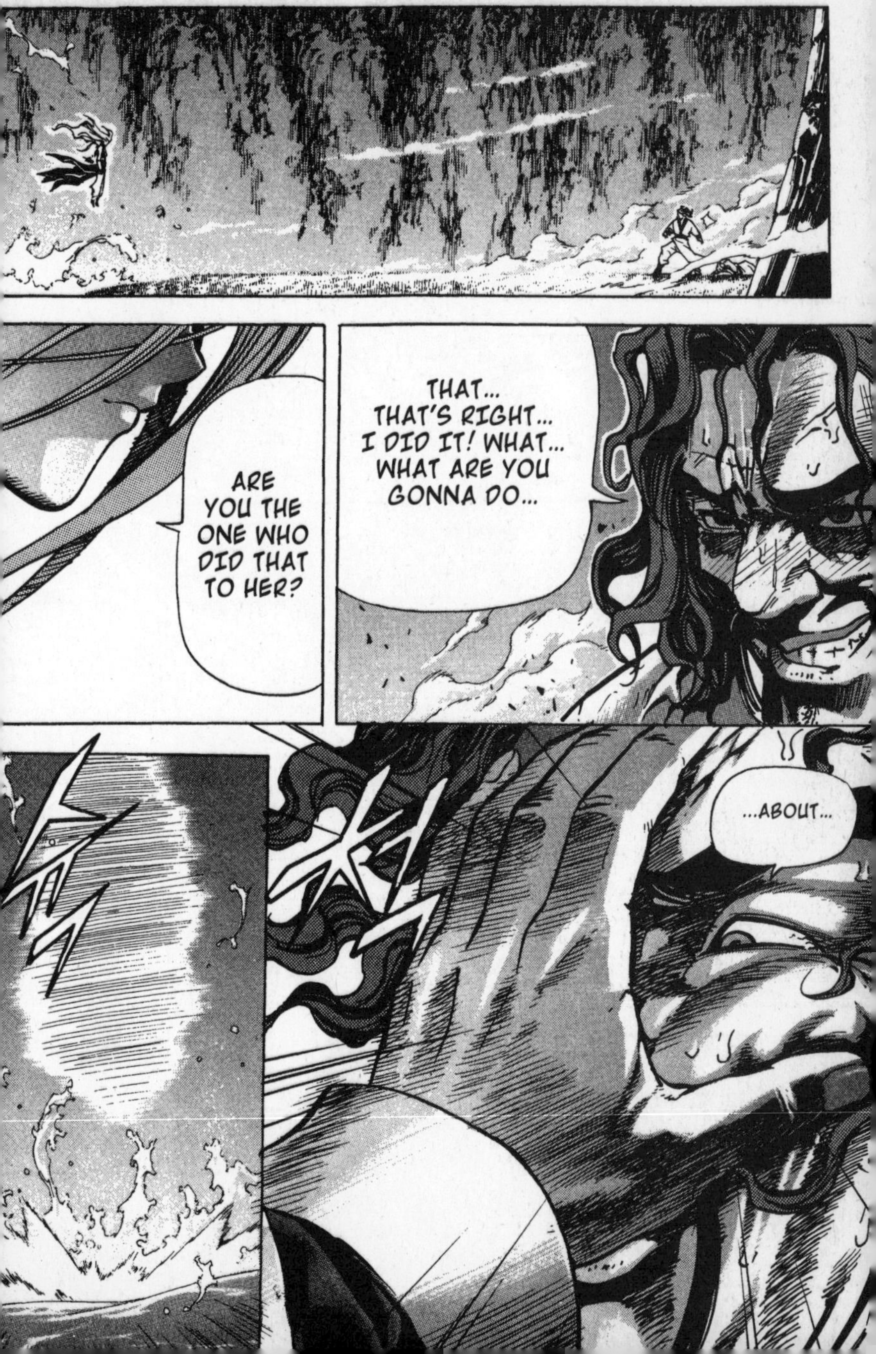
ARE YOU THE ONE WHO DID THAT TO HER?
THAT... THAT'S RIGHT... I DID IT! WHAT... WHAT ARE YOU GONNA DO...
...ABOUT...

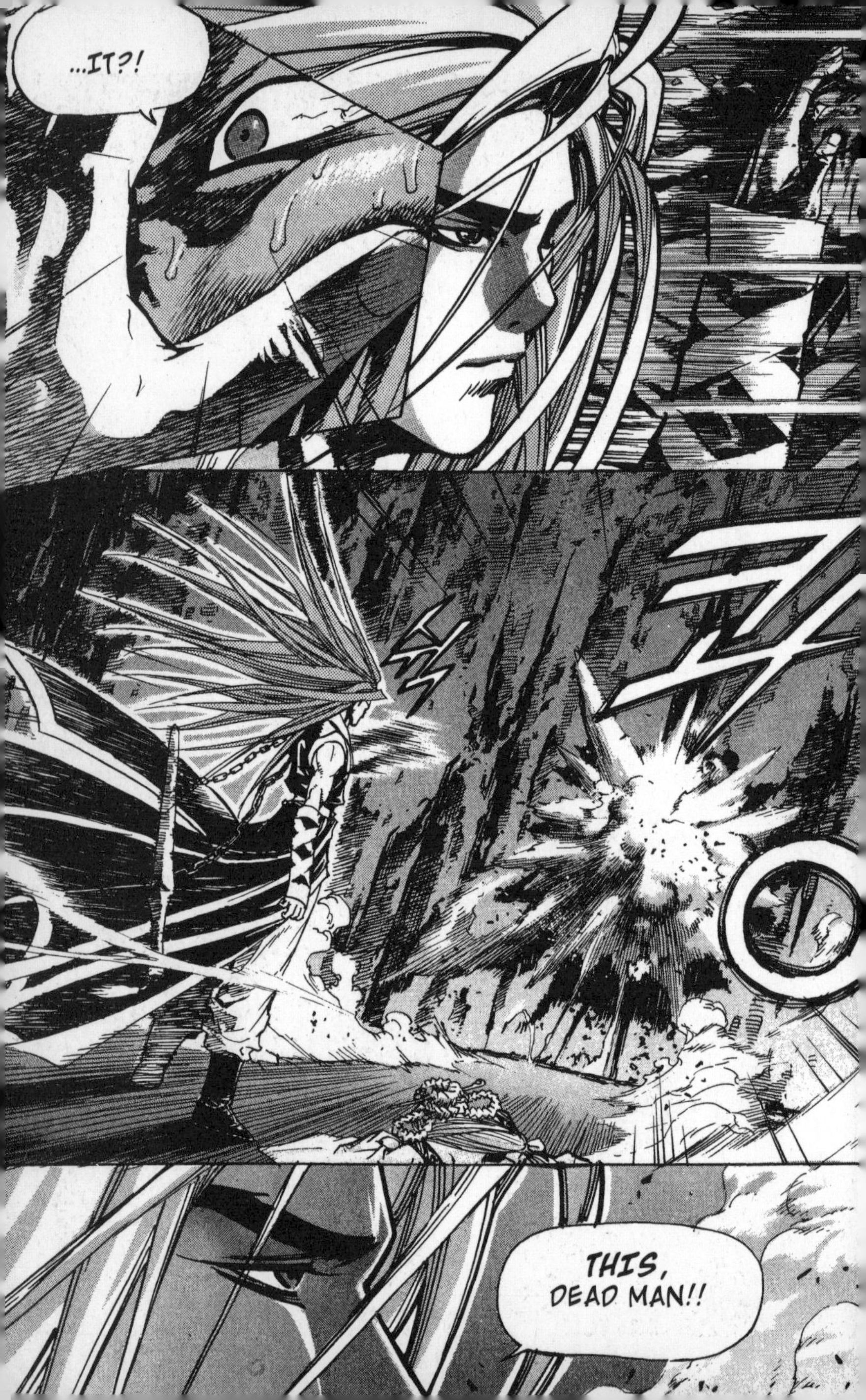
...IT?!
THIS, DEAD MAN!!

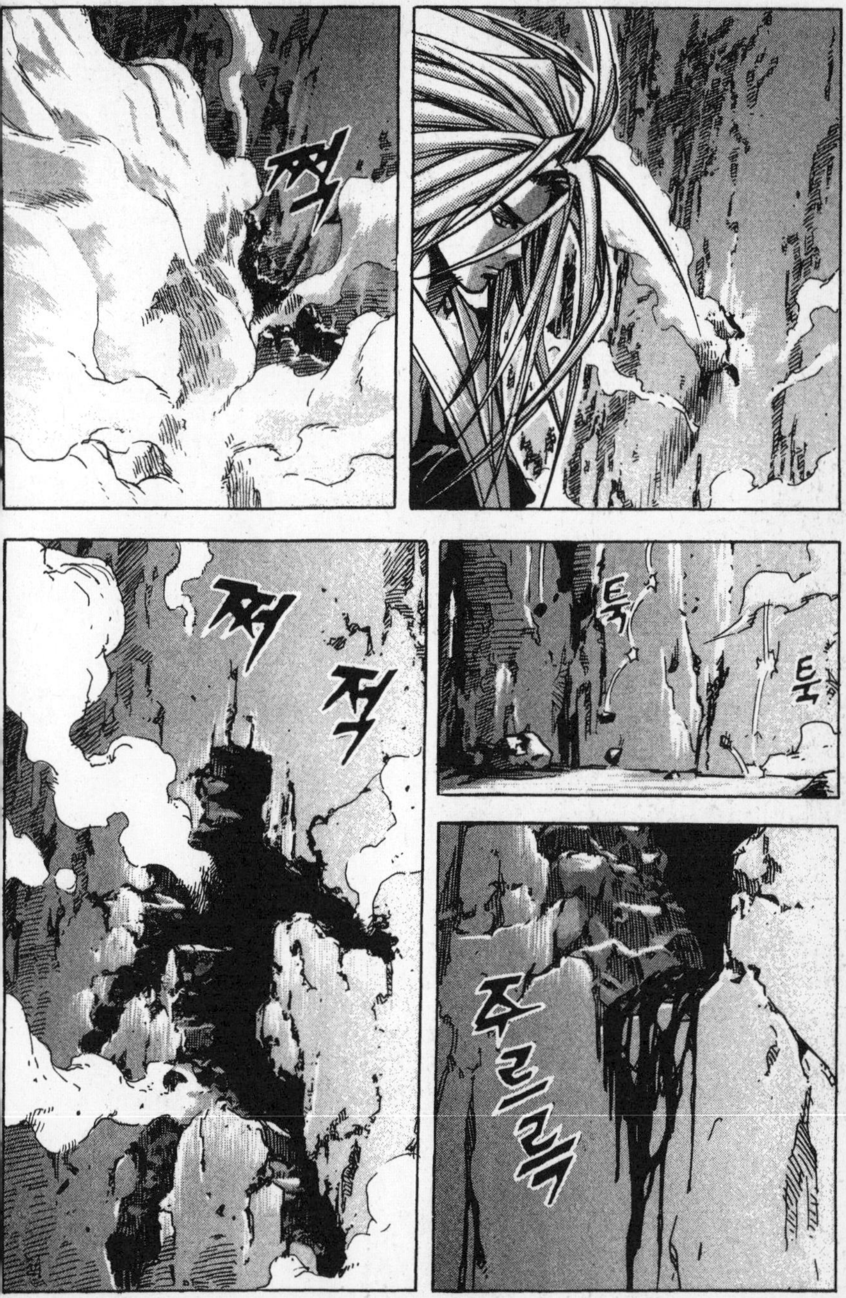
쩍
쩌
적
툭
툭
주르륵

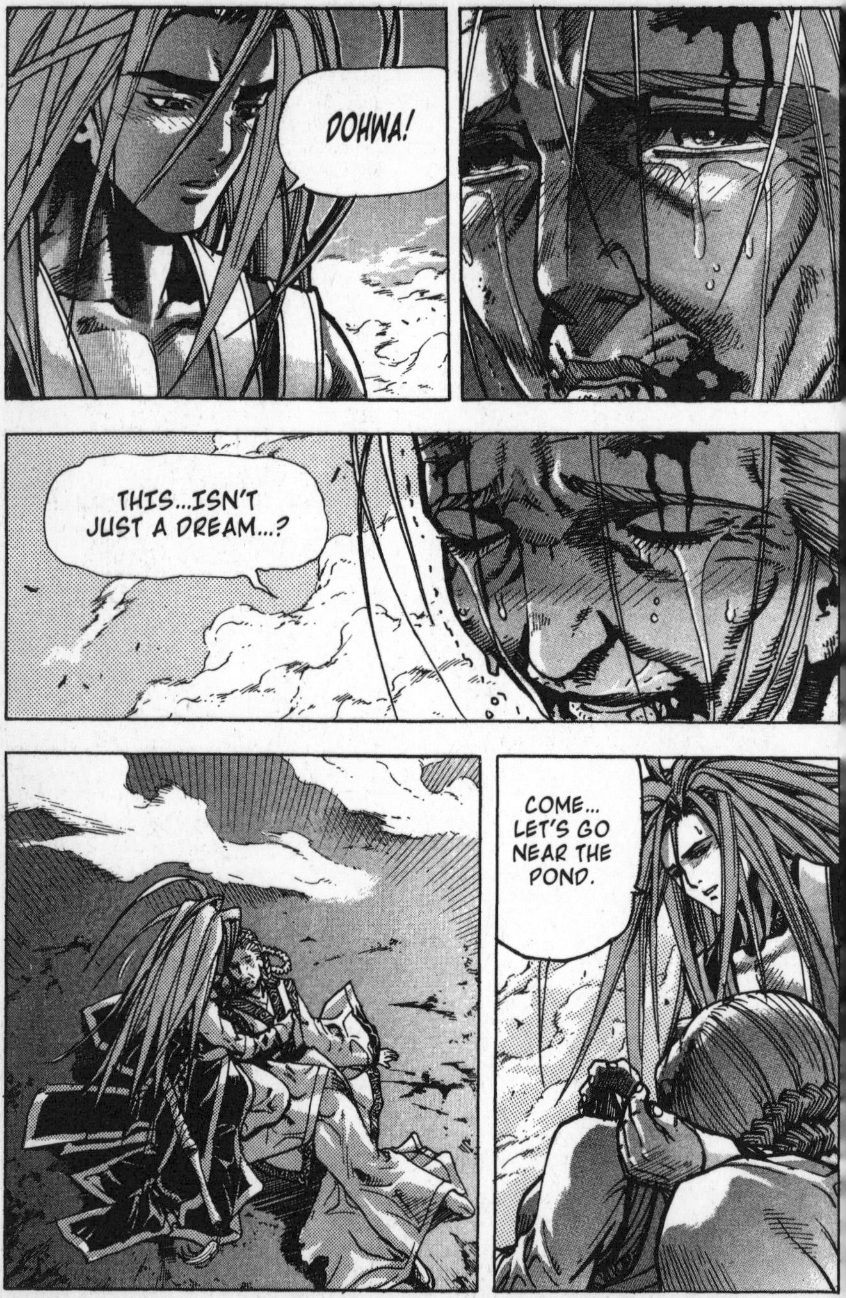
DOHWA!
THIS...ISN'T JUST A DREAM...?
COME... LET'S GO NEAR THE POND.

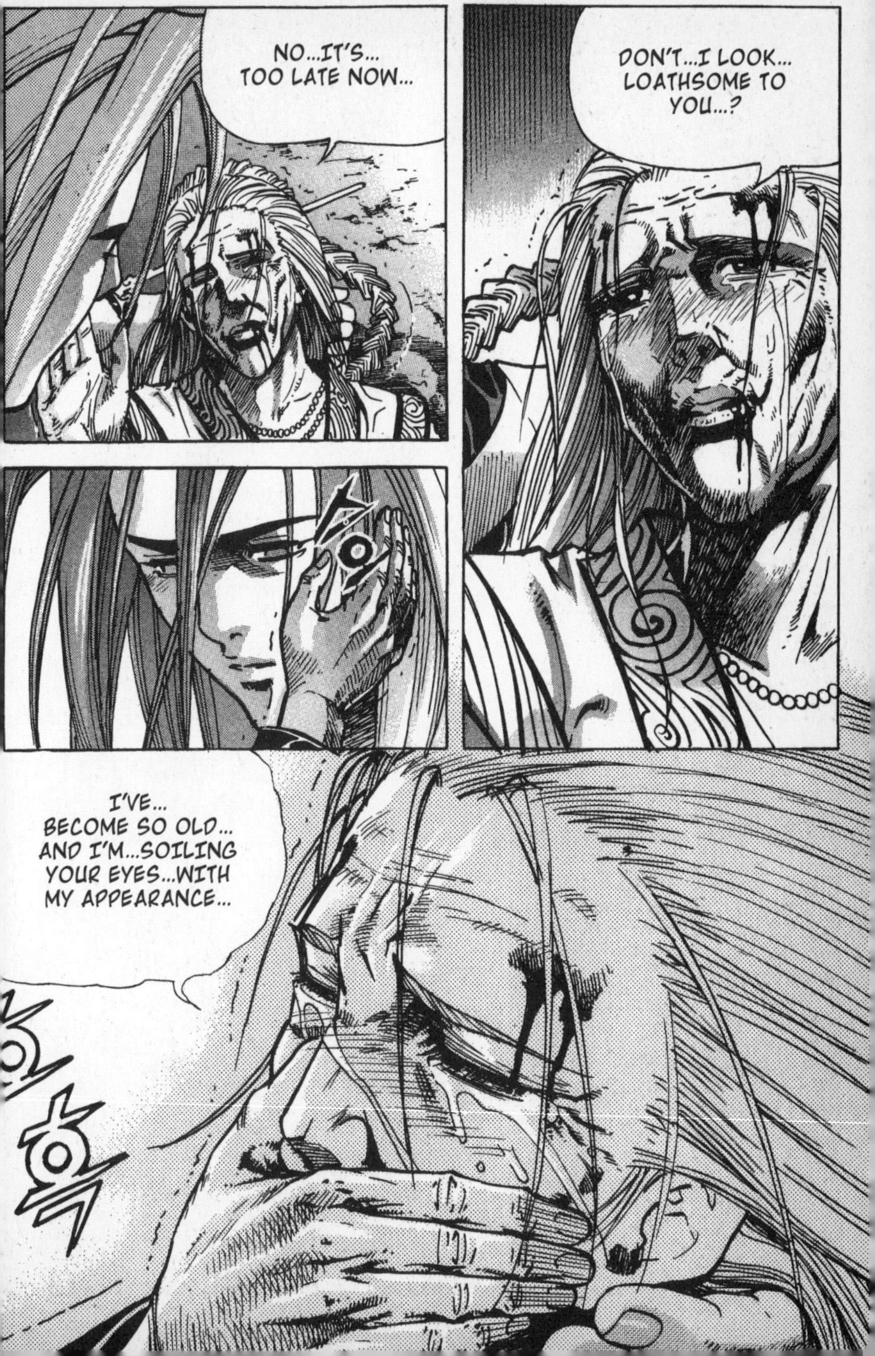
NO...IT'S... TOO LATE NOW...
DON'T...I LOOK... LOATHSOME TO YOU...?
I'VE... BECOME SO OLD... AND I'M...SOILING YOUR EYES...WITH MY APPEARANCE...

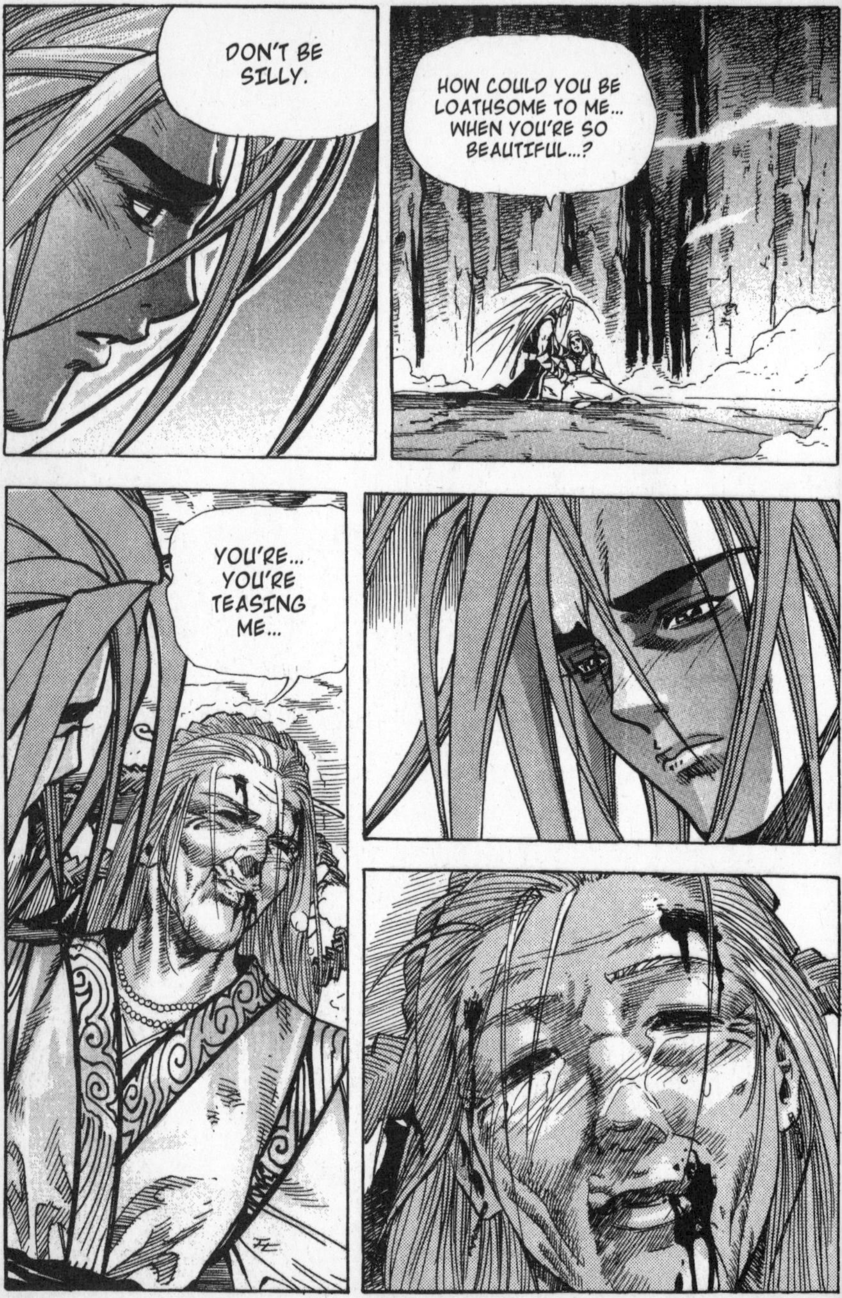
DON'T BE SILLY.
HOW COULD YOU BE LOATHSOME TO ME... WHEN YOU'RE SO BEAUTIFUL...?
YOU'RE... YOU'RE TEASING ME...

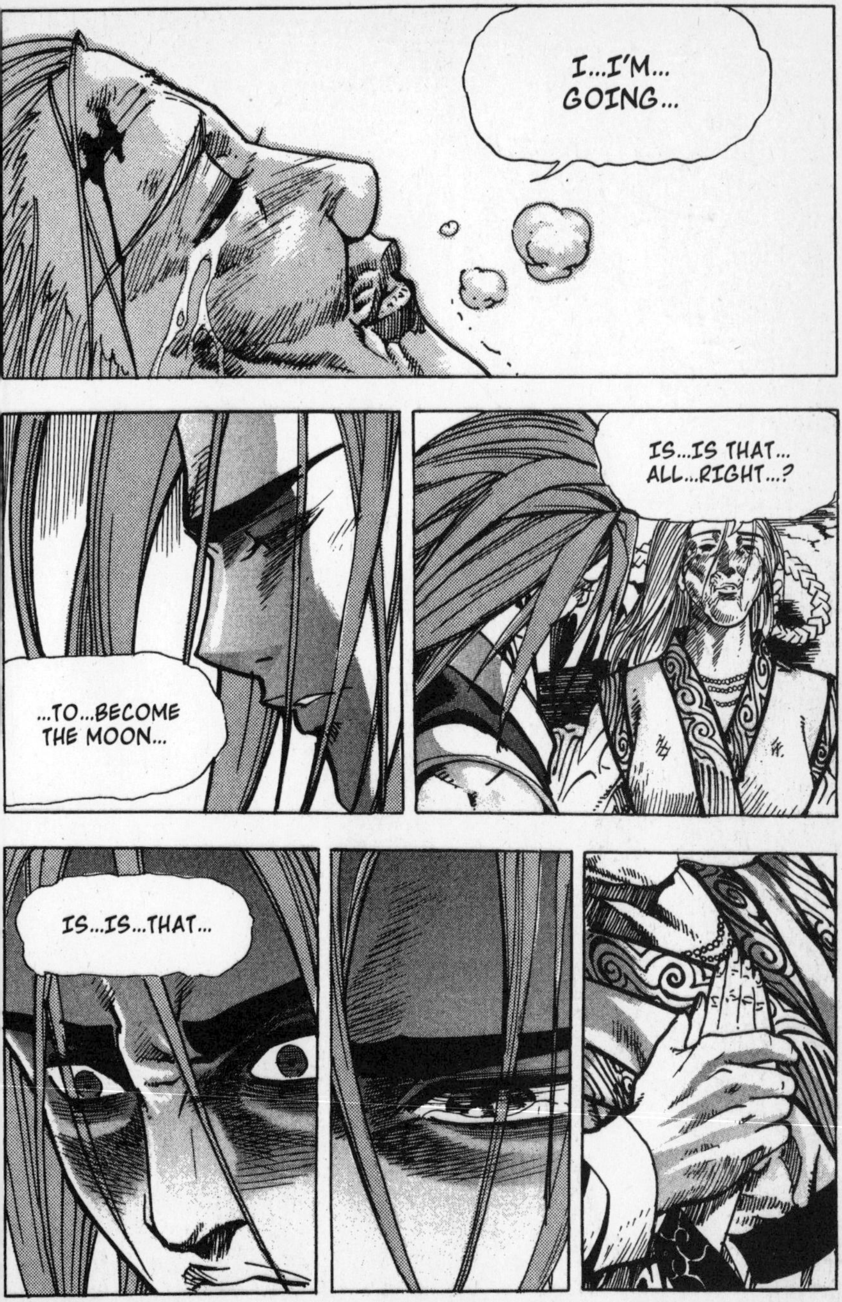
I...I'M... GOING...
...TO...BECOME THE MOON...
IS...IS THAT... ALL...RIGHT...?
IS...IS...THAT...

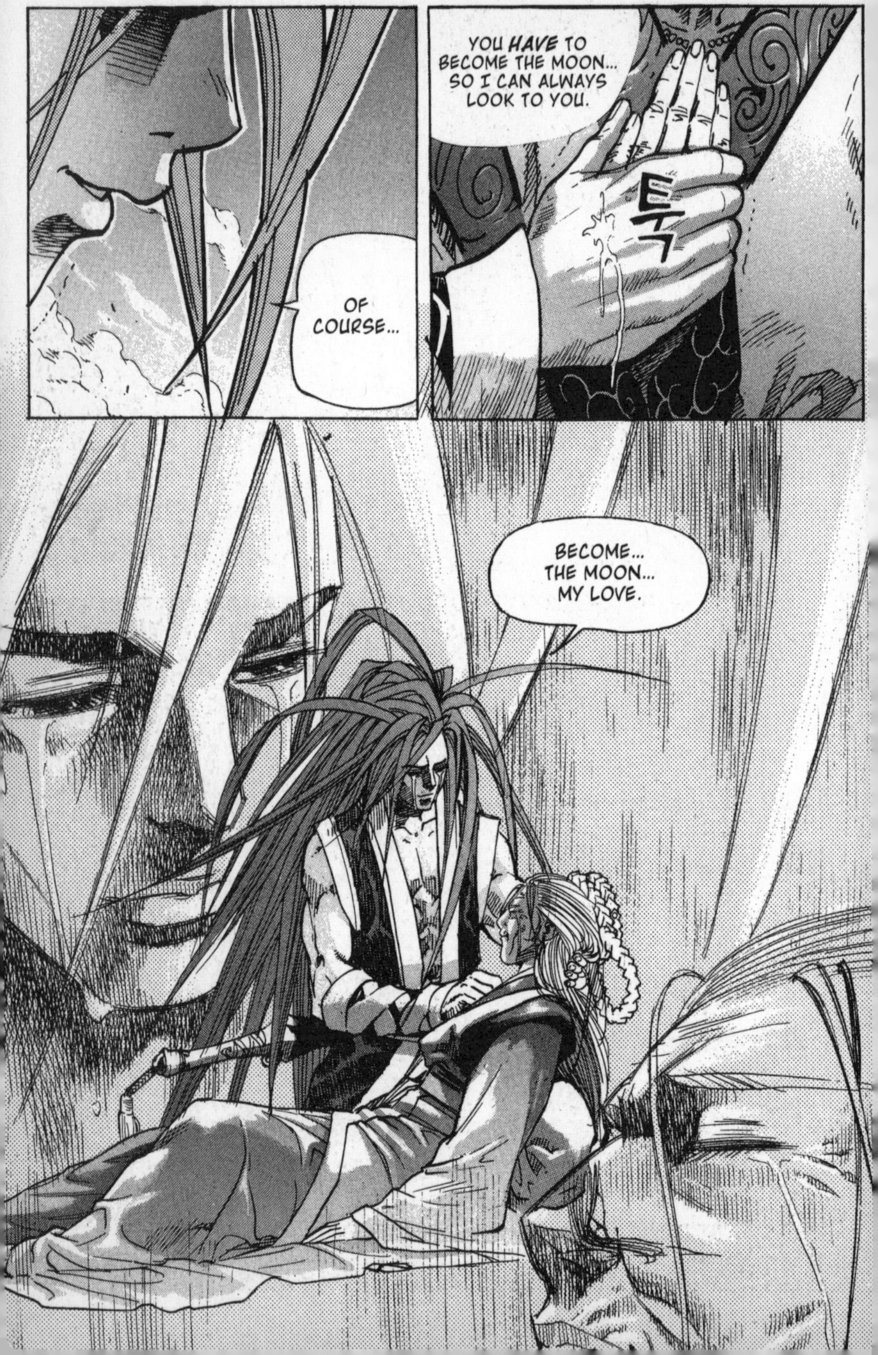
OF COURSE...
YOU *HAVE* TO BECOME THE MOON... SO I CAN ALWAYS LOOK TO YOU.
BECOME... THE MOON... MY LOVE.

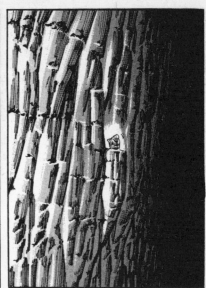

SNIFF...
SNIFF...
SO
SAD.

SNIFF...

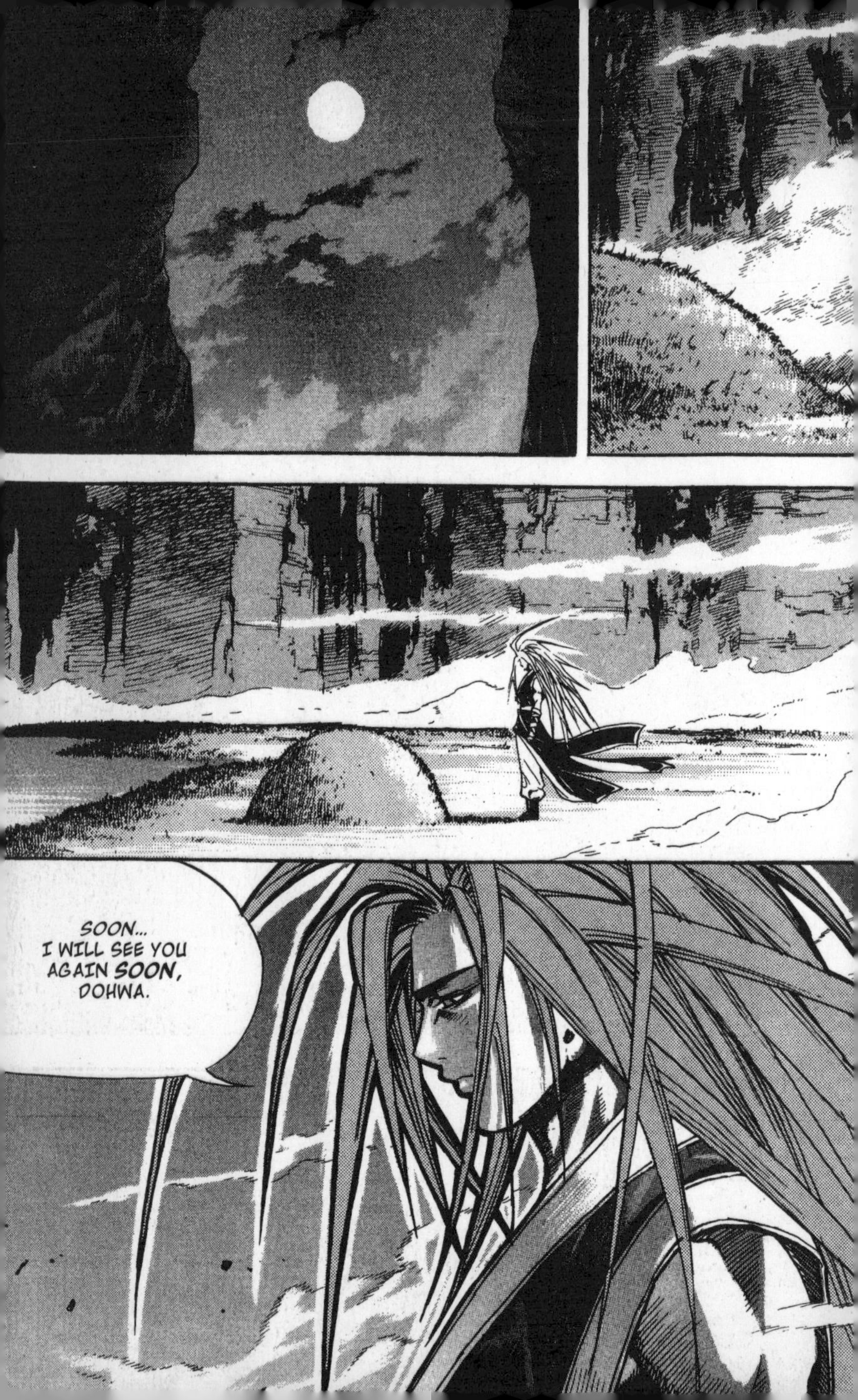
SOON... I WILL SEE YOU AGAIN SOON, DOHWA.

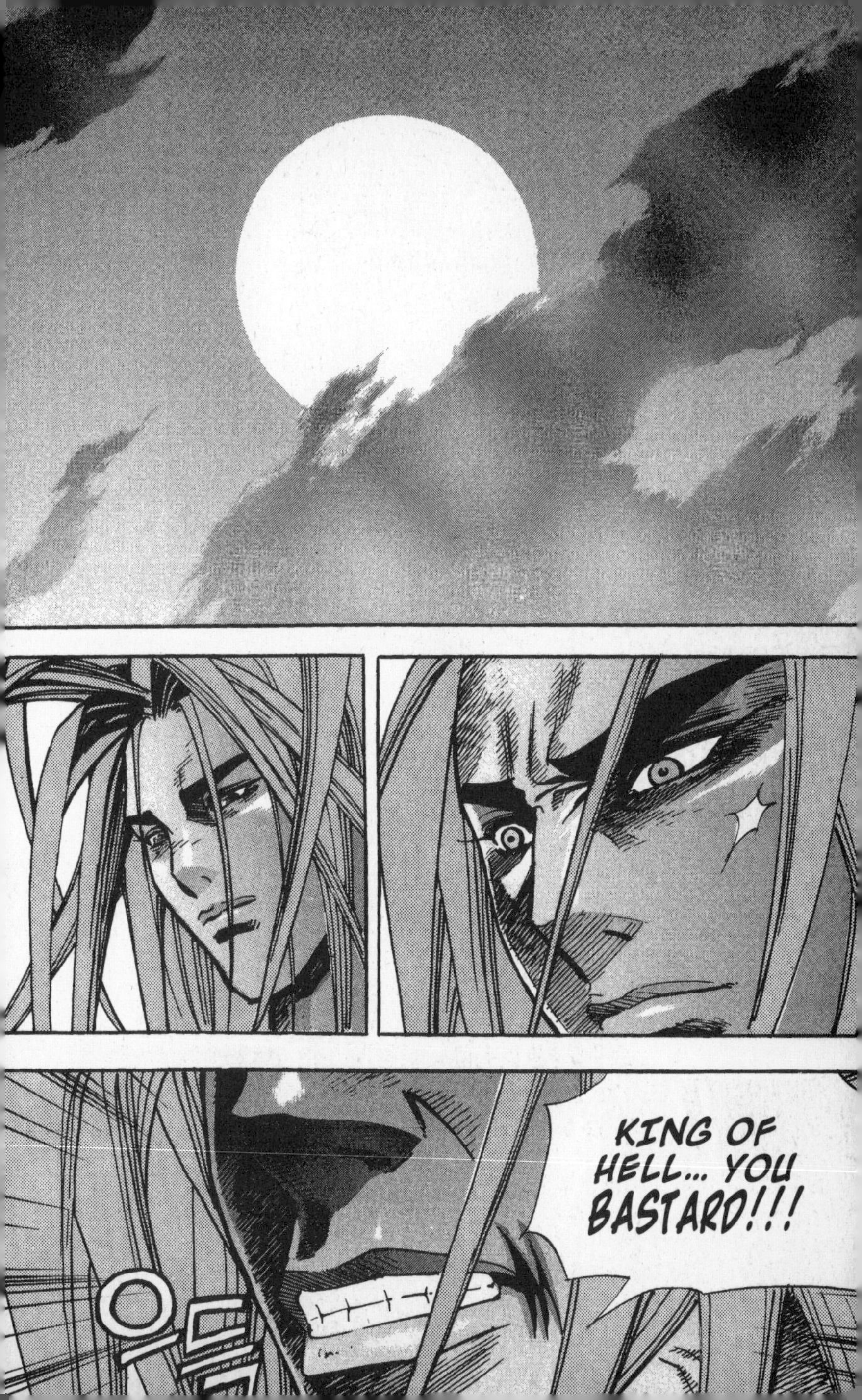
KING OF HELL... YOU BASTARD!!!

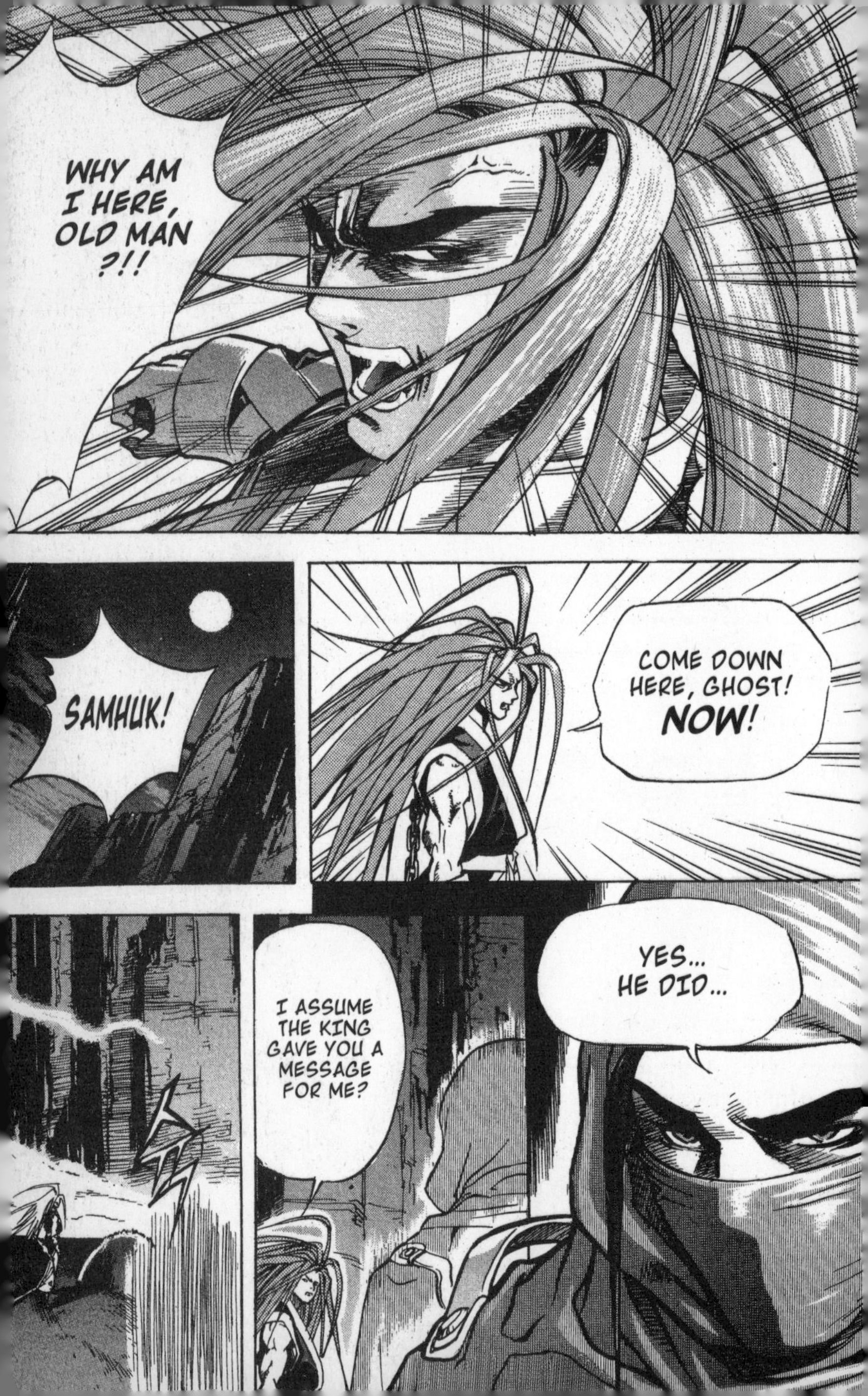
WHY AM I HERE, OLD MAN ?!!
SAMHUK!
COME DOWN HERE, GHOST! NOW!
I ASSUME THE KING GAVE YOU A MESSAGE FOR ME?
YES... HE DID...

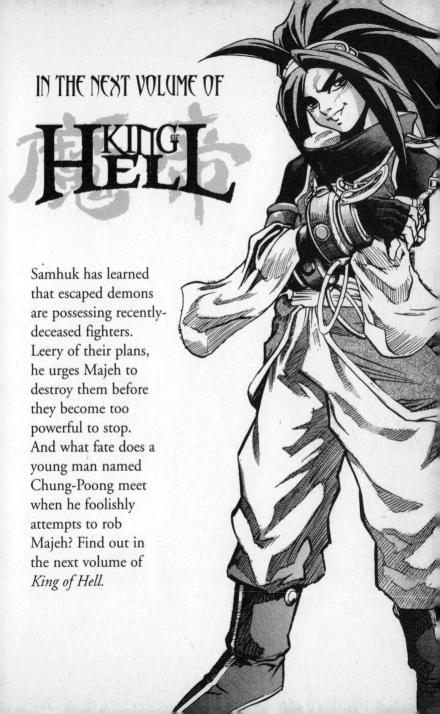

IN THE NEXT VOLUME OF

KING OF HELL

Samhuk has learned
that escaped demons
are possessing recently-
deceased fighters.
Leery of their plans,
he urges Majeh to
destroy them before
they become too
powerful to stop.
And what fate does a
young man named
Chung-Poong meet
when he foolishly
attempts to rob
Majeh? Find out in
the next volume of
King of Hell.

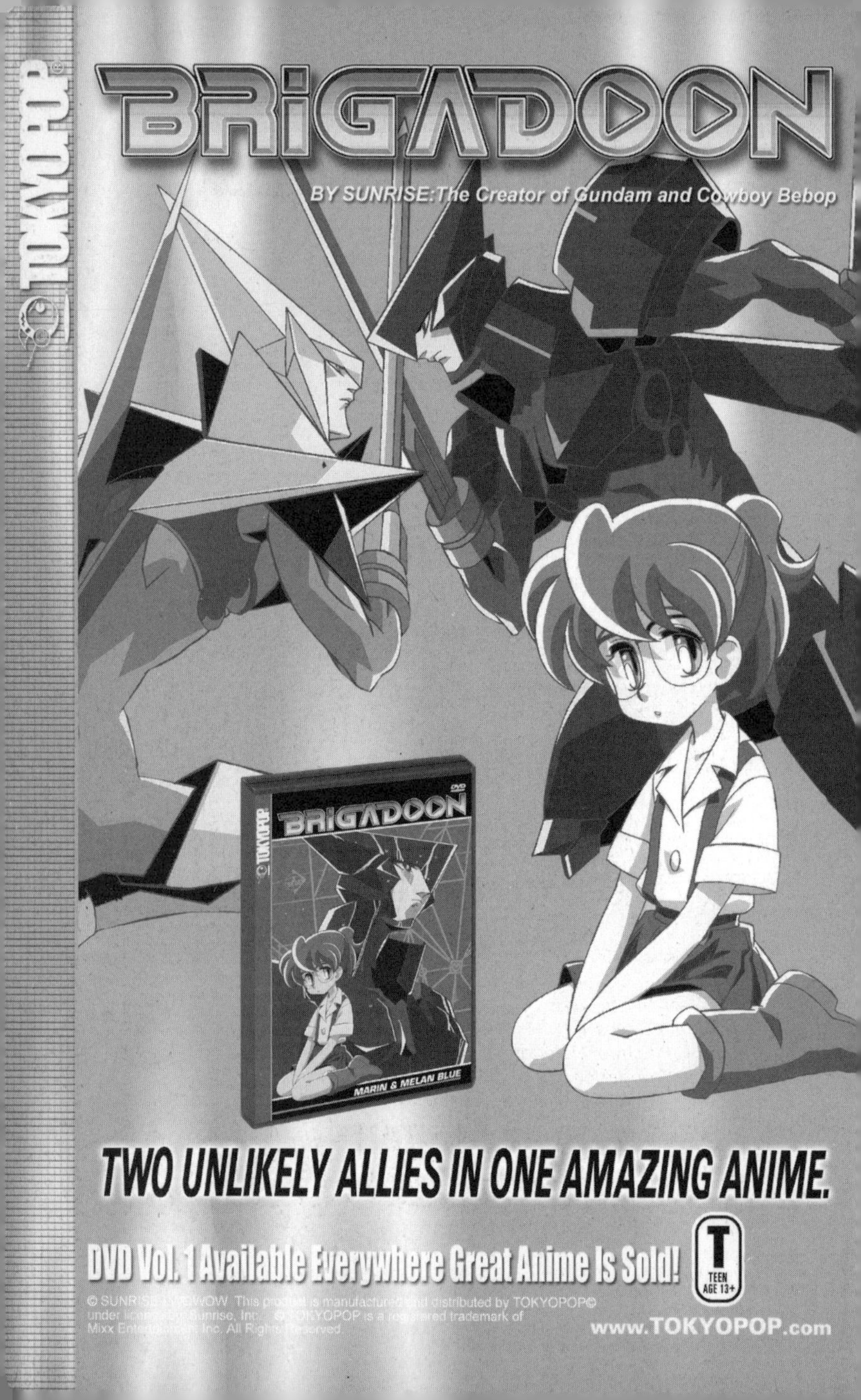

TOKYOPOP
BRIGADOON
BY SUNRISE: The Creator of Gundam and Cowboy Bebop
BRIGADOON
DVD
TOKYOPOP
MARIN & MELAN BLUE
TWO UNLIKELY ALLIES IN ONE AMAZING ANIME.
DVD Vol. 1 Available Everywhere Great Anime Is Sold!
T
TEEN
AGE 13+
www.TOKYOPOP.com

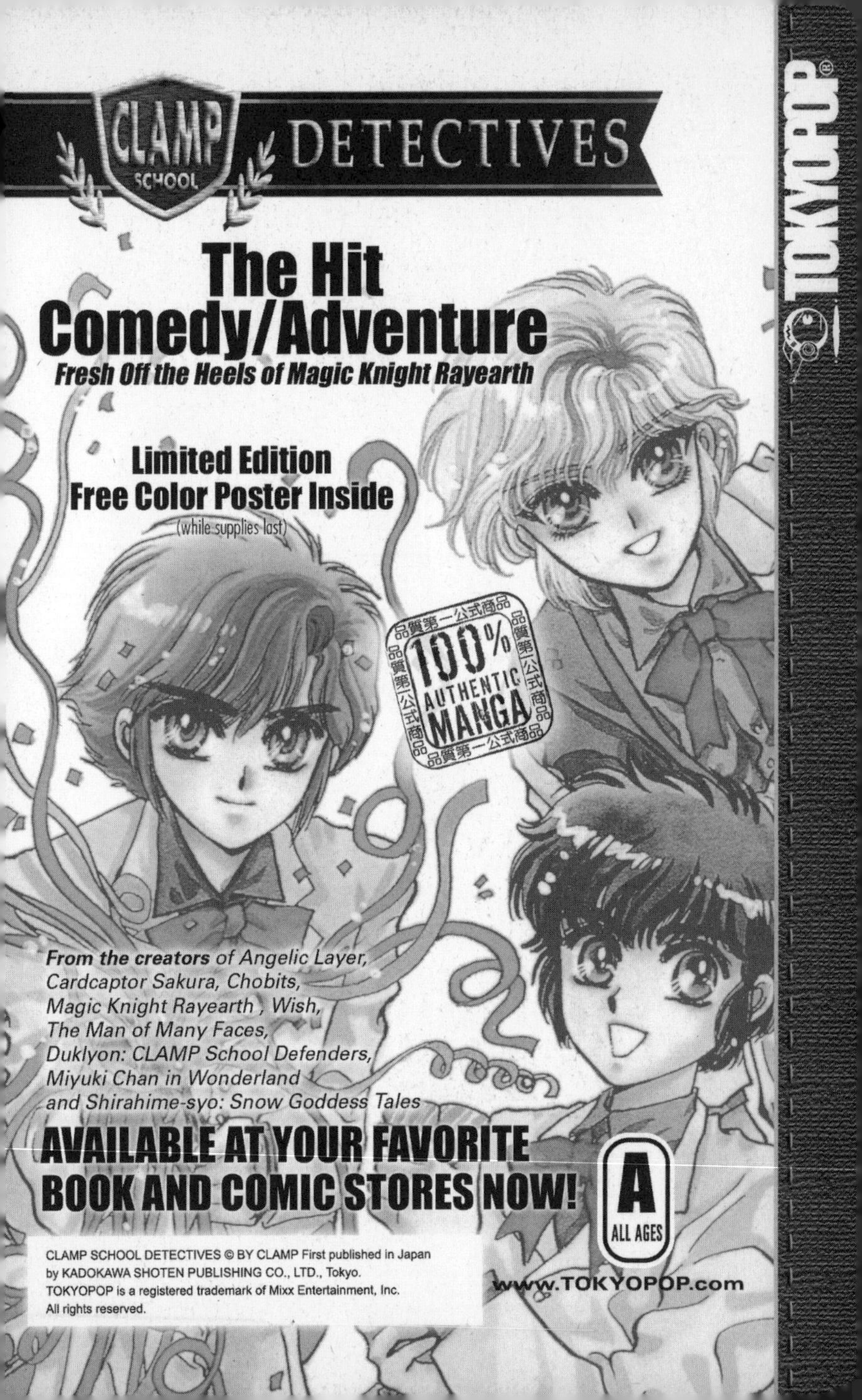

CLAMP SCHOOL DETECTIVES

The Hit Comedy/Adventure

Fresh Off the Heels of Magic Knight Rayearth

**Limited Edition
Free Color Poster Inside**

(while supplies last)

品質第一公式商品
**100%
AUTHENTIC
MANGA**
品質第一公式商品

From the creators of Angelic Layer,
Cardcaptor Sakura, Chobits,
Magic Knight Rayearth , Wish,
The Man of Many Faces,
Duklyon: CLAMP School Defenders,
Miyuki Chan in Wonderland
and Shirahime-syo: Snow Goddess Tales

AVAILABLE AT YOUR FAVORITE
BOOK AND COMIC STORES NOW!

A
ALL AGES

www.TOKYOPOP.com

TOKYOPOP

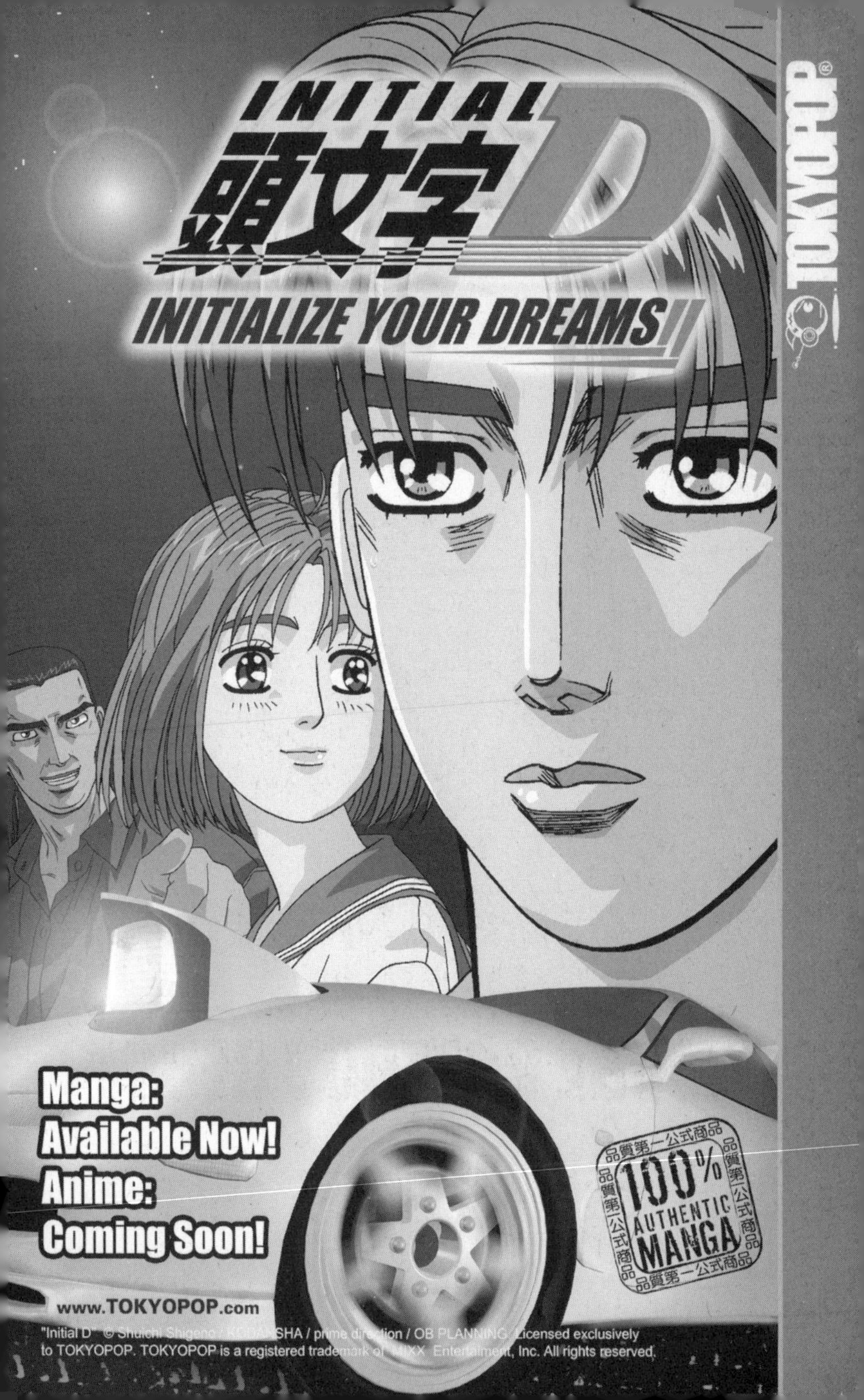
INITIAL
頭文字D
INITIALIZE YOUR DREAMS
TOKYOPOP
Manga:
Available Now!
Anime:
Coming Soon!
品質第一公式商品
100%
AUTHENTIC
MANGA
www.TOKYOPOP.com
"Initial D" © Shuichi Shigeno / KODANSHA / prime direction / OB PLANNING. Licensed exclusively to TOKYOPOP. TOKYOPOP is a registered trademark of MIXX Entertainment, Inc. All rights reserved.

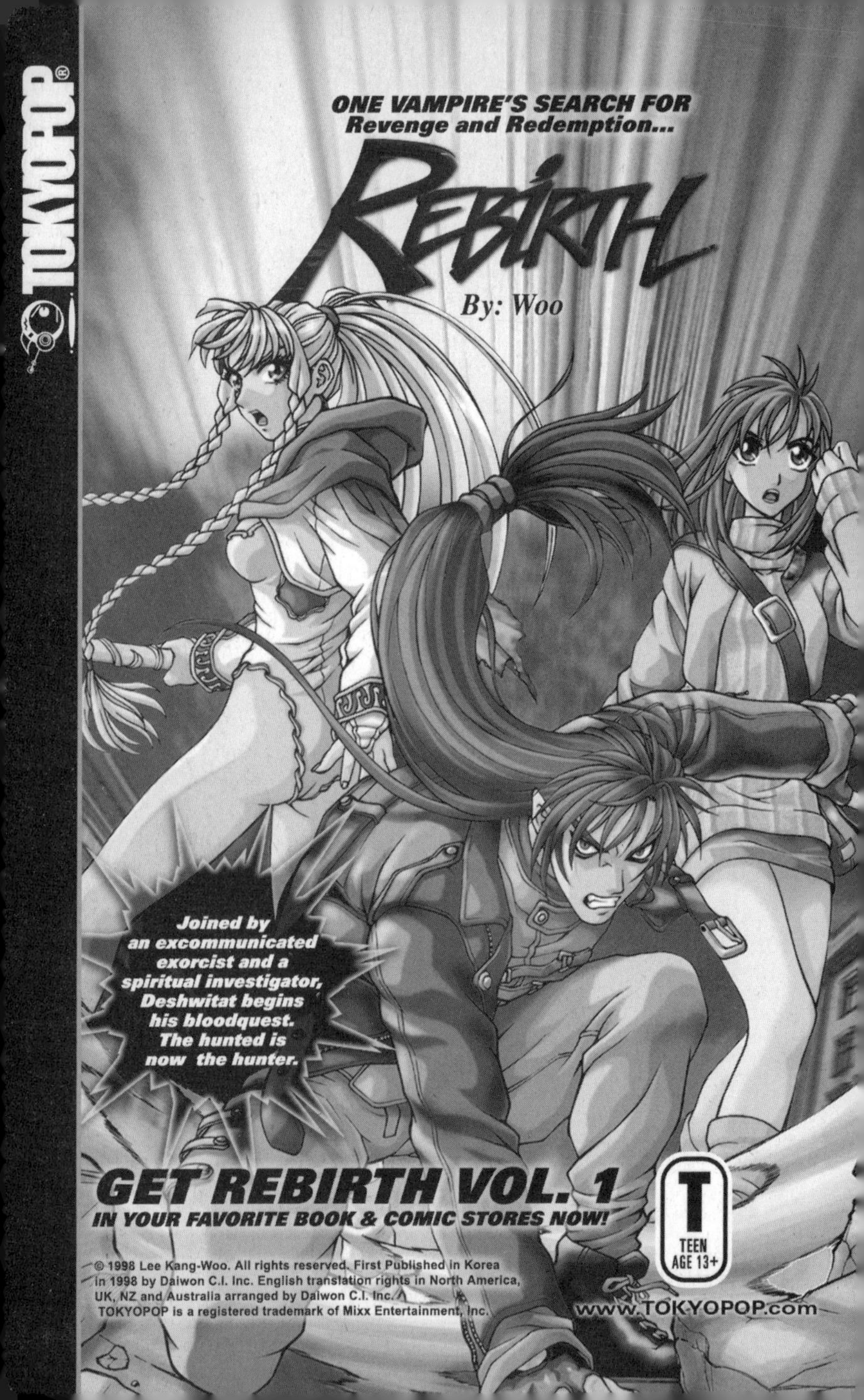

ONE VAMPIRE'S SEARCH FOR
Revenge and Redemption...

REBIRTH
By: Woo

Joined by
an excommunicated
exorcist and a
spiritual investigator,
Deshwitat begins
his bloodquest.
The hunted is
now the hunter.

GET REBIRTH VOL. 1
IN YOUR FAVORITE BOOK & COMIC STORES NOW!

T
TEEN
AGE 13+

www.TOKYOPOP.com

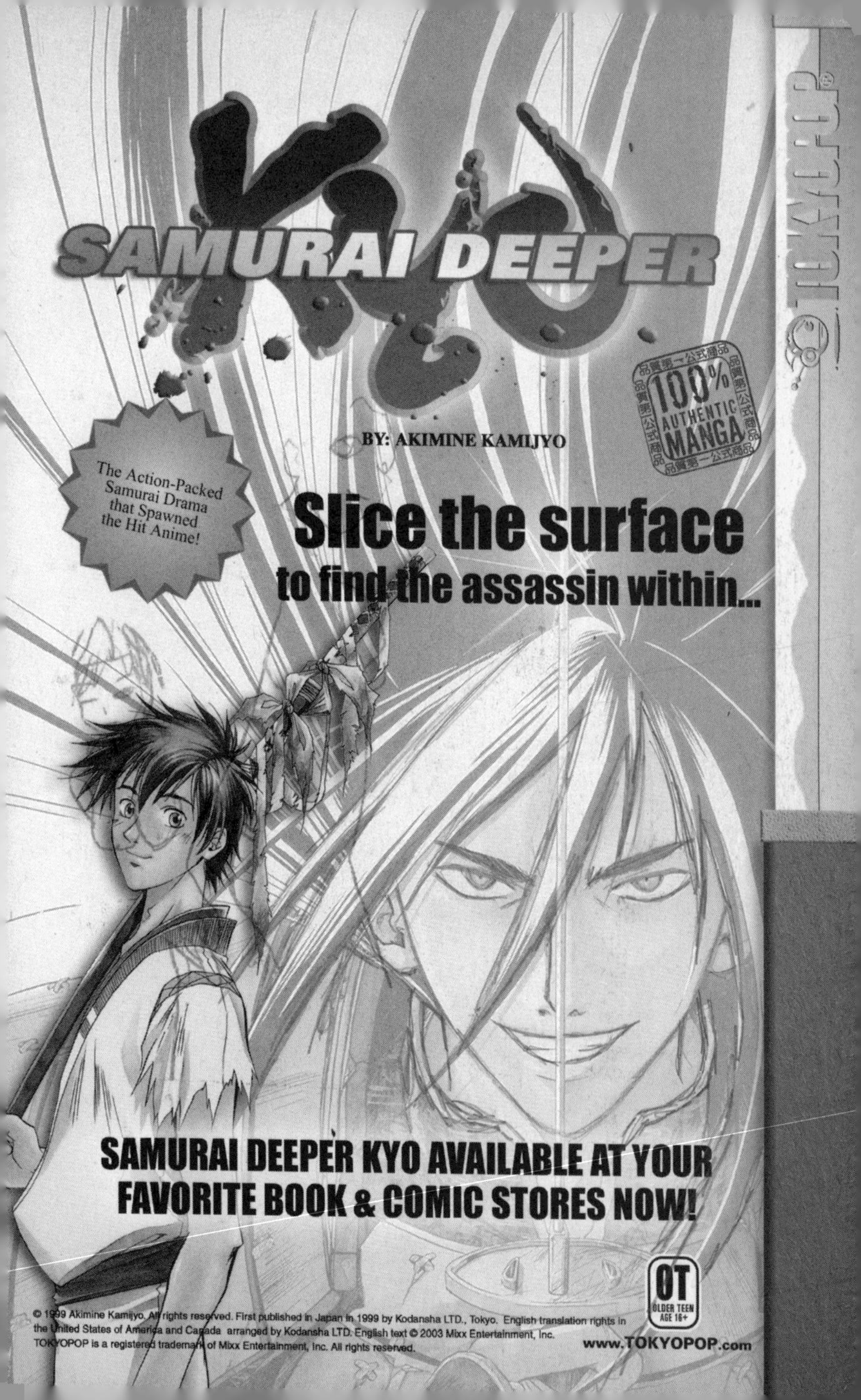
TOKYOPOP
SAMURAI DEEPER
KYO
BY: AKIMINE KAMIJYO
100% AUTHENTIC MANGA
The Action-Packed Samurai Drama that Spawned the Hit Anime!
Slice the surface
to find the assassin within...
SAMURAI DEEPER KYO AVAILABLE AT YOUR FAVORITE BOOK & COMIC STORES NOW!
OT
OLDER TEEN AGE 16+
© 1999 Akimine Kamijyo. All rights reserved. First published in Japan in 1999 by Kodansha LTD., Tokyo. English translation rights in the United States of America and Canada arranged by Kodansha LTD. English text © 2003 Mixx Entertainment, Inc. TOKYOPOP is a registered trademark of Mixx Entertainment, Inc. All rights reserved.
www.TOKYOPOP.com

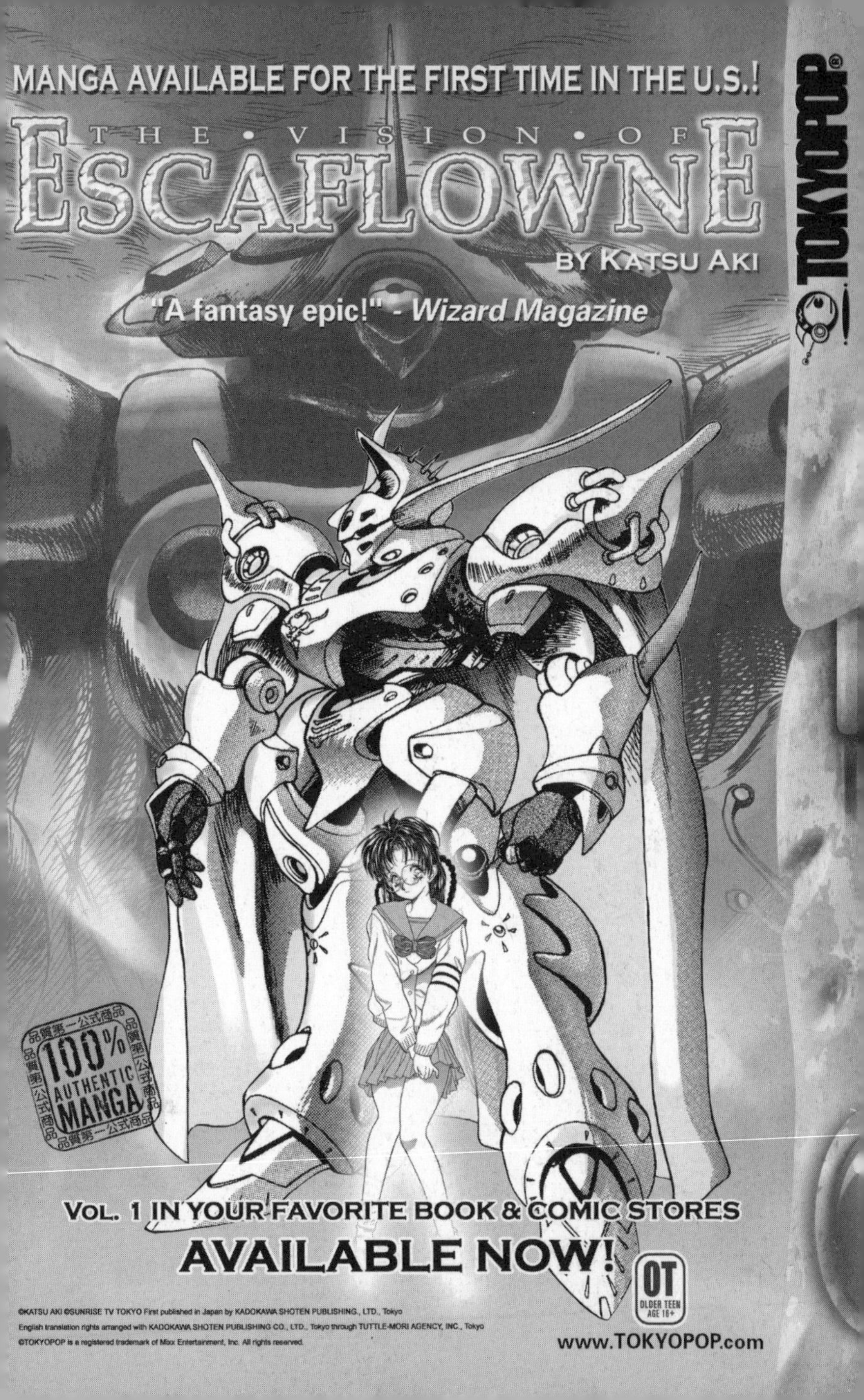
MANGA AVAILABLE FOR THE FIRST TIME IN THE U.S.!
THE • VISION • OF
ESCAFLOWNE
BY KATSU AKI
"A fantasy epic!" - Wizard Magazine
TOKYOPOP®
100% AUTHENTIC MANGA
品質第一公式商品
VOL. 1 IN YOUR FAVORITE BOOK & COMIC STORES
AVAILABLE NOW!
OT
OLDER TEEN AGE 16+
©KATSU AKI ©SUNRISE TV TOKYO First published in Japan by KADOKAWA SHOTEN PUBLISHING., LTD., Tokyo
English translation rights arranged with KADOKAWA SHOTEN PUBLISHING CO., LTD., Tokyo through TUTTLE-MORI AGENCY, INC., Tokyo
©TOKYOPOP is a registered trademark of Mixx Entertainment, Inc. All rights reserved.
www.TOKYOPOP.com